WHAT HAVE I DONE?

Also by Ben Elton

Stark

Gridlock

This Other Eden

Popcorn

Blast from the Past

Inconceivable

Dead Famous

High Society

Past Mortem

The First Casualty

Chart Throb

Blind Faith

Meltdown

Two Brothers

Time and Time Again

Identity Crisis

BEN ELTON

WHAT HAVE I DONE?

MY AUTOBIOGRAPHY

MACMILLAN

First published 2025 by Macmillan
an imprint of Pan Macmillan
The Smithson, 6 Briset Street, London EC1M 5NR
EU representative: Macmillan Publishers Ireland Ltd, 1st Floor,
The Liffey Trust Centre, 117–126 Sheriff Street Upper,
Dublin 1 D01 YC43
Associated companies throughout the world

ISBN 978-1-0350-5994-2 HB
ISBN 978-1-0350-5995-9 TPB

1 3 5 7 9 8 6 4 2

A CIP catalogue record for this book is available from the British Library.

Typeset in Minion Pro by Six Red Marbles UK, Thetford, Norfolk
Printed and bound in the UK using 100% Renewable Electricity by CPI Group (UK) Ltd

Visit **www.panmacmillan.com** to read more about
all our books and to buy them.

For my wife Sophie and our children

Bert, Lottie and Fred

Contents

2012 to 2014

More slaggings and a funeral

I've been quite resistant to the idea of writing my autobiography. There seem to be so many of them these days. If you've appeared on the TV or played a bit of sport, you do an autobiography. Often more than one. My dear friend Stephen Fry's done three and I'm not sure he's got out of short trousers yet. But I've just turned sixty-five, which is starting to feel really quite not young any more. My mother also died recently, leaving me a very old orphan. And, frankly, there's a lot of dementia about, so, if I am ever going to tell my story, I'd probably better get on with it.

I did think about it once before, in the early summer of 2014. In fact, I got quite fired up about the idea. There were two reasons for this: the splenetic media reaction to a sitcom I'd just done and the death of Rik Mayall.

I know that sounds wrong. Putting a bunch of shitty reviews next to the deeply tragic passing of a lifelong friend as if they're of equal importance. I mean, they were *seriously* shitty reviews but all the same. Tragedy-wise, me getting a public pasting is hardly in the same league as the loss of one of the greats of British comedy. Except that, as it happens, the two things were connected. Rik was supposed to have starred in that sitcom. And the fact that he didn't wasn't because he died but because the BBC rejected him. And the intersection of the two things got me thinking a bit – about fame and failure and triumph and disaster and how much Rik and I had both hated reviews (except good ones, of course). You know, all the big important stuff.

So I started messing around with a biography, but soon realized that

I was in the wrong mood, which was sad and angry, and since I am rarely either of those things (and never for long), it was clearly not in fact a good time to reflect on what had been in general a very happy life. So I dropped it.

The show Rik was rejected from was called *The Wright Way* and it was a traditional studio-based comedy about a pedantic health and safety officer. You probably missed it. As I say, it was comprehensively savaged and went out at 10.30 on a school night, thus cunningly avoiding its target family audience by a good two or three hours. The lead was played (brilliantly) by David Haig. David was Inspector Grim in my '90s sitcom *The Thin Blue Line* and is one of my favourite comic actors, but the role of Mr Wright was originally written for Rik. Sadly, the Beeb didn't want him.

It happened like this. In late 2011, the BBC asked me if I'd like to pitch a sitcom idea to them. This was a very pleasant surprise. I'd been in telly wilderness for years and had not expected to be given another chance. I certainly wasn't going to miss this one. To a writer of my generation, a sitcom on the BBC is the Holy Grail of comedy writing. In the days when TV was restricted to just a handful of channels, the great sitcoms lived in the affections of the nation in a way that no other TV did or ever will again. So, of course, I said I'd love to and told them that I'd like to write something for Rik. Ever since our time working together in the early 1980s, I'd felt that my creative partnership with Rik had been unfinished business. Here was my chance to finish it.

And the BBC said 'Well, o-kaaaaaay' and those extra A's are intended to imply a tone of nervous doubt.

I imagine you're surprised at that.

Since he died, of course, there has been a general recognition of Rik's unique greatness. The many glowing front-page tributes published on the morning after his death took it as a given that he was not merely a man who had once been great but one who had *remained* fiercely and uncompromisingly great.

Well, let me tell you that wasn't how it felt before he died. Back in 2012, Rik, like me, hadn't had a major TV gig in for ever but, unlike me, he couldn't spend his days and make his living writing in other mediums, and so he had experienced some creatively deeply undermining and financially challenging years – particularly after he pulled off his spectacular tragicomic pratt fall in which he threw a quad bike into the air and tried to catch it with his head. Rik and I used to call each other the 'hasbs' – as in has-beens, laughing over the inevitable fading of the lustre of those who have once been thought hip.

Although actually the hasbs joke dated back to the summer of 1983, a time when we were at our newest and *most* hip, the golden year between the first and second series of *The Young Ones* when Rik and I shared a stand-up season together at the Edinburgh Fringe. I gave him a good luck card which featured a photograph of legendary Hollywood comedian and drinker W.C. Fields on stage mid-performance, holding his habitual whisky bottle. I wrote on the card 'Rik Mayall comeback season Edinburgh 1993' and added cat-call notations – 'Why aren't you funny any more?' and 'Fuck off, Hasb'. Twenty-five-year-old Rik laughed till he cried and he carried that card around in the little suitcase he kept his notes in for years. I sometimes think about that.

Anyway, in the spring of 2012, it looked like the BBC were giving us both another chance.

Rik was so excited. He loved the character of Rick Wright and he loved the script. He already saw us back in studio together as we had last been twenty-six years before with *Filthy Rich & Catflap*. I tried to manage his expectations, warning him that it was just the start of a process and that we would have many hoops to jump through before getting a series commission. Developing comedy at the BBC had become a much more drawn-out and gruelling business, central to the process being a 'table read', that grim practice in which a group of actors gather in a meeting room and read from scripts to a fiercely non-committal comedy politburo. Rik was amusingly outraged that such a couple of 'comedy ledges' as us should be put through this trial, but he promised to be good.

Here's an email he sent me in February 2012 (Rik didn't own a computer himself. He used to dictate his messages to his wife Barbara).

6 WHAT HAVE I DONE?

28/2/12

My dear, darling, talented Farty

Your fabbo script is simply knob enlarging my dear. Anything the Nazi BBC demand of you I shall, of course, do.

Onwards and upwards comrade!

King

I had been 'Farty' and he had been 'King' since the 'Rik and Ben' stand-up tours of the early Eighties. I pinged back instantly.

28/2/12

Dear King

Your note made me hard with man love.

The Beeb are currently discussing dates for the read. Once that's done, I can come over and whip you into shape (and after that we can have a fag and a shower and start work on the show).

All power to the Soviets.

Farty

My wife isn't entirely sure about me revealing my and Rik's juvenile and perhaps rather un-PC style of communicating. But all private humour looks foolish when exposed to outside scrutiny and, in an age when mobile phones have made secret recording and subsequent exposure of unguarded moments a fact of life, I think it's good to remember that.

Rik and I had such fun preparing for that table read, as ever laughing and laughing at silly 'doobles' (as we called double entendres) and feeling just like we were twenty-two again, except that Rik no longer drank. We did the read itself at the old Television Centre in Wood Lane, that same wonderful doughnut building into which Rik and I had first walked together as Young Ones more than thirty years before. Television Centre was our Emerald City, that magical place which had been the engine room of British popular culture since 1960 – although, by 2012, it was on the verge of being sold off.

Of *course* it was being fucking sold off.

Because *obviously* London needed more luxury residential investment properties and yet *another* Soho House SO much more than it needed the largest and most comprehensive multi-studio film and TV production complex in Europe. May Margaret Thatcher for ever live in infamy for unbottling the privatization genie which, even years after she left office, was still stripping Britain of its publicly owned national treasures. As I write, another ten years have passed since they flogged the BBC's crown jewel, Thatch is long dead and human turds are bobbing about on Britain's privatised waterways. Her cold, dead reach is long.

But back to Television Centre in 2012. It felt so sad as we entered it that last time, with most of the rooms and corridors, which we'd known when they hummed with creative energy, already empty and ready for the wrecker. The place where they'd made *Hancock* and *Steptoe, Dad's Army, Python* and *Morecambe and Wise* was now full of ghosts, the laughter of a thousand studio audiences already a distant memory.

Perhaps I should have read the signs.

Except that we thought the read went terribly well. Rik was (as ever) on fire. His character was that of a good-hearted but endlessly pedantic rule-follower, furiously at a loss in a world where you couldn't get served in a shop because all the staff were busy stroking their phones. I can see him now, sitting in the middle of our little group of actors, a big man in every way: big heart, big face, big comedy. His massive, exuberantly scene-stealing performance so bold and so grotesque it seemed to be pushing at the very walls of the mean little meeting room into which we were all squeezed.

Perhaps that was the problem. He was just too big for that small room. Not that we realized it in the fun of the moment. In fact, as the stone faces of the execs broke into smiles – occasional laughs even – we thought we had been a success.

'I think they liked it,' I said, 'but they were very inscrutable.'

'Just as well,' Rik replied, 'because you wouldn't want to screw 'em.'

This was a quote from the act he'd done on the tours we'd shared together so long before. It was often said that Rik's quad bike accident had affected his memory, but I can't say I ever noticed it particularly.

That evening, the inscrutable ones rang me up and told me they wanted the show but they didn't want Rik. Rik was 'too rich a presence' for a mainstream piece.

Don't get me wrong, I'm not complaining or pointing fingers. Hindsight is a seductive and distorting glass through which to review events. I know that the decision was taken with regret and much soul-searching. Their reason was that the commission was for BBC1 and family viewing and they just thought the mix was too wild. To the Beeb's credit, the following year they would recommission Rik and Ade Edmondson's show *Bottom* for BBC2, which is another story and not mine to tell.

But the knock-back on *The Wright Way* was a hammer blow for Rik and telling him was *so* hard. He'd been convinced that the read had gone brilliantly and that we'd won the day. It was an awful, awful shock. We'd both pinned so many hopes on it – the two of us working together again on telly was a dream come true. Besides, as I say, Rik really needed the work.

This time Barbara wrote the email.

21st April 2012

Dearest Ben

To say we were shocked would be a real understatement.

All utterly devastated that you won't be working together after the lovely warm feeling we all had when we thought that it would be happening.

Love to Sophie, the kids et al

Barbara XXXXX

Rik wanted me to carry on without him. Why wouldn't he? He was the most utterly kind and generous of friends. He still loved the script and he wanted it to be a hit.

It wasn't.

The media consensus, pronounced with venomous certitude after a single episode, was that it was so bad as to be beyond and beneath contempt. Criminally bad. Disgracefully bad. They even had a discussion on *Newsnight* about why I was so utterly shit. *Newsnight*, for fuck's sake. The website Vice headed their round-up of the press reaction with a headline suggesting that I should be placed on suicide watch.

You think you'll get used to it, but you never do. The morning the notices (and subsequent commentary on them) hit was just terrible. I try hard to avoid reviews, but the internet makes that difficult and my children read them and they were pretty upset. They'd been too young the last time I'd copped a real pasting so this was their first proper taste of it. In my case, reviews are always pretty personal, they kind of review me via the actual piece. My eldest son was thirteen and he said, 'Dad, if I ever read anything like that about me, I don't think I'd bother trying ever again.'

Which, of course, is why it's really, *really* best not to read them if you can avoid it.

But even if you do manage to avoid them, enough seeps through. More than enough. You see things by accident or some well-meaning friend insists on quoting a slagging in order to express their outrage at it.

So *The Wright Way* was savaged out of all proportion to its quality (even if it was shit) or its ambition (which was light entertainment) and Rik was furious on my behalf – such a good mate, always so hurt at his friends' pain while appearing to be indifferent to his own. He sent me a text (from his ancient Nokia, his only form of electronic communication) offering to 'kill the cunts'.

Rik's own final notices were, as mentioned, glowing. It was a bittersweet pleasure for those who knew him to read the fulsome newspaper tributes written about him after he died. Most of them hadn't 'got' him in life and they didn't get him in death either. A columnist tweeted: 'To grasp how huge the impact of Rik Mayall was, you really need to sit through the decades that preceded him.'

I know this was meant well, but that's the problem with obituary tweets. They're usually just so *silly*.

Rik *loved* the decades that preceded him. *The Crazy Gang*, Laurel and Hardy, *The Goons*, *Hancock*, Tommy Cooper, *Carry On*, Pete and Dud,

The Pythons, *The Likely Lads*, *Dad's Army*, Billy Connolly and so much more.

It was the decades which *followed* that Rik had a problem with.

Anyway, *The Wright Way* turned out to have been my last chance to work with Rik because, eighteen months later, completely out of the blue, the bastard died on us. I'm still stunned. It's just so very strange that he's gone.

The funeral was in Devon and my wife Sophie and I spent the night before with Ade Edmondson and Jennifer Saunders. That was important to me. It was really good to be with Ade. Of course, Ade's personal and professional relationship with Rik ran even deeper than mine and was even more complex and intense.

The four of us – me, Ade, Jen and Sophie – spent a long and tearful night, drinking far too much, awash with regret over Rik's unfinished life, reflecting on bonds of friendships that had lasted all our adult lives and which had been severed so utterly suddenly.

The funeral day was beautifully organized by Barbara and the children. It was gut-wrenchingly emotional but also truly uplifting. Ade and Pete Richardson spoke at the church and I spoke over the grave, along with Rik's brother Ant. Alan Rickman read very movingly. Rik was buried on his own bit of land in Devon, on a hill facing west, and we all sat around and (literally) on his grave, drinking long into the night as the sun set on a shooting star.

Twentieth-Century Lives

If it wasn't for Hitler, I wouldn't be here

So it's the spring of 2024 and in sunnier mood I have decided that this time I really will write my autobiography. I'll start with my mum, Mary, because no interviewer ever has.

She was born in Northwich in Cheshire in 1929 and she was the first person in her family ever to get a degree. That was a very big deal to her parents, Harold and Kitty Foster. They were enormously proud of her and always put 'BA' at the end of her name when they addressed an envelope to her. Gran had left school at fourteen and Gramps at fifteen; he got an apprenticeship as a research chemist at ICI in Northwich where he worked for his entire life. We still have the cutlery service his colleagues gave him for a wedding present in 1924 and the clock he got when he retired in 1964. I don't suppose a single person in Britain today will work in the same place and for the same company for their entire lives. How many will even be in constant employment for such a span?

Harold's was one of those twentieth-century lives fortunate enough to miss fighting in both world wars; born in late 1899, he was only old enough to enlist towards the end of the first one. He joined the Royal Flying Corps (about to be renamed the RAF), but was still in training when the war ended. He joined the Home Guard in 1940 and I used to love reading the certificate he received in 1945 saying that he had been prepared to sacrifice his life *if need be*. It was a bit of a family phrase.

Kitty had a beautiful voice and, as a teenager, sang at Great War recruiting concerts, something she looked back on with sadness in later life. In the 1920s and '30s, she was very involved with Northwich amateur operatics. That was how she met Gramps, who played flute in the Gilbert and

Sullivan Society orchestra for which Gran played many leading roles. One time, Gran had a rich admirer who had made his fortune with a local underwear business. After a performance of *Iolanthe*, he sent her a gift of a very posh corset from his factory with a note saying that it was 'a jewel case'. Gran sent the gift back without a note and refused to speak to him. The very *idea*!

Harold and Kitty lived through many great and terrible events: the Great War, the Spanish Flu pandemic, the fight for Irish independence, the introduction of female suffrage, the General Strike, the Great Depression, the Second World War, the Cold War and the social revolution of the 1960s. But, through it all, their own circumstances were relatively comfortable and secure (apart from in 1940 when they thought Hitler would invade) with a steadily increasing prosperity which allowed them to end their days in a nice bungalow in Farnham, living off Gramp's ICI pension. It seems to me that they lived classic twentieth-century British lives. Born into working-class families, they themselves became middle class and lived to see their daughter's opportunities and circumstances improve vastly on their own.

My father's parents' life journey was very different. Theirs was not a steady progress; no gentle upward curve for them, rather a Richter scale zig-zag of spectacular reversals and revivals. In many ways, it was as much a classic twentieth-century Continental European progress as Gran and Gramps's was British.

My dad's parents, Victor Ehrenberg and Eva Sommer, were both born into the German Jewish middle class, which was largely integrated with German society as a whole. In fact, believe it or not, my grandmother's father Otto went to school with Kaiser Wilhelm II. The German royal family had a habit of installing its sons for a few years in 'ordinary' grammar schools, presumably to give the future ruler some knowledge of his subjects (or, at least, the middle-class ones). My great-grandfather and the young crown prince of Germany became close school friends, perhaps because they both felt 'othered', as we would now say – Otto as a Jew and Wilhelm as, well, crown prince. I don't know if Otto ever saw Wilhelm again after leaving school, but they certainly maintained some contact throughout their lives. When Otto died, the Kaiser sent flowers from his exile in the Netherlands 'in memory of a friendship'. This friendship might seem puzzling to modern eyes because the kaiser was a notorious anti-Semite. But that was the way with 'civilized' European anti-Semitism. It wasn't vitriolic and murderous in the manner of Hitler, rather more casual and dismissive in a way which allowed the kaiser and so many of his class to make a distinction between the despised Jewish race and the Jews they knew personally who were 'decent Jews'. The British aristocracy was the same, considering the 'race' as a whole to be utterly foreign and different in a most unpleasant manner but making exceptions for any that they happened to like or to need.

In the cultural, intellectual and economic powerhouse of Germany at the beginning of the twentieth century, Jews were tolerated, some even celebrated and there were no legal bars to their advancement – although, as we shall see, like all Jews of that time, my grandfather still faced the obstruction of antisemitism in the job market.

Nonetheless, Victor and Eva had every reason to look forward to lives of security and ever-increasing prosperity in their home town of Kassel. It would have been unimaginable to them that they would end their lives as British citizens living in a small flat in London.

Grandpa and Grandma fell in love when he was a wounded soldier and she a volunteer nursing assistant. Grandpa had enlisted in 1914 and served for the entire war on the Western Front. Like most men of that generation, he rarely spoke of his experiences and scarcely mentioned it in his private memoir. He won an Iron Cross and was wounded with a piece of shrapnel in the leg. The Iron Cross is long gone, buried by Grandma in a backyard in north London after she was shocked to find it among the things Grandpa brought with them to England (owning an Iron Cross in Britain in 1939 was not a good look, particularly if you had a German accent). But we still have the piece of shrapnel, a jagged splinter of metal terrifying with its numerous razor edges. That splinter of shrapnel brought Victor and Eva together.

Dad was born in Frankfurt in 1923, a year of utter and all-encompassing revolutionary chaos in Germany, which resulted in the greatest inflation any country has ever known. The once mighty German Mark became literally worthless. Savings and pensions were worthless.

Wages were worthless if you did not spend them within minutes of being paid. And this in a country which, more than any, had built itself on the solid morality of good business practice. The shock would have been simply stupendous. And what a time of chaos in which to have a baby! My grandparents must have been so scared. Little could they have known how much scarier things were going to get for them.

Grandpa was a classical historian and ambitious for a professorial chair. However, he had trouble rising above the level of senior lecturer and was quite matter-of-factly told the reason after one unsuccessful application: 'We already have enough Jews'. So Grandpa looked further afield and, in 1929, took up a post as professor of ancient history at the German University in Prague. He, Grandma and their two sons Gottfried and Ludwig moved to Czechoslovakia. They all imagined it was just a foreign gig for Grandpa from which they would return in a few years to their extended family, friends and the German homeland they loved.

But after Hitler came to power in that homeland and passed the Nuremburg Laws of 1935, which deprived Germany's Jews of all their human rights, the family could see there was no future for them in Germany any more. Then, after the Munich appeasement and with Hitler threatening invasion, it became clear there was now no safety in Czechoslovakia either. The family tried, with increasing desperation, to organize a way out of the trap they now knew themselves to be in. My grandma wrote literally hundreds of letters to all over the world, trying to find a situation that would lead to the granting of an entry visa to a country not threatened by Hitler. Most of Prague's Jews did not make such efforts. They could not believe that even 'he' could be as terrible as the prospect of leaving everything and fleeing to a strange country without a penny or a friend or a future. My grandma guessed different. She knew that it was a matter of life and death. And now the names of all her Czech Jewish friends, and those of my father and uncle's schoolmates, are written on the wall of the Prague Holocaust Memorial. My father and I visited in 1998 and read each one. That his own name was not on it was due entirely to my grandmother's prescience and tenacity – and then to the kindness of strangers because, eventually, having received endless rejections (including one from an Australian sheep farmer to whom Grandma had offered her and Grandpa's services as maid and stockman!), the family struck lucky. A small charity had been set up in Britain in 1933 to help academic and scientist refugees. This charity (which still exists today) was able to secure my grandpa a grant which was sufficient for the Home Office to issue entry visas to him and his wife. But not their dependents. Their sons Gottfried and Ludwig still had no entry visas. The family was still trapped.

Then, by an astonishing piece of luck, they were saved. On a train in Wales in late 1938, two complete strangers fell into conversation, a Welsh Methodist minister and a German woman, Netty, who was on holiday with her Dutch husband. Before the First World War in Kassel, teenage Netty had been taught English by a young English woman, Irene. Netty and Irene had become friends and Irene had also made friends with Netty's friend, my grandmother Eva. In the long years since Netty had lost contact with Irene, but now on that train making idle conversation it emerged that the minister she was chatting to knew Irene's husband, who was also a Methodist minister, the Chaplain of Rydal Penrhos, a school in Colwyn Bay. So Netty reestablished contact with Irene and fortune smiled – Irene remembered Eva and, remembering also that she was Jewish, asked if she needed help. Letters were exchanged, which resulted in Irene's husband appealing to his headmaster, the Reverend A. J. Costain, to offer assisted places to two Czech/German Jewish boys currently in fear of their lives. It's a complex story and I've done my best to shorten it from Grand-mother's account in her memoir, at the end of which she writes:

I have described that miracle so minutely because it marks the begin-ning of the time which we survived by miracles alone.

These places were sufficient for the Home Office to provide my father and uncle with the extra two entry visas which allowed my family to escape to Britain. My grandma called the Reverend Costain her sons' guardian angel because not only did he save them, but he cared for them and guided them in the first year in their new world.

Here's an ironic bit of family history. Before the UK would issue the life-or-death visa, they required copies of the family birth certificates. These were held in the Frankfurt public records office. Grandma duly wrote to Frankfurt politely requesting copies and, this being Germany, the civil administration worked efficiently, despite its institutionalized anti-Semitism. The fee was paid and the certificates dispatched. Being copies, they were officially stamped, a stamp which, of course, featured a swastika. My father's stamped copy remained his birth certificate all his life. The chap at Guildford bus station was quite surprised when Dad presented it for his old-age bus pass but, as Dad explained, *without* that swastika, the certificate would not be a legal document because the Nazi government had been the legally recognized authority at the time of issue. And this was as true in 1989 as it had been in 1939.

To get to Britain, the family needed to travel through Germany. Having by now taken Czech citizenship, they were allowed entry but, being still Jews, they were allowed only forty-eight hours to pass through and were required to stick to their train route via Frankfurt without deviation. The family took a big risk and visited Kassel to say one last farewell to my remaining great-grandmother Emilie. The night they were in Kassel, Himmler was also in town. All day and all night, the SS and Gestapo conducted house-to-house searches for communists and Jews. None of the family ever forgot the fear that they would be caught. That evening, my grandma tried to persuade her sister Elisabeth to organize an escape. Grandma was confident that, once in Britain, she would be able to find someone within the supportive group she was in touch with who would help her get a permit by creating employment as a domestic servant. But Elisabeth was in love; she was a lesbian and would not leave her friend Imme. This is a passage from my grandma's own memoir.

Elisabeth cried: 'Let them come and kill me!'
They came, they killed her, they shot her together with a children's transport. That was in 1941. I heard of it through a cousin in America; I did not know how to bear it.

Elisabeth worked in a Jewish orphanage and went, with fifty-five children in her charge, to be loaded onto the cattle trucks at Frankfurt station. One can only imagine her journey as the only comfort and security to so many terrified, traumatized children, while also dealing with her own grief and fear. It's a small, if bitter, mercy that the agony ended there. She was shot along with all the children directly on disembarking in the town of Kaunas in Lithuania. Quite recently, I learned from a researcher in Munich that Elisabeth's lover Imme (who was not Jewish) had followed Elisabeth to Kaunas and lived for a while in the vicinity of the wretched remains of the Jewish ghetto in the hope of somehow finding her again, not knowing that Elisabeth was already dead.

Another brief family story. Great-Grandma Emilie, whom the family visited in Kassel, was not murdered in a camp. Mercifully, she died before the final round-up of German Jews. Shortly before she died, she was visited by a German soldier. He was her grandson, my uncle Heinz who would one day own the farm in Langenhain on which I spent my childhood holidays. Heinz wasn't Jewish. He was my dad's cousin by adoption and while his entire family were either murdered or scattered as refugees by the Nazis, he was required to serve six years in Hitler's Wehrmacht. He became an elite alpine commando and it was in this uniform while on leave in 1941 that he visited his Jewish grandmother in Kassel. This was a very brave thing to do, but braver still was that earlier on that same day, he had visited Gestapo headquarters and appealed to them, saying (and I quote his own words) 'Why not just let the old woman die in her bed?'. It must have taken incredible nerve (and a lot of love) to express Jewish sympathies in Gestapo headquarters, even if you were an alpine commando. Nobody knows if Heinz's appeal had any effect, but Emilie did die in her bed, spared the horror of a cattle truck and the gas chamber.

Later in the war, my uncles Heinz and Geoffrey might easily have shot each other because, in 1943, they were both in Italy on opposing sides. My mixed-up family is living proof of the utter imbecility of both racism and aggressive nationalism. Two of my uncles fighting each other in the Second World War, just as my two grandfathers were on opposing sides in the First World War.

If you're wondering about the name, it was changed from Ehrenberg to Elton on British Army advice when Uncle Geoffrey joined up. In fact, according to Geoffrey, it was couched almost as an order: 'If you're captured with a German accent and a Jewish name, you're buggered. Get rid of them both immediately.' So Gottfried Ehrenberg went back to his barracks, thought about it and, deciding on keeping the same initials, applied next morning to be renamed Geoffrey Elton. My father (who, being a physics student, had had enlistment deferred) decided to join his brother in the clean break and became Lewis Elton. My grandparents remained Victor and Eva Ehrenberg until their deaths in London in the 1970s.

So that's a bit of the history of how I came to be and, of course, without Hitler, I wouldn't have been at all because my dad would never have met my mum. Britain gave my father's family sanctuary and, eventually, the chance to live full and rewarding lives. I think that subsequently they made their contribution. When they arrived in 1939, only my grandmother could speak English, but Grandpa and the boys learned quickly. Grandpa was soon teaching again and, after the war, published in English his celebrated work (well, celebrated among ancient historians) *From Solon to Socrates*. Eventually, both boys became professors in Britain. Uncle Geoffrey became Sir Geoffrey Elton, the leading Tudor historian of his generation, and my father was first a professor of physics at Surrey University and, later, a pioneer in the field of education and the first professor in that subject, winning *The Times Educational Supplement*'s Lifetime Achievement Award. Throughout their lives, both brothers were deeply grateful for the sanctuary and opportunity Britain offered and, of course, I share in that gratitude.

Jew? Half Jew? Not a Jew? A question of identity

People often think I'm Jewish because Dad was Jewish. But I personally don't *identify* as Jewish and I don't think Dad did either, not in the modern sense of the word. As far as I'm concerned, Judaism is a religion, like Christianity or Islam. It's not a race. How can something be a race if you can convert to it? And what's a 'race' anyway? Apparently, all human DNA is nearly identical and we're only a few chromosomes away from being brussels sprouts. The human race is one race. It is societies and cultures that differ.

To Hitler I would be a Jew. To a rabbi I wouldn't, because to qualify to be a Jew your mother has to be a Jew. Personally, I feel no sense of racial or religious identity beyond that which is thrust upon me, as it sometimes is. Some people want me to be a Jew either to claim me or to condemn me, and nothing I can say will change their minds.

Of course, there is Jewish *culture*, but it's as diverse as Christian culture. The archbishop of Canterbury and the grand wizard of the Ku Klux Klan are both Christians, but they're scarcely of similar outlook or experience. So I don't know what being 'culturally' Jewish means either. I suppose you could say that Dad grew up in *one* Jewish culture, the largely secular, partially integrated culture of the pre-Hitler German Jewish middle class. But I didn't grow up in any kind of Jewish culture at all. My home life was entirely secular and, like every other state school kid in the 1960s, I sang Christian hymns at assembly and studied bible stories in Religious Knowledge. The only time I ever heard the word 'Jew', as in race or religion, was in nativity plays and I wasn't remotely aware of any connection with me. Of course, I often heard it used as an insult to mean a tightwad. We all used to say that. If a kid wouldn't share, everybody called him a 'Jew', including me. I don't think any of us were aware of the racist derivation of this abuse. It was just a word.

If you're interested in my faith, I'm an atheist, which as far as I'm concerned, means I don't believe in a personified god or the teachings of organized religions. That doesn't mean I lack awe or humility in the face of the great mysteries of the Universe, which I'm sure are as humbling to me as they are to any person of 'faith'. I'm even happy to call that which surpatheth all understanding 'God' if you like. What I'm not prepared to do is claim it looks like me or to imbue it with my own opinions and prejudices. I simply cannot follow the thinking of those who speak of an almighty creator and then presume to know how that creator thinks, or how it feels about homosexuality, or its views on who should win US elections, or what's 'modest' for a woman to wear, or what type of meat we should eat. To me, it is self-evident that every word and opinion that has ever been ascribed to any 'god' in human history is a projection of the views of the human person doing the ascribing. God didn't make man in his image, as the Bible teaches; man has made assorted gods in *his* image. To me, that seems to be stating the bleeding obvious. But, hey, whatever floats your boat.

1959 to 1975

Life in black and white

I was born at University College London Hospital on 3 May 1959.

Elvis was in Germany doing military service. John, Paul and George were members of a drummer-less Liverpudlian three-piece called Johnny and the Moondogs. JFK was still only a US Senator and Harold Macmillan was assuring the British public that they'd never had it so good.

I mention these things because pop music and the study of history have been and remain two of my great pleasures in life. Perhaps I should also mention that beer was a shilling a pint (5 pence), since beer has also been a lifelong source of solace – although I do find in the last ten or fifteen years I've switched largely to wine. I hope to die with a nice cold glass of champagne in my hand or a rich fruity red.

We lived in Catford, a district of south-east London, and I was the youngest of four children. We certainly weren't poor, but we weren't well-off either. Until I reached my teens, I didn't wear a thing that hadn't previously been worn by my two older brothers. They were twins, but one of them was quite a bit bigger than the other so I got clothes third-hand. Like most households in those days, we were a one-income family and Dad was the bread-winner. He was a lecturer at Battersea College of Technology and my mother, who was a school teacher, had paused her career to become what was called a housewife and bring up us four kids. It was a totally different economic world. To my knowledge, I had only one friend at infant school whose mother worked.

I have very few early memories and nothing of note. I know that I was a chatterbox because my mum has often told me since. In the mornings, once my older siblings had gone to school and while I was still too young

25

to go, Mum had a rule that she had to have poured her second cup of tea before I was allowed to start talking at her. After that, she says I chattered continually for the rest of the day.

South London in the early '60s was still in black and white. Things might have been swinging into Technicolor on Carnaby Street and down the King's Road, but in Catford and Lewisham, it was still the 1950s, except for the bomb sites which we owed to the 1940s.

The Second World War still loomed large. 'Playing war' was pretty much the only game in town for me and my mates. We played football, of course, but it certainly wasn't remotely the obsession it has become today. Boys were into war – or at least our vague understanding of it – which consisted of running around shouting 'Donner und Blitzen' and 'Eat lead, Fritz'. The Blitz had been a whole generation earlier, but most kids still knew a Messerschmitt from a Heinkel and owned armies of tiny plastic Airfix soldiers. That's the first thing I can ever remember buying with my own money: a little cardboard box of Airfix soldiers for half a crown, which I'd saved from my 6d-a-week (two and a half pence) pocket money. I can still remember walking over Blythe Hill to the local newsagent in the gathering dusk of a school evening to buy it. I was only seven and, because it was getting dark, Mum said my brother had to go with me. He was nine. I got Rommel's Africa Korps.

I went to the local state infant and junior school in Stillness Road and was very happy there. They gave us school dinners, which arrived in vast steel vats stamped 'LCC', for London County Council. You had to take in dinner money, but many of the kids got it free, about which I don't remember any stigma at all. There were enough kids from poorer families for it not to be a matter of note. Jamie Oliver would not have approved of LCC dinners – spam fritters, fat wrapped in fat and fried in fat – and I can still recall gagging over the vast glutinous lumps in the custard. But it was a proper hot meal with pudding. We all got free school milk too. A third of a pint in little glass bottles with foil tops which you poked a straw through. This was back in those halcyon days when governments of all parties saw the health of the nation as a community responsibility.

Immigration was gathering pace, so there was some ethnic mix in my school, although nothing like as varied as today. There was only one

Muslim in my class as I recall and he was my friend, a boy called Metin. His family hadn't been in Britain long and they were very poor. He had no plimsolls for 'Movement with Music' and my mum tried to offer his mum a pair of mine that I'd grown out of (I was small but Metin was tiny). I can still remember Mum trying to put the offer without giving offence: 'silly to throw them away when they're perfectly good'. The shoes were declined and Mum felt mortified.

Stillness School and Catford are where I got my accent – obviously. Where else would I get it? But the idea that I put on a 'common' voice to disguise a presumed poshness has been a recurring troll across my entire career. I think grumpy old Paul Merton was the first to do an actual routine on it in the mid '80s. He pointed out that my dad was born in Germany and was also a professor, so clearly my true voice must be that of a posh middle European intellectual. The idea still comes up occasionally as evidence of my presumed inauthenticity.

Well, excuse me, but come *the fuck* on.

I mean really.

Come the fuck on and then fuck the fuck off.

It would be a pretty pathetic jibe, even if there were any truth in it. I mean, what performer doesn't affect a stage personality? But people get their accents from their school and their neighbourhood. Nobody ever said Brummie-born Lenny Henry was a hypocrite for not speaking like his West Indian parents, because if they did, they'd sound like an idiot (and a racist). My accent is the same as my brothers and sister – the accent of where I was brought up and where I went to school.

So, Catford, south-east London.

What do I remember?

I walked to school on my own from the age of about six. Mum didn't drive – lots of women didn't then. I loved running along in some private fantasy, a secret agent or a commando storming the cliffs of Navarone. I've always been both an enthusiastic walker and a dedicated day-dreamer. I still stride along in a fantasy world to this day. I'm not a soldier any more. These days, I'm pretending that I wrote the whole of the Lennon–McCartney songbook or am accepting an Oscar or giving a speech in Parliament, but apart from that it's just the same.

In today's society, letting a kid out and about on their own at six or seven would be called highly irresponsible, even criminal. But we all did it back then. As for stranger danger, everybody knew you didn't take sweets from people you didn't know, but that was the full and absolute limit of any discussion of paedophilia I ever heard. In fact, although I knew the rule about sweets and strangers, I had really no idea about *why* it was the rule.

To be honest, the big fear for us wasn't paedos. It was fridges. Mums, including mine, were always warning us about them. *Never* get into an old fridge. It was good advice, of course; these were the days when there were council dumps where you just dumped stuff (the clue's in the name). Fridges from the 1950s had proper twisting handles and there wasn't one on the inside (why would there be? So the cheese could let itself out?) and kids really had died in them. Our local dump was actually straight across the street from our house and Mum suffered agonies at the thought of one of us dying a lonely death trapped in one of the ancient fridges that were scattered about there. The pop group Madness (who are all about the same age as me) wrote a song called 'Time for Tea', which I think was about this and which I found very haunting and moving. It was a fear unique to my generation. The law soon caught up and mandated that fridges must be escapable from within.

Once a year at Easter, Dad would give Mum a break by taking us camping in the New Forest for three days. In those days, he could literally just pull our '62 VW caravette off the road, drive into the woods and set up camp. Us four kids used to swim naked in a stream. In the New Forest! Imagine doing that now. But we scarcely ever encountered another soul. There was a bouncy tree to which we returned year after year to set up camp and we always had it to ourselves. One year, I stepped out of the VW and straight onto a much-loved penknife (fortunately closed) that I'd lost the previous holiday! It was completely rusted but still a magical find.

Our summer holiday was always a trip to Uncle Heinz's farm in Germany. Those truly are golden memories. Langenhain was a small family farm with one ancient tractor and a yard of cobblestones worn almost smooth with age. The haybarn was 300 years old and we used to spend all day jumping from its ancient beams onto the haybales beneath. If I close my eyes, I can still smell the hay and taste my Aunt Nini's *Apfelsaft*.

What else can I tell you about my childhood?

Not a lot, really.

I know I was happy. Maybe that's why I can't remember a huge amount. In my small experience, it seems to me that if you're unfortunate enough to have a sad childhood – or, worse, a brutal one – you remember the detail, but if you were happy, it all sort of blends in. Perhaps that's just me.

My good friends Richard Hannay and Bertie Wooster

I remember Mum always read to us at bedtime and I loved it so much. The Narnia series was a favourite and I adored *The Wind in the Willows*, but she made other less obvious choices. She read us the Richard Hannay adventures, not just *The 39 Steps* but also *Greenmantle*, *Mr Standfast* and *The Three Hostages*. I didn't know at the time that Mum was discreetly rewording John Buchan's occasional lapses into casual racism and anti-Semitism. These are pretty unpleasant to modern ears, but I forgive old John, he was writing in a different age and he wrote a cracking yarn. I've read *The 39 Steps* to my own children (also changing 'Jew' to miser, etc.) and I've read it twice for my own pleasure on sleeper trains to Fort William. I love the Scottish Highlands very much and there is nothing like lying in a cosy sleeper with a large Scotch in your hand accompanying Richard Hannay on his first adventure as he thunders north through the night from London in early 1914.

George Orwell's *Animal Farm* was another of Mum's inspired choices. I still remember crying when Boxer is taken away to be boiled for glue while his once-mighty hoofs can be heard beating feebly on the sides of the knacker's van. Orwell is for me the bravest and most prescient of all British twentieth-century writers. He saw Stalinism for what it was and had the courage and imagination to denounce it in brilliant, compelling fiction. At the time he was writing, the majority of the British Left were still stubbornly refusing to acknowledge that in Russia, Marx's dream had turned to genocidal nightmare. We now know that the dire warnings of *Animal Farm* and *1984* were not dystopian fiction but terrible contemporary reality. As a child, I just thought *Animal Farm* was a wonderful, funny, heart-breaking story.

I read mainly comics myself. Graduating from *The Dandy* and *The Beano* to the exciting (and very well-drawn and constructed) war stories of *Commando* magazine and *War Picture Monthly*. I used to go to jumble sales and buy huge piles second-hand for a penny and binge in my room all day. I read books occasionally when off sick from school. I remember devouring Eric Linklater's *The Wind on the Moon* while recovering from chickenpox. But I only got a proper reading habit myself from about the age of eleven when my dad bought me a book of P.G. Wodehouse short stories called *Eggs, Beans and Crumpets*. It was one of the most pivotal moments in my life. I became a devoted Wodehouse fan and remain so to this day. For me (and many others), Wodehouse is the greatest comic writer in English literature. He understood instinctively that life is absurd and people are ridiculous, and he *celebrated* that. He viewed humanity not with anger and despair but with deep tolerant affection.

From Wodehouse, I got into further reading. I read all of Sherlock Holmes twice or three times and remember absolutely adoring Spike Milligan's wonderful war memoirs (although I could never get into *Puckoon*). I still loved comics but by now only humorous ones; I always bought the annual Giles compilation and Andy Capp and *The Perishers* from the *Daily Mirror*. I also loved showbiz biographies, most notable of which was David Niven's *The Moon's a Balloon*, a brilliant actor memoir. *A Talent to Amuse*, Sheridan Morley's biography of Noël Coward, was also a very big thing for me; I read it several times in my early teens. I fell in love with Coward's life before I experienced his work. His commitment to the art of entertainment inspired me. For fifty years, Coward was one of the most famous people in the world. He personified the 1920s in almost as fundamental a way as the Beatles were to represent the '60s. Yet when I spoke to a group of drama students recently (that's *drama* students), none of them had even heard of him. Everyone gets forgotten in the end; even Elvis is fading.

My main reading, though, was history, which has been a lifelong passion. I lose myself in history in the way many people lose themselves in a novel. I'd read history books even before discovering fiction, the classic *Our Island Story,* and R.J. Unstead's *Looking at History* with its wonderfully exciting drawings of how people used to live. I think the Department of Education would do well to take a look at some of Unstead's work. I wasn't the only kid who actually read him for pleasure. After him, I moved on to the extraordinary A.J.P. Taylor. I read his history of the First World War when I was thirteen and every word of it was to inform my attitude to *Blackadder Goes Forth.*

Brothel creepers and baggy trousers

In 1968, we moved from Catford to Guildford.

Harold Wilson was expanding higher education and they were building a new generation of universities, the first since the great 'red-brick' expansion of the late Victorian era. These 1960s universities were called 'yellow-brick' and Surrey was one of them. My dad's old department at Battersea College of Technology morphed into the department of physics at Surrey University and Dad was the new professor. I was very proud to be the son of a professor. Dad was one of the few academics who the students were prepared to negotiate with during the sit-ins which marked the university's first year. 1968 was a year when revolution seemed a genuine possibility. We now know that you can't run a revolution if the only activists are middle-class students, but for a minute back then, it really seemed you could.

In those days, Surrey had the old system of dividing kids at the age of eleven between secondary modern schools and grammar schools. I passed my eleven-plus and so went to a grammar school. This fact has occasionally been used against me as evidence of some kind of hypocrisy. How can I, having enjoyed the privilege of a grammar-school education, then support the principle of comprehensive education?

Well – leaving aside the obvious fact that kids don't choose where they go to school and the system was what it was whether you liked it or not – for what it's worth, I don't think my education was much of a privilege. I'd have much preferred to have gone to a forward-looking, socially inclu-sive, better equipped comprehensive than a tired, dusty, faintly ridiculous institution dedicated to pretending it was a tiny bit like proper private schools. Because that was my experience of a state grammar school in the 1970s. Godalming Grammar was *all right*, in a bored, baggy-trousered, platform-heeled early '70s kind of way. But it certainly didn't feel remotely like a centre of excellence. Its principal redeeming feature was that it was coeducational, which personally I feel is the best way to educate kids. I had good mates there and there were some great teachers to whom I will always be grateful, but the headmaster was an out-moded snob who used to lift boys up by their sideburns.

I remember there was a kind of school council to which I got elected as a junior school rep. I tried to introduce a bill to allow girls the right to wear trousers. It was what my (female) constituents were asking for and it seemed a self-evidently logical step to me. I made an impassioned speech about the archaic inequality of forcing girls into these impractical gar-ments which left them at the mercy of wind, weather and little boys trying to see their knickers, a common practice at school to which I publicly admitted my own guilt, which took some nerve I can tell you. I really tried with that speech, but at the end of it, the headmaster just sneered and said, 'I suppose, Elton, you'll be asking if you can wear a skirt next.'

How things have changed.

There was the cane but I never got it. I wasn't a goody two-shoes, but I had enough sense not to do stuff that would get me physically assaulted.

I got by with deeply average marks and a few absolute clunkers. My English Language work was terrible; a teacher wrote, 'Benjamin's writ-ing is very creative. Unfortunately, so is his grammar and spelling.' They don't write reviews like that any more. I was terrible at languages too. My French teacher wrote, 'Benjamin came to this school determined he would be unable to learn French and he is succeeding admirably'. Another bad review. Perhaps it was good that I got used to them early in life – although they wouldn't often be so wittily written.

In fact, I don't think my failure at languages was my fault. You see, I went to grammar school not knowing any *grammar* at all. I was of that unfortunate generation who went to junior school at a time when it had become suddenly unfashionable to teach formal grammar. So, I went on to big school not knowing even what a verb or a noun was and since these were the first terms I heard in my very first French lesson, I was essentially being taught a foreign language *in* a foreign language. Some kids caught up. I just switched off.

It didn't seem to matter much. My memory is that most kids got average marks. Nobody was hot-housed. I didn't know a single kid that had extra private tuition. In fact, parents had very, *very* little to do with their kids' education. There was home and there was school and they just didn't mix. Parents didn't really get involved at all. Imagine that? Parents did not spend their weekends watching their children kick balls around and they weren't encouraged to 'share' in their kids' homework either.

As someone who brought up kids in the modern era, it sounds like heaven to me.

I can't really remember my parents bothering much at all about my very average marks. There was no pressure at home to excel academically – and, frankly, very little at school either. Everybody just bumbled along. Hey, it was the '70s. I think it was a symptom of the general presumption that you could always get a job doing something, even if 'only' working in a shop. Now there are no shops.

The 1970s was a great time to be a teenager. There seems to me to have been less stress and, in terms of popular culture, it was one long party! Even the fashions were ridiculous and fun. Just think of it: we went from prog rock, to glam rock, to punk rock, to ska and Two-Tone, to power pop and New Romantics in just ten years!

It was back in the early '70s that my love of pop and rock, and also comedy, was really nourished. We only had three TV channels but they had a lot of good stuff on all of them. My absolute favourite was *Morecambe and Wise*, but there was so much else: *Dad's Army*, *The Likely Lads*, *Man About the House*, *Fawlty Towers*, *On the Buses*, *Please Sir!*, *The Two Ronnies* and *Porridge* to name but a few. And there was also *Top of the Pops*, an absolute must every Thursday night for every single schoolkid in the UK.

And do you know what? I'm not being clever after the event, but I didn't know *anyone* who liked Jimmy Savile. Everybody absolutely knew he was a weird, repulsive, arrogant dick that you just had to put up with to get to Slade, Sweet, Bowie and T. Rex. I'm not suggesting for a second that anybody had any idea of the gothic horror of his secret self, but you simply knew he was a smug, arrogant shit. It was just obvious. Nobody could understand the ubiquitous hold he had on TV with his overweening vanity and blokey ineptitude.

But that aside, *Top of the Pops* was just brilliant. Even when it was crap, it was brilliant. I loved the naff panto style and I loved the fact that you could have Val Doonican and David Bowie back-to-back on the *same* show, or St Winifred's School Choir straight after a punk band. It was truly inclusive community entertainment, Sir William Beveridge's vision for Britain dressed in silver platform boots and woolly cardigans. I loved glam rock then and I still do – hod carriers dressed in Bacofoil and their mums' feather boas. For all their fey/yob posturing, those glam rockers were often hugely talented people – great songwriters, brilliant musicians and the penultimate generation of musicians who understood that rock 'n' roll is supposed to be *fun* (the New Romantics would be the last), for which, of course, they were critically despised or at best horribly patron-ized. T Rex blazed the trail, then Slade (my favourites), Bowie (the genius who of course progressed far beyond Glam), Sweet (the foundation of all US big hair rock), Wizzard (with Roy Wood, inspired songwriter and pro-ducer, and multi-coloured beard), Suzi Quatro (so much more than the token woman), Roxy (crazy cool) and even Mud, who must have been the ugliest band on earth but *Lonely This Christmas* remains a classic for me.

Yes, Glam was truly great, but in fact, Elvis was my first love. I was very late to the party, but like many who came before me, I fell in love with rock 'n' roll via Elvis. It was his '68 *Comeback Special* that did it for me. I didn't know who he was, why he was coming back or where he'd been, but my brother said it was important to watch it, so I did.

I was transfixed. Twelve years after *Heartbreak Hotel*, I was poleaxed by Elvis.

After that, I educated myself on the whole history of rock 'n' roll, saving up paper-round money to buy Chuck Berry, Little Richard, Buddy Holly and Eddie Cochran. The early '70s was a good time to get into rock 'n' roll because it was going through its first major revival with bands like

Showaddywaddy and Sha Na Na, as well as brilliant rock 'n' roll nostalgia movies *That'll Be the Day* and *American Graffiti*. Teddy boys were back in fashion and everyone whose mums would let them was swapping their platform shoes for brothel creepers.

After Elvis, Buddy, Little Richard and Chuck, I caught up with the '60s and began a lifelong love affair with the Beatles. For me, the Beatles are not just the greatest popular musicians of the twentieth century (obviously), but the greatest popular artists full stop – greater even than Chaplin. The blinding light of the Beatles' artistry and personalities changed *everything*, not once but on a six-monthly basis for seven incredible years between 1963 and 1970. They did it effortlessly (or so it seemed) and with such humour and humanity that, while leading (by example) an artistic, cultural and even political revolution that changed the world, they still managed to charm the grannies. I really enjoy my friend Richard Curtis's movies, but I couldn't get on with *Yesterday* about a world in which the Beatles had never existed. In the movie, all this is taken to mean is the absence of an incredible canon of songs (which just one person remembers); apart from that, every aspect of culture is unchanged. Of course, if the Beatles had never existed, *nothing* about today's culture would be the same. I put this to Richard and he said, 'Oh yes, but I just have to ignore that'. I'm afraid I couldn't.

My Artful Dodger shows promise

Apart from rock and pop, for me those early teenage years were all about amateur dramatics. Before I discovered theatre, I really didn't have any hobbies or interests apart from toy soldiers and history (aged eleven, I tried to write a history of Britain and managed about fifty pages, but it was basically *Our Island Story* regurgitated).

I was never into sport at all. When people ask me what football team I support, I tell them I'm a musical theatre fan and would rather see a good production of *My Fair Lady* than a cup final any day. And I would.

Once I got the theatre bug, it was all I wanted to do.

My road to Damascus was Onslow Village Hall in Guildford. I was ten and the epiphany came courtesy of a little amateur dramatic society called The Curtain Raisers who were asking for children to audition for *Peter Pan*. I went along and got the role of 'Slightly Soiled', one of the Lost Boys. From that moment on, I had 'caught the bug', as my Gran announced.

My interest ramped up even further after I played the Artful Dodger in the school production of *Oliver!*. This was memorable for two reasons. Firstly, because Lionel Bart's *Oliver!* is a work of true greatness and sparked in me a lifelong love of musical theatre. And second because it resulted in me falling in love for the first time. With Oliver, in fact, who – due to lack of interest from enough boys in the idea of being in a musical – was being played by a mischievous and very pretty girl called Gabby whom I became instantly besotted with. She was eleven and I was twelve and although she rejected my romantic advances (in favour of a handsome football player called Mick – obviously) we became lifelong friends. Her full name was (and is) Gabrielle Glaister and, in 1985, I was very happy to be able to recommend her to John Lloyd, the producer of *Blackadder*, for the role of 'Bob', which she played absolutely brilliantly, holding her own even when enveloped in the hurricane of comedy that was Rik's Lord Flashheart.

Another reason that school production was so important for me was because Tony and Pat, the teachers who staged it, were also in the biggest am dram company in the area, The Godalming Theatre Group. This was a much bigger and better-funded outfit than The Curtain Raisers and it turned out they were planning to mount *Oliver!* for an astonishing ten nights that Christmas at the local Borough Hall. The group's directors, Desmond Holt and Keith Thomas, came to see me in the school production and afterwards they asked if I'd like to play Dodger for them. When I got home and told my parents about it, I was so excited I could hardly speak. Ten nights in the local hall! It really felt like I'd scored the lead in a West End run.

Christmas '73 remains an utterly magical memory for me. Slade were at Number One with their mighty Christmas anthem. The Morecambe and Wise Christmas show featured Laurence Olivier and Vanessa Redgrave. Hula Hoops had just been introduced in the UK. And I was singing 'Consider Yourself' and getting big laughs off the dialogue night after night at Godalming Borough Hall. The *Surrey Advertiser* review said I showed great promise for the future. When that future came to pass, there would be a long, lo-o-o-ng period of it during which I would have killed for such a positive review.

After *Oliver!* I just lived for am dram. I remember playing Lancelot Gobbo in *The Merchant of Venice* at Guildford Castle and also The Common Man in *A Man For all Seasons*. It was while rehearsing this in 1974 that I heard the bombs going off when the IRA blew up the Horse & Groom and the Seven Stars pubs in Guildford town centre. I can still hear that muffled crump, the silence that followed and then shouts and sirens filling the night.

Keith Thomas and I formed a comic double act to perform at the various old-time music halls that the group presented. He was six or seven years older than me and was, for some years, a professional entertainer. I visited him in Bournemouth when he was appearing in 'The Lulu Show' at the Winter Gardens in 1974. I'd had a huge crush on Lulu since 'Boom Bang-a-Bang' and watching her from the wings, as I was privileged to do one night, was a real adolescent thrill (oh, those hot pants!). Keith was a big influence on me in those early days, giving so much encouragement and advice. He and his future wife Muriel really believed in me, even offering to help me out financially if I tried to make it in showbiz. They're both still friends and I'll always remember their support and kindness. In fact, I saw Keith's production of *Joseph and his Amazing Technicolor Dreamcoat* just the other day at the same old Godalming theatre group of which I am proud to now be president.

It was at this time (when I was about fourteen) that I really began to start writing comedy in earnest. I tried my hand at sketches for my heroes Eric and Ernie, but never actually submitted them. I wrote short stories too, although I don't think I ever finished one because I always just started without having bothered to think of a plot. For many years, I retained a tendency to run off with the gags and dialogue without properly considering structure. I only came to fully understand this when I started working with Richard Curtis on *Blackadder*. He is such a master of construction. I'll never forget him arriving at my place one morning with the plot for the 'Dictionary' episode of *Blackadder the Third* already in his mind. He said

'Benj, what about this? It took Dr Johnson twenty years to write his dictionary. What if he lends it to Blackadder, then Baldrick puts it on the fire because he thinks a book is a kind of loosely constructed log and Blackadder is left with a weekend to rewrite the whole dictionary?' How brilliant is that? It's a plot *and* a gag.

1975 to 1977

All alone in the world

I left home in September 1975 when I was sixteen. This sounds a bit more dramatic than it was. I was no teenage runaway; my parents supported the move. I'd been getting increasingly restless at school, absolutely convinced that the sooner I began carving out my career in theatre, the sooner I'd achieve the success I was dreaming of. My head was full of the sort of naive self-confident fantasy that all stage-struck youngsters indulged in before the era when the venue for success switched from the real world to the virtual one. 'I'll knock on theatre doors and offer to sweep the floor until they put on my play' was the kind of bullshit I'd tell myself.

My parents could see I was serious about wanting to leave school, but they wanted me to remain in education and, by good fortune, my dad had spotted an article in *The Guardian* about a visionary educator called Gordon Vallins. Gordon's big idea was that theatre should be a part of education and he had managed to set up the first A level in theatre arts. These days, higher education is jam-packed with media, TV, theatre and even stand-up comedy courses, but at the time, Gordon's dream was unique and original. Particularly because he didn't see his A level as vocational, there were plenty of drama and movement sessions (he once took us out in a thunderstorm to read the storm scene from *King Lear)* but no actual acting classes. Gordon thought theatre and drama were worthy of study in themselves, like history or English literature. He also believed that a course with drama at its core would impact positively on student development in general, building confidence and cooperation and helping with the study of other subjects.

He'd set up his shop at South Warwickshire College of Further

Education, which was a technical college in Stratford-upon-Avon, and in 1975 I applied to go there to do A levels in history, English and drama. The fact that Stratford was Shakespeare's hometown didn't register with me much at the time. I certainly never would have imagined that, more than forty years later, the Bard and his works would become so central to my own creative life.

The grandly titled Department of Drama and Liberal Arts (DLA) occupied a small hippy corner of a college that mainly specialized in hotel and catering courses. Our small cohort used to go to the refectory for lunch in our flared loons and tie-dyed T-shirts – some girls even barefoot in their leotards and tights after a movement session – and be roundly laughed at by 200 teenagers in platformed shoes, chequered trousers and big tall white hats. It was good fun all round – both sides thought the other lot were the weird ones.

Going to DLA meant leaving home and living in 'digs'. We chose one from a list supplied by the college student services, so Mum thought it would be all right. It *seemed* all right (ish) when Mum dropped me off, driven by my brother in my Gramps's Ford Anglia. I would have my own room and it seemed clean. That, however, was all that could be said for the place.

The husband-and-wife team who ran it were aggressive, money-grabbing shits – 1970s versions of Dickens characters. I suppose it's hardly surprising that they tried to give as little as they could for the rent they extracted, but they could have been more pleasant about it. They were surly and scary and made no effort to make me or either of the other 'guests' (two bewildered-looking African guys learning English who were much older than me) feel remotely at home. They gave us very little to eat and held loud boozy parties with their friends on school nights. One night, I summoned up the courage to ask them to turn the music down. They were too stunned by what they clearly considered was an outrageously unreasonable request to reply, but as I turned to scurry back up to my room, I could hear them saying that I needed teaching some manners and they should get me out of bed and do it there and then. I was too scared to sleep for most of the long night that followed. It was a drab, lonely, hungry and intimidating start to life as a grown-up, aged sixteen and four months.

Looking back, it seems even grimmer than I felt it was at the time. My wife Sophie thinks sometimes I'm a bit detached from my emotions. If I am, I guess it can be a useful characteristic when you're scared and hungry.

I left that first digs after about a fortnight. I was genuinely afraid of my nasty hosts and went to student services who found me a room with another DLA student two years older than me called Roger, who became my friend. He was a big, bushy blond-haired, flashing-eyed eccentric who had a great Pythonesque sense of humour and fearsome temper (which emerged only very occasionally). I think he was impoverished country posh: a cut-glass accent and holes in his huge woolly jumpers, and a talented musician obsessed with Elton John. I visited him once at his parents' home in Gloucestershire, a large, run-down old farmhouse, and I remember the cheese which his dad had made himself was crawling with maggots, but they happily ate it anyway because after all 'the maggots are just made of cheese'.

The new boarding house was a bit better than the previous digs but not much. Us student tenants were clearly still seen as a slightly resented necessity and rations remained very, very stingy. I remember my mum coming to visit and being shocked by the full 'cooked supper' that she and Dad were paying for. That night, it consisted of a single fried egg, a single wafer slice of packet ham, about half a dozen chips and one of those foil-wrapped, chocolate-coated marshmallow 'tea cakes' that were such a popular 'treat' in the 1970s.

Depressing though my living arrangements were, I was soon to face a greater personal challenge than short rations, dispiriting digs, isolation and loneliness. In fact, something which briefly looked a lot like ostracism.

I'd come to Stratford equipped with a full-length, three-act comedy that I'd written during my O level year at school. DLA had a studio theatre, a big black box of a space with lighting bars and rostrums for both seating and staging. I'd found it incredibly exciting when I first saw it at my interview the previous spring and, since that day, I'd dreamed of putting on my own play there. So, shortly after arriving, I asked Gordon if I could do exactly that and he smiled and said I was welcome to try.

So I pinned a notice on the department board asking for expressions of interest in a student theatre group I was forming. Can you imagine it? I'd been there about three weeks. Also, being the product of am dram societies, and also completely uncool, I announced that my group was to be called The Studio Players. Further to this, my notice explained that the first production of the company would be a three-act original play called *Once More with Feeling*, written by me.

It would also be directed by me.

And any students interested in being cast in the play should apply to me.

Why on earth would that piss anybody off?

All I can say is that it genuinely didn't occur to me at the time that it would. I had no idea then, and still have very little idea of how to play it cool.

And I was completely unaware of the feathers I was ruffling. DLA had been going for seven years at that point and to date no student had tried to put on their own production of anything, let alone their own full-length, three-act play three weeks after arriving.

After my notice had failed to solicit any response, I persevered by asking around personally and made the mistake of trying to cast second years. They were, after all, the cool and confident ones, the ones who knew where everything was, the ones who shouted ostentatious greetings at each other across the common room and hugged each other and shared cigarettes while we newbies grinned sheepishly on the fringes. Surely these golden creatures would just love to be directed by me in my play.

Some of them even said they would. But not for long. There was soon to be a whispering campaign against me and a lot of laughter behind my back. One by one, every single person who agreed to be in my cast dropped out again.

Even I knew by this time that it had been a big mistake to try to cast second years. I was a snotty little fresher and I'd tried to align myself with the cocks of the walk. So I asked around in my own year and, although I made some headway, my grandiose over-reach had by this time turned me into a bit of a joke. And a bad joke at that.

In fact, within our arty little college community, I'd gone what these days would be described as somewhat toxic.

This obliviousness to some people's resentment of and irritation with me has been both a blessing and a curse over the years. It makes me kind of thick-skinned through ignorance, which is a sort of defence but it's brutal when I finally work out what's being said about me.

Anyway, whether I deserved it or not, I was given no quarter. I can remember walking into Stratford's famous Dirty Duck pub after about a month in Stratford (no ID needed in those days – you had to be actually pre-pubescent not to get served), seeing a group of fellow students and the conversation stopping dead as I approached. Even with my socially tone-deaf sensibilities, I knew that they'd been talking about me and, from the smirks on several faces and the guilt on one or two others, I knew that they'd all been laughing at me.

Everyone was laughing at me.

That was when even I could not avoid the realization that I was truly fucked. My great project would end in ignominious failure and, in creating that failure, I had made myself a joke, a figure of isolation and contempt. This was a very unhappy feeling for a lonely sixteen-year-old living in cold digs a hundred miles from home.

Then something really interesting happened.

I got thrown a lifeline. And from a most unexpected source.

There was one person in the second year who was very different to the rest. He was more like our year really, not at all 'showbiz-y' but long-haired and hippy. He played guitar and was incredibly handsome with a little moustache and piercing blue eyes. He carried about him an air of amused tolerance as if quietly laughing at a joke that only he got. John Stone was cool. Some people just are. He even had a cool name. And he lived on his own in an old caravan on the edge of a field on a farm a couple of miles out of Stratford.

I mean, come on. How cool is that?

Anyway, one day, he floated dreamily up to me in a cloud of tobacco smoke. I don't think he'd said a single word to me up until that moment.

'This play you're doing,' he said. 'I'll be in it if you like.'

I can picture his face in front of me as I write, icy blue eyes framed by long black greasy hair, that strangely knowing half-smile playing on lips between which hung, as if by a miracle, a ragged little hand-rolled cigarette. Even at the time, I guessed that he'd made this offer for his own amusement and I guessed his game. John Stone was well aware that a lot of people had dropped out of my play and that the majority of the kids on the course were currently feeling a certain degree of schadenfreude at my discomfort. Clearly sitting in his caravan, smoking his rollies and listening to his Roy Harper records, he'd decided to put a cat among the pigeons.

It's a funny thing about being cool, a quality which I generally consider highly overrated. John hadn't really done much at college, he wasn't outstanding academically and he wasn't a 'star' actor. He was just cool. You either had it or you didn't. I didn't and never have had. But John had it and, for his own amusement, he had decided to lend me a bit of his. Now that is proper cool.

From the moment of John Stone's stunning intervention, the whole vibe around me and my play changed. The leading second years didn't like John and they liked him less now he'd played his maverick move. But I was looked at with more interest among the first years. I know that a lot of them had felt some social pressure to avoid me, but with John's patronage, that changed. I think there was even some sympathy for me by this time. I had been looking pretty stupid and very isolated (always last to be picked when we had to partner off for drama exercises), but I hadn't given up even after losing most of my cast and I hadn't cried about it either. Not when anybody could see anyway.

So, things started to turn and, as the term progressed, I felt a certain tolerance towards me emerging. Affection, even. I was still something of a joke with my Mickey Rooney-style 'Hey, let's do the show right here' enthusiasm and over-eagerness, but no longer a bad joke. With John in the leading role, I was able to recast the rest of the play and this time everybody stuck with it.

The play was about a well-meaning vicar who is attempting to put on a play in his church hall and has to deal with two domineering local 'grand dames', both of whom expect to be cast as the lead. In the play, the vicar solves the matter by casting both women in the same role with all the attendant confusion. It was set in the 1920s, a result of my Wodehouse and Coward fascinations. Nobody actually said 'Anyone for tennis?', but they might as well have done.

Teenager in love

So, in the autumn of 1975, I got my play on. We even ran for two nights. We had costumes and a proper set and it got lots of laughs and on the whole – for a first play, starring a teenage hippy with shoulder-length hair as an elderly, bewildered 1920s country vicar – it went very well indeed. Gordon Vallins sent me a letter in which he talked about how he was aware how hard it had been for me and how impressed he was that I had seen it through. I'm not sure he actually thought much of the play – he was a Bertolt Brecht fanatic, so not really up for sub-Coward pastiche drawing-room comedy – but I treasured his letter and still have it.

And after that everything was okay.

The second years got used to me and I began to make real friends in my own year. I also got a girlfriend, a lovely fellow student called Nicky. I remember I bought her a knitted tank top from a boutique in the high street for Christmas. Tight tank tops were the thing for girls then, worn over white blouses with puffy sleeves and huge jumbo collars. I was pretty pleased with that and I think she was too. It was wonderful to be sixteen years old and buying a Christmas present for a real girlfriend. It doesn't get much better than that.

I look back on my two years in Stratford with gratitude and joy. Gordon was an inspired educator. Besides studying theatre theory (lots of Brecht), we did plenty of practical. Street theatre was big in those days with hippy-style 'happenings' still (just) considered interesting and new. I really threw myself into it, producing two street theatre shows of my own. Not surprisingly, they were about things I was interested in: one was a history of rock 'n' roll and the other a history of the Second World War. I don't know what the citizens of Stratford made of my Elvis impression in the Memorial Gardens, or of us re-enacting Pearl Harbor with toy planes and boats in front of the fountain, but we had a great time.

Occasionally, Gordon took our shows out of Stratford to the real world. I remember we did my Second World War show in a Coventry shopping precinct. As ever, before the show could start, you had to go through the excruciating process of drumming up a crowd, prancing about shouting

'Come and see a show' at busy shoppers and laughing youths. I've got some balls in this area, but let me tell you, it's a grim thing to have to do. This show featured a number of national flags, including a swastika. I suddenly looked up to see one of my cast marching off towards Boots waving a large Nazi banner shouting 'Support our group!'. This was 1975, still only thirty-five years since the dreadful night in November 1940 when Coventry had been so utterly devastated in a German bombing raid. Plenty of people in that precinct had experienced it. Fortunately, I was able to stop this particular bit of crowd-drumming before we were all lynched.

After Christmas, Roger (of the maggoty cheese and cheesy maggots), Mick and John (two other mates from our shared boarding house) and I moved out together and rented a cottage on the same farm as cool John had his caravan. I was sixteen and living with my mates in an old brick cottage in a field. It was like an Enid Blyton fantasy, but with beer and masturbation. I made furniture out of planks and bricks and cardboard boxes. It was freezing and horribly bleak, but we loved it.

My parents gave me ten pounds a week, of which five went on rent and the other five had to cover everything else – food, transport, clothes, the lot. Once in a while, we'd treat ourselves to a trip to the Dun Cow pub or the Snitterfield Arms and I'd have a pint of mild and a Cadbury's Creme Egg. Simple pleasures.

I kept writing. And I put on another show in the spring, a musical which Roger and I wrote together. One of my biggest personal frustrations is that I can't play an instrument. I'd so love to have been able to write music, but it will never be. But Roger could – really well, in fact – so he wrote the songs and I wrote what in musical theatre is known as The Book. The show was called *The Dancing Silhouette* and was set in a run-down New York nightclub full of cynical good-time girls and tough fatalistic guys – which obviously, as a seventeen-year-old from Guildford, I knew loads about. I remember my dad asking 'Why not write what you know?' and me replying that Shakespeare never went to Venice – to which he said, 'You're not Shakespeare'. Too-flipping-shay.

Around about this time, there began perhaps the most gruellingly intense and emotionally distraught time of my life. I fell in love. It was not like my earlier crush on Gabby. It was like no emotion I'd previously experienced. Nicky and I had had fun together, but this was proper all-consuming love, absolute and agonizing.

And it was unrequited.

I was doomed.

I break my own heart

It started so inconsequentially towards the end of my first year when, one day outside college, I bumped into the mother of one of the locally based students, Ali, who was in my year. Ali's mum told me that Ali was a bit down at the moment and it would be nice if some of her friends came to visit her.

I scarcely knew Ali. In fact, I hadn't really noticed she'd stopped attending college, but I am someone who feels the burden of social responsibility quite strongly and felt I should respond to her mother's request, so I visited her.

I think I was pretty smitten even on that first visit and it soon became a habit. I'd spend long hours in her room drinking instant coffee, listening to Bob Dylan and Nick Drake and talking about life and stuff. Pretty soon I was hopelessly in love with her. And there was much to fall in love with – she was tall and willowy with beautiful long, thick brunette hair cut in a fringe over her twinkling, clear blue eyes. She was a fascinating and complex girl who suffered somewhat from adolescent depression, the seriousness of which I only slowly gathered; to me, she seemed just beautifully sad. We were both seventeen and I was filled with youthful romantic notions, a broken heart waiting to happen. And God did it happen. Because Ali didn't love me. And, to be clear, she never once pretended she did. But she *liked* me, which kept us together and provided ample fuel for my desperate hopes and desires. I became her principal companion and friend, with me always hoping that it would develop into something more, no matter how many times she gently but earnestly assured me that it wouldn't. That's the thing about unrequited love: hope springs eternal, with every small kindness and shared confidence making the sufferer imagine they still have a chance.

I went through agonies over Ali, agonies of romantic frustration that made me feel physically sick. But I wouldn't let go.

I was the agent of my own destruction.

I broke my own heart.

Of course I did. All unrequited lovers do. And the fact that Ali valued my friendship was her only complicity in my self-perpetuating crisis. I ended up feeling that I actually had a *duty* to be faithful to this entirely one-sided love, that if I let it go, then all the pain would have been a lie. As I say, it went on for more than two years.

But I'm a resilient sort of a bloke and, while nursing my broken teenage heart I was still managing to get a lot out of life at South Warwickshire College of Further Education.

At the beginning of my second year, I inherited Cool John's caravan. Imagine it! I was seventeen and living in my own extremely hip private space. I was on my own, but in no way a loner. I had lots of friends and I had a Honda 50 to whizz into college on. The Cara, as it was known from then on, was from the 1950s, a steel shell with an all-wooden interior featuring lots of little nooks and cupboards. It was very worn and a bit mouldy, but still fabulous if it's yours and you're seventeen. It had a cold-water tap and a little gas stove and a two-bar electric fire. The winter was harsh and I couldn't afford to keep the fire on for long, so every morning for months, I woke up with white frost on my bumfluff moustache. I was literally frosted over and the top blanket on my huge pile of bedding was stiff and glittery with it. Years later, my mum told me how sometimes she'd lie awake at night worrying about that ancient electric heater causing a fire with all those blankets and with me burning to death. Looking back, it does seem amazing that I had such careless independence. I don't think I'd have wanted any of my kids living in such circumstances at that age. The 1970s was a different world.

Oh, I loved that Cara and had I not been so bloody broken-hearted, it could have been the perfect setting for romance. I did manage the odd tryst, but mainly I was faithful to my one-sided love affair and I spent many lonely evenings listening to Dylan and The Beatles on my little mono record player and writing appalling anguished poems about my desperate love. I put a lot of this self-obsessed, self-important, grandiose, theatrically miserable teen angst into the character of Rick the Poet in *The Young Ones*.

When Rik died, a lot of people tweeted the speech I wrote for Rick imagining his own death (as many teenagers do) . . .

This house will become a shrine, and punks and skins and Rastas will all gather round and hold their hands in sorrow for their fallen leader. And all the grown-ups will say, 'But why are the kids crying?' And the kids will say, 'Haven't you heard? Rick is dead! The People's Poet is dead!' And then one particularly sensitive and articulate teenager will say, 'Other kids, do you understand nothing? How can Rick be dead when we still have his poems?'

I'm still very proud of that.

Two plays, a B and two Cs

Between self-pitying poems and doing a bit of coursework, I did write another couple of plays during my A level year. Both were historical and both very serious, a brief departure from my dedication to comedy. I suppose, what with being in love and everything, I was going through a serious phase.

The first of the two was set in the First World War (and the first of a number of times in my life I'd write about that historic world tragedy) and it was called *Cannon Fodder*. It featured a fellow student and unique comic spirit called Dave Thompson, who went on to play Tinky Winky in the *Teletubbies*, and remains a dear friend. The other play was called *The Bear Hunt* and was about Stalin's purges! Well, I guess you only get one chance to be an earnest seventeen-year-old.

And then there was the little matter of A levels. They were fast approaching and I was in danger of screwing up badly. This wouldn't have bothered me at school, but my attitude had changed. I no longer even slightly wanted to be an actor. All I wanted to be was a writer – a playwright, in fact. My father, as ever good with his rare but timely advice, suggested that for a writer the most important thing was reading. And where better to read than at university? Once more, I was persuaded that the sensible thing for me would be to remain in education and, again, drama was the lure. For a second time, I decided to delay my anticipated rapid ascent up the showbiz ladder and apply to do drama at university.

There weren't many courses in those days. Bath offered one, along with Hull and Manchester and one or two others. I applied to all of them and got offered various interviews, to which I travelled on my Honda 50, top speed 48 miles an hour. All my university interviews were conducted with a very sore arse. Hull had a beautiful, brand-new theatre with professional lighting and sound and comfy seats and everything. I thought it was amazing and while I was being shown around, I asked if the students put on their own shows in it. The reply was that such a splendid facility was reserved for coursework only and tutor-directed productions. Manchester, on the other hand, didn't have its own theatre. All it had was a run-down former church called the Stephen Joseph Studio. It was battered and forlorn with a few lights, a tape recorder, some rostrums and not much else. It was, however, available to any student who wanted to use it.

I knew which course I wanted to get on to.

It turned out to be a life-changing decision.

But, to find that out, I had to get in.

Manchester offered me a place, but it was dependent on me getting a B in English A level, which was just not looking likely as I have had lifelong problems with spelling and punctuation. A lovely man called Tim Clarke, who taught English at DLA, said that there was no way I was going to get a B unless I made a concerted effort with my essay writing. I guess, like lots of kids, I was pretty good on ideas and opinions, but a lot less focused when it came to spelling, grammar, structure and form. But I really, really wanted to get into Manchester, so I agreed to buckle down.

Tim kindly set me extra essays (which meant extra unpaid work for him, for which I'll always be grateful) and I tried to focus. I didn't have a desk in my caravan, just a little table that was permanently cluttered with dirty dishes and teen anguish poems about Ali, so I borrowed an ironing board from two stable girls who lived in a nearby cottage and set it up outside as a desk. The spring of 1977 was pretty glorious and I remember vividly sitting at that borrowed ironing board on the edge of a cornfield as the insects hummed and buzzed and I tried to concentrate on *A View From A Bridge* and *King Lear*. The day that Tim gave back one of my extra essays with the note 'This looks like B material to me, Ben' was a great moment.

This was also the year that punk rock exploded – not just in music but in fashion and general attitude. It was what Mick Jones of The Clash memorably called the 'one-hundred-day battle of the flares'. Almost overnight, every young man in the country cut off his hair and bought a pair of drainpipes. Nothing has ever been as out of fashion as a pair of flares was in the Jubilee summer of '77. One day, *everybody* wore them, boys and girls. The next day, absolutely nobody did. It was that instant. Funny to think how much more of a cohesive national community we were then, even sartorially. Fashion isn't remotely as uniform any more. I think it was *Top of The Pops* that bound us together.

I got my B in English and my two years in Stratford ended – a glorious start to life and I will be for ever grateful to Gordon Vallins and his team. Years later, when the government ran a campaign in which celebs were invited to name a teacher who had changed their lives, I was proud to name Gordon. He told me that he thought the tribute was better than a knighthood, which made me very happy.

I spent most of the summer holidays of '77 writing yet another play (about two people in a private fallout shelter settling down comfortably to sit out the aftermath of nuclear war and finding they have a squatter) and also working as a barman in the Jolly Farmer on the River Wey back in Guildford. The landlord was a terrifying man, huge and violent, who had lost a finger in a fight. He also used to hint darkly that he was a member of the National Front. I've never been more relieved to finish a job in my life – and I've presented a documentary on carp fishing.

One very formative thing I did that holiday was to read Robert Tressell's *The Ragged Trousered Philanthropists*. This book affected me like nothing since *Animal Farm*. It chronicles ordinary working-class life in a seaside town during the Edwardian era and is generally considered to be the first and most important British Socialist novel. There's a passage in that book where the hero suggests that if air was a commodity that could be owned and sold, then workers would be as short of breath as they were of food, warmth and shelter. Twelve years later, I would base my first professional play, *Gasping*, on this brilliant and illuminating observation.

The golden summer holidays of 1977 came to an end and I said goodbye to genteel Stratford-upon-Avon and got ready for life in a big city. I'd be leaving many friends and happy memories behind me, but one thing I wouldn't be leaving behind was the principal source of my anguish. By coincidence, my friend Ali was going to Manchester to do English. If she'd gone elsewhere, no doubt my great unrequited passion would have faded much sooner, but as it was, I took it with me to Manchester where it would continue with equal emotionally destructive, self-inflicted fervour for more than another year.

1977 to 1979

'Hi, I'm Rik Mayall'

I rode from Guildford to Manchester on my Honda 50 in September 1977 and moved into a hall of residence called Grosvenor House. It wasn't the traditional university 'hall' with dinners and black gowns and that kind of boarding-school vibe. Manchester had a few of that sort, but Grosvenor was just a big, modern rabbit-warren block with corridors of tiny rooms and communal kitchens and showers. I knew I wouldn't be staying long; I was still only eighteen, but I'd already been living away from home looking after myself for two years and I didn't want to live on a communal corridor.

I mentioned the Stephen Joseph Studio which I'd liked the look of when I did my interview. Well, I soon discovered that not only were students allowed to use it, but they were encouraged to. Every Monday night was 'Studio Night', an evening when any students could present any work they felt like. Isn't that a wonderful thing? And on the very first studio night of my first term, a comedy team from the third year called 20th Century Coyote put on a show to welcome us freshers. It felt like an exciting night even at the time but, in retrospect, it takes life-changing significance.

How can I describe the first time I saw Rik Mayall?

Well, frankly, it was a form of love at first sight. Of all the talented and successful people that I have met in my life, Rik's star quality was the most obvious and the most immediate. Rik just *shone*.

He opened that freshers' show with a little welcome address. Strolling into the light, slightly scruffy, a woollen scarf knotted round his neck and tucked into his buttoned-up jacket (we were *always* cold), and just *standing* there. He really waited it out, looking at us for a looooooong moment before raising his eyebrows in the tiniest expression of surprise, as if to say 'Well, where is the ovation that is my due?'.

We didn't need a bigger hint than that. The place erupted in cheers.

The second and third years of course knew Rik and knew the role he had invented for himself, the role of a man who was *already* a star and who was merely waiting with bemused tolerance for the world to catch up with the idea. But we first years got it too, instantly. It was all in that one pause and that raise of the eyebrows. Rik's comic moves were instinctive and we reacted instinctively. We cheered and shouted, joining in the joke of the scruffy student who stood there as if to say that if the world wasn't at his feet, it should be.

And he hadn't even said a word yet.

And goodness he was handsome! More than handsome, in fact. He was beautiful. I am not one who normally takes much notice of male beauty, but Rik as a young man was riveting. Ask anyone. He had a very big head – almost too big but not quite – the face was lean and chiselled with high cheekbones and his deep-set eyes so mischievous and roguishly sexy. Confidence is always attractive and Rik had more than his share. I never knew a person who was happier being themselves than Rik, the epitome of that old cliché – the guy who women want and who men want to be. I may be wrong, but I think everybody admired Rik at uni. There were, no doubt, some who were jealous too, but I don't think anybody doubted his charisma.

Anyway, Rik waited until the applause had died down and then said four words which I can hear in my mind as I write them down almost fifty years later. The first words I ever heard him say.

'Hi. I'm Rik Mayall.'

Not the funniest line ever delivered you might think. Well, all I can say is that it seemed like it at the time. It was perfect. There was a tiny beat after the 'Hi', a beat that told us something significant was coming. And it was – the momentous sentence 'I'm Rik Mayall', said with the sort of effortless, self-effacing (but actually self-loving) cool that perhaps Brad Pitt might have used if he were addressing a group of theatre arts students at UCLA. Except Brad Pitt is a superstar and universally acknowledged to be one of the world's sexiest men, while Rik was a slightly spotty third-year drama student wearing a threadbare jacket and standing in a run-down and freezing former church in Manchester on a dark autumnal night. But that's the point. Brad, Rik. Rik, Brad. The *tone* was the same, a tone that said 'You know who I am. I know who I am. Let's all just get the hell over it and celebrate.'

I laughed till it hurt. I thought he was as funny as Monty Python. And he'd still only said four words.

'Okay, I want to talk to you freshers,' he went on, with the same natural presumption of status. 'Just a little bit of advice about getting on here at the drama department, which I know must seem like a big and scary place right now. But, believe me, it's really simple to relax and fit in. If you're a girl fresher, all you need to do is shag Rik Mayall. And if you're a guy fresher, just try to shag a girl who's shagged Rik Mayall.'

Maybe that doesn't sound funny to you, particularly in a different age when we view bullish male sexual posturing very differently. But please believe me when I tell you that it was a joke instinctively *calling out* bullish male sexual posturing, laughing at the male ego while celebrating the *Mayall* ego. And the women were laughing even harder than the men.

And it was so *original* back then. Don't forget, this was decades before celebrity wankers began adopting the excruciating affectation of referring to themselves in the third person. Rik nailed it back in '77. It was hilarious on two levels. We all knew he was playing the biggest kind of arrogant arsehole, which was funny enough, but the fact that you kind of felt he half meant it, *and with good reason*, made it truly irresistible.

The rest of the show was pretty good too, sufficiently offensive and bad taste to satisfy any wannabe punk freshers in that grim dark autumn of strikes and racial tension that was late '77. And, astonishingly, Rik wasn't the only towering comic talent in that little student troupe because no sooner had he left the stage than Adrian Edmondson appeared, also so striking, lean and handsome and so *intense*. Ade was leading a First World War sketch where a group of eye-bandaged men led each other across the stage whistling 'Tipperary', the classic image of soldiers blinded by gas, until the punch line revealed they'd all gone blind because of too much masturbation. I remember thinking this was very funny but also pretty tasteless. But then if you can't be tasteless in student revues, where can you be?

I didn't get to know Ade properly until after uni, but Rik and I became friends in that very first week. I bumped into him the day after that first show. He was shaving in the studio toilets and suggested I admire the spots on his chest to see what a real man looked like, the first of many zit gags we shared. I remember writing a page in *The Young Ones Book* as a joke advert for a makeup pencil to deal with the embarrassment of teenage spots (use the makeup pencil to draw a ring round it with an arrow pointing at it and write 'Look at my lovely spot'). In the book, I gave the gag to Ade's character Vyvyan, but it could have been Rik on that first day I met him.

He used to have a joke of pretending not to know my name and calling me Fresher. 'Hey, Fresher, shagged any chicks yet?' Again, don't judge. You had to be there.

It may actually have been the pursuit of girls that first led Rik to properly befriend me. True to habit, I put on my first show within a week of getting to uni and, with the influence of Gordon and DLA still strong, it was a piece of street theatre. The idea came to me on my second day when all us first years were summoned to a 'student meeting' from which tutors were excluded. There we were solemnly informed by a couple of the more pious and humourless third years that there was a campaign to improve the Stephen Joseph Studio. We were informed in hushed tones that the space might even constitute a *health hazard* as there were problems with damp and we might all die of rheumatoid arthritis in the middle of an improv session.

Anyway, that evening, back in my little hutch at Grosvenor House, I decided to spin this urgent political campaign into a piece of agitprop street theatre.

I wrote the show in its entirety that night. It was a history of the Studio, mixed with a righteous polemic about how desperately hard done by we students were to have to do our improv in a damp space. Fortunately, I wrote it as a comedy, framing the whole thing as a TV game show in which poor students were promised gleaming amenities but ending up with a shitty damp old church. The next day, I put up a sign on the department noticeboard saying that I was presenting a show, just as I had done two years before. This time, however, I didn't meet the same hostility, perhaps because I wasn't mounting a full-length play but just a little lunchtime sketch to augment an ongoing protest, and also because I concentrated my casting efforts on my own year. And maybe because I didn't announce I was forming my own theatre company and calling it 'The Studio Players'. That would have helped.

Anyway, I soon had a group together who thought it sounded like a laugh and I put on my little twenty-minute bit of street theatre. That in itself was quite noteworthy within our little department, but what really caught Rik's attention was that I decided to flank my cheesy male TV game show host with two female assistants – assistants who, in a vigorous satirical blast against sexist stereotyping in the media, were dressed in tinsel-trimmed bikinis. I honestly think that the fact that I managed to persuade two first-year girls to perform in glittery bikinis *outside* in the University Precinct in the autumn term in the north of England in the cause of anti-sexist satire is what really first endeared me to Rik.

All I can say in my own defence is that I really did mean it as satire on the objectification of women in light entertainment ('70s game show hosts were exclusively middle-aged and male and always flanked by sexily clad young female assistants).

But I guess you could also say I was having my cake and eating it.

The kindness of strangers

I loved being at Manchester University, but my first term wasn't all plain sailing. There was one setback early on, which is another example of how I can rub people up the wrong way without realizing it.

As I've said, having arranged my own accommodation for the previous two years, I didn't want to spend a year in a student residence. The blokes on my 'corridor' were nice enough, as were the girls on the corridor below and above, but it was a dull, featureless place and I'd been used to more characterful living spaces. So, when I saw a sign on the drama department noticeboard saying a group of third years were renting a house in Fallow-field and needed one more drama student tenant, I applied. They invited me round for a cup of tea and it seemed I'd passed my audition because they offered me the room. I handed in my notice at Grosvenor House, packed up my stuff and moved.

Three days later, I was asked to leave.

What a shock. I'd thought it was all going great. I'd sorted out my room, put my shampoo on the edge of the bath and claimed my bit of the shelf in the kitchen. That's how it had always been in my experience of communal living; you had your own stuff. When I'd lived in the farm cottage with Roger, Mick and John, we'd basically lived off toast. I got my main meal at the college cafeteria and, apart from that, it was a loaf of bread every three days, a carton of marge once a week and a jar of Marmite once a fortnight. In my caravan, I'd upgraded slightly to the occasional package meal (I remember proudly inviting Ali to dinner and doing her instant Vesta chicken chow mein), but that was where I stopped. I had been away from home for two years and had never once cooked a proper meal. What I put onto the bit of shelf I'd claimed for myself in my new home was cornflakes and white bread. I *suppose* I noticed that all the other available shelf space was loaded with *communal* food straight from a health food shop, and what's more a '70s health food shop: beans that needed soaking for a week, brown rice that was impervious to mastication, muesli that would prize open the buttocks of a concrete elephant (quoting my own lines there). I suppose I should have realized that these people cooked together and that what they cooked was very, *very* healthy. But I didn't think anything of it. I had my stuff, they had theirs. I didn't see how there could be a problem.

But there was a problem and, two days later, my fellow housemates invited me to join them in the communal 'space' and told me that it had been a mistake and they wanted me to leave.

Looking back, of course it's obvious what it was about. They wanted a like-minded individual to be a part of their little community. They were kind of conservative hippies, a bit smug, well-heeled, very into themselves. They found me a jarring note. I lived for the department and the students' union, while they just did their coursework, then went home to boil rice.

I liked to drink beer and talk about pop music, politics and theatre. They liked to sip green tea and talk about themselves.

I'm not saying they were exclusively arseholes or that I was perfect. I'm sure I talked too much; I've always talked too much. And now they were asking me to move out. And I did.

Immediately.

I scarcely gave them time to squeeze my hand earnestly and say 'It's not you, it's us'. I could hear them protesting behind me that I didn't need to leave at once and that they'd be thrilled for me to stay till I found somewhere else, but I was already at the door. For one thing, I was really worried that I was going to burst into tears. I certainly felt like it. I was appalled, convinced that this would mark me as an outcast at the department. I thought that the fact that a group of older, established students had only been able to stomach me for *three days* before throwing me out would condemn me to be a social leper for ever.

I grabbed my military greatcoat and walked out into the night, leaving all my stuff behind me to be collected God knew when. I was outside, alone on the street within ten minutes of being summoned 'for a little talk'. What's more, it was raining. I mean, really raining. It was a proper storm, like the one Gordon Vallins had had us shouting 'Howl, howl, howl' into, a gaggle of teenage Lears. My coat was heavy with rain in minutes, but all I could do was stride along with rain pouring down my face, mixing with the tears that I could now safely let go.

Maybe I really was an irredeemable arsehole. I couldn't help thinking about what had happened to me in my first term at DLA. Maybe this time there'd be no cool John to save me, this time I'd remain an outcast for my whole three years at Manchester.

But never mind the next three years. There was the immediate problem to consider. It was past eight in the evening on a dark, cold, stormy October night and I had *nowhere* to stay. I couldn't go back, I absolutely couldn't. But I had nowhere else to go. I'd only been in Manchester for a few weeks. I had a few friends in the first year that I might have asked to help and, of course, there was Ali, but they all lived in halls of residence where overnight guests were strictly not allowed. There were no mobiles in those days and no way of appealing to anyone, even if I'd had an idea who to appeal to.

I really had got myself into a fix. I suppose I could have gone to a hotel of some sort, but hotels were not in my consciousness. I don't think I'd stayed in one in my entire life – guest houses sometimes on family holidays, but not hotels. Besides, this was Rusholme in 1977. There *weren't* any hotels. Manchester's cultural renaissance was still at least a decade away. As were credit cards. I had a cheque book, but it was with my stuff and, anyway, a sodden eighteen-year-old with no luggage fronting up at some guest house reception (presuming I could find one) and asking to pay by cheque would have caused the cops to be called. Besides which, I had very little money in the bank anyway.

In the end, history repeated itself. I was saved by the cool kids.

Through Rik, I'd met some second years who were occasional members of Rik and Ade's 20th Century Coyote comedy troupe and general free spirits. Well, for some reason or other, I had their address. I don't know why they'd given it to me. Maybe they thought I could conjure up more first-year girls in glittery bikinis, but for whatever reason, that address was still in the pocket of my greatcoat. I really didn't know these guys at all, but I knew that they were laidback types and it seemed to me that they were my only chance of avoiding either drowning or dying of exposure on a park bench in the small hours. So I decided to appeal to them.

I was in Rusholme and the house was in Didsbury, a couple of miles' walk up the Oxford Road.

I was a drowned rat, a sodden, friendless, homeless outcast. It was an inauspicious way to approach a house. Didsbury is actually a rather posh part of Manchester and the house was a semi-detached one, set back from the street by a front garden. The reason it was being rented to scummy students was because it was extremely run-down. I made my way up the heavily overgrown front path, screwed up my courage and knocked on the door. It took a while for anyone to answer and, when they did, I was dismayed to discover that none of the people I knew were in. The door was opened by two strangers – a boy and a girl in a state of stoned semi-undress – and it was obvious that I'd disturbed them mid-shag. Not a great start but, despite that, after I'd blurted out my story, they were kindness itself. They were, like many students at that time, sort of punk hippies, very much into the ideas of sharing and love but also with a burgeoning political edge. They listened to what had happened and although neither of them knew me, said that I was welcome to stay. The girl was particularly outraged; she would turn out to be something of a firebrand and saw my sudden eviction as an act of social injustice. So they invited me in, told me to make myself at home and then went back upstairs to continue shagging while I sat on the couch and waited for my recent acquaintances – Mike, CJ and Mark – to come home.

I slept on their couch for three weeks.

When the story of what happened got about, none of my fears about being branded a leper materialized. In fact, it was quite the opposite. The general view was that I'd been appallingly treated. The next day in the department, people were sympathetic and, the day after, the guy who'd chucked me out apologized unreservedly and asked if I'd come back. Peace was made but I didn't return. I was having too much fun. Mike, CJ and Mark became good friends. Mike was at Rik's funeral, thirty-seven years after that night of the stormy outcast. Mark appeared in *The Young Ones* as Neil's hippy friend. Chris Ellis, or CJ as he was known, and I became particularly close – a short, skinny guy from Leeds with an enormous broken nose, the streetwise youngest son of a big working-class family who reminded me of Dustin Hoffman's character Ratso in *Midnight Cowboy*. He played the glue-sniffing kid complaining about being too young to drink in the first episode of *The Young Ones*. I was CJ's best man in 1981 when he married a lovely American girl. He's a film editor in LA now. He was always going to do something cool.

Besides providing temporary shelter, that house in Didsbury would become quite a significant address for me. I'd live there myself in my second year and Rik and Ade had lived there the year before. Apparently, Ade had ridden his motorbike through the front door and up the stairs. If any house was the prototype of *The Young Ones* house, it was this one.

Plays, pot and a new girlfriend

I didn't get to know Manchester at all when I was a student. My whole life was bound up in the drama department and the students' union. And Ali of course. I was still in love with her and visited a couple of times a week, constantly rekindling a fire that existed only in my own heart. I used to dedicate all my writing to her, getting each new play typed out and copied at the library and then slipping an extra dedication page into her copy 'For Ali'. She had quite a pile. I wrote a lot of plays.

That was who I was when I was a student. A playwright. I never thought about TV writing at all. I was always very practical in my approach to impossible ambition and I knew that if I wrote a play, I could stage it. This also made me a director, but I didn't think of myself as one. Directing was a means to an end: getting my writing onto a stage. I never had the slightest interest in directing anybody else's work.

I did minimal coursework, as usual doing what I needed to do to get by and that was all. I found it interesting enough and I liked my tutors, but all I really cared about was my own writing.

Midway through that first term, I put on my play *The Bear Hunt*, the dramatic critique of Stalinism that I'd written in my last term at Stratford. I put up another sign on the department noticeboard, just as I'd done two years before, announcing that I'd written a play and wanted to direct it. This time I encountered no social resistance.

The next play I wrote was called *Man of Woman Born* and, get this, it was a feminist take on the Ancient Greek tragic drama *Hippolytus* by Euripides. The original play is a blood and sex fest featuring murder, suicide, incest, vengeful gods and a chorus of nagging married women furious with men. It's all about the corrupting power of the female sex and so obviously I decided to make my reinvention all about the corrupting power of men and of sexism.

Right on, matey boy! – as I would later write in *The Young Ones*.

Around this time, I got into smoking weed.

Or dope as we called it. Or spliff. Or pot.

At the time, the word 'pot' was an archaic '60s hippy word and so we found it funny to use it in what would now be called a postmodern meta manner. For a year or two, I really, *really* enjoyed smoking pot. It was cheaper than beer and made you giggle a lot more. Of course, this was '70s stuff, usually quite weak and benign. Super-strong skunk and hydroponic weed were decades away. But it was strong enough for me! I remember we had a game called 'Cosmic Blowback' in which one of us would stand on their head with their feet against a wall and someone else would put the burning end of the spliff in their mouth and blow down it, sending a stream of pot smoke straight into the head-stander's mouth. Straight after this, two more willing assistants would whip the head-stander back upright, leaving them feeling like they had left the galaxy before crashing back to Earth in a giggling heap.

I never took anything stronger, but for a couple of years I got stoned pretty regularly. I'd sit around with my mates Dave, Johnnie, Martin and Zani, smoke a few joints, get the giggles, then get the munchies, then get burger and chips, then crash out. I remember asking myself if I was on the slippery slope to a wasted life and decided that, as long as I was getting up the next day and writing half a play, I couldn't be doing myself much harm.

And always on the lookout for opportunities to stage these plays, my attention turned to the university student theatre company, Manchester Umbrella, which became absolutely central to my life.

Umbrella (which was open to all students, not just drama ones) was already quite a large and ambitious organization when I joined it. The previous year, they had mounted a season at the Edinburgh Festival, taking over a little hall just off Leith Walk called Zetland Hall and creating what they called 'a festival in itself', putting on an impressive six shows in all. I couldn't think of anything better than going to the Edinburgh Fringe Festival with my own play and so I got involved with the group as quickly as I could.

It was through Umbrella that I met the girl who finally broke the spell of my self-created, one-sided, non-consummated (not even a flipping kiss!), three-year solo love affair. Of course, everybody knows the most certain way to fall out of love is to fall in love with someone else and this is true, even in the case of unrequited love affairs like mine. This new girl's name was Kate and we would be together for nearly eight years.

Kate was a law student but loved art and music and theatre, and had just taken over as Umbrella's administrator, publicity officer and occasional clarinet player. She was funny and sharp and suddenly we were a couple. Ali and I remained friends, but drifted apart in the end as friends often do, particularly when they have shared a friendship so deep that there is no real way to conduct it in a less intense manner. It's funny to think how fervently we live our lives when we're young. I reconnected with Ali again recently, both of us in our sixties, looking back with fondness. She still has all the plays I gave her which made me happy and gave me permission to tell our story in this book.

My two Edinburgh seasons as a student in the summers of 1979 and 1980 remain among my happiest memories, a whole gang of us living and sleeping in an old run-down hall and putting on shows. It was like a Mickey Rooney and Judy Garland movie but with marijuana joints.

We slept on the floor of our 'auditorium', pooled money to provide tea, coffee and cornflakes in the morning and the rest of the time lived off deep-fried haggis and chips. The boys did at least; I seem to recall that some of the girls made salads. There were toilets which we shared with the public but, for a proper wash, you went to the public baths. I don't know if municipal public baths even exist any more, but the Edinburgh ones of the early '80s were brilliant. We couldn't believe them: for 50p, you got your own room with a colossal and spotless stainless-steel bath full of steaming hot water. Of course, there was much fantasizing about sharing one, but there were stern notices and stern old bath ladies banning such practices. I don't think anybody ever dared try it.

Umbrella presented four plays in Edinburgh, plus a lunchtime play and a kids' show. I wrote and directed the lunchtime show and one of the main evening plays for both the '79 and the '80 seasons.

My first lunchtime show was a spoof musical comedy called *Golly Bobby You're So Dashing and Divine*, set in an English country house during a weekend party, which I suppose is evidence of my continued love of Coward and Wodehouse.

My other play in Edinburgh that year was a comedy called *Angels Out of Tune*, a left-leaning farce set in a guest house from hell and very loosely based on John Bunyan's *The Pilgrim's Progress*. Scotland's poshest paper, *The Scotsman*, said it was 'brutally rewarding and thought-provoking with a strong last punch'.

Can you imagine how thrilled I was?

I was walking on air up Leith Walk.

Golly Bobby got great notices too.

'A recipe for success, very funny and a splendid way to pass an hour,' said Radio Forth.

I'd been writing consistently since the age of fifteen, always believing that I had something to offer and now I had proof! My first-ever proper reviews and they were really good.

I thought it was the greatest thing ever.

Rik and Ade were up in Edinburgh in '79 too. They'd left university the previous year and were returning as fully fledged unemployed adults. Their show was called *Death on the Toilet* and God it was funny. I can still remember the opening gag. Ade answers the door to Rik dressed as the Grim Reaper.

ADE: Who the fuck are you?

RIK (in Cockney accent): I'm deaf!

ADE: All right, I'll speak up. WHO THE FUCK ARE YOU?

Death on the Toilet was also a success, with every seat sold each night (which was about fifty, I think). I vividly remember Ade telling me how excited they were and what a great time they were having. They'd do their show in the afternoon, collect all the cash and go straight to the pub. No one had ever been able to afford to get pissed on a daily basis before and Ade and Rik were making the most of it. I thought it sounded like they were living in heaven. In fact, they were living in a single, shared two-man tent for *three weeks* – which no doubt was part of the reason they spent so much time in the pub.

They used to come around to see us at Umbrella in our little hall (not least to use the loos) and I remember sharing a spliff with Rik in the little basement storeroom I used as a bedroom. It was so damp that it had mushrooms growing on its walls and was dark and cold even in the summer. We'd talk about comedy, of course. Perhaps it's romantic hindsight, but I think we both felt that sometime, somehow, we were going to get somewhere and that perhaps we'd do it together.

Someone who was already getting somewhere was a bloke called Rowan Atkinson. He was up in Edinburgh doing his show with another bloke called Richard Curtis and having a huge success in a proper big room. Big success, not beer-money success – the sort of success that had people talking about BBC offers and being the next big thing. Rowan was the talk of the Fringe and a number of our group stumped up the cash and got tickets. I didn't. I was doing my own comedy; I wasn't really interested in anybody else's. I remember everybody said that it was brilliant, telling stories of this weird, rubber-faced genius, but I didn't think Rowan Atkinson sounded like my sort of thing at all.

The importance of being earnest

Towards the end of my second year at uni, the UK changed for ever, not that we were fully aware of it at the time. Margaret Thatcher was elected on 3 May 1979. It was my twentieth birthday. I remember that election very well, but funnily enough not because of any awareness of the social and economic earthquake that Thatch would unleash. It wasn't Mrs T that scared us; it was the fascist National Front. Throughout the 1970s, the far right had been on the rise and had made such a strong showing in the second 1974 election that they had earned themselves the right to a televised party political broadcast this time around.

Party political broadcasts, eh? That weird TV institution seems a distant irrelevance now in our multi-channel zero-focus world. But they used to be a part of everybody's lives. You couldn't avoid them – the BBC and ITV had to show them at prime time. The whole nation's evening would be interrupted by these strange five- or ten-minute lectures delivered by some wooden-voiced, middle-aged man speaking very slowly and clearly.

'Good evening. I should like to take a little of your time to speak with you about inflation.'

Anyway, now the National Front were going to get one. Nobody could believe it: Nazis were going to be advertising their racism *on the telly*.

These were the days of the Anti-Nazi League. *Everybody* wore the badges and danced to the rhythm of ska and Two-Tone.

In fact, the threat from the NF, as we knew them, fizzled out at the '79 election. Thatcher drew their sting by giving her famous speech about people being fearful of communities being 'swamped'.

Anyway, shit was getting real, as people didn't say then, and I rose to the challenge. In the autumn of '79, as Mrs Thatcher's new government began to flex its muscles, I wrote a play called *If Turnips Were Horses*, all about debt-driven consumerism and unemployment.

Well, I was still a student. You're allowed to be a bit earnest.

In my own defence, this was in the days of what was called agitprop theatre. Agitprop is short for agitation and propaganda. Sounds like a lovely night out, doesn't it? Agitprop had its routes in the brilliant work of Joan Littlewood and her Theatre Workshop Company and it could be very good – *Oh! What a Lovely War*, for instance, is Agitprop. Sadly, with one or two honourable exceptions, by the late '70s the form had become hectoring, humourless, lefty bollocks. State-funded theatre companies touring the country trying to bring down the state that was funding them.

And the funny thing was that these theatre companies were flourishing under a *Labour* government. But, *of course*, not one that was sufficiently left-wing for them. They saw Labour Prime Minister James Callaghan as a Tory. A lot of people on the left did at the time in those balmy days before Mrs Thatcher showed everybody what a real Tory fucking looked like.

There was an awful lot of left-wing posturing going on back then. Universities were much more political places than they are today, Gaza and trans rights notwithstanding. And, in those days, it was all about *class* politics. Left versus right. Or, more tellingly and depressingly, left versus left. Then, as now, progressives were far happier hating each other for not being pure enough than taking on the real foe. The students' union steps of the 1970s were crowded with earnest middle-class young people selling competing journals representing their various versions of communist and revolutionary socialism.

Ah! Those long-gone earnest voices of another age. I hear them still.

'*SO-cialist Worker*. Get your *SO-cialist Worker*.'
'*SO-cialist Challenge. SO-cialist Challenge*.'
'*Morning Star! Morning Star!*'
'*Marxism Today. Marxism Today*.'
'*Sparticist Separatist Gazette*.'
'*Communist Syndicalist Times*.'
'*Socialist Sparticist Syndicalist Communist Marxist Advertiser*.'

I think I may have made the last couple up but, believe me, the choice on the left was bewildering and all of them hated each other with far more passion than they ever hated the Tories – and they hated the Labour Party most of all. I tried to take an interest for a while. I'd buy the odd paper and sit in the union tea bar with a skinny liquorice paper roll-up feeling important and pretending to be Trotsky. But the truth is that while I definitely agreed with many of the grievances outlined in those ancient red inkies, I absolutely rejected their desired revolutionary solution. As such, I was considered worryingly right-wing and reactionary by many politicized students at the time.

My last two efforts at student play-writing were more satisfying. They were both presented on my second season in Edinburgh with the Umbrella company in the summer of 1980.

Again, I wrote a comedy for our lunchtime slot, a kind of Jane Austen spoof called *Oh, Be Still My Palpitating Heart*. One interesting footnote is that, five years later, Richard Curtis and I used a couple of the gags from it in the opening scene of the second series of *Blackadder*.

My play that year was a two-hour three-acter for which I used the same title as my first-ever play *Once More with Feeling*. This was a very different story, although also still set in an amateur dramatic society between the wars. This time the local vicar was a Shakespeare nut who put on a Shakespeare play every year and always insisted on playing the lead role. Unfortunately, he was also a fascist, a huge admirer of Hitler and a fervent anti-Semite. This was causing him anguish as the only play he hadn't yet done was *The Merchant of Venice*. Refusing to portray a Jew, he decides to mount a version of the play where Shylock is a Christian and all the other characters are Jews.

Much hilarity and a little bit of politics ensued. It would be thirty-five years before I used Shakespeare for inspiration again, but I suppose my sitcom *Upstart Crow* has a sort of genesis here.

Around that time, I also nearly got a break with the BBC. One of my uni tutors got me an introduction to a drama producer at BBC Radio Manchester, who said that if I submitted something, he'd be happy to read it. What I did was a good example of both my strength and my weakness as a writer. I wrote a full thirty-minute 'play for radio' over the next twenty-four hours. I say it was a play, but really it was just a kind of gag-fest panto. I don't really know what I was thinking. In fact, I wasn't really thinking at all beyond the idea that I must hurl words at this opportunity as quickly as possible. The reply I got was very fair. The BBC bloke said he'd enjoyed the piece and it had some good jokes, 'but of course you realize it's not a play'.

I hadn't realized.

The same tutor who'd made the recommendation to the BBC said something to me about my work, which I've thought about a lot over the years.

'Ben, you may one day make a decent playwright if you can just forsake your ruthless pursuit of the one-line gag.'

At the time, I just didn't agree. It seemed to me that tutor and the department itself represented a culture that I thought was anti-entertainment.

But, actually, I think he had a point. For years, I didn't trust my writing and thought the only way to sell it was gags, gags and more gags. I'm quite good at writing gags and I think perhaps that facility allowed me to put less thought into form and structure, sometimes obscuring a good idea by hiding it behind gags that weren't actually worthy of it. In short, I haven't trusted myself.

So while I rather resented the comment at the time, I came to see that he definitely had a point. And it's one which I'll probably still be struggling with to the very last word I ever write.

The Early '80s (Part One)

London calling

I graduated from university in the summer of 1980.

I am so grateful for my time at Manchester; it was the most wonderful and intense three years. These days, three years pass in the wink of an eye but, back then, each year – first, second and third – seemed like an entire lifetime. I lived the experience to the full in my own way, making great friends, enjoying a modest portion of the traditional student delights of sex and drugs and rock'n'roll, and, above all, writing and presenting play after play, each of which at the time meant everything to me and for which I cared as passionately as I have ever done with any professional work.

I know I must have sat some final exams but can't really remember doing them. I suppose I also must have made an effort at revision, but I don't really remember that either. Something must have sunk in, though, because I do find that I retain some knowledge of the theory and practice of theatre to this day, even though I haven't turned a page of Grotowski or Stanislavski since.

Anyway, university life was over. It was the autumn of 1980 and Kate and I travelled directly from Edinburgh to London in the cold grey dawn of Thatcher's Britain.

Isn't that a phrase and a half?

Thatcher's Britain.

What prime minister before or since has had the entire country named after them? None. Not Peel nor Palmerston. Not Gladstone, Disraeli, Lloyd George or Atlee. Not even Churchill. Only Margaret Thatcher got the whole country named after her. She was a political colossus and my generation came of age in her shadow.

I could have had dinner with her, you know.

It was after she'd retired and the invitation came from Andrew Lloyd Webber. He's a mischievous bastard and I could see he thought it would be a laugh.

'Come on, Ben. You *have* to meet her'.

But I said no. And not out of some angry piety either. I don't refuse to talk to people just because I don't agree with them. In fact, I really wanted to go. I love history and I knew that I'd never again get the chance to meet anyone who had had a more titanic influence on Britain (I choose that word deliberately).

So why didn't I go? I'll tell you why. I was worried that I'd *like* her.

And I didn't want to like Mrs Thatcher.

I tend to get on with most people I meet and I knew she would be interesting. How could she not be? She was the most powerful and influential British woman of the twentieth century. And good company too, according to all accounts – witty, confident, gossipy and, of course, very bright.

I knew Mrs Thatcher would be fascinating and that there was a good chance I might actually like her. Besides which, even if I'd hated her, I'd still have been polite. I try to be polite to everyone.

But I didn't want to slink away thinking I'd let myself down. And, more particularly, I didn't wish to have all the other diners (who I was pretty sure would be Tories) grinning behind my back, mistaking my good manners for fawning cowardice.

So I didn't go. But I still very much regret that missed chance to sit face to face with history.

The passions have faded so much now that it must be hard for younger people to have any idea of the political polarization of the decade in which I began my adult life, the economic and cultural *shock* of the gears of society being shifted so suddenly and so brutally.

Looking back, I think it's possible that even Mrs Thatcher might concede that the society she created (despite not believing in such a thing) did not develop entirely along the lines that she'd hoped it would. But no one can say that she lied about her intentions. She did what she said she'd do. Her great (and in my view deeply damaging) achievement was to shatter what was then known as the 'post-war consensus': that universal assumption that the political centre of Britain had shifted permanently leftward; a cross-party acceptance of the founding principles of Atlee's post-war Labour government, that six-year whirlwind of change that had established the NHS, nationalized coal and the railways and empowered the trade unions; the shift in priority from the individual to the community, the idea that in fact the individual can only *truly* thrive and prosper if the whole community thrives and prospers.

That was the post-war consensus and Tory prime ministers, right up to Edward Heath, recognized it to a greater or lesser extent. Even Churchill, who stormed back in straight after Atlee's single term, did not try to reverse the establishment of the NHS, even though it was only three years old at the time and would, I imagine, have been easy to kill.

Thatcher changed all that. In her ten years in power, she shifted the political middle ground of the UK all the way back rightwards and we have lived with that ever since. The post-*Thatcher* consensus, and Labour governments since, have legislated under that new reality.

That's one hell of a change and I was young when the gears were crunching. From the Brixton riots of '81 to the Poll Tax riots of '89, with the miners' strike and the City's Big Bang in between, the '80s *made* modern Britain.

Is it therefore any wonder that I was interested in 'a little bit of politics'?

A flat in Hampstead

But I most certainly didn't want to *be* a politician. I chose showbiz, as I had done since I was ten, and, as such, was super-impatient to establish myself as a writer. I had no idea that my big break was hurtling towards me. I was going to be in exactly the right place at exactly the right time.

The principal reason for that lucky circumstance was because in 1976, my dad inherited his parents' flat in Hampstead and decided not to sell it immediately in order to help give us four kids (and many friends) a base in London if we needed it.

I cannot express enough how much of a lucky break this was. The UK is still London-centric but in those days, before the internet and the resurgence of the regions, you really *had* to be in London. Being in the right place at the right time has so much to do with a person's chances in life and there's no doubt that being part of a family that owned a flat in London gave me a huge start and one that is denied to most people. I know privilege when I see it and that mouldy, run-down, little basement flat bought in the early '50s courtesy of the pensions that Germany paid to its lost Jews gave me a substantial portion.

Kate was also moving to London to study for the Bar so we moved into the flat together. We also gave a roof to assorted uni buddies. I don't really remember what I did that first grown-up autumn, except that I wrote another play. About Mussolini – as you do.

I remember sending it off to many theatres but I got no takers. I'd also written to pretty much every theatre in the country trying to get work as an assistant stage manager, but had had no luck there either. I still have all those rejection letters in a file, with their bright confident letterheads announcing the names of regional theatres, many of which have since died slow, sad deaths. If I were in control of the Arts Council, I'd put every penny into the regions and education. I don't believe in government-sponsored centres of excellence, but that may be personal. August institutions like the National Theatre, the Royal Court and the RSC have certainly never wanted anything to do with me. Believe me, I've tried.

But back to the autumn of 1980. I was a broke, unemployed aspiring playwright. I signed on the dole, an experience which was as depressing then as I imagine it is now, and wondered what the fuck I was going to do.

Then things started to happen. Very, very quickly.

Rik had moved to London by this time and I had seen quite a lot of him, most memorably when he and Ade came to Hampstead to do their cabaret show in the upstairs theatre room of a pub called The Three Horseshoes. Rik had come around to my place beforehand with a plastic carrier bag full of beer and we got afternoon-drunk, a totally different vibe to evening-drunk because you still have the evening to get through, an evening which, for Rik, included doing a show. He didn't fuck up completely, but Ade certainly wasn't happy and for years thereafter, Rik didn't drink before shows – or not to my knowledge, at least. But it was an early sign of how booze would one day become a serious factor in Rik's working relationships, the most intimate of which were with Ade and with me.

That Hampstead show had in fact been a double bill – Rik and Ade (who I think by that time were billing themselves as The Dangerous Brothers) and a duo called The Outer Limits, made up of Nigel Planer and Pete Richardson. The two double acts had met performing at London's fledgling Comedy Store.

The show was pretty good as I recall, despite Rik being still a bit pissed. Pete and Nigel did the first half, the highlights of which were Nigel's very fledgling 'Neil the Hippy' character and the two of them doing a human impression of Space Invaders, the first cult video game.

Then came Rik and Ade, who were electric. They had already developed an early showstopper in which Rik's furious psycho tries to tell Ade's even more furious psycho a joke about a gooseberry in a lift and Ade questions the logic – 'But how does it reach the buttons?' 'It fucking jumps!' – until it descended into splendid comic violence.

I also remember there was a lovely mad punk poem by Ade in which Rik played a furious (there was a lot of fury) commuter who's so familiar with his soul-destroying daily Tube journey that he doesn't realize he's dead and doesn't have to do it any more.

But, unquestionably, the highlight of the show was Rik's solo performance as a pretentious feminist poet and theatre tragic getting ever more furious (ha!) at the audience's refusal to take him seriously. 'I'd like to do another poem about Vanessa Redgrave. SHUT UP!!'

After the show, I met Pete and Nige for the first time. Pete was already well-advanced with his plans to open his own comedy club using the cream of The Comedy Store talent. He intended to call this club The Comic Strip. The pieces of what was to be something of a comedy revolution were falling into place.

'Once in every lifetime / Comes a chance like this'

Christmas came and went and New Year's Eve 1980 blurred into New Year's morning 1981, presenting no more promising a prospect than the previous autumn had done. The only bright note was that one of the collective of people currently crashing at the Hampstead flat had a Christmas job and was able to supply booze at New Year. Then, quite suddenly, in January it all started to kick off. One cold wet depressing morning, Rik rang me. 'Come to the pub NOW, Fresher! I've got something to talk to you about!'

That was exciting in itself. I loved hanging out with Rik and I loved making him laugh. But I had no idea how exciting it was about to become.

And also how painful.

We met at the George Pub in Wardour Street. The Comic Strip had opened by that time around the corner in Brewer Street and the George had become (and would remain) the major Comic Strip watering-hole. It's a small pub and always crowded – you really had to wrestle your way in and the bar was always jammed with people who'd got their drinks hemmed in by people trying to get their drinks. I bought two pints of lager and went to secure us a place. I knew I'd be first. I'm always first. Punctuality is important to me – time matters, and we're never born with enough of it. When Rik did arrive, he wasn't alone. There were to be three of us at the meeting. Me, Rik and Rik's girlfriend, Lise Mayer.

I can't remember if I'd met Lise before that day, but if I had, I certainly didn't know her. It's often presumed that she was on the drama course with us in Manchester, but in fact she went to university elsewhere. She and Rik had met through her dad who was a tutor at Manchester and they had only quite recently started going out.

Anyway, Rik had something incredibly exciting to tell me. He had been approached by a producer from the BBC called Paul Jackson who had said that if Rik could come up with a TV idea, Paul would pitch it to the Light Entertainment department. By this time, The Comic Strip was beginning to attract a little bit of media attention. Rik in particular was getting noticed in a *Time Out*-ey, fringey sort of way. At the time, Paul was producing *The Two Ronnies*, but he was young and ambitious and keen to develop something of his own. He'd checked out The Comedy Store and The Comic Strip and thought Rik was going to be a star. I don't think Paul gets enough credit for his role in bringing the underground 'alternative' phenomenon to a wider public. He was a visionary but also a populist and for that reason I don't think his unique and brilliant contribution to television arts has been sufficiently celebrated.

Rik told me that he wanted to pitch Paul a sitcom set in a student house based on the four embryonic characters that Rik and the other guys had been developing in their respective double acts: Rik's angry poet, Ade's psychotic anarchist, Nigel's pathetic hippy (as we have seen already called Neil) and Pete's kind of pseudo cool team leader. Rik had no script but he had lots of ideas and had already thought of a name for the show. He had decided that his character (Rick) should be a Cliff Richard fan (Cliff was already a mums' or even grannies' favourite by 1981, the joke being that Rick thought he was still hip) and he wanted to call the show *The Young Ones* after Cliff's hit from 1961. Cliff seemed like an old man to us then, but in fact he's only nineteen years older than me.

I was listening to Rik with growing excitement. He was describing a sitcom in which there would be a weekly band, comic violence, cartoon elements . . . In fact, anything at all could happen, which was to apply as much to the dialogue as the plot.

'Rick should get it all wrong, but weirdly,' Rik said. 'Like if someone insulted him, he'd reply "I'm not a fridge you know".'

I can still remember him busking that line. For some reason, it just seemed so funny. Perhaps it was as simple as the tiny speech impediment Rik affected when doing Rick 'I'm not a fwidge, you know', except it was much subtler than that, almost 'thwidge'. Actually, I don't think I can even spell it phonetically, it was so distinctive – the tiniest comic lisp used to devastating effect.

Like Rowan's 'B' words.

Anyway, after the third pint, Rik got to the point, a point I'd been desperately hoping he'd get to since he'd asked me to come out for a drink.

He wanted me to be a part of it. In fact, he wanted me to write it.

That moment was one of the most exciting of my entire life. 'Me and

Lise have loads and loads of ideas,' he said, 'but you're a writer. An actual writer. You've done bloody *plays*. Millions of plays so now you can do a bloody sitcom.'

All of those student plays had paid off much sooner than I'd dared to hope and in a totally unexpected fashion. I remembered me and Rik sitting in my little mushroom room in Edinburgh sharing a joint and him telling me how much he had admired *Angels Out of Tune* and *Golly Bobby*.

He hadn't forgotten either and now, on the strength of them, we were discussing a potential BBC sitcom together!

I went straight home that night, sat down at once and, working through the night, I wrote an entire episode draft.

I called the episode 'Demolition' and it would become episode one of *The Young Ones*. I mentioned that I tend to instantly throw a lot of words at a project. This time they well and truly stuck, every single one of them. That script would be recorded for television largely unchanged almost exactly a year later. I wrote it long hand in blue biro and I still have the manuscript. It just flowed out. I felt I was on fire. Many of the terms and phrases that would shortly become part of British youth culture emerged that night.

Young Ones-speak, which was developed out of the private student banter that Rik and I shared, really entered the language: *Yes, it blummen well did matey boy and if you ever say it didn't, you're a total and utter, utter virgin who's never snogged a girlie. Right-on kids! Vegetable rights and peace. Take that Thatch!* The '80s pop mag *Smash Hits*, which sold in millions, was practically written in *Young Ones* style and you still hear echoes of it today. When that total shit Boris Johnson called someone a 'girly swot' in the House of Commons, he was actually quoting a line I wrote for Rick in *The Young Ones* more than forty years before. It was kind of fitting, really. Johnson has always been a bit like a character from a sitcom – just a particularly crap and obnoxious one.

Incidentally, this was *exactly* what Rik wanted his character Rick to be. Crap and obnoxious. Rik was absolutely clear: this was to be an anti-sitcom. The characters must be properly selfish and unpleasant. He even wanted to be ugly and would design himself a truly ugly haircut and stick prosthetic spots all over his handsome chiselled face. So did Ade. And the girls still went crazy for them both. If you've got it, you've got it.

Along with the language, that first script also contained quite a lot of the physical comedy that would define the show. Both Neil's too-hot-to-hold vat of lentils and Vyvyan's first entrance – smashing through the kitchen wall and later biting an exploding brick – all came to pass exactly as I conceived them that very first night.

Also, I'm here to tell you, did much of the detail of how the four characters would turn out.

The four personas Rik had in mind from the two stage double acts, which I'd seen showcased at the pub comedy night the previous autumn, had been very sketchy and actually too grown-up to be students. In the clubs, they were sort of weirdos in their twenties or even thirties. Nigel's stage 'Neil' did a long riff about having caught herpes on an ashram in India. And while Rik's angry theatre luvvie poet could conceivably still be a student, his and Ade's Dangerous Brothers characters (from which Vyvyan would develop) could just as easily have been middle-aged – Pete's straight-man schtick even more so. All four characters needed more breadth and depth and *character*. They needed authentic (if comically exaggerated) voices. And I knew instinctively where to find those voices. The show would be rooted socially, culturally and politically in the youth culture of my own generation: student life in 1981, the second year of Thatcher's Britain. I'd been living it and now I would write it.

Rik's character in particular offered glorious opportunities to lampoon the vainglorious middle-class student political pretensions that I'd myself been such a part of over the previous three years. I switched his poet's obsession from theatre and ramped up the posturing revolutionary aspirations, giving the character his own fantasy life as 'The People's Poet'. The first time I wrote that phrase was a punch-the-air moment.

I rang Rik the following morning and told him I had a script.

'What took you so long, you lazy bastard?! Get the fuck round here and show me it *now*'.

'Righty-ho, matey, and after you've admired my nob, you can have a look at my script'.

I'm not sure Rik and I ever had a single conversation that wasn't peppered with doobles and nob gags. Pathetic perhaps, but it made us happy.

Rik was living in a flat in a grotty tower block in Green Hundred Road, just off the Old Kent Road. I used to take the Tube to the Elephant & Castle and then walk the last mile. The flat was shared but I can't remember who with or whether Lise had yet moved in. I don't think Ade ever lived there, although he was round there a lot too. He and Rik used to spend hours making comedy cassettes together.

Rik made me a bacon and tomato sandwich. He lived largely off bacon and tomato sandwiches in those days and used to claim it represented a fully balanced diet.

I sat down opposite him and Lise, and read them the script out loud. I used to read out all my stuff because my handwriting and spelling are so poor.

Rik *roared* with laughter from start to finish. I mean it, he roared. He was always so incredibly generous with his laughs. If he found something funny, he expressed it with every ounce of his physicality – great throaty explosions of mirth with tears in his eyes and sometimes even rolling down his cheeks.

I was ecstatic. In those days all I wanted to do was make Rik laugh. I absolutely trusted his instincts and always worked towards them, taking his inspired comic muse and spinning it into comic substance, adding content and language, building on the madness. In that early time, we had an *organic* connection, we really did. We *got* each other. In a way, we shared a sort of love. But, like many a shared love, it was a bit imbalanced.

I found him inspiring and exciting and I felt I could give him exactly what he needed.

And he felt the same way.

He thought he was inspiring and exciting and that I could give him exactly what he needed.

'Come on, Farty. Write me some bloody gags, you bastard, or I'll tell the whole world you're a virgin.'

He said that to me in a hundred different ways over many years. Sadly, for many of those years, I didn't respond.

But, in 1981, I did. All I wanted to do was make Rik laugh because I loved him.

And Rik did laugh. He laughed and laughed and when I'd finished reading, he demanded we go immediately to the pub to celebrate.

Going to the pub and drinking several pints of lager was a joy to us and we did it a lot. Later on, booze would become a far less happy thing between Rik and me, but in 1981, drinking in the day still felt great.

I took the Tube home at the end of a momentous afternoon and, if it's possible to float on air in an underground tunnel, then that bloke stinking of Heineken and dancing on the ceiling was me.

Three names on the title page

There was, however, one part of the script that had progressed less satisfactorily than the rest and that was the character of Mike. I knew I hadn't got it quite right yet and so did Rik. As I've mentioned, the original inspiration for the character was Pete Richardson, a witty and inventive man who any lover of '80s comedy will know from his groundbreaking work as film-maker-in-chief of *The Comic Strip Presents . . .* TV series. Rik demanded I should go alone without him or Lise present to talk to Pete about the character before doing more work on it.

I met Pete in The George and what we discussed was the 'being cool by being uncool' thing that underpinned so much of our comedy in those days. We talked about a guy who thinks he's enigmatic and impressive but always gets it a bit wrong. I remember Pete coining a phrase that night that I thought was very promising. He said, 'This guy thinks he's really cool but instead of saying "I'm Mike, I'm cool", he gets it a bit wrong and says "I'm Mike, the cool person".

Mike the Cool Person.

It seemed really funny to me. An uncool man, invulnerable in the conviction that he was the coolest guy on Earth. After that chat, I really felt I had it. Mike would be a man who was always starring in his own movie. I'd known people like that at uni, the kids who wore shades to lectures, geography students who thought they were Lou Reed. I'd have Mike say enigmatic things which were actually just bollocks, like 'Hey, now we're in the same supermarket and we ain't buying frozen peas'. After all, a lot of what the beat poets said would be just bollocks if it hadn't been said by beat poets. Mike would be a poseur but with enough weirdness about him to make him attractive and interesting. I still think it's a great character.

Rik thought I was on to something too and so, with Mike further finessed, the script was complete.

The next challenge was to make it legible.

Fortunately, I had a typewriter which had come with the flat. My grandfather had typed his big hit, *From Solon to Socrates*, on it.

From Solon to Socrates to nob gags.

I remember that Kate was hosting some kind of lefty meeting that day and the other flatmates were at home too, so the only place I could find to type was in the bathroom. It's kind of ironic – considering how many times I have been accused of toilet humour over the years – that my professional career literally started in one. The TV impressionist Bobby Davro once did me writing my material sitting on a toilet. He didn't know how close he was.

Ours was a basement flat created out of the cellar when the townhouse had been subdivided and our bathroom had been dug out under the front steps – a 1950s conversion, completely unlined, or damp coursed, horribly wet and freezing cold. This was January and there was no heating. I sat on a cushion on the three solid concrete steps that led down into this black hole with a loo and a bath in it, with the typewriter on my knees. With slimy mould on the streaming walls, my breath hanging thick in the air, dew drops on the end of my nose and my arse in danger of developing piles, I laboriously typed out my script two-fingered. I still have that typed script too. Rik and I actually read the first few pages of it together on camera in 2011 when I made a documentary about '80s comedy. It took many freezing hours and a couple of bottles of Tippex to complete, but it was worth it.

Shortly after that experience, with Kate's help I learned to type, which was one of the most useful things I ever did.

I gave the typescript to Rik and Lise who gave it to Paul Jackson. I hadn't included a title page, but by the time Paul saw it, Rik and Lise had added one with all three of our names on the front. This was quite a hard one for me to swallow. Give or take a sentence or two, it was definitely exclusively my script, plot, structure and dialogue, and it had already gone a very long way beyond the ideas discussed during that original night in the pub. Rik didn't deny this when I brought it up and assured me that, while we were all to be equal co-originators, he and Lise would be credited as creative advisers and I would be credited as sole writer.

That's what he told me.

I was soon to learn that it was most definitely not what he told Lise.

I'm not blaming Lise. Rik could be very dishonest – as much with himself as with others. He kept his life in compartments and he kept a lot of secrets. He was never deliberately cruel, but he was sometimes cowardly and naive, which could have the same effect. I think that, after his wife Barbara and Ade, I knew Rik better than anyone did. But I never knew the whole man.

Rik created a fundamental confusion between the originators of *The Young Ones*, which would lead to some questionable choices and a very painful confrontation from which I would emerge comprehensively defeated. But I'll get to that.

This is mainly a happy story and 26 February 1981 was a very happy day because that was the day Rik phoned me to tell me some truly incredible news.

I can hear his voice now and quote him verbatim.

'Congratulations, you're a rich man. The BBC want to make the pilot.'

'Rich man' was perhaps a slight exaggeration. The script fee was £1,000 and, after Rik's agent's fee and admin, my share was to be £287.63, which was a third. I genuinely did not mind that at all. The original idea had been Rik and Lise's and he'd brought me into his big break. My joy was unalloyed. It was a career earthquake. I was twenty-one, barely six months out of university and I had a sitcom pilot script commissioned at the BBC. Few writing careers in showbusiness have ever got off to such a flying start. In fact, I remain the youngest writer ever to get such a break and my gratitude for such good fortune remains undiminished. We had Paul to thank for the pace things had moved. He was a human dynamo with a very easy-going boss, Jim Moir, head of Light Entertainment, whom I would later satirize in *Filthy Rich & Catflap* as Jumbo Whiffy, head of Nice Entertainment. Jim was a large, big-bellied, jolly-faced, back-slapping bloke steeped in the traditions of light entertainment. He reminded me slightly of Eddie Large of Little and Large. Jim didn't understand a word of the script and happily told us so, but he trusted Paul's instincts and took a punt. That was all it needed back then. Jim was his own boss; he didn't have to go to a channel controller or a head of programming or a chief scheduler. He didn't have to find his way through the various contradictory levels of the vast top-heavy bureaucracy, which is the modern BBC (so brilliantly satirized in the series *W1A*). If he wanted to spend £1,000 on a hunch, then he could. Of course, taking that script into studio would be a more expensive and complicated business, and it would be January 1982 before we'd record it, but when you consider that the first series was on air the following autumn (eighteen months after the commission of the pilot script), it was still an astonishingly speedy result.

They were simpler times and we were very lucky.

The Early '80s (Part Two)

A fateful career move

On the very same day that I became a professional sitcom writer, I also became a stand-up comedian – because getting a pilot commission from the BBC wasn't the only reason 26 February 1981 was a watershed date for me. That afternoon, I auditioned for The Comic Strip as a comedian. So, I'm going to leave *The Young Ones* for a minute and turn to my strange and totally unexpected career as a stand-up comic.

I say strange and unexpected because I promise you that, a week before I became a comic, I had had absolutely no desire or ambition to be any such thing. Yet my decision to have a crack at it would shape me and my professional life in an infinitely more significant manner than anything that I had or would ever do as a writer, including *The Young Ones*. It would end up defining me in the eye of the media and public. And everything else I would ever do would be viewed through its prism. Even today, after sixteen novels, numerous TV series, three movies, three West End plays and four musicals, I am still seen largely as a gobby, shouty, Thatch-bashing stand-up comic who's written some other stuff. It's diminished slightly as I approach old age but, for a good thirty-five years, I was never able to escape the confines of my sparkly suit.

But it wasn't planned. From the age of fifteen, all I ever wanted was to be a writer. I never had any real ambition to perform. I put on a dozen plays as a student and cast myself in only one of them and even then in a minor role. When my star was at its brightest, I used to get lots of offers to act and I turned down just about all of them. Clearly while I have a decent-sized ego, it isn't one that leads me to any great desire to be on stage or on camera. I can enjoy it occasionally, but any performance ambition I have pales utterly in comparison to my desire to write. In fact, I only appreciate the art of stand-up comedy through the eyes of a writer – as a wonderful medium for ideas. I'm only in it for the material. I would have no interest in performing anyone else's gear. I'm not in it to be looked at. I've never felt remotely powerful or sexy on stage. All I feel is *focused*. A laugh for me means I've been understood.

I only ever became a comic out of the necessity of the moment. If I'd got a job in a regional theatre or the BBC had given me ten grand and an immediate full-series commission for *The Young Ones*, I think it pretty unlikely I'd ever have become a comic at all. But I didn't have any money and, with the very recent exception of Paul Jackson (via Rik), nobody wanted to read my scripts.

I needed to find a way to earn a living and, even more importantly, a means by which I could advertise my talents as a comedy writer. I was a man desperate to be a professional writer, but whose post so far had consisted entirely of rejection letters from theatres. Nobody was reading my plays and nobody was interested in the writing dreams of an untried, untested twenty-one-year-old. Why would they be? *The Young Ones* dream would not become a reality for at least a year (if it ever did) and I was impatient to let the world know what I could do.

The solution was in front of my face. If nobody would read my words, I'd shout them at them. Performance had so far not been a big part of my plans, but suddenly it became so. Prior to the first *Young Ones* meeting, Rik had also been talking about me trying to write him a character monologue to do on stage and I'd been to see him and Ade at The Comic Strip, watching them and Alexei Sayle, Arnold Brown, the Outer Limits and French and Saunders.

It occurred to me that I could do that.

I'd also looked in at The Comedy Store, which was a much scarier place where many of the acts were pretty awful.

If I could find the nerve, I could *certainly* do that.

And what really struck me most was how little *material* anyone had, even at The Strip – or, at least, material that was funny in itself. Most of the comedy relied on the performance to make it funny or the old trope of being funny by being a bit shit, which was a coin that could only be spent so often. I was under no illusions that I was a brilliant performer, but I reckoned I could write better gear than most of what I was seeing.

So I wrote myself a little act and asked Rik if he thought Pete might give me a shot at The Comic Strip.

Rik didn't think much of the idea. He told me I should stick to writing. But I was determined and so he ignored his personal misgivings and asked Pete to give his farty mate from uni an audition.

And thus it was that I turned up on the afternoon of 26 February 1981 at The Comic Strip. This was situated in Paul Raymond's Raymond Revuebar, a strip club in Brewer Street in Soho. Soho was a very different place then to what it is now. The area's adoption by the more exuberant elements of the gay community was still at least a decade away. Back then, it was a '70s-style shithole, the principal feature of which was crappy, sleazy-looking peep shows and strip clubs. Of course, there were still elements of old '50s Soho that had charm, family restaurants, Italian coffee bars and a couple of decent pubs, but basically it was depressing and, frankly, quite scary.

Anyway, Pete agreed to take a look at me and on that dark, freezing cold afternoon, with the heating not yet turned on, I got up on the tacky little stripper stage in the tacky little strip club which smelled of booze, fags and disinfectant and, when the cleaner had been persuaded to turn off her Hoover for a minute, I did my thing. Pete and his writing partner Pete (surname Richens, they had almost the same name) watched me do about five minutes after which, having consulted together briefly, Pete and Pete said I could have an unpaid try-out on the midweek bill.

Maybe they just did it as a favour to Rik, but I will always be deeply grateful to Pete for giving me a shot.

And that first gig changed so much for me.

What a night. The nerves were crippling as I entered the scary environs of the Raymond Revuebar, which felt like something out of the life of the Kray Brothers. I remember finding my way to the cramped backstage area and it being made pretty clear that there was no room for me in the boys' dressing room, which already housed Rik, Ade, Nigel, Pete and a very taciturn Alexei Sayle. Instead, French and Saunders let me share the tiny little room (a broom cupboard, really) that they occupied as the only girls. It was the first time I met either of them, but we hit it off from that very first minute. They were so kind and so friendly. Dawn is, of course, the more gregarious of the two and offered me sweets saying 'Chocolate, remedy for all things, even first-night nerves'. Jennifer was more reserved, but no less welcoming. 'You'll be fine and even if you aren't, at least it'll be over.' We became instant close friends and have remained so ever since.

That first night, I was introduced onto the stage by the Strip's compere, no less a star of alternative comedy than Alexei Sayle himself, an immensely intimidating figure who I think scared the audience almost as much as he scared me.

'Next up is a try-out, so give him a chance, you bastards. Ben Elton!'

And I was on.

My first three minutes bombed. For some strange reason, I'd decided to open with an impression of Ronald Reagan. There was a much-advertised hair dye for men at the time called Grecian 2000 and I think my joke was something to do with him looking like a 2000-year-old Greek but without the respect for democracy. Well, suffice it to say they didn't get it and there was, as we pros say, a strong smell of embalming fluid in the building. But my second half went very well indeed. It was a satirical take on the old-school, working men's clubs, Bernard Manning-style of comedy. I played a big angry man who just insulted women without actually bothering with any jokes. I wore a loud checked jacket, stuffed a pillow up my jumper and put on a Mancunian accent because basically it was a Bernard Manning skit.

When I got off stage, Pete said he'd give me another spot that very week and this time I'd get a tenner!

Just think of the thrill of that? It was insane. Intoxicating.

I'd scored a paid gig! The nervous agony had been worth it. I'd given Kate strict instructions not to attend, but she'd ignored me and snuck in at the back and when we met up afterwards, we literally danced for joy in the middle of Brewer Street.

Pete in fact gave me not just one but three or four more gigs at the Strip. I always followed another guest act, a wonderful comic rock'n'roller called Ronnie Golden, a sweet man who sang a song called 'Stomping on the Cat'. I can close my eyes now and remember the laughter beyond the musty black curtain as he got the audience to mew plaintively while he stomped, while I stood in the cramped darkness of the wings struggling to overcome my nerves, deep in the dark heart of London. Ronnie and I exchanged Christmas cards for years.

Such vibrant and intense nights for me.

But I knew there would be no living for me at the Strip. They were a gang and, guest gigs notwithstanding, I wasn't part of it and never would be. It was like uni all over again. I was a fresher and they were all third years. I knew that if I wanted to get regular work, I would have to try my luck in a much tougher school. I would have to face the infamous Comedy Store.

Baptism of gong

This was a truly terrifying prospect.

I'd been spoiled by starting at the The Comic Strip. Everybody else started at The Comedy Store, including the Strip gang themselves before Pete led them away to create a slicker, less hit-and-miss show, a show with punters in proper seats who knew they were paying to see a group of performers who were already getting real media interest.

The Store on the other hand was a bear pit. A beery, aggressive, angry hell-hole. I'd visited as a punter and sat among the tables full of shouty geezers and baying Hooray Henrys (an '80's term for posh yobs). And I knew that if I had any ambition to pay my way as a stand-up, I'd have to take it on.

So I approached Peter Rosengard and Don Ward who ran the place and, on the strength of the fact that I'd already played the Strip, I got offered £15 for a slot on the early-evening Saturday show. There were only two Comedy Store shows per week in those days, both on Saturday night – the early and the late. The early was quite late (ten-ish) and the late was at midnight.

The early was fucking terrifying. The late reduced the bowels of every comic to liquid.

Despite its status as ground zero of the UK stand-up boom, The Comedy Store in those days wasn't a real comedy club at all – not like the one they have now in Leicester Square with its many rows of seats and a seven-night multi-show schedule with hordes of efficient staff. The original Store was just an add-on night in yet another strip club, this time the Gargoyle Club on the corner of Dean Street and Meard Street. It was a tiny little dive with about fifteen tables and a mean little stage which was just big enough for a girl to remove her clothes on.

It felt like a cellar, but in fact it was on the top floor of a five-storey building and you could only get to it via a lift, a very slow lift which only took four people at a time so there was always a queue of impatient punters waiting in the street, a queue which the performers had to jump in order for the show to start.

Imagine that.

You're an unknown and an obvious ex-student compelled to tell a gang of drunken toughs that you have to push in front of them because you're one of the acts. How's that going to go down?

Well, you'd better be fucking funny then, you cunt, was the obvious and regular reply.

When they did get in, the punters were crammed round the little tables and, unsurprisingly, many of them had no interest in comic arts whatsoever. The idea of 'alternative' comedy was brand-new and many people had only come in because the club had a late licence and they could therefore continue drinking. These were days long before Tony Blair's licensing revolution. *Everything* stopped at 10.30 p.m. in the week and 11 p.m. at weekends, so a late licence was a punter magnet.

And not a very discerning punter magnet.

And every show was a gong show.

A glance at The Comedy Store website tells me that, these days, they only do a gong show once a month. That's once a month too many if you ask me. Quite simply, gong shows are anti-comedy. It's possible that they produce moments of audience wit, but I compered plenty and I never heard any. They are combative and gladiatorial, which is, of course, the enemy of subtlety, light and shade, and *timing*. There is no possibility of confidently exploring and developing an idea or pausing for effect if some drunk arsehole who hasn't even been listening can legitimately shout 'Gong' any time they want.

The way it worked doesn't need a lot of explaining. A large gong hung beside the stage and if the shouting and heckling got overwhelming, the compere would hit it and the comic had to leave the stage. Immediately. No finishing your sentence. Gong! You're off. Of course, some people given power will always abuse it and there was always a section of the audience who preferred to see comics gonged than take the time to appreciate what they had to offer. This made for a very loud, shouty and frankly intimidating atmosphere. It was, of course, particularly hard for women and very few bothered. This was a time when it was still possible to shout 'Show us your tits' at a woman on stage without looking like you came from a different century. Jenny and Dawn played the Store only once and that was it. Never again. Why the hell should they? It was such a shame for all those genuine punters who might have seen them because, of course, even at the Store, most of the audience was made up of reasonable (if drunk and excitable) people. Most people *are* reasonable. But as we all know, it only takes a few.

And there was always a few.

The memory of that first night at the Store still makes me feel faintly sick as I write. I'd felt desperately nervous about The Comic Strip, but this was proper terror. All comics go through this and it takes a long time to get used to it. You have to make sure you eat breakfast on the day of a gig because by lunchtime you won't be able to eat. You lose count of how many times you go to the loo and yet, despite that, before you go on stage, you really do still want to shit yourself.

I wrote a bit of material about it at the time.

Mother Nature has the best sense of humour. She's located the nervous system in the same place as the digestive system. The arsehole of a stand-up comic ages at twice the speed as the rest of his or her body. I may only be twenty-one, but my bum can remember the war.

You notice that 'his or her' in there? Yes, I had my PC self-correct button on even in the midst of that early terror. I didn't presume all stand-ups were male and, in fact, despite the brutish sexism of some audiences, they weren't. Pauline Melville was a founding member of the

Alternative Cabaret and Jenny Lecoat, Jenny Eclair and Helen Lederer also started around the same time I did. And, of course, there was Jenny and Dawn.

So Saturday 14 March 1981. My first gig at The Comedy Store.

My guts were absolutely churning as I went up the escalator at Leicester Square Tube. I have always thought that, on that first night as I emerged from the station, I could actually smell burning because, south of the river, Brixton was in flames. But I just looked it up and discovered that the riots began on my fourth Saturday at the Store, so I must have melded the memories together. Still, it gives you some idea of what London was like that spring, a city on the edge. *Britain* was on the edge. Nobody knew it, but when Brixton and Toxteth and St Paul's went up in April '81, an entire *decade* of strike, protest and riot had begun.

I walked out of the Tube and made my way through Chinatown, crossing Shaftesbury Avenue and up Dean Street, plunging into the grimy sullen grimness of pre-pink pound Soho.

Struggling to steady my churning guts. New material running round my head, stuff written specifically for that night. I still intended to end with the sexist comic thing, but I'd dropped the Reagan bit (what was I even thinking?) and replaced it with comic observations in my own voice, taking on all the important issues of the day.

McDonald's? Fast food? If you want it fast, why not just flush it straight down the toilet? Cut out the middle man! Triple thick shake? You need a suction pump to get it up the straw. If everyone sucks together, the windows of the shop cave in. People are walking out with bleeding earholes.

McDonald's had only been in the UK for a few years and, believe it or not, when it first arrived, it had seemed glamorous and cool. Don't forget, we'd only had Wimpy up until then and McDonald's was proper American. I can remember the first Big Mac posters on the Tube saying 'Betcha think about it all the way home' and you did! It felt so new and exciting. So slagging off Maccas was quite an original pose back then.

Why'd they put that bit of gherkin in? Everybody hates it, we all have to fish it out and put in on the table so the next poor bugger puts his elbow in it!

Observational comedy was quite unusual in the UK entertainment scene. Comics told jokes. I was kind of riffing on life, finding the funny in the shared experience, which was very different. I'm not saying I was the first person to do it, but I don't really remember anyone else at the time.

Everyone's going on about proper beer. They call it real ale. What's that supposed to mean? I was drinking lager and some student says 'Don't drink that, man, it's not REAL . . .' I says 'Try telling that to the taxi driver when you've thrown it up all over his cab on the way home! Don't worry, mate, it's not real.'

I can close my eyes now and remember it all. The compere announced me: 'A new face making his debut at The Comedy Store so give him a chance for fuck's sake! Ben Elton!' Walking onto the tiny stage, the glittery tinsel curtain behind me and the audience scarcely two feet in front, I could have reached down and picked up a drink without stepping off the stage. I almost feel I can see those young, early '80s faces before me as I write. I remember taking the mic from the compere as he headed into the wings, then standing alone in the bear pit, enduring perhaps the most testing and formative moment of my youth.

'Yes indeed, ladies and gentlemen! I was having a fag outside to stop the nerves and I got run over by a jogger!'

Joggers were another new phenomenon in early 1981. It's hard to imagine now, but literally *nobody* went running in the streets before then. For a start, you'd have kept treading in all the white dogshit. The Britain of my childhood and early youth was a different planet. As I say, the '80s changed everything. And I guess, in a small way, starting that night, I was part of the change.

The ten minutes passed in a blur. I pumped out my routine while pretending to be tough, getting good laughs and (more importantly) the audience's attention. I won't say I grew in confidence, but I was aware that the gear was landing. I was going to be okay. I wasn't gonged. I wasn't even heckled. In fact, I kinda stormed it, as we used to say. I got big proper laughs and left the stage to loud applause, even cheers – cheers which the compere happily milked for me. 'Ben Elton, ladies and gentlemen. Shall we book him next week? Yes!!!'

And they did. Don and Pete immediately offered me both shows for the next four Saturdays. £30 quid a night, for a month, guaranteed. Yes indeed!

That night, for better or worse, and from a standing start barely a fortnight before, I turned myself into a real comedian. Or, as we were called then, an *alternative* comedian. I think with the exception of the day I met my wife, it was the most significant day of my life. And, in fact, I only met her because I'd become a stand-up comic.

But I'll get to that.

Me and Benny Hill

This term 'alternative' is something I suppose I should try to 'unpack' (as we say these days) because it followed my generation of comics around for years.

I guess it does have a slight whiff of arrogance about it. After all, it suggests a kind of superiority, as if whatever it's an alternative to needed putting in its place. But I don't think anybody really saw it in those terms. In fact, I never once heard anyone actually refer to themselves as an 'alternative comedian' (except in massively inverted commas). I know I didn't. It was something the media latched onto.

As far as I know, the term was actually coined by a group of actors and anarchists who called themselves Alternative Cabaret. This was a distinctly far-left-leaning group made up of Tony Allen, Pauline Melville, Jim Barclay and Andy de la Tour, all of whom I became friendly with – particularly Andy who I was very close to. I reckon that we must have done a pub and curry together at least once a fortnight throughout the entire '80s, putting the world to rights over beer and masala.

Alternative Cabaret was formed with the idea of subverting the traditional tropes of variety entertainment. They had a proactively left-wing agenda, but in a more general sense it really boiled down to a rejection of racism, sexism and homophobia in comedy. I would say that that was the one thing which defined all the various artists who found themselves collectively defined as 'alternative'. Prior to the 1980s, UK stand-up had been an almost exclusively male art form practised in tough working men's clubs and was all about telling a string of jokes.

And racist, sexist and homophobic humour was absolutely central to it.

I don't think many of those comics actively saw themselves as being anti-non-white people, or hating women or gays, but many of their jokes relied on at best a contempt and at worst a full-blown hatred of those people. As Trevor Griffiths put it in his brilliant play *Comedians*, 'that is a joke that hates'.

There was a hugely popular ITV show in the '70s called *The Comedians* in which a lot of the material was pretty reactionary. The undisputed star of that show was Bernard Manning, a brilliant joke-teller with exquisite timing who could be genuinely hilarious but whose material was often deeply racist and sexist – and, I would say by most standards, deeply offensive. I saw him live in Blackpool once and he did material that included casual references to gang rapes and lynchings. What he said about Yoko Ono combined xenophobia and misogyny with a sneering aggression that was genuinely shocking. And, yes, he got huge laughs on all of it.

It's easy to forget but when I was growing up, women in variety (as opposed to comic actresses) were either singers, dancers or decorative 'dolly birds' (as they were called). They never got the laughs, although their bodies and personalities were endlessly the butt of laughs. Of course, there were exceptions. The great Joyce Grenfell springs to mind, along with Gracie Fields. By the '70s, there were a few more – Marti Caine and Faith Brown – and comedy goddess Victoria Wood had already made her breakthrough by the time we all started. But these were rare exceptions. I really do think it's impossible for anyone under about fifty to really understand how deeply entrenched sexism and racism were in entertainment back then. They were stand-up comedy's DNA.

And we were against it.

Well, actually most acts weren't so much proactively *against* it on stage. They just didn't indulge in it. But I was against it and based quite a lot of my early comic material on calling it out, particularly sexism. And because of that, I have often found myself characterized as some kind of joyless zealot who tried to take the sex, the sauce and the cheekiness out of laughter. This is just such bollocks. I love comedy about sex and have written too much of it to count. It's sexism I don't find funny and I tried to use that idea to actually *be* funny. Not sexist comedy but comedy *about* sexism, which I guess is alternative comedy. It's a rich vein and I was the only man at the time trying to mine it. The first routine I ever did on TV was called 'Big Tits', in which I imagined a woman unable to even get dressed in the morning because she was laughing too much at her own body, at her big tits.

It was this sort of material that led directly to me finding myself an early combatant in what we now would call a 'culture war'. It led to a lot of misunderstandings about what I was actually trying to do, which was to use my own attitudes and beliefs as a source and inspiration for my comedy, rather than basing it on perceived stereotypes and prejudice. The worst of these misunderstandings was an idea that dogged me for many years and which still comes up occasionally: that I set out to kill Benny Hill. And succeeded, kind of literally.

It happened like this.

Sometimes in early interviews, I used to kick back against the idea that I was against 'sauce' in comedy by pointing out that I loved the *Carry On* films (which I did), but I didn't love Benny Hill. The reason for this was because the women in *Carry On* were as funny as the men, but the women on Benny Hill were not funny at all and were used exclusively as decoration and titillation. *Carry On* stars Hattie Jacques, Barbara Windsor, Joan Simms, Liz Fraser, June Whitfield, Wendy Richards et al were not 'dolly birds' and were every bit a match for Sid James, Kenneth Williams, Kenneth Connor and Charles Hawtrey. Together they made sublime British silliness packed with enough doobles to satisfy even Rik and me. But Benny Hill's girls were just there to show their knickers and their knockers.

Now I'm not some grim purist. I don't mind being titillated. And I don't mind a bit of lingerie in entertainment. Anyone who's seen the 'Fat Bottomed Girls' dance in *We Will Rock You* knows that. On the whole, sex and sexiness on stage and screen is fine by me.

But by the late '70s, Benny Hill – who had, in the '50s and '60s, been a hugely original talent – had fallen into a very specific rut. His 'funny little man' had become a leering creep, a particularly blatant example of something that had become the norm in variety in those days, which was basically the sexual harasser as a lovable (if flawed) comic character.

It really was a different world. The 'old man in a dirty brown mac' was a sketch show staple. 'Flashing', as it was known, was seen as something almost endearingly quaint and funny.

I remember a line from *Man About the House*, a generally pretty good '70s sitcom where a young woman complains of a bus trip in which her bottom has been constantly pinched and slapped by men. Her friend replies eagerly: 'Ooh, what number bus was it? I'll take it myself tomorrow.'

And that was in a show considered quite progressive at the time – a woman eagerly embracing the idea that it's *flattering* and *fun* to have random strange men pinching and groping you. That kind of thing was absolutely part of the cultural wallpaper. It passed without comment.

Anyway, after I became quite suddenly famous in early 1986, I was interviewed by Terry Wogan, who suggested that perhaps the likes of Benny Hill were just a bit of harmless fun. The answer I gave has come to haunt me ever since, but I stand by it. At the time, there had been a whole string of truly shocking judgements in rape cases in which old male judges had firmly laid the blame on the victims, with senior judges telling young women that if they hitch-hiked in a mini skirt, they might very well expect to be raped and they should have thought twice before provoking the poor defendant. I suggested to Terry that ours was clearly a culture in which women felt unsafe to walk out in parks at night and that perhaps a contributory factor to this culture might be one of Britain's top comedians ending every single show by chasing a bunch of mini-skirted young women round a park, by the end of which they had all ended up in their lingerie.

Incidentally, it has often been pointed out to me since (always as if a trump card is being laid) that the girls were *chasing Benny*. Which is true, but *only* after he'd appeared to be harassing them. Beside which, during the course of the 'chase', they did tend to lose all their clothes.

I think my point is still sound and it was one I made a couple of times in my actual stand-up act.

At the time, my observation was spun as if I was accusing Benny Hill of encouraging rape, as if he was directly responsible for it. Which made me sad on his behalf. I had been talking about Benny Hill as symptomatic of a culture which viewed women as sex objects, a mind set, the extreme end of which resulted in elderly judges blaming women for getting assaulted. Benny Hill wasn't personally responsible for rape, *obviously*. But, frankly, there could also be no denying that by the 1980s, his comedy had become lazy and formulaic, and, yes, deeply sexist. And sexism has consequences, particularly when it's the absolute flagship of the ITV light entertainment schedule.

Well, sometime shortly thereafter, Thames Television axed *The Benny Hill Show* and some people blamed me. It was as if somehow, I, a twenty-six-year-old Channel 4 newbie, had ordered his sacking, that some jumped-up, humourless lefty scarcely out of uni had hounded a much-loved icon from the screen. To his *grave*, in fact, because when he died the majority of the obituaries in serious newspapers named me as playing a central part in destroying his career and bringing about what was apparently a sad lonely end. *The Independent* made this accusation against me on their *front page*.

For what it's worth, Thames axed *The Benny Hill Show* because a once-great comic had got tired, repetitive and, in a rapidly changing social climate, incredibly old-fashioned. There were, of course, those who regretted the show's passing; one of their main arguments was that apparently the show had a large following in America. This was used as a reason to suggest that his sacking had been motivated only by political correctness, ignoring commercial reality. But British broadcasters did not make their programmes to service cult followings for bulk buys on US cable TV (which earn very little for the originator). In the UK, Benny Hill had done his dash.

When change comes in mainstream entertainment, it always seems very sudden, almost arbitrary. One minute you have a show, then you don't. Look at Noel Edmonds and his *House Party* – from king of Saturday night to home on Saturday night *overnight*. One minute, he appeared to be what he'd been for years, the king of the Beeb, the next minute, totally yesterday's man. Everybody gets axed in the end. It certainly happened to me and when it did, I could honestly have argued that a pretty big audience was still watching me. Of course they were. I was on the telly. My last TV stand-up show was in 1998. It got an average of six and a half million viewers on BBC 2 and, as such, was a big hit, but shortly after that I couldn't get arrested for a TV gig. It just happens. The vibe just changes. After twelve years as a constant star presence on mainstream TV, I was out of fashion – or, at least, I was as far as programme commissioners were concerned. I'm not complaining. Nobody gets a meal ticket for life and I had a long run – although not quite as long as Benny Hill's.

Did alternative comedy make any difference in the end?

Hmmm. Not sure.

For a while, I guess – for comedy, certainly, and also as a part of a broader cultural and societal shift. We fought the battle of the 'c' word back in the '80s (that's cunt, not Conservative, by the way). When I was young, using 'cunt' as an insult was done exclusively by men (really, you *never* heard a woman say it) and thus it implied contempt, even hatred for women. And in the '80s, among comedians it became actually socially taboo.

By 1990, nobody used it. If you did, it sounded aggressive and Neanderthal. Then, of course, the proudly anti-PC male warriors of shock comedy (i.e. easy laughs) beloved of *Loaded* magazine brought it straight back. They started using the word cunt again and making jokes about rape, except now it was *postmodern.* They presented as brave cultural revisionists taking an edgy stand against politically correct conformism. What bollocks. At least Bernard Manning was honest about who he was.

The '80s really was a good time in terms of growing awareness of the reality that society was at best appallingly sexist and at worst actively misogynist. Suddenly, the use of half-naked women on advertising hoardings started looking desperately sad, uncool and totally out of date. There was a car poster that had the slogan 'If it were a lady, it would get its bottom pinched' which some fine female wit famously sprayed over with 'If this lady was a car, she'd run you down'. That bit of graffiti became quite famous and as the decade drew to an end, no advertiser would have dreamed of using near-naked female flesh to sell their products. It would have looked ridiculous.

That didn't last long, did it?

My urge to speak, act and create in a manner consistent with my principles certainly presented challenges. Trying to recognize what we would now call the non-binary nature of sexuality could really mess with the timing of my saucier material. I'd be building to the climax of some glorious nob or fanny gag (or nob *and* fanny gag) and yet feeling I had to stick in a disclaimer that not everyone in the audience will be viewing it from my straight male perspective. I knew I could sometimes come across as pious, which doesn't help anybody. On the other hand, the pursuit of principle sometimes leads to an even better comic perspective on the gag. So, ya know, swings and roundabouts.

Change is never easy; it requires effort and a bit of sacrifice. People tend to think the so called 'outrageous' comics are the brave ones, those comics who claim they will 'say anything' and be cruel to anyone. But, in fact, it's *easy* to say anything. Deciding what *not* to say is hard. Bullying soft targets behind the guise of breaking taboos is witless and lazy.

On a whim, sometime in the early 2010s, Andy de la Tour and I went to The Comedy Store. One male comic's opening line was 'I hate midgets'. The whole audience cheered. None of them *actually* hated midgets. They just enjoyed being part of the mob. The next guy said he hated poor people.

Recently, of course, the pendulum has begun to swing again and people are starting to mind their language and their subject matter. And, as ever, this has resulted in the old whinge that political correctness – or 'woke', as it's now called – is killing comedy and that 'you can't say *anything* any more'. Well, undoubtably there has been a whiff of Maoism in the air of late as cultural revolutionary zealots attempt to police language and attitude. But I was there the last time culture jumped through this hoop and in my experience you *can* say anything, it just doesn't hurt to think a bit harder about how you say it and *why* you're saying it. In the end, your comedy might be the better for it.

The Early '80s Keep on Giving

Becoming who I'm not

My onstage character was formed on stage. He was kind of forced upon me by the audience. I didn't realize it was happening at the time.

By the summer of '81, I had become the compere of The Comedy Store, a massive step-up in profile and status within the tiny pool into which I had dived. I also started getting offered many one-off gigs around London. Between March and December, I did 112 of them (I have a lifetime of appointments diaries on my shelf). In those early days, I dreaded doing the actual shows, walking out onto a tiny stage or often just a pub floor, a complete unknown with everything to prove all over again with every gig. But I loved the aftermath, the sense of achievement, of succeeding in a scary and edgy world. I'd conjured up a career for myself and found a speedy route off the dole. It was exhilarating. I vividly remember the almost euphoric feeling of sitting in a taxi, driving home through London at 3 a.m. after compering the midnight show at the Store. In the three years that I had been in Manchester, I only took one taxi and that was paid for by my gran to get to the station to go home for my gramps's funeral. Now I was taking taxis home from work and I was paying for it with my own money! Gliding through a near-empty, moonlit city (there were, of course, no late Tubes), the sweat of the gig still damp on my shirt. I was in the *scene.* Playing clubs, *hip* clubs. And dawn was just a couple of hours away. And I was still only twenty-one. How good was that? I used to sit back in those cabs, in a lovely beer buzz, smoking a cigarette and feeling like I *owned* London.

I didn't realize that, in the terrifying cut and thrust of those early gigs, I was developing a stage personality that would come to define me absolutely and not necessarily in a good way.

The personality that found fame five years later on *Saturday Live*, which was considered by many columnists and commentators to be ranting, angry, over-opinionated and aggressive.

The funny thing is that in real life I'm not any of those things. I'm passionate but I'm not angry. I talk a lot but I certainly don't 'rant'. I have opinions but I know how to listen and learn. And nobody who knows me would *ever* describe me as remotely aggressive.

How did I manage to so comprehensively become something I'm not?

It was the bloody Comedy Store.

In those gong shows, you either won or you died, and if you died, you very soon stopped getting paid. Don Ward didn't mind 'gong fodder', but he wasn't going to pay for it.

So I got on that stage and I *unleashed*. I swore hard and loud and if there was even the hint of heckling, I'd step out of my routine and confront it with all my might.

What did it say on the poster? An evening with some of London's top comedians? Or an evening with some of London's top comics PLUS ONE FUCKING IDIOT WHO CAN'T KEEP HIS MOUTH SHUT! Did anyone pay to hear what you've got to say?! Were they queueing up downstairs saying to each other 'Oh, I do hope some random pissed-up dickhead is going to wake up in the middle of someone's act and FUCK UP THE PUNCHLINE!' Is that what these people have given up their Saturday night for? No, it fucking isn't, so have another pint of piss and SHUT THE FUCK UP.

It was funny, in a shouty, strutty kind of way, but it's not me. Like I said, I'm not remotely aggressive. I've never been in a fight in my life I'm pleased to say, not even at school. I don't think I'm a coward, but I don't like violence, physical or verbal, and I don't find it impressive. What I did to hecklers was an essential defensive mechanism. I knew that my material *was* my act, that my success depended *entirely* on people hearing what I had to say, and for that to happen, I had to shut up the loudmouths in the audience. I do not have a funny face or obvious comic physicality. I can't get a laugh with a hop and a skip, a shrug or a smirk – at least not unless those things emerge from the material. I'm all about the ideas, and ideas-led comedy is delicate and demanding; the audience has to *listen*. If they miss a sentence or two, the whole thing collapses. So I protected my gear by saying it loudly and forcefully.

And fast. That was another defining aspect of my style that I fell into overnight. I wasn't going to give them a *chance* to get in. I'd roll over them.

Maybe if I'd started doing comedy at an Oxbridge smoking concert, like Fry and Laurie or Rowan Atkinson, I'd have found a gentler and more reasonable voice – still fast, I think, but not *aggressive.* But I didn't. I did what I needed to do and in so doing developed a voice that would take decades to calm down. Long after my TV stand-up career had come and gone, I was still struggling to trust an audience to listen without being bludgeoned into it. The fear and tension of those Comedy Store days went very deep.

These days, I have learned to trust the audience, to slow down a bit, to shout and swear a bit less. Pause even. But I'll never quite be able to unlearn those early habits.

The gong casts a long shadow.

Early warning of trouble to come

I was seeing a lot of Rik as ever, not because of *The Young Ones*, the pilot script of which was grinding through the BBC, but because I began to write little bits and pieces for his stage act. We experimented with new characters and I also wrote some lines for his fabulous Kevin Turvey creation. And I wrote a monologue that he performed on Victoria Wood's sketch show *Wood and Walters* plus one or two other bits and pieces for various outlets. We had so much fun. It was just Rik and me – sometimes in the pub, sometimes at my flat – laughing together in one long improvisation.

And it was from Rik that I got the first hint of some particular trouble to come, trouble of which, as with my ruffling of feathers in my first term at DLA, I was supremely unaware.

Rik and I were on the Tube on our way up to the flat in Hampstead to go to the pub. Usually when Rik and I wandered round London together, as we often did that year, we pretty much laughed the whole time but, on this occasion, Rik was uncomfortable, staring at his shoes. Out of the blue, he started talking about Alexei Sayle and about his style and about my style, the upshot of which was that he said some people thought I was getting into Alexei's territory, that I might even be copying him.

By that time, Pete Richardson had given me a few more gigs at the exalted Comic Strip (so much cooler than the Store) and he had recently offered me the actual compere spot for midweek shows because Alexei wanted to start taking Wednesday nights off. He was the celebrated and unchallenged compere and alpha male of the Strip; he was billed in *Time Out* for the whole week and in retrospect I think Pete rather relished the idea of teaching Alexei a lesson by giving me the gig. All I can say is that if that was Pete's plan, it worked, because I only ever compered the Strip once and then only for half the show. Alexei had been watching from the back and, to my complete surprise, he came back at the interval and told me he was taking over.

So I should have seen it coming but I didn't. Because I'm me and clearly there's something lacking in my brain. And now Rik was sitting beside me, staring at the stubbed-out fag between his shoes (yes, we smoked on the Tube) and saying that some people thought I was copying Alexei.

Boom. Sucker-punched.

'Do *you* think I'm copying Alexei?' I asked angrily.

'No,' he replied.

'So who? Who thinks I'm fucking copying Alexei?'

He didn't answer but he didn't need too. It was obvious.

Alexei thought I was copying Alexei. And he had told Rik to get his little mate to pull his fucking head in. Alexei was a truly powerful force at the Strip, the only working-class person in a company of middle-class farties. Working-class Liverpudlian, no less. And on stage, he ran the shows. Rik admired him and I think was slightly scared of him too. He felt obliged to deliver the message, even though I can assure you he didn't agree with it.

I admired Alexei too and I still do admire him. He came first and I don't deny that I learned something from him. His high-energy mod tirade that culminated in the 'Ullo John! Gotta new motor?' riff was giddily good, an inspired rhythmically developing fusillade of invective which was original, game-changing and utterly compelling. And I'm sure that my own dynamically structured material owed something to his example. My 'Big Tits' routine was an accumulative riff and perhaps my most celebrated bit of early gear, 'Double seat, double seat', a routine about not wanting anyone to sit next to me on a train, even more so. These were routines that grew in passion and volume with plenty of rhythm and repetition, just like Alexei's 'mod' routine. But neither of us had a copyright on routines that gathered in rhythmic outrage (look at Eric Idle's routines on the Pythons – 'Bleedin' Watney's Red Barrel' or his frustrated punter in a cafe which sold only dishes containing Spam or Basil Fawlty unleashing on his German customers). But, more importantly than that, the *content* of our acts was utterly different. My stuff was based on a shared recognition of common experiences or the exposition of a principle, while his stuff was a kind of series of brilliantly surreal non sequiturs. The real problem for Alexei was that I was another shouty, lefty stand-up and, up until then, his only competition had come from three apolitical ex-uni-type sketch teams: Rik and Ade, Pete and Nige, and Dawn and Jenny (plus gentle self-effacing Jewish schtick from Arnold Brown). Briefly, he'd been unique. Now he wasn't.

I was really upset with Rik, so upset in fact that I just got up and got off the Tube. I don't know which station – Camden or Chalk Farm. I suppose I'd thought I'd walk home and find him in the pub later. Anyway, he jumped off the train after me as the doors were closing and, instead, we went straight to the nearest pub together.

'Come on, Farty. You know I don't really think you copy him. Forget about it.'

Well, clearly since it's more than forty years later and I'm writing this now, I didn't forget about it.

Nor, unfortunately, did Alexei.

But, at the time, I didn't think any more of it. Our industry was riven with jealousies. I almost never shared a bill with Alexei and I felt I had nothing to apologize for.

Trying to write for everybody at once

With my entry into the embryonic alternative comedy scene, my writing prospects had expanded overnight. Other people besides Rik began to ask me to write for them. I wrote a routine for Pete Richardson, in the character of a sleazy pornographer ('My friends call me Lady Di 'cos I like working with children'), which actually made it onto the *Comic Strip* album, definitely earning the few quid he paid me for it.

Also, Nigel Planer asked me to write a radio sitcom with him for a group of actors he'd known in his musical theatre days (not many people know that 'Neil' was once understudy for Che in *Evita*). Nige and I had become good friends, but our efforts to create a show together didn't quite click. He wanted to improvise the thing in a group and as I think you know by now, that's not really me. I like to go home and write.

And then there was Tony Allen – celebrated Ladbroke Grove hippy anarchist, original Alternative Cabaret member and compere of The Comedy Store before me. Tony was a big personality and self-proclaimed 'Guvnor' of The Store. He was a big ego but I liked him. He suggested we try to write a sitcom together and I visited him a number of times in his flat on Ladbroke Grove, a road which was known then as 'The Front Line' because of its reputation as a tinderbox in relations between the police and Notting Hill's black community.

It didn't work out, but you can see Tony as the guy who spray-paints Rick in the 'Party' episode of *The Young Ones*.

And there's a little Tony Allen story that's lived with me all these years because it speaks so loudly to the nature of the times. During that summer of '81, in which I often shared a stage with him, Tony would berate me for the formal nature of my act: formal in as much as I wrote stuff at home, learned it and then delivered it. There were often departures from the script, but I definitely worked from pre-prepared material. 1981 was the high tide of the purist alternative ethic which, like punk rock five years before, valued the supposed 'integrity' and 'authenticity' of just getting out there and fucking doing it (although why making it up on stage should be considered 'purer' than making it up at home has always been beyond me).

Tony was always on at me to improvise more. He'd berate me as I came off stage. 'Free-form, Ben! Fucking free your mind and fucking free-fucking-form!!'

Tony had the same objection to my politics that he had to my comedy. He knew I was Labour and being an anarchist (whatever that is), he was against all traditionally organized political parties. Well, on one very memorable night, for some reason I did go on and genuinely improvise, discarding my prepared routine and winging it. I'd been for an audition that day and I found myself riffing on the experience and getting big laughs. When I came off, Tony – beaming from ear-to-ear – was waiting in the wings. He enveloped me in a hug, towering over me. He was a big, fit man who must have been at least six foot three.

'You see!' he said triumphantly. 'You free-fucking-formed and it was brilliant, wasn't it?

'Yes,' I agreed, feeling quite pleased with myself.

'You opened your mind to its infinite possibilities and went to places you didn't know existed,' Tony said, hugging me again.

'Yes, Tony, I did.'

'Good,' he said, releasing me and jabbing an angry finger at my chest. 'Now apply that to your fucking politics!'

I wonder if they still have debates like that in the wings of comedy clubs.

As to on-stage improvisation – well, of course it's great as a theatre sport and it can also have a valid place in a prepared routine. Some of my best riffs have been developed on stage with key lines coming to me unbidden in the moment. But it can only come from a place of strength; good prepared material can beget great new material. A journey is rarely worth taking if you don't know where you're starting from.

Boasting to my butcher

In May 1981, I made myself a hostage to fortune.

My captor was our local butcher's. I'd often bought sausages from them, but never been able to afford much else. Then I finally got my third of *The*

Young Ones writing money. A cheque from the BBC for £287.63! I know the figure exactly because until I got an accountant, I kept a careful note of every penny I earned in my appointments diary. Paying your tax is very important to me and I'd read enough showbiz memoirs to be well aware of the perils of forgetting that the earnings of an artist are irregular and sporadic and the tax is *never* paid as you earn.

Anyway, suddenly a cheque for nearly £300 had dropped through my letterbox. And it was from *the BBC*. It was amazing. Wonderful. Thrilling. Another pinch-yourself moment! Kate and I and the rest of the flat would celebrate! I bought wine, I bought beer and decided that I would buy fillet steaks! Steaks were truly special. I doubt I'd eaten even a dozen in my whole life. Mum never cooked them. My experience of steak was confined to my gran giving me a treat for mowing her lawn, and a couple of teenage visits to Berni Inns with girls. But I *loved* them and now I had £287.63, so I went straight round to the butcher's and asked for five of their very best steaks. I was friendly with them and, since they knew me as strictly a sausage man, one of them asked me what I was celebrating.

'I've sold a script to the BBC!'

Stupid move. Never do that.

Selling a script is absolutely no guarantee of getting a production and, even if you do, it can be a long time in coming. This was spring 1981 and *The Young Ones* would not be broadcast until autumn 1982, by which time I'd long since had to give up using that butcher.

I stood it for a while . . .

'Ohh hello, here's Mr TV Writer. Can we interest you in a guineafowl and some foie gras?'

'How's it going at the BBC then? How about a chateaubriand, lovely for two?'

'What? Sausages again? Thought you were a BBC millionaire.'

They never let it drop. In fact, it got worse, their comic double act growing ever more joyful as the months went by with no sign of my show on TV. In the end, I just stopped visiting and bought supermarket sausages instead. The moral of the story? Don't boast to your butcher till you're in the *Radio Times*. Better still, become a vegetarian. If we all did, we'd save the planet. I will if everyone else does.

The trouble with Mike

There were two principal battles for me over *The Young Ones*. One was about how the scripts should be written and the other was about who should play Mike. I lost both and personally I think the show was the worse for it. There you go. Said it. It's taken me forty years. I never broke ranks at the time and not since either. But most of the people involved with *The Young Ones* have done plenty of interviews about it over the years and this is my autobiography.

The Mike thing came to a head in the summer of '81. The actual tele-recording of the pilot episode had been scheduled for the first week of January and so the question of who would play the fourth role was becoming more pressing.

But what's that you say? Surely Pete's playing Mike – he who coined the key phrase 'Mike the Cool Person'. Well, obviously, you don't say that, because if you're reading this autobiography, then you're interested in my work and so you know that Pete Richardson didn't play Mike as had originally been planned.

So what happened? To be honest, to this day I don't really know why he didn't – except that it was absolutely *nothing* to do with me. In fact, of the principal players at that stage, I think I am the *only* one who had absolutely nothing to do with it.

I *think* it had quite a lot to do with a clash between Pete and producer Paul Jackson. Paul is a brilliant and inspiring producer and, by this time, Pete was becoming a hugely original TV producer himself, already in the early stages of developing what would be his decade-long run on Channel 4 with *The Comic Strip Presents . . .* These two 'big beasts' were never going to work well together.

Perhaps the BBC felt there was a conflict of interests with Channel 4. Perhaps it was the reverse.

Group dynamics probably played a part. Pete was The Comic Strip's supremo. He had founded the club and, for the previous year, had effectively been Rik, Ade and Nigel's *employer*. If he joined *The Young Ones*, then inevitably a lot of that authority would have joined with him. *The*

Young Ones would have looked like another Comic Strip project. Pete playing Mike would have fundamentally altered the power balance.

The truth is I just don't know what happened.

It was all very murky and I was not included on any of the discussions.

All I know is that, one day in the pub, Rik told me 'Pete's not playing Mike' and that was it.

Pete should have played Mike. I wanted him to. He *was* Mike in many ways. He 'got' the joke. I wrote it for him and, frankly, he had inspired it.

Anyway, for some reason we'd lost the person best suited to playing Mike and the clock was ticking.

Guess who was slated to play him next?

Me.

Yes, I was going to be Mike in *The Young Ones.*

At least that's what Rik said to me through the early autumn of '81. But he told me he wanted to keep it to ourselves for the time being.

I know Paul Jackson knew of the plan and was very happy with the idea. After all, I'd written the one existing script in its entirety and, as compere of the London Comedy Store, I had plenty of credibility as a comedian. And he knew me to be diligent and professional. I think Paul Jackson would have loved me to play Mike.

And, of course, I would have absolutely loved to have done it. The thought hadn't occurred to me until Pete was dropped, because as far as I was concerned he was cast, just like Ade and Nigel. But once the role was free I was thrilled at the prospect of doing it myself. And, frankly, I think I *was* the next best choice after Pete and I think Rik thought so too. Like Pete, I *understood* the role. I, as an added bonus, was also, crucially, *the right age.* Pete was already thirty-one but at just turned twenty-two, I was basically still a skinny student myself.

It was a lovely dream but it didn't last.

One day, I turned up for a meeting with Rik and Lise at their flat and Rik took me straight to the pub. Lise didn't come.

I can remember that moment like I had a film of it. We walked in and, before we'd even gone up to the bar, Rik turned round, pointed his finger in my face and said 'You're not playing Mike, okay?'

I was pretty surprised.

'But what do you mean? You said . . .'

'I know what I said and don't want to discuss it. You're not playing him. Forget it.'

'But you promised.' (And he bloody had too).

'I know I promised, but you're not playing him. So shut up about it and let's have a pint.'

Then he went to the bar and that was that. Rik was the boss in '81. There was no doubt about it. He was the golden one, a huge star about to happen. He was the only reason *The Young Ones* had been commissioned in the first place. Paul had originally approached Rik and Rik alone, and it was Rik who brought in first Lise, then me, then Ade and Nigel. I led on many aspects of *The Young Ones* in those early days, but *only* for as long as Rik let me.

So what had happened? Well, it wasn't Paul Jackson, because he was very happy for me to play it, as indeed Rik had appeared to be. So I guess it was the result of a decision made between Rik and Lise, but I'll never know the detail because Rik made it very clear that he was not prepared to discuss it ever again and we never did.

It still makes me sad. I really think I could have made Mike work. I was absolutely in the same supermarket and I wasn't buying peas. Mike was always the problematic Young One. But he really hadn't needed to be.

Anyway, now, of course, we again had the problem of who *was* to play Mike.

If not Pete and not me, then who?

I knew who I thought should play it. My old mate CJ, the guy from the original Young Ones student house in Didsbury, the guy who'd given me sanctuary on that stormy night of my brief homelessness. Honestly, he'd have been perfect. I'm good at casting and I *know* he was right for it. In fact, when writing a lot of the Mike stuff, I'd had CJ's dry Leeds-accented voice in mind (he talked like Jarvis Cocker from Pulp, who I know comes from Sheffield). CJ was also one of the gang, an occasional member of Rik and Ade's first comedy company, 20th Century Coyote. As mentioned, he was very small and skinny with a huge broken nose, but handsome too in a sad-eyed way and very smart. And, like Rik, he always carried himself like a star, posing for shots in his own private movie, just like I wanted the character of Mike to do: 'He walks in the room. He's looking good.'

And, again, *he was the right age.*

As I think I mentioned, CJ plays the glue-sniffing character in the vox pop bit of the '*Nozin' Aroun*'' skit in episode one. Have a look and tell me he wasn't a Mike.

I campaigned hard for CJ and he was given an audition, but I could see in retrospect that he was never going to get it because he was my mate and my choice, and also a part of Rik's gang at uni. The dynamic of *The Young Ones* creative team between me, Rik and Lise was changing. My influence with Rik was waning. As Burr sings in *Hamilton*, you need to be in the room where it happens, and Rik and Lise shared a room.

So, after CJ got rejected, we ended up auditioning proper actors for the role. It was the very last thing we should have done because if ever there was a sitcom based on a shared communal comic vibe, it was *The Young Ones*.

Chris Ryan, who was eventually chosen, was without doubt a fantastic actor, a truly gifted artist who played the role with consistency and integrity. He was brave and lavished his considerable talent freely with immense patience and goodwill.

But he wasn't *right* for it.

He was just too grown-up, too solid a presence. Already in his early thirties, he just wasn't *farty* enough. In my view, we gave him a poisoned chalice.

From the moment Pete was dropped, the character of Mike had got less clear by the day until, in the end, I don't think anybody really knew who he was (although I certainly fucking knew who he had *been*). Some of the creative decisions were just ridiculous. I was on the back foot by then and didn't play any further part in the development of Mike, but when I saw the golfing outfit that Rik and Lise had decided to put Chris in, I nearly wept. Talking rats and random stuff aside, the central quality of *The Young Ones* was that it was *recognition comedy.* It held up a highly self-aware mirror to the posturing pretensions of youth; a very, very exaggerated mirror, certainly, and a very specific bit of youth (house-sharing middle-class students), but it shared a common understanding with its audience – an understanding of being young in Thatcher's Britain. Where on earth did a pristine clean golfing kit, £1,000 sets of clubs and immaculate pinstripe suits fit in? Mike should have been a penniless twenty-year-old post-punk hipster in skinny ties, skinny jeans and scuffed Kickers. He was supposed to want to be Joe Strummer, not Arnold Palmer.

On the page, Mike had been a *real character*. Just like Rick, Vyvian and Neil, he was rooted in truth. The students' unions of 1982 were full of Mikes.

The ridiculous direction it took still makes me sad a whole lifetime later.

And as for the landlord character

I did my best. I honestly did.

But, blimey, it was a hard brief. Right from the first meeting in the pub – a footnote to Rik and Lise's basic idea of a sitcom featuring a student house shared by the four stage characters of Rick, Ade, Nigel and Pete – had been that Alexei would play their landlord.

And, at what I believe was Alexei's suggestion, the character of this landlord was to be that of a Soviet defector who was laying low in Britain.

Because that would be a *really* familiar trope to add to a cast of characters whose principal strength was that they reflected various shades of post-punk British youth styles!

Maybe it was Rik and Lise's idea. All I know is it certainly wasn't mine.

The comic aspect of this Soviet landlord was to be the by-now-rather-familiar *Young Ones* idea of someone trying to be hip but getting it wrong. Both Rick and Mike's characters were spending elements of this now rapidly diminishing coin and Jerzy Balowski (as I ended up calling him) would attempt to disguise his true Russian defector self by trying to sound like a groovy Londoner. The added texture being that Balowski had defected in the early '60s and therefore his language was to be mired in a hapless mash-up of the Swinging London 'fab and groovy' speak of fifteen years before.

I guess it *could* have been funny, but since we had already covered that kind of cultural cringe by making Rik's posturing proto-political punk character a Cliff Richard fan, I had my doubts.

I did my best in that pilot script to service this pretty exotic brief, but as far as I was concerned, despite an energetic and compelling performance from Alexei, Jerzy Balowski was not funny, the reason being that, just like Mike's ridiculous golf kit, it was a weirdly inorganic bolt-on to the purity of the original (already multi-layered) idea. We could have taken the land-lord figure in so many interesting directions (a high bar having been set by Leonard Rossiter with Rigsby in *Rising Damp*), but in my view, an ex-Soviet Russian émigré wasn't one of them.

Writing it and not writing it

On a cold January night in 1982, we made the pilot of *The Young Ones*.

At Television Centre! The home of dreams!

It's hard for young people today to understand just how much the BBC meant to British people fifty years ago. It was the heart and the brain and the conscience of the nation. The BBC was, by a thousand miles, the coun-try's most important cultural institution. It towered above everything.

And, for those like me devoted to the comic arts, it *was* everything. There were no cool clubs, no eclectic internet, no niche streaming services. ITV played an honourable and occasionally ground-breaking second fiddle, but for those who wanted to create new comedy, there was really only the BBC. Peter Cook and the *Beyond the Fringe* team had briefly taken boundary-pushing sketch work into club and theatre culture in the 1960s, but with that very brilliant exception, since the Second World War everything interesting in comedy had happened on radio or television and almost exclusively via the BBC.

And now I was at the heart of it!

Oh gosh.

I still gasp at my good fortune, the sheer mad luck of it all.

At the time, it was all happening too fast for me to reflect upon much, but as the years pass, I become more aware.

I recall peeking out at the long audience queue that snaked round the inner circle of the Television Centre doughnut, trying to spot my guests, the collected smoky breath of 200 foot-stamping people hanging in the bright lights that illuminated the famous 'Helios' statue in the middle of the circle.

I wasn't queuing. I was in! I'd been there all day rehearsing.

I don't think anybody went to the refectory in the pre-recording break. Too strung out to eat, we gathered together in 'Green Assembly' (or perhaps it was Blue Assembly or Red Assembly, the colour-coded tea hubs dotted the inner doughnut). Nervous faces hunched over horrid little plastic cups. Crisps for supper. Paul's urgent final notes. The cast all trying to look cool like it was just another gig.

Because I was appearing in the show (we pre-recorded my turn as Baz in 'Nozin' Aroun'' in the afternoon), I had my own dressing room! Eighteen months, earlier I'd been a student. Kate came to see me with her tickets and VIP pass. I can remember us standing there together in a sort of awe; the tiny room with its mirror and chair felt like a presidential suite.

My mum, dad and gran were in the studio audience.

I did part of the warm-up, delivering my 'Big Tits' routine, which I think Gran just sort of blanked in her mind. She was so proud. She didn't follow a single word of what she saw that night, but she loved every minute of it. She died two years later and, on my last visit to her in hospital, she introduced me to the nurse as 'my TV grandson'.

I can't really remember much about the recording itself – only flashes, like the lovely first laugh Rik got on 'I'm not a fwidge, you know', his brilliant improvisation from that first meeting in the pub. I'd been the first person ever to laugh at that and now there were 200 more. Soon there would be millions (we hoped). I do recall a sense of slightly abstracted wonderment watching Nigel dropping the lentils, Ade's dramatic entrance through the wall, Nigel trying to kill himself on the toilet – these were scenes I'd imagined alone and typed out on a cold stone step in a mouldy bathroom almost a year before. And now they were actually happening, brilliantly engineered by Paul and the BBC special effects department, and getting huge laughs. I confess that I also felt, for the first time, that small tinge of disappointment that all comedy writers feel at the point when they disappear behind the performers. I had written those scenes, created the dialogue and imagined the slapstick exactly as they were now being presented. But the laughs belonged to Rik, Ade and Nigel. In the end, the performers must own the laughs – the *real* laughs, anyway, because if you're thinking about the writing, then it's not actually funny enough.

After the recording, we all went for the first of many after-show Indian meals. That was a major tradition in those days, all of us gathered together over lager and poppadoms. We were happy. Paul was happy. Would the BBC be happy?

I discovered later that they were just bemused. None of the powers that be 'got it', but then they didn't see it as their job to 'get it'. They were looking for youth programming and I actually think they felt that it was their job not to 'get' their youth programming. They hadn't liked punk rock much, but they still put it on *Top of the Pops*. I imagine dusty old half-pissed BBC execs shook their heads in bemusement over the Crazy Gang, the Goons and the Pythons too and then let them get on with it. It was a great system.

And so the BBC commissioned a series, an incredible career advance for everybody concerned.

My personal joy, however, was somewhat tempered by a sudden change in *The Young Ones* working model.

I should have seen it coming. But then, why would I? Rik was still keeping the truth from me and possibly also from himself; he had a lifelong habit of avoiding difficult decisions and situations. After we made the pilot, and even now that a six-part series had been commissioned, Rik continued to allow me to think that, for the five other episodes, I would be the sole writer and he and Lise would be creative script editors, just as it had been on the pilot (whatever the actual billing might have said).

But things had changed. Once more, Rik summoned me to the pub. And, once more, his finger was in my face before we even got to the bar.

'We're all writing it together. Equal input, equal billing. Okay? I don't want to discuss it again.'

'But you said . . .'

'I know what I said, but I'm telling you now, it's the three of us or you're out.'

Yep, that's what he said. I could have called his bluff. I knew they couldn't write it without me and I knew he knew it too. But it was his show and while it couldn't happen without me, it had ONLY happened because of him. It was my big break and I owed it exclusively to his faith in me.

I did try briefly to argue my case. I asked Paul Jackson to broker a meeting between Rik and Lise and myself. The meeting took place in yet another pub and it was absolutely horrible. To this day, I regret my insistence on asking for it. Rik was half-pissed when he and Lise arrived. Dutch courage, I think. He knew he was massively going back on his word and had hence decided to make himself furious and brutal. He accused me of ingratitude and disloyalty, betrayal even, and I collapsed completely. The conclusion was forgone and I could have saved myself a horribly upsetting encounter.

But it really wasn't about me trying to grab more credit.

Maybe you think it was. But it wasn't.

I genuinely didn't think it would work if the three of us tried to write the show together and, of course, in the end we didn't. I wrote my stuff and Rik and Lise wrote theirs, and in the main they were the ones who bolted it together. This was a source of real sadness for me, real proper pain. I got marginalized and so lost a very large part of the thing I loved most, busking with Rik and making him laugh.

But *The Young Ones* turned out to be a smash hit.

Hits are rare things and often you can't explain them. I hated a lot of the stuff that ended up in *The Young Ones*. I still do and certainly, if I'd had my way, much of it would have been different. But who knows what might have happened then? In the end, you can't argue with a smash hit. And flawed though the show was, that was what we got. An absolute whopping great hit. Who knows, perhaps it took the very elements I hated to make it so.

Chemistry is a funny thing.

And, for the record, let there be no doubt that together Rik and Lise wrote at least half of those other eleven *Young Ones* scripts. More than that on some, less on others. I just submitted stuff and Rik and Lise did the selection and editing. The only other two episodes over which I exercised anything like the control I'd had over 'Demolition' were the episodes called 'Bambi' and 'Summer Holiday'.

The real casualty of the whole bruising encounter was my creative relationship with Rik. That magical youthful period – which had begun in 1977 with 'Hi, I'm Rik Mayall' and which, by 1981, had blossomed into something truly dynamic – would never be the same again. And it causes me nothing but pain to say this, but in the long run, I think that damaged Rik more than it damaged me. It's my view that Rik only ever found two people with whom he could truly improvise freely and hilariously towards a script, people who were capable of writing stuff for *and* with him that flattered and expanded his immense and unique comic energy, stuff that he embraced unequivocally with his exhilarating gleeful passion. That's me and Ade. Ade can speak for himself and has done so in his excellent memoir *Berserker*. As for me, mine and Rik's creative partnership never recovered and although we were to share many joyful times together, particularly as stand-ups on the road and briefly on the *Young Ones* book (and, of course, socially), we were never able to recapture the creative spirit we had shared as collaborators. It still makes me very sad.

But there was still fun to be had. We rehearsed *The Young Ones* in the famous old BBC North Acton rehearsal rooms and we'd always go to the pub at lunchtime. Everybody did, crew, producers, everyone. And next to us at the bar would be a bunch of *Top of The Pops* dancers and half the cast of *'Allo 'Allo*. Script discussion with senior execs would take place in the bar. I honestly don't know how we did it. If the government thinks the middle classes are drinking more than they used to, then they never went to a pub on a midweek lunchtime in the '70s and '80s. Or the House of Commons Bar for that matter.

I'm glad to be able to pay a little nostalgic nod to those North Acton rehearsal rooms. In their way, they were almost as evocative and exciting as Television Centre and as redolent of a national culture which is already a distant memory. The building was a pretty anonymous-looking seven-storey concrete block, quite a number of stops up the Central Line, but the handwritten noticeboard in the lobby, detailing what was going on on those floors, was just stardust. *The Two Ronnies* on one floor, *Only Fools and Horses* on another. *Russ Abbott, Are You Being Served? Top of the Pops*, of course. We used to live in hope of sharing the lift with the *TOTP* dancers.

Still the Early '80s . . .

'Still to come, teenage abortion and youth unemployment, but first, let's have a laugh with Ben Elton!'

In talking about *The Young Ones*, I've skipped ahead of other stuff that was happening for me in '81 and into '82. Looking back, it's incredible to think how much did happen. It seems like a dream now. At the time, it was a dream come true.

Constant gigging led surprisingly quickly to TV work as a stand-up. ITV ran a much more vibrant national network in those days and there were lots of regional magazine shows, some with a 'yoof' mandate and all looking for content. I did a gig for Thames and one at Granada.

Granada TV was, of course, located in Manchester, so how good do you think it felt for me to be going back to my old university town just a year after graduating in drama to *perform on TV*?

Kind of weird to reflect that, at that point in my life, I must have been quite hip.

I didn't *feel* hip.

Just a nervous ex-student anxious to please. Still do really.

My third TV gig was also based in Manchester and it turned out to be quite significant. This time it was for the BBC and for an evening show which was to be broadcast nationally! What's more, I was offered a semi-regular slot. Another amazing break. The show was called *The Oxford Road Show*, after the BBC's Oxford Road studio, and it had elements in common with *Saturday Live*, which five years later would make me a celebrity overnight. Those common elements were the ones that were least attractive to the performers: I'm talking about the presence of a live audience of 'young adults' standing less than a metre away from the performers with their heads at the level of your crotch. This was a *big* thing in '80s 'yoof' broadcasting – lots and lots of real 'kids' being herded around studio floors by crazed floor managers who had to get the cameras from one side of the studio to the other every three minutes without mowing down a skinhead. The thing about people, any people, is that they are, on the whole, very self-conscious. And all those 'kids' standing around on the *ORS* floor were as aware that they were on TV as I was, so of course they all defaulted to standard 'cool' pose number one – that is, looking bored and hard to please. This was at least a generation before any semblance of American-style enthusiasm was to infect UK youth culture. It was post-punk and the default attitude was that everything was shit and anybody who was remotely successful was a sell-out.

Particularly middle-class ex-students scarcely older than they were who were trying to be funny.

It was an awful feeling, waiting on my little podium watching the floor managers herd groups of confused young people to stand around me while elsewhere in the studio a band was playing or a pre-recorded segment on gonorrhoea was showing on the monitors as the seconds ticked away until my humiliation began.

I'd hear the previous segment being wound up 'and don't forget, if you have been abused by your father and want to discuss incest with a trained youth worker, write to us including a stamped addressed envelope. But now it's time for some laughs . . .'

My principal camera would already be in place, I'd be staring into it with what I hoped was an unimpressed 'don't give a fuck' face while, in my peripheral vision, the other cameras were sweeping across the floor, smashing rastas and skins and mods out of the way, lassoing many more with the cables that followed them. The red light came on and a floor manager waved their arms. The punks, new romantics, rastas, skins and mods reset their expressions to aggressive indifference and I'd say something like 'All right! Yeah! Looks like we've got just about enough angry young people in the studio to have our own inner-city riot.'

This *would* have been followed by deathly silence, except I didn't give them a chance for that. Instead I'd plough on with my damage control: 'Ooh, little bit of politics, eh? Can't handle that, can we?'

It was all very unpleasant. They were trying to look indifferent and I was trying to look even more indifferent. Unfortunately, they were the audience, so they kind of held the high ground.

I always ended my act with 'My name's Ben Elton, goodnight!'. Most comics end like that now, but for a long time, I was the only one. I don't know why, but it actually sounded quite original at the time. Maybe it's because previously comics on TV had ended with things like 'God Bless, drive safe, look after Mum'. Name-checking myself was kind of cocky, but in a good way, and it made sense too. I was an anonymous segment in a wildly eclectic show. Nobody was going to guess my name from the credits. I needed to tell them.

ORS (as they liked to call it) was quite good. They had lots of excellent bands and covered interesting topics and events. Nonetheless, I very quickly started using the experience as material for gags. My routine '*Nozin' Aroun'*', which I performed on the first episode of *The Young Ones*, was of course a piss-take of shows like *ORS*, but with the benefit of hindsight, *ORS* didn't deserve such ridicule. Viewed from our post-truth, fame-obsessed age, it was sublime. It's incredible to imagine, but in all the shows I did with them, I can only remember *one* item about celebrity. I took the piss out of all those worthy five-minute segments on unemployment, STDs, race and politics, but when you look back, in terms of youth programming, it was a golden age of intellectual and cultural rigour.

ORS was a very tough gig for me and I honestly don't think I ever got a single laugh, but I look back on it with affection and respect, even if one time I had to do my act while being completely engulfed in aerosol string. Well, it was the Christmas edition.

The start of a big pile of broken crockery

I have written many scripts that never saw the light of day, easily as many as those that did.

The first of my many failed screenplays came about when, one day, a production company rang me and asked if I'd like to write a movie for Channel 4.

'Yes' was the short answer.

This was to be my first experience of a process known as 'development', a terrible and soul-destroying experience for writers which begins with huge enthusiasm and then slowly erodes over successive re-writes until the script is unrecognizable from the thing that caused so much enthusiasm in the first place. At that point, somebody says 'Maybe we need to go back to the first draft' and then you're dead.

My idea for this first screenplay was based around the Greenham Common dispute.

The memories are fading now but Greenham was a *huge* thing in the early '80s and rightly so – a women-only peace camp outside the US missile base at Greenham Common in Berkshire. In that amazing decade of civil conflict, in which literally *no* nightly news was complete without a top story featuring massed ranks of police officers advancing towards some large group of angry citizens, women's peace camps were a big deal.

My idea was a love story between a young woman protestor and a soldier on guard on the other side of the wire. A promising start I think (and one I returned to in my novel *Blast From the Past*), but I wanted to play it as a kind of Ealing comedy/*Dad's Army* style and they wanted to play it as a serious bit of Film on Four realism. Actually, I think they were probably right, but I was very much in a *Young Ones* frame of mind at the time, still focused on 'the ruthless pursuit of the one-line gag'.

Anyway, after three or four drafts and a shitload of work *Common Ground*, as I called it, withered on the vine. It's all still in a file in my study, the first of a forty-five-year pile which I have come to refer to as 'broken crockery'. I'm always working on a number of things at once, probably to the detriment of all of them. Sophie and I have, for a long time, referred to all my ongoing punts as 'spinning plates'. Because so much stuff fails to reach an audience, I often lament that one minute I have four or five plates spinning, the next I'm up to my ankles in broken crockery.

Common Ground was broken crockery.

My next pile of ceramic shards was a screenplay written for Rik. It was called *Ironic Monty*, a spoof showbiz biography about a failed comedian called Monty who discovers irony one day and builds an act around saying weird ironic things. He is embraced by the critical elite as a brilliant surrealist and becomes a huge success, but (ironically) never understands why.

Rik loved the idea when I told him about it and we pitched it to the BBC. They assigned us a producer who Rik and I met in the bar at the National Theatre where Rik was appearing in *The Government Inspector*. The bloke had a file full of notes and he did the usual producer thing of saying there were lots of good ideas but 'of course, as it stands, it's not a movie'.

He may have been right and he may have been wrong, but young as I was, I knew enough to at least listen, take some notes and then do a second draft. This would have performed the essential function of including the producer in the process, making us partners rather than adversaries. Rik, however, was having none of it. It was post-show, he'd just given a massive comic performance and received rapturous applause, and the lager was flowing. I could see he was getting ready to blow and I really didn't want him to because I'd done all the bloody work and knew that it wasn't going to help.

RIK: Who the fuck are you to fucking tell us how to write our script?
HIM: I'm your producer and please don't take that tone.
RIK: Well, what does a fucking producer do?
HIM: It's my job to tell you when I don't think that certain elements are working and to encourage you to develop them and change them. And I think you have a very great deal to do to make this into a movie.
RIK: Why do you get to say what elements aren't working?
HIM: Because I'm the producer.
RIK: Well, I think you're a fucking Nazi.
HIM: I resent that deeply. I am Jewish.
RIK: Well, then you're a fucking Jewish Nazi.

That's what Rik said. I give you the last four lines word for word as I have never forgotten them. Unsurprisingly, development ended there.

Gigs, more gigs and Edinburgh!

Through all these various bits of writing, I continued to do stand-up – lots of little gigs and a few slightly bigger ones. The big ones were benefits. Lots of benefits. Sometimes it seemed like the '80s was one long benefit concert. Nicaragua was the big thing in '83 and my close mate Andy de la Tour was very involved. A popular revolution led by the Sandinistas (which was a revolutionary collective years before it was a Clash album) had overthrown the evil psychopathic dictator Somoza, but was now being undermined by a US-backed counter-revolutionary war. That's honestly how it was and you didn't have to be a rabid commie to be on the Sandinista side. So it was definitely a good cause, but God it led to some bloody awful gigs, gigs which felt like they lasted longer than the actual eleven-year Sandinista regime. I'd turn up at 8.30 p.m. to do my spot planned for the top of the second half, only to discover that the first half had barely begun, the opening musical act having done five numbers instead of the allotted one and the Nicaraguan poet who followed was in the process of reading his complete works in Spanish which were followed by an English translation. The hours I've spent hanging around in some depressing backstage 'hospitality' (a shitty storeroom with six empty lager cans) picking over the curling sandwiches with various salsa musicians and street poets while some selfish socialist juggler, who has got totally over-excited by the fact that he's actually playing to an audience of more than five passers-by, is using up all the audience goodwill.

Benefit gigs were a constant pull on my conscience. Thatcher may have put a lot of people out of work, but she certainly stimulated the market in unpaid stand-up gigs. Miners, printers, nurses, oppressed South American countries, a woman's right to choose, anti-nukes, prisoners of conscience, Amnesty International, the beaten-up and on-the-ropes Labour Party . . . they all filled up my '80s. Every lefty cause in the country seemed to want me to crack nob gags on their behalf and I always tried to answer the call.

But sometimes I got to gig on my own behalf and, in the summer of '83, I returned to the Edinburgh Festival. It was Andy's idea and, at the time, a pretty original one. Back then, stand-up comedy was not the

Right: Mum and Dad in 1968. They had been invited to a Royal Garden Party. Gran was so proud. Mum insisted they borrow Gramps's Ford Anglia because she didn't want to go in our camper-van.

Left: At twelve and performing in an am dram old-time music hall. Not the coolest kid in school. Start as you mean to go on.

As the Artful Dodger with The Godalming Theatre Group at fourteen at Godalming Borough Hall. It felt like the West End to me.

Sixteen and giving my Saucy Hitler in a student show at Stratford College.
I think we were trying to be satirical.

1979 and playing Mercutio in a Manchester Uni student production of *Romeo and Juliet*.
I'm about to die. The audience may have felt the same way.

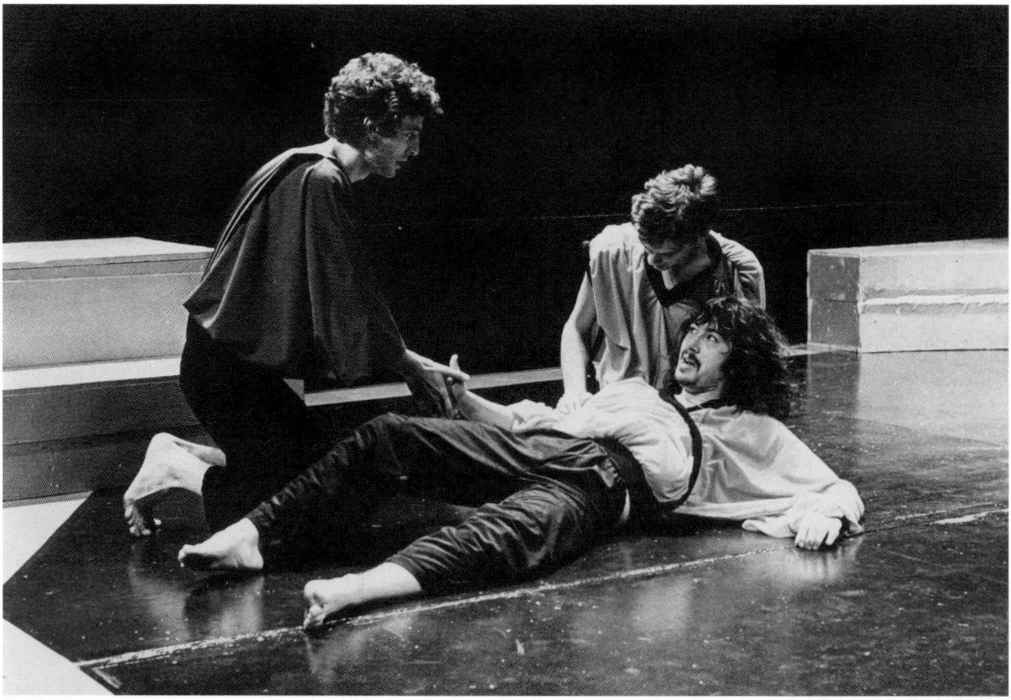

Right: Nineteen and in the Ducie Arms, the drama department pub, no doubt imagining the album cover.

Below: *Oh, Be Still My Palpitating Heart*, Edinburgh Fringe, 1980. A few lines from this ended up in *Blackadder* (never waste a good gag).

1982. Hosting one of thirty episodes of the regional culture show *South of Watford*. Can you spot me?

Alfresco, 1982. Me, Stephen, Robbie, Hugh, Emma and Siobhan. I had a very big TV hit that year – this wasn't it.

The Young Ones, 1982. To paraphrase the title song: once in every lifetime, comes a chance like this.

With Rik, Ade and Andy de la Tour, taking publicity shots for our 1983 Edinburgh season of 'Stand Up Comedy'. We didn't use them because Ade dropped out. We thought we were the comedy version of The Clash.

1984 or 1985. Me and Rik after a gig.
We were so happy together on the road.

Camden's finest. A meeting with Madness in 1984 on our failed sitcom project.
It was fun while it lasted.

Happy Families, 1985. Ade, Stephen, Helen Lederer, Dawn and, yes, that's Jennifer in front, aged twenty-six and suffering for her art under about an inch of prosthetics. It was a hot summer – no wonder she looks so pissed off.

Me, Harry, Stephen and Hugh about to do the last *Saturday Live* of 1986. We're trying to look cool but our bowels would have been quaking. Those ninety-minute live broadcasts were nerve-shredding.

The Jam Tarts in 1986, the year they supported me and Rik on our Australian tour. They were as much fun to hang with as they look, and I married the bass player (the one on the left in the leopard-print leggings).

On our tours together Rik and I played Little Richard in our van after every single gig. We couldn't believe it when we got to meet one of the true founding fathers of rock 'n' roll.

all-conquering popular art form it is now. In fact, it was rare enough for us to decide to call our show 'Stand Up Comedy' so that people would know what they were getting. Imagine that – a time in Edinburgh when you had to say that you were a stand-up! Now you have to say if you're not.

I was so excited. My student memories of Edinburgh were very recent and very rosy, and I could think of nothing better than going back as a comedian, this time able to afford beer. I signed up at once and Andy, who knew a promoter, got onto all the booking and accommodation stuff.

Then it got even better! Rik said he wanted to come too.

Wow, that was exciting. Rik was now a star of *The Young Ones*, which meant a much higher profile gig, to say the least. Also, our somewhat fractured writing partnership notwithstanding, Rik and I were still very close, so sharing a stand-up season together sounded like pretty good fun. And it was.

Rik, Andy and I went up to Edinburgh in the August of '83 and it was just wonderful, doing three weeks as proper professional comics in the most vibrant place for alternative theatre arts on the planet. And also the best party.

The three of us stayed in this flat right close to the Assembly Rooms where we were performing to packed houses. It was on the top floor of one of those magnificent stone Edinburgh townhouses. We all had our own big spacious rooms with huge windows and we felt like kings in a castle. 'Stand Up Comedy' was a big hit and basically the whole season was one long party, going to other shows and meeting up with mates old and new. Our flat was a social hub and we'd drink the night away with whoever had dropped in. I remember having to talk comic/drummer Rowland Rivron in from the window ledge where he'd decided to enjoy a can of lager. It truly was horribly dangerous: he was completely pissed, seven floors up and one slip from death. I understood his motivation. I too have a slight compulsion to start climbing things when drunk. I've done a few lampposts and bus stops in my time and I remember once Rik having to stop me climbing into a skip ('There could be needles in there, Farty. You'll get AIDS'). So I know a bit about stupid and Rowland was being horribly stupid. If he'd slipped and died, it would have ruined our whole night.

There's nothing to worry about (actually there was)

And now I must leave my 1983 self, getting drunk after gigs in Edinburgh, and go back to the dying days of 1981 and begin another story.

As you know, 1981 had been a huge year but as Christmas approached, there was one more momentous development to come, one that would lead to professional associations that would span decades and the forming of enduring lifelong friendships.

And the production of a pretty terrible TV show.

On 17 December, I attended a meeting in London with two guys from Granada TV, producer Sandy Ross and researcher Jon Plowman. Also in the room as I entered were two very tall young posh boys in sensible shoes and tweedy jackets, who seemed a bit wary although very polite, and also a very friendly girl in dungarees with extremely short hair and a wide toothy smile. They were Stephen Fry, Hugh Laurie and Emma Thompson. All of us were at the beginning of our adult lives. Emma, Hugh and I were twenty-two and Stephen was twenty-three.

Stephen was even taller than Hugh. And very slim. He was slightly sad-eyed and had a face that looked as if somebody had held his large chin with one hand and the top of his head with the other and given a very slight twist in opposite directions. His large patrician nose was also slightly skew-whiff. Stephen has often said that he despised his appearance when he was young but, in fact, he had a rather romantic look about him and was actually really quite handsome. And although in those days he could occasionally be quite spiky (being young and impatient), even then he exuded that irresistible avuncular warmth with which the world is now so familiar. I began calling him Bing Bong almost the moment I met him. It just emerged as a sort of Wodehousian tribute and he has been 'Bing' to me ever since.

Hugh – or Huzzer as he soon became – *was* handsome. It didn't always show in photos back then, but he was a proper heartbreaker: piercing blue eyes, strong chiselled features and a rangey, wiry athletic frame. He'd been head boy at Eton and a Cambridge Blue at rowing. It was as if a young James Bond had decided to pursue a career in sketch comedy.

Given all that, you'd have imagined that Hugh would have been the more confident and relaxed of the two, but that wasn't how it seemed to me at all. He was equally charming, funny and erudite, but it seemed to me so much less happy to be *him*. Even on first acquaintance, there was an inner anger about Hugh, a large proportion of which was firmly directed at himself.

Emma was simply breathtaking. Not in any conventional sense. She is beautiful, of course, but I don't remember being aware of that at first meeting. Emma makes no great display of her very striking physical charm when not 'on duty', so to speak. She dresses for comfort and scarcely wears makeup. It was her beautiful *spirit* which shone, her immense enthusiasm for life and her kindness. She seemed to *care* about everyone and everything. I soon came to recognize her wit and intelligence, which was the match for any of us, but at first meeting, it was her open-hearted enthusiasm which bowled me over.

So there we all were. I loved them all at once and I love them still.

Shame about the show.

Sandy Ross had gathered the four of us together because Granada TV were trying to put together an ITV answer to *Not the Nine O'Clock News*, which had been a huge success for the BBC and set a very high bar for sketch shows. *NTNON* was assembled almost exclusively from Oxford and Cambridge graduates both in front of and behind the camera (I think only Pamela Stephenson wasn't one) and so that was where Granada had started too. Stephen, Hugh and Emma had had a great student success in Edinburgh in the summer of '81 with their excellent Cambridge Footlights revue 'The Cellar Tapes' and Sandy Ross very sensibly booked them wholesale. However, by this time, alternative comedy had appeared and a new sketch show peopled exclusively by Cambridge Footlights would have jarred a bit even then, so Sandy looked further afield. His first port of call was, of course, Rik Mayall, the hottest new face in British comedy. But Rik was busy doing Kevin Turvey on *Kick Up the Eighties*. Being the generous soul that he was, Rik recommended me.

There's Nothing to Worry About was the pilot title of a programme that would eventually emerge as *Alfresco*, a sketch show on ITV which ran for two series in 1983 and 1984. The utterly unique and original creative spirit that was Robbie Coltrane joined us soon after that first meeting, a fat, full-strength unfiltered cigarette clamped between his fat, full-strength fingers. He was a bit older than the rest of us and scarily worldly, a proper grown-up among us slightly overgrown students. Rob was effortlessly stylish; he drove a vintage open-top sports car and wore exquisitely cut suits. I remember once, out of the blue and for no reason, he gave me a beautiful silk tie from the 1950s, which of course I still have. A perfect combination of erudite elegance and uncompromising masculinity, he could quote Robbie Burns while fixing a car engine. He had genuine natural cool. Our ensemble was completed by another Scot, the wonderful actress Siobhan Redmond. If ever there was a show that was *not* greater than the sum of its parts, *Alfresco* was that show.

In fact, *Alfresco* was a turkey – trimmed, stuffed and presented to the public with all the trimmings – but, oh, what a wonderful two years of fun and friendship we had cooking it up, putting on stupid costumes in the parks and streets of a city which had only two years earlier been my student world, or eating large fried breakfast butties from the film location catering van, stamping our feet in the cold of a frosty dawn.

For the pilot period we all stayed at Manchester's famous Midland Hotel, bang in the middle of the city, and in the evenings we'd get drunk, eat vast quantities of roast meats in the carvery (or at least us boys did) and play stupid games. This was before the Midland had its big modern refurb and the creaky old place, with its long corridors and threadbare carpets, was a faded version of its pre-war heyday (when my gran took my mum for special-treat teas after a Christmas shopping day in the big city). Our single rooms didn't even have loos, but for us it was magical luxury. We all laughed so much. There's a photo in Stephen's autobiography of him, me, Hugh and Emma all in bed together (fully clothed), collapsed in a paroxysm of hilarity. There was a lot of that sort of thing. We'd get drunk over dinner and then go out into St Peter's Square and play the game where you have to approach strangers with an enquiry and attempt to slip an inappropriate phrase into the question without them noticing. We were very young.

Sadly, when our efforts at comedy reached the screen, it was a comprehensive flop. Looking back, I can see that the reason was simple.

I wrote too much of it and Stephen, Hugh and Em wrote too little.

Whose fault was that? Well, mine for trying too hard and Stephen and Hugh's for not trying hard enough. I don't think Em at the time was expecting (or expected) to write much at all. The Footlights still definitely had a very sexist vibe about it and the vast majority of the writing had always been done by the men. I believe that the writing of 'The Cellar Tapes' had followed that pattern, with Em having to work hard to get her stuff in.

Funny, really. Out of Em, me, Stephen and Hugh, there was only one of us who at the time was definitely *not* considered to be a principal writer. That would be the one who would go on to win a screenwriting Oscar. Emma 1, Patriarchy 0.

There was no doubt that Sandy was looking to Stephen, Hugh and me to lead on creating material, which was reasonable since all three of us had done quite a lot of writing already. But while I was stepping up to the plate, Stephen and Hugh were stepping away from it.

I think I've mentioned that, throughout my life, I have thrown an enormous number of words at any opportunity. *Alfresco* was no exception.

I would turn up with a whole bunch of sketches and say: 'I have ten sketches to offer you today and personally I think they're all bloody brilliant'.

Stephen and Hugh would turn up with one half-finished sketch and say: 'Well, we've got this thing, but really it's probably dreadful and it might be best if we just didn't even bother to read it.'

That's honestly how it was. It's a matter of upbringing and schooling, I suppose. Stephen and Hugh both went to private schools and then to Cambridge, places where it was simply presumed that students would succeed and so it wasn't done to be too bullishly energetic and certainly not to shout about it.

In my life, if I wanted to get something done, I had to get doing it and, if I wanted anybody to take notice, I'd had to shout.

So I shouted. Or, at least, leaped at every challenge with unbridled enthusiasm and confidence. Stephen and Hugh just kind of shrugged and left me to it.

When, in despair, Sandy drafted in John Lloyd, the producer of *Not the*

Nine O'Clock News, to sprinkle a bit of his stardust on our permanently frustrated writers' room, John pulled no punches. He has a big streak of scary anger in him and I can remember his eyes flashing fire as he bollocked Stephen and Hugh over their lack of effort.

'Ben's written far too much and quite frankly a lot of it is complete shit,' he said. 'But at least he's *trying*, whereas you two don't seem to be bothering at all. *Now pull your fucking finger out.*'

I don't think any of the three of us felt very good about that particular intervention.

The truth is, I think my prolific enthusiasm threw them.

Back in the Footlights, everyone was like them but less talented, so despite their agonizingly self-deprecating self-criticism (which, in Hugh's case, seemed sometimes to border on self-loathing), their stuff still got done. With me around plucking sketch after sketch of varying quality but with consistent confidence from every orifice, I think they retreated into their shells.

I really wouldn't have minded at all if they'd said 'Benj, you're wrong. There's half an idea here which might amount to something if you do some work on it.' I'm actually good with criticism and script notes, particularly from people I respect. And I *really* respected them.

But they never did give me notes. They just hummed and hawed and stared at their brogues and sucked on endless cigarettes. Stephen sometimes also sucked on a pipe.

But, as I say, the creative impasse which largely existed between us didn't prevent us from becoming instant best mates. For a while, in fact, we were almost inseparable.

I even briefly started wearing a tweedy jacket and brogues. I went to the Oxford and Cambridge Club with them and drank port at the end of the evening. And I went to Cambridge with Stephen. It was my first visit, even though my uncle was Regius Professor of History at Clare. Stephen showed me round all the little lanes and tea shops. I just loved it and began to understand the magical hold that it has on its graduates.

I think I influenced Stephen and Hugh as much as they influenced me. I know I did in Stephen's case, because he's been generous enough to say that it was me who first swung him towards the political left (I think he'd been a kind of libertarian at Cambridge).

And I became very close, very quickly with Emma. She is, as you would imagine, an immensely impressive person, her intellect as keen as her personality is charming and surprising. In fact, I fell in love with her. It happened a couple of months into the process of making our show. We'd become fast friends already but then, suddenly, I just woke up one morning truly besotted. I can still remember the look of exasperation on Stephen and Hugh's faces when I confided in them. 'Oh God, you too! Every man falls in love with her in the end. Even the gay ones.'

It was a strange interlude, being in love with Em. Kate and I were still together but living rather separate lives at that point, so had my sudden passion been requited, who knows what might have developed. But Em, while definitely loving me as a friend, had no interest in romance whatsoever, let alone helping me out with my sudden romantic lust. We did have one snog in a cab, but I think it was a pity snog and I guess I was mature enough by then to know it was a crush on my part, the almost inevitable result of our intimate working proximity. Talent is always attractive and Emma is about as talented as it's possible to get. What's more, she was performing *my lines.* That's pretty heady stuff and I just fell head over heels. There's no doubt that, in theatre and film, developing feelings for colleagues is what I guess you might call an occupational hazard. The professional relationship is so intense and relies so deeply on mutual emotional support and understanding. Anyway, it was excruciating for a while, an agonizing throwback to my adolescent days with Ali. I remember one night sitting in a little service apartment (we'd all moved out of the Midland when we began spending longer stretches in Manchester). I was experimenting briefly with contact lenses at the time and in my romantic misery, I cried one out onto the bar of the electric fire I was huddled in front of.

I remember watching it sizzle through my watery eyes and blurred vision, and feeling like a right prat.

I got over my obsession as quickly as I'd fallen into it. One morning, I woke up and, while I still loved Em very much, I was no longer *in* love with her. I think this was quite a relief for Em, who had put up with the whole incident with great charm and patience. Our previous close friendship resumed its course and has continued ever since.

Two other friendships were forged during the making of *Alfresco*. I got close to John Lloyd at once. I mentioned John's temper, but he also has great personal charm and an impish sense of humour. Later, when I joined *Blackadder* (which John produced), things would become more fraught between us, but back then it was just fun.

We hit it off immediately. Our first script sessions were conducted in Edinburgh where Stephen, Hugh and Em were again performing a show. One night, John and I started drinking in the bar of the famous George Hotel, where all the BBC types hung out. Suddenly a Hoover was being shoved between our feet and it was 6.30 in the morning. The two of us had sat drinking for the entire night. It wouldn't be the last time.

And Robbie Coltrane became another very special new mate. We all loved him so much, with his angry, acerbic wit and tough, no-nonsense attitude. He was also just such a brilliant comic actor. You only had to look at him and laugh. He was supremely irreverent and contemptuous of any and all sacred cows. He said what he wanted to say, always. I'll tell a small story of one of our many shared jokes (although perhaps you'll think it tasteless). We were in the studio and, for some reason, the set for the sketch required a hedge. I was standing in front of the hedge, dressed as a schoolboy and, as the studio manager called for silence for a 'take', I heard a rustling behind me and a very large hand emerged from the hedge holding a fiver. A deep, mellow Glasgow voice said: 'Would you like to buy some sweeties, little boy?' Look, I know it wasn't the greatest gag in the world, but it was so *perfectly* timed and executed that I absolutely broke up as he'd known I would. For many years thereafter, I put a fiver in his Christmas card.

I've always liked a drink, but Robbie was in another league, particularly since he mainly drank Scotch which, if you drink at the rate of wine, is heavy stuff. How often have I heard Rob enquire 'Shall we have a wee Mickey Mouse?' referring to The Famous Grouse, his favourite blended Scotch. Sometimes we worried about Rob. He was such a big man and, as mentioned, also smoked untipped full-strength fags. Most of us smoked back then, but as with everything in his life, Rob did it on a bigger scale. A few years after *Alfresco*, in the late '80s, Robbie said to me that his doctor had told him that if he carried on as he was, he'd be dead in ten years.

'But what a ten years it'll be!' he added, raising a glass and cigarette at once in the same huge hand.

Robbie actually survived for another thirty-five, defying medical gravity for most of them. I saw much less of him in later years after he moved back to Scotland, but I miss him very much nonetheless. An enduring legacy of our relationship is my friendship with Rhona, the wonderful woman he married and who is adored by all who know her. Rhona was kind enough to ask me to speak at Robbie's memorial at the Actors' Church in Covent Garden and I was deeply honoured to do so.

Granada had high hopes for *Alfresco* and were heavily invested. They gave it a pilot and two series, which showed real commitment. But it just didn't click.

It still has its fans, but is now largely forgotten – and probably deservedly so. But, oh my gosh, I'm so very grateful to Granada for the incredible contribution it made to my life.

1984 and 1985

A hit single, a spin-off book and Girls on Top

So, what next? *The Young Ones* was over, but there were a couple of fun spin-offs still to be done. The Comic Relief record 'Living Doll' with Cliff Richard was fun. I had to provide the jokes and I remember sitting listening to the old Cliff seven-inch single over and over again, wondering how to fit gags in. The intro I wrote for Rik remains one of my favourite *Young Ones* moments.

> *'Hey, kids! Stop snogging and pay attention to me! If you're a wild-eyed loner standing at the gates of oblivion, then hitch a ride with us cos we're on the last freedom moped out of Nowhere City and we haven't even told our parents when we'll be back! So pull on your dancing trousers and get down to the total and utter king of rock 'n' roll. Cliff Richard!!'*

I had to write a sketch for the B Side too.

> RIK: This'll be the biggest thing since the Beatles split up.
> NEIL: Oh wow. Have the Beatles split up?

It still makes me laugh to this day and the gold disc I got for it hangs on my study wall. I reckon I blummen well earned it, matey.

And then there was the book. Writing *The Young Ones* book is a generally happy memory. It was a brief swansong for the gleeful, almost childish exuberance that had been our joyful creative relationship. The book sold

149

three quarters of a million copies. It's only through the figures that I can really remember how big *The Young Ones* was.

Also, around this time, Jen and Dawn had hooked up with Ruby Wax to write a sitcom for Paul Jackson called *Girls on Top*. It was about some flat-dwelling young women and Tracey Ullman, a huge emerging talent, was to co-star. They asked me to be the script editor, which was very flattering. I don't think I made much difference, but it was good fun hanging out with the girls for a few evenings and I've been kind of mates once removed with Ruby ever since. We made a pact way back then to have a proper evening together, just the two of us talking comedy. 'Two Jews with booze,' as Ruby put it. It's been forty years and we haven't done it yet. But maybe we will one day.

The Rik and Ben tours. It was the best of times. It was the best of times

And then there were 'the Rik and Ben tours'. These came about as a result of our Edinburgh season in the summer of '83, when Rik and I decided that we'd like to do more tours together.

There would be five in all and they remain among the happiest memories of my life. Yes, our creative relationship was well past its peak, but our friendship was undiminished and our shared sense of humour was as mutually and happily robust as ever.

Our tour posters still hang on my wall. They don't seem like so much now – just three weeks of one-night stands in city halls – but they felt huge to us at the time.

And there's a name on every one of those posters which was to become as significant in my life as even Rik's has been: Philip McIntyre.

Today, Phil is one of Britain's most important media figures. He's a highly successful West End producer, Britain's top independent comedy and variety promoter, and a significant film and TV producer. Also, to a very select group of whom I was the first, he has been an agent. Almost my entire professional life has been bonded with Phil's, starting in the autumn of '83 and continuing to this day.

But, back then, Phil was a young rock promoter. He'd done a bit of comedy (he promoted Billy Connolly's first-ever English gigs) but, basically, he, his junior partner Paul Roberts and his brother Nigel were in the live music business. And, from the very toughest of working-class beginnings, Phil had built a successful company in a traditionally ruthless, cut-throat business.

One day, Phil was sitting in his house in Preston watching *Kick Up the Eighties* and he saw Kevin Turvey. 'Nigel,' he said to his brother, 'get down south now, find out who that bloke is and say we want to promote him.' That was the beginning of a career in comedy promotion that would take Phil McIntyre Entertainment to massive, multi-arena-filling success with pretty much every major name in the field. And it started with Rik.

And with me. Because when Phil asked Rik to let him promote a live tour, Rik and I had already decided to tour together as a double bill.

We met Phil together at The Famous Cock pub just by Highbury & Islington Tube station. Rik and Lise had moved to Islington by this time and The Famous Cock was a favourite of ours – and not just because its name was a single entendre. Phil is a tall, pale, freckly bloke of Irish descent with a strong Preston accent. He and I liked each other immediately although, of course, neither of us were aware what a truly significant moment in both our lives this meeting was. It was simply agreed that Phil would promote that first little tour. Phil has promoted, produced or negotiated pretty much every single thing I've done ever since.

So Rik and I were off on the road.

These days, of course, live comedy is a massive deal and an act of Rik's celebrity would be playing multiple arenas. But that just wasn't how it was then. Britain didn't have the live bug the way it does now. Consider this: *The Young Ones* (featuring Rik, Ade and Nigel) had actually done a few live gigs the previous spring and they'd played *students' unions*. I'm talking 500 people tops. Now, remember that, on TV, *The Young Ones* was absolutely mega – were such a phenomenon to occur today any live version would play multiple nights in 10,000-seat arenas, whereas Rik, Ade and Nigel did single nights to 500 students.

Personally, I think it has a lot to do with the increasing social isolation caused by the internet. In the old days, we all watched the same things. Watching telly was actually a community activity. We didn't need live gigs to feel connected with our culture. More than 20 million people watched Morecambe and Wise at Christmas, but when Eric and Ernie did live gigs, they did one-nighters in civic halls and local theatres. Incredible. I don't think it's a coincidence that, as TV audiences shrink, live audiences grow. People who are used to watching fragmented multi-channel broadcasting on letterbox-size smartphones crave the big communal experience, being part of a tribe of likeminded people celebrating a shared love. Sitting in a 10,000-seat concrete car park watching a solo comic might not make for great comic art, but at least it's real and you're part of it.

Arenas would have to wait for another generation of comics. Nonetheless, Rik and I loved our city hall tours *so* much. They were just the *best* thing. The feeling of freedom was absolute. We were in a van together, just me and Rik, Tony our tour manager and Phil or Paul to take care of business. Playing the *same* venues that Slade, T. Rex and Bowie had played when we were teens. The same local halls the Beatles and The Stones had once played even as they conquered the global charts.

Such carefree days! Making money, stopping at service stations to eat huge greasy meals and buy stupid stuff from the shop. Doing gigs to kids who really loved us. Piling back into the van and sticking Little Richard on full volume – *A wop bop a loo bop a wop bam BOOM!* Staying up until dawn, smoking fags, drinking lager and talking complete bollocks in some threadbare hotel lounge or guesthouse.

And just *laughing* all the time. Ridiculous, schoolboy banter. One tour, we actually tried to invent a board game called 'Dooble' where you would get cards with everyday situations and phrases and try to turn them into nob gags.

CARD: Yorkshire is the biggest county in England.

EXAMPLE ANSWER: No, it isn't! The biggest county in England is my nob!

That sort of thing would reduce us to tears and we didn't even take drugs. We did it all on beer, a few whisky chasers and youth.

We were having fun, but the times were heavy. Our first two tours together coincided with the year-long miners' strike and Britain was being torn apart. There were striking miners everywhere with their buckets and their Coal Not Dole badges, angry men getting thinner and more desperate as the year dragged on. On the motorways, through the window of our van, we often saw the hired coaches filled with blue rows of police, often from London, hurtling up the road to support some regional force in pit-gate battles. My girlfriend Kate was on picket lines many a weekend as a strike supporter and a legal observer, and, of course, Rik and I were 100 per cent on the side of the unions against Mrs Thatch and her battle to break them. We managed to do a couple of miners' galas, which were very moving occasions. The strike caused such immense suffering and deprivation for the miners and their families.

Of course, looking back, with all our knowledge of climate change, it's clear that coal mining could never have been sustained anyway. But for Thatcher and the Conservatives, the struggle was never about coal. It was about the deliberate and brutal destruction of working-class solidarity and the trade union movement. She won, but the country paid a heavy price in the shattered communities in which all hope was lost and the relationship between the public and the police, in which for many all trust had gone.

Fucking lefties

I must tell you about one miners' benefit I did in London because it's a classic example of how the often joyless, puritanical, holier-than-thou instincts and the suspicion of success among people on the left so often derails the very causes we all wish to support. It drives me completely bonkers. As far as I'm concerned, intolerant lefties who'd rather destroy their own side than fight Tories are *worse* than Tories. Mind you, those sort of lefties all think I *am* a Tory because I wrote a musical with one.

Anyway, there was this big London benefit at The Royal Festival Hall.

It was a posh venue, but the line-up was the usual Red Wedge suspects: poets, alternative comics and Latin American salsa bands. I don't know, maybe Paul Weller was there too. As ever, it was a rather pious line-up – short on star power and utterly lacking in any showbiz sparkle. In fact, sparkling would have been considered selling out.

And then something utterly amazing happened. The back doors of the auditorium burst open and Wham! appeared – George, Andrew, Pepsi, Shirley and the whole backing band, all in fabulous white! I guess the organizers must have known but none of us did. It had been kept super-secret. This was Wham! in 1984, Wham! in the glorious pomp of their all-conquering youth. They ran down the aisles and leaped onto the stage, kicking into their life-enhancing, joyful, uplifting power pop classic 'Wake Me Up Before You Go-Go', which had only been out a few days. Just think about that! This was the biggest pop group in the UK playing the biggest hit in the UK *for the striking miners.* Nobody knew they were going to do it. Nobody on the planet could have expected it. They just decided they would.

Go George and Andrew. In fact, go-go George and Andrew!

Watching from the wings, I was ecstatic. What a message to send to the wavering population. It wasn't just grumpy, slightly shit, left-wing alternative cabaret artists who believed in trade unionism. It was proper massive fucking stars for whom such a statement was bravely off-brand and risky. George and Andrew's endorsement would shift more hearts and minds in a single headline the following day than Red Wedge could achieve if we toured the UK for a thousand years. This was epic.

And then I realized some people in the audience were booing. And some fellow artists in the wings were sneering. For a moment, I simply couldn't understand what could have provoked such a reaction. Of course, I knew Wham! were miming. They were performing a highly complex studio track and doing an energetic dance to go with it at the same time. They'd had no opportunity to soundcheck or bring in a sound rig that could remotely cope with their production. They were a five-minute pop slot on a fucking awful three-hour bill using the in-house PA. *Of course* they were fucking miming. They had no option. And so what if they were? They were *here* and, even miming, they were more professional and entertaining than the entire rest of the bill put together times ten, including me.

But that wasn't good enough for the Stalinist tankies and Guardian-istas, either in the audience or backstage. How dare they *pretend* to sing. It wasn't *authentic*. It was that most terrible of all things: *selling out*.

But, of course, the fact that Wham! were miming wasn't *really* these idiots' problem. That was just a convenient excuse to hate on them. The real problem was that Wham! were *happy*. They were optimistic. They were charmingly uncomplicated and unself-conscious. They were without guile or cynicism. And, above all, they were mega fucking successful and hugely fucking popular. *That* was their real crime. God forbid that any-thing associated with the left should be an actual success.

Succeeding. Could there ever be more concrete evidence of *selling out*?

I was so angry, so depressed. Wham! had come down to the Festival Hall to support the trade union movement in its most bitter struggle in at least fifty years. And they got booed. At the end of the song, George said 'If you're booing us for not singing live, you're here for the wrong reason' and they left.

And then the compere came on with a superior grin and said 'Wham! – doing a gig for the *Mime*-ers'.

Fuck me, he was pleased with that. And he got a huge laugh and a mas-sive cheer, after which he no doubt introduced a communist poet or a Maoist juggler and the audience went back to sleep. I wouldn't know. My head was in my hands.

Madness, Madness, they call it Madness

While society was fracturing and the post-war consensus going to hell in a basket, I was having the time of my life.

I started working on a sitcom featuring the pop group Madness. You won't have heard of it because it never happened (another one for the pile of broken crockery), but it is nonetheless of supreme importance to my life because it was my first collaboration with Richard Curtis, with whom I would end up co-writing *Blackadder*.

I'd heard a lot about Dick. He was supposedly the 'brains' behind Rowan (you won't be surprised to hear that Row also has his own brain). Dick had written lots of sketches for *Not the Nine O'clock News* and, at the time I first met him, was in development with Rowan and John Lloyd for a sitcom called *The Black Adder*.

I'm not absolutely sure how we first got acquainted. Dick has a slightly different story to mine, but in my memory, he just rang me up and suggested we meet. The idea of our collaboration was definitely his, so I owe him plenty.

The first record I have of a partnership that would eventually produce the fully formed *Blackadder* is on Thursday, 21 July 1983. My diary says *Richard Curtis 6.00 – 6.30*. Now this *might* mean that Dick was being a bit vague about when he could get to our meeting, but it might easily mean that he was suggesting a half-hour slot. That would be Dick all right, the most famously busy man in the world. Whenever I see him, he's dashing from some meeting with a head of state and going on to chair an ideas session with Bono at the UN. For such a private man, he's led an extraordinary life of public service. I try to do my bit charity-wise, but Richard's not just in another league but on a different planet. His capacity to organize and inspire is incredible.

Anyway, Dick and I met up in July '83. He came round to mine, that same flat in Hampstead with the mouldy loo in which I'd typed out the *Young Ones* pilot, and yet another lifelong friendship was born, a friendship which, for the first six years, was also a very close and intense artistic collaboration.

As I mentioned, the idea Dick proposed to me was that we should try to write a Monkees-style sitcom for Madness. I thought it was a brilliant idea and leaped straight into it. I note that, a week after our first meeting, my diary says to meet at 11.30, 'having done ten minutes' dialogue each'. That's Dick again; there's always something of the kindly schoolmaster about him. I often feel that he's gently putting me in line. He got a First at Oxford, which I imagine takes a bit of discipline, and he's very disciplined about work. That early diary note actually sums up our whole working relationship, right there on our second meeting. We would always bring stuff to the table. It was never a case of writing together in the room. Certainly we'd chat and talk about ideas and directions, but the hard work was done alone at our separate desks. That's also how it would be with *Blackadder*.

Doing the Madness thing was fun. We met the band a few times in Camden, which is of course where the Nutty Boys all hail from. We'd go to the Dublin Castle, where they'd had their famous career-kickstarting residency in '79, or we'd meet at their office. The band were, as you would imagine, as inventive and as witty as their music (and their famous videos), so if nothing else we had a laugh.

The Madness project bumped along through the rest of '83. I was busy and so was Dick, but eventually in the new year we managed to persuade the BBC to give us a pilot. Sadly, however, not a proper pilot. By this time, the Madness star was fading a little and they weren't enjoying quite such guaranteed chart success. It was to be just a ten-minute, non-broadcast tester with one camera in any location we could find. I remember we all met up early one morning on Primrose Hill with our director, Geoff Posner. Geoff is a brilliant television artist and he and I would work together many times subsequently, but this was not our finest hour. Madness did great, but the whole exercise was neither one thing or the other. We needed an audience. The tape still exists and, to be honest, it's pretty grim. It was mine and Richard's fault entirely; not Geoff's and definitely not the band's. Anyway, the BBC passed and that was that.

Richard and my next collaboration would be rather more successful. But I'll get to that.

I write Jen her first lead – not quite as successfully as the one she would end up writing for herself

Also in '83, while in Manchester on *Alfresco*, I began work on what was to become a show called *Happy Families*, a comedy inspired by the classic Ealing comedy *Kind Hearts and Coronets*, in which Alec Guinness played multiple roles. It was a story about a mad and wicked old granny who has four granddaughters, all of whom have flown the coup, leaving only the grandson. The story begins with Granny sending the lad off to find the four girls in order that a terrible family secret may be revealed. The idea, of course, was that one actress would play Granny and all the daughters.

Paul Jackson read the script, liked it and offered to pitch it to the BBC. The next question was who should play the multiple lead role. We both had the same idea. Jennifer Saunders.

Jen and I had already become very good friends. My appointments diary for 1983 contains many 'meet Jens'. I'd also got much closer to Ade by this time. My first 'meet Ade in pub' entry occurs in the spring of that same year, the first of hundreds that were to lubricate and enliven the next forty years and counting. It's so funny to look back and think I was hanging out with them separately before they were a couple. It's hard to remember now that they've been together so long.

Jen and I had started playing squash together. She belonged to a posh club called The Hogarth (Jen always does things in style). She was fiercely competitive and as focused and aggressive with a racket as she was calm and serene when letting her mind wander while you thought she was listening to you. We were playing one time and she made a massive backhand swipe with her racket, the final trajectory of which connected with my right eye. Rackets were wooden in those days and there was quite a lot of blood. I still have a scar on my eyebrow.

If this was a biopic instead of a book, it would be as I got up off the floor, bloodied but unbowed, that I asked her if she'd like to play the lead in *Happy Families*. It certainly happened around that time.

And for the role of Guy, the grandson, we asked Ade. Ade was a much bigger star than Jen at the time and hence actually a bigger casting catch. He's also a talented and really thoughtful actor and I relished the opportunity to show a completely different side to him than the one that the public knew from *The Young Ones*. The rest of the cast was just as talented. Dawn played the mad old cook and we had Stephen and Hugh as the village doctor and his assistant. Helen Lederer was Dawn's kitchen maid and love interest Flossie. I still laugh to remember Dawn's delivery of the line

'I'm exhausted. I've spent the whole afternoon up to my elbows in Flossie's duff.' Dawn could deliver a dooble as brilliantly as the great ladies of *Carry On*, who of course set the standard.

Because the piece was episodic with all four granddaughters having pursued entirely different lives, we had the chance for amazing guest appearances in each show and Paul got us the best. Rik played a Nazi priest, Nigel Planer a pervy French cafe owner, Jim Broadbent a David Hamilton-style soft-porn photographer, Una Stubbs was a mother superior, Chris Langham a documentary film-maker, John Sessions an American soap star and Chris Ryan his harassed producer. Lenny Henry did a brilliant Hollywood dude.

Paul himself directed on film on single camera – I think the only time he ever did that. The whole production came together for a glorious summer in and around Uttoxeter in 1985.

I wonder if you're saying to yourself 'Sounds interesting. Why haven't I heard of it?' Well, I can't say it was a huge hit, but it did pretty well at the time. I wish it could be seen again, but the reason it's never been repeated or released on DVD is (I think) because Paul used proper pop music for the soundtrack. This sounded brilliant at the time, but the rights were only secured for one broadcast so unless somebody ever strips the tracks off and re-scores it with original music, I don't think it will ever be seen again. Maybe I'll make that a project for my fast-approaching old age.

Never do a bloke a favour

One thing I'd forgotten about from the years '81 to '85 – but which looking at my old appointment diaries has brought back to me – was that, throughout that time on most Saturdays, Kate and I had a lonely old man called Joe to tea. Sometimes I did it, sometimes she did it, often we both did it. Those Saturday cuppas were so excruciatingly dull that for forty years I've blocked them from my mind. Kate tells me she'd forgotten too and yet there it is in my appointment's diary – 'Joe for tea' – over and over again *hundreds* of times.

It began in '81. I was out but Kate was in when he knocked on the door, a virtual down and out living in a shelter, sixty-five or seventy years old. He wanted money, so Kate gave him a couple of quid, but being Kate – who always had time for every lost cause – asked him if he would like a cup of tea and a bit of toast.

Well, that was it. Once you've formed a bond, you're stuck. P.G. Wodehouse put it brilliantly when he said (something along the lines of) 'Never do a man a favour. You'll owe him for the rest of your life.' This was in a fantastically astute story about a man who saves a friend from drowning and, from that point on, the friend holds the man responsible for him being alive and so expects his benefactor to sustain him.

Joe kept coming year after year, for his tea and biscuits and, of course, a few quid. I wish I could tell you that he was fascinating company, that we grilled him about his memories of the war and ancient loves lost and won, but sadly he had no stories to tell or at least none that we were able to access. He was a single man who'd lived a life of various manual jobs and bedsits, ending with semi-homelessness and penury. He had no family. There'd been a brother but they hadn't got on and he was long gone. I presume he had a state pension but I couldn't say. If I was Alan Bennett, maybe I could spin a memoir and a play at the National out of it.

'Old Joe smelled strongly of urine. He had nothing to say for himself and so we conversed in a serious of pauses broken only by silence.'

Old Joe did smell, I'm afraid. Of sweat and wee. As I write, I can recall it vividly. I guess such a thing will come to us all.

In the end, Old Joe stopped coming. I can only presume he became incapacitated, died or just possibly got as bored with us as we were with him – although I must say I rather doubt that since each visit ended with him getting a fiver, which I rather think represented our principal attraction to him. When he stopped coming, we couldn't enquire after his welfare because, in all those many teas, we never knew a thing about him beyond his first name. Kate and I did try at first, ringing various hostels and the police, but understandably they asked for details and we had none to give. So we gave up and forgot about him. It's strange to be rediscovering that interlude now. *Joe for tea* – how my heart used to sink reading that.

Voice of the London scene

One other strange and rather wonderful job came my way in '83. I was asked by a great guy called Mike Chaplin at London Weekend Television to front a regional arts programme called *South of Watford*. Again, I look back with sad nostalgia at the quite extraordinary breadth and variety of regional broadcasting that existed in the days before multi channels drew the teeth of licensing legislation. *South of Watford* was well-funded, well-researched and excited about reporting exclusively the London scene. I fronted thirty editions over two years. We did shows on anything and everything: the original pop-up clubs, which were being thrown for a single night by groovy people in weird and wonderful locations; 'gender bending', as it was called (and this was before Boy George hit the charts); the psychobilly rock scene; the new fashion for rubber and bondage clubs; street car racing; the artists Gilbert & George; the Dungeons & Dragons gaming scene; London's carp-fishing community and many, many more.

Just think of it: this was a *local* show just for London and it really dug deep into any emerging scene, be it cool or naff. I remember we did one on something called 'music sampling', a new development where DJs were dropping bits and pieces of old songs into new songs. That was more than forty years ago, long before digital. These kids with mohican haircuts and Afros were cutting up tapes with razor blades and telling me 'One day no new songs will be written. Only mash-ups of old ones.' You heard it first on *South of Watford*.

I interviewed some amazing people too: Morrissey, Marilyn, Shane MacGowan, all before they were famous, and many others equally amazing who never would be. It was such an extraordinary job to have, a job that thousands of broadcast journos would have killed for and yet I had it as a hobby. I was leading a charmed life. The stupid thing was, I was working too hard to appreciate my good fortune. Or to be aware of how much some people were starting to resent it.

1985 and 1986

Well now, 'Bob' . . .

When Richard and I decided to have Edmund Blackadder fall in love with a girl called Kate dressed as a boy, we gave the girl's male alter ego a name, which on Rowan's lips would turn into one of the funniest single syllables in the history of sitcom.

'Bob.'

Row has a very slight stutter on B and P words. It's the tiniest hesitation, a sort of 'mm' from the back of the throat as the word seems almost to be gathering up courage to face the world. Row is a bona-fide performance genius who uses every element of his personal physicality to build his comedy, including minor speech impediments. Row knows all about those B's and he uses them to devastating effect.

So. *Blackadder*.

I wrote it with Richard Curtis. Or, at least, we wrote series two, three and four. I'm not going to go into who wrote what because neither of us can ever remember and if we do, we have a rule never to divulge. We were a team – truly, deeply and absolutely collaborative and mutually supportive.

One thing I will mention about the division of labour is that there used to be a presumption that I wrote the rude bits and Dick wrote the cute bits. This isn't the case at all. I can do sweet and he can do rude. He probably *tends* towards the former, while I am perhaps sometimes too quick to scurry to the latter, but we are both ambidextrous when it comes to sweet little noses and dick-shaped market vegetables.

So, me and Adder. I wasn't involved to begin with. When Dick approached me about the Madness idea in '83, the BBC were already broadcasting his and Row's co-written sitcom called *The Black Adder*.

I remember enjoying it quite a lot. Kate and I watched it together in our flat and used to sing along to Howard Goodall's extremely catchy title music. There are good things in it, but it's also no secret that the show was something of a disappointment. It didn't quite click. I felt this watching it and I think the audience in general felt the same. So much had been expected of the show: Row was the stand-out star of *Not the Nine O'Clock News* and major film production values had been expended on this, his first effort at sitcom. John Lloyd, who produced it, famously said of *The Black Adder* that it looked like a million dollars but unfortunately cost two million dollars.

Clearly this general feeling of potential unfulfilled was shared by the creatives themselves, because when the BBC offered Row a second series commission, he and Richard decided to shake things up a bit. Richard and Rowan had been a creative team since meeting at Oxford. They'd done a lot of sketches together, but *The Black Adder* had been (I think) their first effort at writing a sitcom. It was also to be Rowan's last. In my experience at least, Rowan's genius, like Rik's, lay in performance. They can both write but they are principally *enablers* of scripts. I'm pretty sure neither of them ever put 'writer' on their passport. Anyway, Rowan volunteered to drop out of writing the second series, leaving only Dick. Now if it had been me, I'd have tried to do the whole thing on my own, but to my eternal good fortune, Dick didn't want to do that. He wanted to co-write the second series and, rather wonderfully, he wanted to do it with me.

I was immensely flattered and I remain so. Dick is a brilliant writer and a deep thinker, and while he has worked with one or two other collaborators (on *Mr Bean* and *The Vicar of Dibley*), I'm the only person he's ever invited to join him at the ground floor of an idea as an equal partner. And this really was to be the ground floor. We were determined to remake this historical sitcom idea pretty much entirely.

So Dick and I sat down at once and started thinking about how best to build and improve on the previous effort. I think it's fair to say that, by the end of the very first meeting, we'd decided on the most significant changes that would turn *The Black Adder* into *Blackadder II* and set the style and tone for what people now think of as *Blackadder* in general.

We agreed that there was no advantage in the whole 'cinematic scale' thing that had been such a feature of *The Black Adder*. My first TV love was the traditional three-set, studio-based sitcom recorded live in front of an audience – *Dad's Army, The Likely Lads, Porridge* and *Fawlty Towers*. I felt that the scale of *The Black Adder* and the use of locations had been somehow alienating. I imagine that they had been going for something like *Monty Python's Holy Grail*, but that had been made for cinema, not TV. I just couldn't see what was gained comedically from that kind of scale. Rowan falling off a horse in a panoramic wide shot at 200 metres was no funnier than if it had been the unit caterer falling off a horse. For Rowan to be funny, you needed to see the detail.

But, for me, Rowan was in fact the core problem. Whisper it quietly, but Rowan in *The Black Adder* is not actually very funny. He's *quite* funny, but not hilarious in the way we know Rowan to be. He is one of the greatest comic talents of the twentieth century. But not everything a person does can be as good as their very best efforts and I think it's fair to say that Edmund of *The Black Adder* was not Rowan's best effort.

The truth is, I've never enjoyed Row's village idiot schtick as much as I've enjoyed his authority characters. I *like* Mr Bean, but I don't love him the way I love Row's Adder or the various vicars, headmasters and judges that he has played in sketches. I remember remarking to Richard that Row is often at his most comically potent when sitting behind a desk answering to a knock. He looks up with weary face and says 'Ah, come in, Simpkins . . .'

Then you know you're in for a treat.

And Row can chew a word like no other.

Of course, Row's an extraordinary physical clown but, even then, I think it's at its best when there's a warped intelligence to the character – Mr Bean's amoral cunning, for instance, or, better still, the French mime artist he did on *Not*, his face a mask of bored superiority juxtaposing the crazy physicality of his limbs.

In *The Black Adder*, Rowan's character was the idiot while Tony Robinson's character Baldrick was quite clever and sly. Richard and I agreed that, for this new effort, we would reverse the dynamic and make Edmund Blackadder clever and sly and Baldrick the village idiot. Without doubt, that can be marked down as the most significant decision made on the entire series, even more so than bringing the show back into studio and a live audience.

Rowan and John were enthusiastic about the direction we wanted to take things and so Richard and I set to work. We very quickly developed a writing model that served us throughout our whole time together. The idea was that I'd write a draft of an episode and he'd do the same and then we'd swap and work on each other's. The most important rule was that neither of us was allowed to look back. If Dick cut some section or other of my script, then I had to accept it and move on, and vice versa. There was to be no talk of 'Oh, you cut my favourite joke. *Please* let me put it back.' We arrived at this method mutually and very early on, and it was wonderfully liberating. Most collaborative writing sessions are about everybody fighting for their favourite lines with a lot of 'I'll let you keep that if you'll let me keep this', which means that you end up with a script full of jokes which half the creative team hate. You have to learn to love the cuts.

This was years before email, of course, and even slightly before personal computers. *Blackadder II* was done with biros and typewriters. I think it's lucky we didn't have the internet and Zoom because if we had, we might never have had to meet at all and much shared fun would have been missed.

Dick was renting a lovely little cottage in the gorgeous Oxfordshire village of Great Haseley and sometimes I'd visit. I look back on those times almost as some kind of Rupert Brooke-style idyll. Dick had that kind of effortless patrician charm and easy-going authority, which only seems to come from private school and Oxbridge. Stephen and Hugh have it too. It's a culture that's done a lot of harm in the world, but at its best, it's winningly inclusive and gentle and inspiring. To a boy from Catford, Dick's Oxfordshire village felt a tiny bit like Grantchester in Brooke's famous poem. Like Brooke, we were even living in the shadow of our own impending Armageddon, in as much as nuclear war felt like a real possibility as Reagan and Thatch squared up to the pre-Gorbachev Soviet dinosaurs.

It was just so *nice* going to Dick's place to work: the run-down, rambling little cottage with its garden bursting with summer fruits and buzzing insects (and tended by Dick's mother Glen), and the long summer evenings with scripts and gags and dinner to come. We probably only did this half a dozen times over the whole three series but, like all the summer joys of youth, when looked back on in later years, it seems to have stretched out for ever. The two of us would do a bit of work on each other's scripts, but mostly we'd chat, often about music. I vividly remember, on one visit to his cottage in '84, he'd got his hands on what was just about the first copy of Prince's 'When Doves Cry' sold in the UK. He was *so* excited about its game-changing genius that he played it for me three or four times in a row.

I think Dick was probably the most excited person in Britain about the Live Aid concert in 1985. It combined his two great passions – pop and altruism. He organized a big all-day party for it at his cottage. I don't suppose any of those attending could have guessed that he would take that long afternoon and evening of pop as his inspiration to build Comic Relief, which must by now be one of the biggest charity organizations in British history.

When Richard and I felt we had six good drafts, we took them to John Lloyd.

That's where the idyll would end.

John's a hard taskmaster. He always has been and always will be. Of course, being a very clever man, he's right a lot of the time. On the other hand, he *thinks* he's right *all* of the time. Well, you don't get to be as successful a producer as John without believing you know best. It's part of the job. But that doesn't make it any easier to take when you're on the receiving end of one of his lectures and you just don't agree. John's favourite line with us, when questioning some plot twist or joke, was to say – with a weary and irritating sarcasm – 'Dick, Benjy, *you* are the geniuses. I am just a poor foolish producer tasked with the job of enabling your *inspired* muse. *You* know everything, I know *nothing*. I humbly accept that. But will you *please* allow me to know fucking better than you on this *one small fucking point*?'

It was always just one small point he wanted us to concede on, nothing more. Until he moved on to the next. And the next. Sometimes he won, sometimes we did. Sometimes he was right no doubt, but sometimes he was *fucking wrong* and we had to square up to his smouldering fury. It was always a painful battle. Dick and I took to calling John 'Mad Jack', which he took as a compliment. To this day, John signs his emails to me 'Mad'.

But we got there in the end.

And we reckoned we had a winner. From Kate's arrival at Blackadder's door calling herself 'Bob' through Queenie pardoning a prisoner whom Blackadder had already executed. The Adder's attempt to rival the voyages of Walter Raleigh without leaving England. The blackmailing of the baby-eating Bishop of Bath and Wells. The Whiteadders' dinner party with the false breasts. Blackadder and Melchet's sojourn in a German dungeon and plenty more besides. Dick and I had our series written and we were really rather pleased. But then . . .

Comedy bombshell – Blackadder cancelled

One morning, when we were ready to submit *Blackadder II* to the BBC, Dick arrived at my flat for what had been planned as our final-check script meeting and he was grim-faced. As ever, Dick was much closer to the loop than me and he'd got the news first.

'They've cancelled it.'

I could scarcely believe it.

'What do you mean?'

'What I say. They've cancelled the Adder. They're going to pay us for the scripts because those were commissioned, but they aren't going to make them. Not now or ever.'

It was true. I got my letter through the post the following morning. I still have it. Framed.

BBC TV Centre
23rd October 1984

Dear Ben

After BBC 1 Comedy Offers with Michael Grade yesterday, we unfortunately had to cancel 'The Black Adder' for the next financial year and I suppose, in realistic terms, that means for ever. It is a great sorrow to me and I know you will be bitterly disappointed. I will be speaking to you personally about it when I have the opportunity, but I just wanted you to know that there is no other consideration but money and resources which led to this rather bleak decision being made.

Kindest regards
John Howard Davies.
Head of Light Entertainment Group, Television.

It was down to regime change, that corporate canker which bedevils all artistic careers, the utter curse of all writers. You spend months and years getting a project up, then – bam! – a new boss comes in and only wants to see new stuff. Michael Grade had come in as the new controller of BBC 1 and he didn't want *Blackadder*. So he cancelled it.

And hereby hangs a showbiz myth.

Michael Grade has claimed subsequently (I think it's even in his autobiography) that the show was never cancelled, that what he actually did was *threaten* us with cancellation. His story (which has made it into Wikipedia as fact) is that he cleverly manipulated us, sternly letting us know that if our scripts didn't offer a radical alternative to the excess of the *The Black Adder*, he wouldn't make them. The demands he claims to have made on us (principally do it cheaper and stick to the studio) are, of course, two of the very elements that played a crucial part in making *Blackadder II* a better series than the *The Black Adder* had been. I scarcely know Michael personally, but I know enough about him to respect his contribution to broadcasting. I also think that, over the intervening forty years, he has honestly come to believe his version of events. He genuinely sees himself as the brilliant, 'tough love' enabler of our stubbornly self-confident youthful talents. The man who turned around the Adder.

But I can assure you, it's complete bollocks.

You've read the letter. He cancelled it without a word of debate.

I get it (and I got it then). Michael Grade had come to BBC1 and spotted a large slab of his entertainment budget earmarked for a show which had drastically underperformed on its first outing. Rowan was a star, but he was nothing like as big a star as he was to become and Michael just didn't think the percentages on another *Black Adder* added up.

If I'd been him, I'd have probably made the same call.

But what we knew, and Michael Grade didn't, was that we were way ahead of him. We didn't want to make *The Black Adder* again either. Dick and I had spent months working *away* from it. The stories were firmly anchored in studio, the characters were all new, the budget required was much less. It was a totally different show.

We had in fact already decided to call it *Blackadder II* to flag the change. No other sitcom previously had done such a thing. There was no *Man About the House Six* or *On the Buses Twelve*. We felt that by putting II on the end (and turning the title into a surname rather than a nickname), we were signalling not a continuation but a fresh start. Not so much number two as *mark* two.

In the wake of the cancellation, Dick and I were desperate to make Michael Grade aware that he was cancelling a show that in effect we'd already cancelled. Nowadays, Dick is so connected he could probably do that in a couple of phone calls – no doubt via the prime minister, the Dalai Lama, Steven Spielberg and Bono – but back then we had no clout (I still don't). Fortunately, John Lloyd did have a bit and Rowan's agent had even more. Richard Armitage was an old-school showbiz legend who had probably dandled Michael Grade on his knee. John and Armitage went back to the BBC armed with our scripts and explained to Michael Grade that if only he'd give us a second chance, everything would be different.

And here, of course, is where Michael Grade truly can call himself the man who saved the Adder. Personally, I think the true story reflects even better on him than his own version.

Because Michael reversed his decision.

That is a really huge thing for a big boss in a new job to do. He'd made his big move and now, just because the star's agent had made a special plea, the boss was flip-flopping. That could have marked Grade down as a rubber-spined flake. Reversing the reversal took a big man. Michael Grade truly did turn the Adder around, just not in the way he claims.

So, the cancellation was cancelled and we began to make the show which would turn out to be the biggest TV hit of any of our careers.

The *Blackadder* ensemble seems a foregone conclusion now, but at one point it was a question of casting just like for any show. Tony Robinson and Tim McInnerny were retained from the earlier version, but with their characters much changed. I loved Tim as an actor and Dick and I had a lot of fun creating Percy Lord Percy for him. It was actually the closest we came to using a character from the original *The Black Adder*. We just made him even stupider and added a larger dollop of naive pomposity. Nobody does wounded ego like Tim. The rest of the roles were entirely new. Dick and I had written Lord Melchet absolutely with Stephen in mind and, of course, only Rik could play Flashheart. I've mentioned that I was thrilled to see Gabby Glaister winning the role of Bob and, of course, I was a very enthusiastic advocate of Hugh and Ade in various roles. The principal women, though, I had nothing to do with. And, oh, what brilliant choices they were. The late Patsy Byrne as Nursey was wonderful and then there was perhaps the most inspired casting coup of the whole series: Miranda Richardson as Queeny.

Oh my goodness she was good. And utterly and completely her own creation. There has been some talk over the years from Blackadder actors about having busked bits of stuff in rehearsal, but Miranda was the only player who created something new and truly unexpected beyond what Dick and I had written. Her Elizabeth was an alarmingly quixotic child/woman, both playful and chilling, constantly surprising us with crazy intonations, random emphasis and sudden bursts of manic pace. It was an entirely unique performance and she did it without once questioning or seeking to change a single syllable of the script. When writing all the other roles, Dick and I had a pretty good idea of how the lines would be delivered. We knew what we wanted from the actors and so wrote towards their styles and skills. Even Rowan's extraordinarily original performance was still well within the parameters of how we'd been hearing the lines when we wrote them. It was the same with Rik's legendary Flashheart. But Miranda constantly took us by surprise. She was simply sensational, an absolute original. John's decision to cast her is one of the greatest masterstrokes of his long and illustrious career.

It is often thought, bearing in mind the amount of talent involved and the amount of laughs generated, that rehearsals must have been an absolute giddy whirlwind of hilarity. Reader, I hope you won't be too dis-appointed when I tell you that sadly this was not the case. In fact, they were grim.

I stopped going but Dick was at every single one and he assures me that it was all pretty fucking awful, particularly for *Blackadder the Third*. They'd have the table read on the first morning, at the end of which – instead of some small congratulation followed by a move towards a bit of staging – there would be a collective weary sigh, fags would be lit, cof-fees replenished and they'd embark on some long and gloomy discussion about whether 'vole' or 'gerbil' was the more amusing small animal. This actually sounds like it might have been a funny conversation but, in fact, such a question defies analysis; most comedy does and the moment you try, it soon starts to feel like nothing will be funny ever again – particularly when the principal participants are staring furiously at their scripts as if they'd been asked to perform *The Tibetan Book of The Dead*. I remember Dick's primary frustration was always that these (often circular) discus-sions tended to begin before anyone had actually tried simply rehearsing what was written.

Now, I don't deny that some good things did come up in rehearsal, as indeed they should when clever comic actors have parts written spe-cifically for them, but something that only Dick and I remember now is that all those weary deconstructions didn't always improve things. On the contrary, often they made things worse. This is most noticeable in *Black-adder the Third*, which was set in the Regency period, the highlight of which for me was Hugh's Prince George. To my mind, this is the series in which the scripts were subjected to the most tortured micro-tinkering. The process reached its nadir between the third and fourth series when we made *Blackadder's Christmas Carol*. That's my least happy memory on the Adder. I'd attended the table read of what was to me and Dick a fan-tastic and fully formed script and, by the time I attended the recording, about 50 per cent of it had been fucked up in the rehearsal room. I mean, it's still *okay*. But I'm telling you now, it could have been *so* much better. I remember that's the only time I ever got as angry with John as he regularly got with us.

Sitting at Rowan's feet

In talking about the subsequent series of *Blackadder*, I've got ahead of myself a bit, but the show started for me in 1985. Another big writing gig I did in that busy year was to co-write a new stage show for Rowan. Getting asked to do this was such a lovely surprise. We'd only just completed the *Blackadder II* scripts and Rowan and I hardly knew each other at this point, yet he and Richard had already decided that I would be invited to become a part of something which had so far been exclusive to them. Rowan's stage work.

Dick and I got right down to it, creating the sketches that would very soon make up 'Rowan's New Revue', his first since that famed breakthrough Edinburgh set of '79 which I hadn't gone to see. We worked in the same way as we did on the Adder, swapping pieces and working on each other's stuff. There were perverted school teachers, smoothie presenters, visitors from space, politicians, comedy vicars (of course), a father of the bride (of course), Satan, a man plagued by an invisible man, a dopey guy on a first date, a harassed waiter in an Indian restaurant, a member of a church congregation, a guitar hero miming an interminable solo. All human life was there – or at least a large slab of the middle-class bit of it. Not all of the material would necessarily work today. The Indian waiter sketch required Rowan to play an Indian, which would at the very least come under scrutiny, even though the butt of the joke was the invisible table of drunken lads he was dealing with. There was a funeral oration monologue called 'Tom, Dick and Harry' which Dick and I just loved writing. It was about a blind man, a deaf man and a mute man who lived together sharing senses. I wonder again if we'd embark on that idea today, fraught with political peril as it would be.

Anyway, having assembled a big bundle of sketches, the two of us went to see Row at his place in Waterperry which, like Dick's cottage, was also in Oxfordshire.

Fuck me, that was a grim afternoon.

Row is the sweetest of men, and kind, but God he can be stern. We sat down together in his study, him in a big armchair with a large pile of pages on his knee, us perched on the edge of slightly less comfortable chairs. He began to read.

He read them all.

One after another.

In silence.

He placed the pages that he'd finished with on a little table beside him. I can see him now as I write, those long delicate fingers very precisely and neatly discarding one hard-won idea after another.

The process lasted at least an hour and he never laughed once. His brow was furrowed, his lips pursed, a slightly pained expression on his face, a study in concentration, exactly like a schoolmaster reading a pile of less than adequate essays (well, he does play schoolmasters very well). Every now and then he'd murmur 'I *quite* liked the first half of that one' or 'Mmm, there's an idea here *somewhere*'. I have to say, as getting-your-script-marked sessions go, I preferred John Lloyd's flashing-eyed fury to Row's frozen stillness. At least Mad Jack would roar with laughter when he wasn't insisting furiously that we could do better.

Anyway, Row finally got to the bottom of the pile.

'Well done,' he said in the tone of a man who was really saying 'Well done for trying'. Then he added, 'Some good ideas, I think, but it all needs work.'

Row wasn't being mean. He was just being Row. He's a very thoughtful and focused man who takes his work very seriously. But it was a hard day. Rowan and I have now been friends for forty years and have worked together many times, but back then I didn't know him so well and it felt like Dick and I had failed utterly.

Twenty years later, when our kids were little, Sophie and I took them round for tea at Rowan's and I reminded him of that awkward and uncomfortable afternoon.

'Oh Benj, I'm so sorry,' he said as he poured the tea. 'I'm sure it was all so much better than I indicated.'

Yes, it blooming well was, I assured him. In fact, the changes we subsequently made were relatively minor (if crucial) and the West End run was a huge success. We won a Cable ACE Award for best live show. Row used to dip into those sketches when required for years.

I reminded Row of all this and he took it well. He always takes being ribbed well. Beneath the seemingly serious exterior, he has the most playful sense of humour. As he served the cakes, his cat made an appearance. Row deftly removed the fondant fancies before the cat could snaffle one and then, scarcely realizing he was doing it, he did a mime of the cat's angry reaction to this disappointment – a brilliantly instinctive, fully rounded impersonation of an outraged cat. The kids were very thrilled. It was their own private Bean moment. That sort of thing happens all the time with Row. He can't help falling into instinctive moments of inspired mime to the delight and privilege of anyone who happens to be in the room.

Working on that revue was a particular joy for me because, for a few gigs, I was Row's straight man. Yes, on stage! Richard had played that role back in their student and post-student days, but now Dick had retired from the stage permanently and I got the gig – just for the try-outs, a few shows here and there, small colleges and the like, but what a thing to have done, eh, doing a whole two-man show with Rowan Atkinson? I was the very first concerned father to learn that his son had been beaten to death by Row's schoolmaster in the 'Fatal Beatings' sketch.

One sketch I recall that caused a great deal of discussion was 'Rude Schoolmaster'. This was a comic reboot of one Rowan's most famous early riffs when he simply read out names from a school register and yet managed to make every syllable funny. I had an idea to do a sort of *homage* to this in which every name was either a dooble or even a single. 'Herpes . . . Gonad . . . Russian exchange student Suckmeoff.' The idea was that the master was trying to lecture the boys about smut and rude jokes but that, by a cosmic coincidence of which he was sublimely unaware, they all had names which *were* smutty and rude. 'Any more of this nonsense and I will send you all straight to the headmaster, Mr Greatbighardcock.'

It was a very silly idea and one which Row was deeply suspicious of, but he embraced it in the end and, of course, delivered with absolute stony-faced brilliance.

The show tried out in Manchester before moving to the Shaftesbury Theatre in London for a season, with Angus Deayton now providing Row's splendidly dry foil. For the first time, my name was on a theatre hoarding on Shaftesbury Avenue, a thrilling moment for a boy who had grown up wanting to be Noël Coward.

Ibiza

So it was that, in 1985, I shared stages with the two most important comic performers of their generation: Row and Rik. Rik and I were still touring. We did spring, summer and autumn tours that year, each one as much fun as the last. Back in the van, Little Richard on the stereo, 'Let's dd-o-o-o-o it!'

Phil McIntyre and Paul Roberts promoted all of them and were often in the van with us.

One interesting interlude was a summer season in Ibiza. Phil had come to us after our spring tour and pitched a brilliant idea. He has spent his life trying to think up brilliant ideas and has come up with many. This one concerned the death of that once-great British showbiz institution, the summer season.

Before cheap air travel, the Brits had holidayed at their own seaside resorts and every single town on the coast boasted at least one four-month long summer season show of music, comedy and variety. It was a beautiful thing, and I'm lucky enough to have seen it before it died. I saw Lulu and Mike Yarwood at the Winter Gardens in Bournemouth in '74, and then in the '80s I saw Cannon and Ball, The Nolans, Freddie Starr and Little and Large in Blackpool. But those glory days were gone, the British now holidayed in Spain, but Phil reasoned they'd still want entertaining and thus the Rik and Ben three-week residence at The Heartbreak Hotel, Ibiza was born.

It only *kind* of worked. Ibiza holidaymakers weren't bored families shivering after a day in the Blackpool drizzle. They were sun-baked nihilists pissed-up on endless jugs of free sangria which they got courtesy of their tour packages. By the time I went on stage at about 11.30 p.m., they were a rowdy bunch to say the least. But my Comedy Store training served me well and, of course, they all adored Rik whose act did not require much concentration.

Gigs aside, though, we had a good time, as you can imagine. Finishing work at two in the morning made for a night-time existence and we used to end up having breakfast at the little cafe near our chalet block – egg and chips washed down with coco locos, a rum and pineapple cocktail. They had a pool table in that cafe and I well remember Rik bending over to lean along it to take a difficult side shot and crashing to the floor like a sack of potatoes and lying there, pool cue still tucked under his chin as if he was going to take the shot at floor level.

On the morning of our departure, we had a final coco loco session and got comprehensively drunk before heading for the airport. At the departure gate, Rik joined a completely different group of people thinking it was us and nearly got into an actual fist-fight having embraced a woman he thought was Lise. Phil's effort to revive the traditions of British variety nearly ended up in Rik's arrest at Ibiza airport.

The start of Comic Relief and corresponding with the GOAT

I actually had yet another writing gig in '85. It was a one-off comedy half-hour for Lenny Henry at the BBC. It was about an inept motorbike dispatch rider who's having a terrible day. His Honda 50 breaks down and he has to take it on the Tube. I called it *Pratt Outta Hell.* Looking back, I was clearly spreading myself too thin, but at the time everything was too exciting to stop and reflect. I'd met Lenny through Dawn, of course, and we were friends. He's great company – warm-hearted, extremely sharp and perceptive, and endlessly funny with his brilliant mimicry and stories of his Birmingham childhood.

And speaking of Len, Comic Relief also kicked off in '85. I was quite involved at first and was one of the people at the very first meeting organized by Richard Curtis. It was fun in those fledgling early days. Stephen and I did a little publicity tour together in the Midlands and Northern

Ireland. There was the *Young Ones* single and, in the spring of '86, the first live concerts. That was fantastic. I'd just got famous and so I was on the bill as a celeb in my own right. When I came off, I saw Billy Connolly standing in the wings.

'I'll have to raise my game after that.' He actually said it.

Wow. I mean, *Wow.* With a big shovel full of O-M-G.

Maybe he was just being nice, but he said it. I think Billy Connolly is the greatest stand-up comedian Britain has produced in my lifetime. I wrote him a fan letter a couple of years later. It was after he'd won some award or other and when he accepted it, he had talked about how much he enjoyed *Filthy Rich & Catflap* and mentioned me by name. I was so happy. So I wrote to thank him and also to give my reasons why I thought he was our greatest living stand-up. I got a lovely personal note in reply; this was in the days when you had to get a stamp and an envelope and find a postbox, which was quite an effort. Late in Billy's stand-up career, I saw him perform in Perth. By that time, he was living with Parkinson's, but he was just the same brilliant, life-affirming, deeply *human* comic that he's been for more than fifty years. The wit and the passion burned as brightly as ever and his unique insights into our collective absurdity remained forensically astute. Billy's is an art which, although it can be angry and fierce, loves and celebrates humanity and loves it for all its faults and foibles. And he plays a mean banjo. We exchange very occasional emails. When he announced he was finally quitting the road, I sent him a little letter and he sent a one-line reply: 'I always knew you were one of the good guys.' And guess what? Just the other day, out of the blue, I got this: 'Dear Ben, I was thumbing through my iPhone address book and I came across your name and it cheered me up just to think of you. Keep making strangers laugh.' He signed it 'Your fan. Sir Billy'. I'm not sure I have ever, or will ever, get a more wonderful, touching or humbling note from a fellow professional than that.

I carried on doing Comic Relief stuff for a few years and was on all the early Red Nose Day TV nights, but I was never very comfortable with the whole ethos. Perhaps it showed because, in the end, Dick dropped me. He's absolutely ruthless about maximizing the money and having studied the way the phone donations went while I was on, he concluded that I wasn't the sort of act that made people donate. My stand-up vibe just wasn't warm enough for the job and I don't think I could quite disguise my inner conviction that the really urgent necessity was to seek political solutions. So he stopped asking me to perform. A relief for both of us, I think.

More of 1986

You never get a second chance to make a first impression

And so we arrive at 1986, a simply massive year for me. I became a bona-fide TV star, which changed everything for me professionally, and I met the girl I would spend the rest of my life with.

Fame arrived at the end of January. It happened pretty much overnight and I have been famous, at least in Britain, ever since. I already had two successful sitcoms to my name, but success is very different to fame. Fame changes everything. From the moment it hits, you are viewed for ever through its prism, be the light golden or harsh, bright or faded. People's attitude towards you changes utterly, not with close friends, of course, but with everybody else. At the BBC, for instance, I was suddenly a much more significant figure. I'd been one of their most successful writers for years, but I had still been somewhat on the outer edge in the bar. Now that I'd been on the telly, I was centre of the group.

But at the time, I honestly didn't realize how famous I'd become. I'm always focusing on the next project. Years and years later, when people very kindly say 'You meant so much to me on *Saturday Live*', I always think that I wish I'd been more conscious of it at the time. Perhaps I'd have taken time to enjoy it more. The same week I did my first *Saturday Live* on Channel 4, *Blackadder II* started broadcasting on BBC2, two prime-time shows on two separate channels (out of only four) in the same week and both hits. It should have been a moment to savour, an extraordinary career high, but I don't remember even thinking about it at the time. Looking back, I want to shout at twenty-six-year-old me 'For God's sake, enjoy it, you silly bastard'. On the other hand, if I had done that, perhaps I would have also been more sensitive to the shit I've copped when I feel I've been pretty resilient to it. I think in the end I'm with Kipling on this and prefer to meet triumph and disaster and treat those two imposters just the same.

Saturday Live was the brainchild of Paul Jackson and Geoff Posner, a power-house duo if ever there was one. Paul had initially planned to emulate the American show *Saturday Night Live*, in which a house company of comic actors do sketch work with a guest celebrity host. From the start, though, Paul drifted from that template, making it more of a variety bill with established and unknown acts doing their turns.

The pilot was shot in late '85. I wasn't involved. Kate and I were members of the live audience and Lenny was the host. I remember French and Saunders appeared, but I can't recall who else. My memory is that the principal feature was the high-concept studio staging, which involved a multiple of performance platforms and a milling audience, some of whom were sitting on fairground rides.

When the series was commissioned, Paul booked Stephen and Hugh to do a sketch each week, as well as Rik and Ade's Dangerous Brothers and various other regulars, but he didn't ask me at all. I remember feeling a bit frustrated. Paul and I were good friends and had by now done *The Young Ones*, *Happy Families* and *Pratt Outa Hell* together. And he'd seen me gig many times on Rik and Ben tours, in which I did the whole first half of the show. So I couldn't understand why he was giving everyone but me a gig. Maybe he knew I was always going to add 'a little bit of politics'. Anyway, I lobbied Paul for a chance and eventually he gave me a slot. But he still wasn't sure and hedged his bets. While all the other acts were booked for the full ten-week run, I was only booked for the first five.

I was given a slot in the last segment, going on at around 9.45 p.m. The years of live work paid off because it really clicked. I had a year's worth of road-tested and honed material, which cut up nicely into little sections. None of my stuff had been exposed on telly so I could really pick the good bits. Oh, and I also had a sparkly suit. I bought it specially for the show. I didn't want to look cool. I wanted to look showbiz!

I can't remember which riff I did on that first week, probably 'Double Seat Double Seat', which I still get quoted back to me forty years later. It was an early example of observation comedy, of which I think I was a pioneer. I knew that when I was on a train, I was always hoping nobody would sit next to me, so I reasoned that other people would feel the same. So I created a snowballing riff about rushing along the train trying to find a free double seat and then the stratagems I'd employ to keep the seat next to me free, which ended with me claiming that I put my nob on the table 'because people will move a newspaper but they're not going to move your nob'.

Whatever set it was, it certainly got talked about and, after that, I delivered a self-penned five-minute set every week. Paul quickly forgot about only booking me for half the run and I closed every show. To everyone's surprise, not least my own, me and my sparkly suit were the hit of the series.

Some of those early routines were quite game-changing. I did one based around an ad for Renault cars which pointed out the staggering sexism that was endemic in advertising imagery and rarely, if ever, challenged. The ad featured a super-cool (super-smug) man who only tells his wife that he's made a life-changing career move and set up his own company *after* he's done it. He does this after they've dropped off their kid at private school (getting his violin out of the spacious boot to show how sensitive they are). The punchline of the ad was 'Buying a Renault. One of your better decisions.' The punchline of my act was 'Marrying an arrogant, sexist dickhead. One of your stupider decisions.' It might all seem pretty obvious now, but back in 1986, deconstructing the social-political assumptions entrenched in a car advert was definitely something new for stand-up comedy and it struck a chord, not always a supportive one but a chord nonetheless. I remember I was very big with single mothers and got a lot of letters and cards.

There was a routine I called 'Photosynthesis', which was about junk mail deforesting the world. There was one about the royal family being a benefits family in state-funded housing. Another was about sexist architecture and why women always have to queue for the loo in theatres. I had a riff about bouncers in dickie bows turning punters away for wearing jeans, pointing out that while Hitler and Goebbels would pass any club dress code, the Messiah would not ('Fuck off, Jesus. No sandals').

Personally, I think the best routine I did on *Saturday Live* was one about what it would be like if it were men who had periods: 'We'd be down the pub boasting about how heavy our flow was.' This routine was protesting the advertising industry ban on tampon ads. Yes, think of that – as late as the mid-*1980s* commercial TV still had a voluntary code prohibiting the advertising of women's sanitary products. I still find that pretty mind-blowing. That routine definitely caused a bit of a stir and within months the ridiculous (and deeply misogynist) ban was lifted. Coincidence? You be the judge. All I know is that suddenly the ad breaks were filled with joyfully menstruating, rollerblading girls scooting through bursting fire hydrants in exuberant displays of reckless abandon. Of course, I took the piss out of those too.

The show was all done absolutely live, no delay at all. When the red light came on, you were in a couple of million sitting rooms. It was *The Oxford Road Show* all over again, with gangs of kids milling around and nudging each other while I tried to remember my act. This time, however, after four years of gigging, I sort of knew what I was doing.

Well, I knew what I was doing in the moment – how to put my gear across, with sincerity and passion. In a broader sense, though, I was bliss-fully ignorant. I had absolutely no idea that I was also creating a kind of genre which would come to define stand-up in the '80s and define me for the rest of my life.

All I knew was that I was doing my thing and it was going great.

Then, about halfway through the series, I got a massive slap in the face. And it wasn't from the press (even though the hostility which would later become the norm was already emerging). It was from a peer, a colleague I respected.

Alexei had unleashed.

Alexei Sayle pisses on my parade

In those days. Alexei wrote a weekly column in *Time Out* magazine which *everyone* under forty in London read. And that week, he'd devoted the majority of it to saying that I was basically an unfunny, middle-class, posturing hypocritical little shit. Kate and I had gone away for a brief holiday between Saturdays and, this being long before the internet, when I got back to do the next show, I was completely unaware of what everybody else in comedy had been talking about all week.

As previously noted, I'd known Alexei for years and although aware of his antipathy to me, I'd never imagined that he hated me enough to make such a very calculated and coldly focused public attack. It was horrible to think that somebody (and somebody I respected) held me in such contempt. I was also kind of scared. Alexei carried a lot of moral authority; he'd been the first famous 'alternative' and he had proper cred. He was, as we were often told, the child of communists. He was from Liverpool and was working class. He sure had the chops to call out a middle-class ex-student poseur. But such *venom*. It was an unsettling feeling, to be so loathed. It was also *so* unexpected.

I was called a 'sell out' from the very first moment I got on the TV. There was no honeymoon period. The derision from both left- and right-wing critics was instant. I was a silver spoon-fed, middle-class hypocrite preaching revolution while grasping at wealth and celebrity and everything about me was a lie, most notably my accent, a laughable Mockney which I was putting on for purposes of undeserved street cred.

Alexei Sayle led the charge from the left and I did wonder at the time whether he'd noticed that I was getting exactly the same critique from the right. *The Daily Mail* commissioned a piece by no less a cultural icon than playwright John Osborne, the original 'angry young man' who kickstarted 1950s kitchen-sink realism with his play *Look Back in Anger*. The strap-line banner on the *front page* of the *Mail* for Osborne's article was 'Why I hate Ben Elton'. Bit of a shock when you pop into a newsagent for a paper (as we used to do) and get a rack of that in your face.

Alexei didn't let it drop for twenty years either. Not constantly of course, but I'd hear about nasty things being said in interviews. I remember Sophie hearing one in Australia in which he'd described me as being responsible for the downfall of British comedy! Wow.

Throughout all that time, we'd meet very occasionally at dos and I'd always be polite. But everyone's human and I admit I resented it. It's not nice being loathed.

And, of course, I'd been right to be worried about the broader effect of that first attack back in '86. It lent political and moral authority to any-body feeling bruised by my sudden and unexpected ascendance. Not long after, *Time Out* devoted a whole cover to a comedy magician called Jerry Sadowitz throttling my *Spitting Image* puppet, alongside a cover-line lamenting the fact that it wasn't the real thing.

Rik kindly had it framed and gave it me for Christmas.

I'm not saying a lot of that shit wouldn't have come my way anyway, but Alexei sure gave it a good kick-start.

In the end, twenty years after it began, he apologized.

Isn't that amazing? He got in contact with Phil and said he'd like to meet up. Unfortunately, I was away in Australia and Phil only told me about it later because he didn't think I should respond and he knew that I would have done instantly. But, of course, Alexei and I have many mutual friends and one of them, the late and terribly missed comedy musical maestro Simon Brint, was getting married. I knew that I'd bump into Alexei there and, being me, I really wanted to make it nice. Alexei had a novel out at the time called *Overtaken*. I'd read his first book, *Train to Hell*, and had thought it was excellent so I made a point of reading his latest so that I'd have something to talk about. Fortunately, I really liked the new one too, so I started whittering about it the moment he approached. I'll always remember looking across the room and seeing Ade grinning broadly. Ade knows me as well as anyone, except Sophie I guess, and he knows what a people-pleaser I can be. I was doing 98 per cent of the talking, feeling somehow that it was up to me, not Alexei to make everything all right between us. Anyway, when I finally paused for breath, Alexei apologized. He said that I hadn't deserved the things he'd said about me and that he was sorry.

Alexei is a true original, an innovative performer and a fine writer. He influenced a lot of people, including me. He's also a proud man and I imagine that he won't be thrilled that I have chosen to tell this story pub-licly after all these years, particularly the part with him apologizing. But he did it at a large gathering. *Everybody* there knew what was going on and he made no suggestion that he wanted it kept just between us. If he had, I would have respected that. I have soaked up quite a lot of pain because of him and also suffered the collateral damage of his pronouncements lending credibility to greater spite in others. I think that gives me the right to set this story down. Closure is a rare thing in life and I'm grateful to him that he allowed me some.

Still making that first impression

We did three series of *Saturday Live* (or *Friday Night Live* in its final season), thirty shows in all. I was made the permanent compere for the second and third series, linking all the acts and becoming the 'face' of the show.

The biggest change for me being compere was that I now opened the shows as well as closed them, which is when I started doing my 'topicals'. It was these opening routines which more than anything else came to define me. I'd do eight minutes of carefully road-tested and honed material at the end of the show about any number of things – the bottom drawer of my fridge or the strange capacity of small dogs to produce large turds – but it was the opening three minutes that came to loom large in my legend.

That's when Thatch-bashing Ben was born and I don't suppose I'll ever entirely emerge from his shadow. I even unwittingly invented a catch-phrase for him. Sensing audience doubt when I ventured away from non-contentious subject matter, I'd confront it by saying 'Ooh, little bit of politics. You're not too sure are you?' In many people's mind, 'a little bit of politics' became all I was about.

Paul Jackson – being, as ever, insanely busy – had dropped out of producing the show after the first series and a new guy came in to co-produce with Geoff Posner – another Geoff, Geoffrey Perkins. Geoff is a legend in the business, a hugely successful producer who was also about as nice a guy as you could ever meet. I say 'was' because he died at the horribly young age of fifty-five in 2008. The BBC named a conference room after him. He would have smiled at the idea of being turned into a room.

Geoff and I very quickly became close. On *Saturday Live*, we would sit down on the Friday and review the week's news; he had a wonderful knack of finding absurd and interesting things for me to riff on. It was Geoff who suggested I do something around *The Sun*'s almost hysterical campaign to save a single donkey called Blackie who was the tormented centrepiece of some ancient village ritual in Spain. Blackie the Donkey became a bit of a runner for me – him and Tory cabinet minister Edwina Currie. Those Friday night script sessions were always tense. Everyone else would have left after the rehearsal, leaving me and Geoff to worry ourselves silly over the topicals. Then, on the Saturday, between the dress rehearsal and the show, we'd review and I'd tinker with the script, adding stuff if anything interesting had happened that morning.

And then I'd have to learn it.

It still makes me sick to think of. I didn't discover the auto cue until the last series. I think I had some misplaced pride about keeping it real, which just meant that my carefully written gags often came out in a kind of terrified gush as I tried to hit my mark on stage, keep to time and remember gear that I'd written sometimes only an hour before. All the while, floor managers waved their arms at me.

No wonder I came across as a bit hectoring.

One added misery of those terrifying show nights was the necessity of my having to read all my stuff to the Channel 4 lawyer before the gig. I was the only person required to do this. I suppose it was because my stuff was subject to change up to the last minute, whereas everybody else's act was set and scripted so it could be vetted earlier.

Blimey, that was a grim experience. Me and Geoffrey sitting with the stony-faced legal eagle who *never* even smiled. Most of the stuff was entirely non-contentious, but I still had to subject it to the deeply undermining process of reciting it to a piece of human granite.

The smaller the dog, the bigger the turd! Those little yappy ones you see growing out of rich old ladies' armpits. They've got bodies like Doctor Who's Tardis! They're bigger on the inside! Mountainous turds! They block out the sun, Charles and Di are taking a well-earned winter break on its lower slopes.

Not the sort of material that works without an audience.

The smooch at the end of the disco when all the little fun-size Mars bars start getting ground against girls' stomachs.

The lawyer could snap out of his trance at the most unexpected moment.

HIM: Fun-size Mars bars are a product.

ME: So?

HIM: If I've understood your joke correctly, you're comparing them to small penises. Mars could claim you'd defamed them.

ME: It's just a visual image. Obviously, I'm not saying fun-size Mars bars *are* small penises. I'm saying their shape and the contouring of the chocolate is reminiscent of a small penis.

HIM: Then you have to say that. Currently you make a statement. You need to couch it in the form of a comparison and one which is a private opinion, not Channel 4 policy.

ME: So you want me to say: *The smooch at the end of the disco where all the things that in my opinion are reminiscent of the shape of a fun-size Mars bar get ground into the girls' stomachs?*

HIM: Yes. I think I would be prepared to pass that.

We really did have conversations like that, every week. And bear in mind these conversations took place an hour before I was going to have to host ninety minutes of absolutely live TV, which would include me delivering two sets of my own gear, some of which had only just been written and was now being rewritten. I may have looked cocky and opinionated, but actually I was just trying to blurt it all out before I forgot it.

Besides Geoff Perkins, I made another lifelong mate on *Saturday Live*. And one of my closest. It was on that show that I first got to know Harry Enfield. He'd joined us that series and our dressing rooms at the London Studios were next to each other. We bonded over the horrible wait that precedes live TV – long chats, lots of nervy laughs and a shared feeling of the leaden dread that was about to engulf us both, with me endlessly fretting that none of the topicals were funny and him reminding me that at least I didn't have to do them in an amusing Greek accent.

Saturday Live was an incredibly significant show, a real watershed in British entertainment because it created the modern stand-up boom; a boom which is now nearly two generations old and still booming, a boom that led very quickly to pubs in every town in Britain hosting stand-up nights – and, in larger towns, the emergence of actual specific comedy clubs.

Before *Saturday Live*, there was no 'circuit'. The Jongleurs club had started up in London and there was Malcolm Hardee's Tunnel gig in Greenwich, but the acts who appeared were still a quaint and rarefied breed – spesh acts and strange-looking alternative spirits. Julian Clary did his first gig on *Saturday Live* in bondage gear with a dog as a sidekick, while the wonderful Jo Brand debuted with us while still calling herself The Sea Monster. There was no constant supply of confident, skilled comedians, like there is today. Variety had been dying in the UK; the disappearance of the working men's club and the end of the seaside summer season had meant the fading of the old guard of British entertainers. *Saturday Live* breathed life back into the medium.

And it was *fun*. Proper young fun, a pure entertainment show that belonged firmly to youth in the way that I don't think any show had done as clearly since *Ready Steady Go!* more than twenty years before. We always had three great musical acts, all playing live, of course. These days, music on mainstream TV is rare and generally thought to be a programme-killer. A cabaret show such as *Live from the Apollo* (which isn't actually live) doesn't feature any at all. But in the days before the internet gave people instant access to every band on the planet 24/7, telly still had a massive role in introducing people to new music while also giving them a fix of the familiar. And, gosh, it was exciting in the studio, particularly for me. I'd introduce a band (something I loved doing) and then watch as the crane camera swept over the audiences' heads towards the musicians on a stage opposite me, the five or six floor cameras ploughing through the audience in hot pursuit, all expertly wrangled by Geoff Posner in the gallery. I'll never forget, on my first show as the official regular host, introducing The Damned covering the classic '60s rocker 'Eloise' and the excitement of those huge opening organ chords and Rat Scabies' power drumming.

The shows passed by in a blur and afterwards we'd all go to the bar and hang out with Eurythmics, Robert Plant, Paul Weller or The Pogues, before the core team would all pile across the river to The Zanzibar Club in Great Queen Street and drink until 3 a.m. Happy days.

One morning in Melbourne

Saturday Live made me a very public figure and this unquestionably had an effect on my relationship with Rik. I won't say that he was jealous exactly, but it certainly affected him. We'd always been The King and Little Farty, and I was happy to continue to play that game and we did so all our lives, but nonetheless the dynamic had changed. Like they say, fame changes everything.

When I started getting recognized in pubs, Rik would turn on a massive blast of Rikness, flicking V's and pulling faces until everybody forgot about me and focused on him. He did it for a laugh and in good spirit but he was never comfortable with my latterly acquired fame. Dawn told me that she once found him looking thoughtful on some Comic Strip shoot. She asked him what was on his mind and he sighed, 'Ben's the famous one now'. I honestly don't think he was resentful; he was pleased for me. But it definitely changed things.

We did, however, have one more tour to do together where the old relationship of star and largely unknown little pal still held, a tour that would lead to the biggest and most unexpected change of direction in my whole life.

Phil had come to us in the autumn of '85 and asked if we fancied touring Australia.

Did we?! Too bloody right we did, matey.

And now the tour had been organized. It was April '86 and Rik and I were the two most excited people at Heathrow Airport. Barbara was with us; Rik had left Lise Meyer in late '85 and married Barbara shortly after, and they were expecting their first child. Now here we were, boarding our flight to Melbourne.

We loved that flight. We were in business class (a first time for me certainly) and we made the most of it. You could smoke on a plane in those days and we drank and fagged our way across the world.

Paul Roberts was on the flight with us, representing Phil, and about halfway through the flight, he came and squatted down beside mine and Rik's seats. He told us that he had good news and bad news.

'The bad news is that you have to have four Australians on the bill with you. It's a union requirement.'

This was a pretty devastating bit of news. Phil had known it would be so, which was why he had told Paul not to tell us until we were on the plane. Rik and I had a complete show. I did the first half and he did the second. There was absolutely no possibility of their being room in the show for *four* extra comedians. We were horrified and would have certainly not done the tour had we been told in the first place, which was why Phil and Paul didn't tell us.

We started to protest when Paul reminded us that we hadn't heard the good news.

'The Aussie promoter has booked an all-female pop band. Four gorgeous girls called The Jam Tarts.'

Well, this was certainly better news.

'And it won't be a problem at all,' Paul went on. 'The Aussie promoter says it's just a union thing. They've been booked to appear, but you can have them playing in the bar in the interval or even for the ticket queue, as long as we pay them.'

Funnily enough, this actually turned me and Rik in favour of The Jam Tarts, even before we'd met them. There was no way we were going to demean fellow artists by making them play to the queue. If they had been booked to appear, then that's what they would do. We decided that we'd invite them to do a short musical bracket before my set and then another one before Rik's. Then we ordered more drinks and Paul returned to his seat much relieved.

We arrived in Melbourne in the morning and that evening went to a comedy club. I even got up and did a set, performing for the first time in a different hemisphere, which was quite a thrill. I went to bed that night, excited for the tour ahead but never imagining the life-changing encounter that awaited me the following day.

Rik and I met our support act backstage at the Princess Theatre in Melbourne: four girls in their late teens – Jodie, Lucy, Anna and Sophie – and a woman of about forty-five called Kate, who was both the band's manager and the mother of Anna and Sophie.

They were all very pretty, but the skinny girl with the big dark eyes beneath the fringe of bobbed hair, standing behind her double bass, just took my breath away.

It was love at first sight.

Or at least it was for me. And thirty-eight years later, I am writing this at home in Fremantle, Western Australia, where The Jam Tarts were born. Sophie is my wife, Kate is my mother-in-law, Anna is my sister-in-law and Jodie and Lucy are still dear friends.

Quite a forking fork in the road, eh?

Sophie and I didn't get together on that tour. In fact, I never even kissed her. She was only eighteen (*nearly* nineteen) and I was twenty-six, which seemed to me like a very big gap. Besides, I had a girlfriend at home whom I was very fond of – although, in truth, I think Kate and I had both known for a while that our university-based romance was running its course.

I spent the whole tour nursing a secret passion that brought me to tears on the last night of the tour when Rik and I had dinner together in Perth and I confessed my infatuation to him.

But apart from my silent agony, the tour was a blast. We played Melbourne, Sydney, Brisbane and Perth and stormed it. The girls were all brilliant fun and we made a great tour gang. Rik and Barbara became as close to Kate and the girls as I did, so did Paul Roberts. I think even if I hadn't ended up marrying Sophie, everyone would have remained friends.

One particularly exciting day was when Rik and I presented a gong on the Countdown Awards. Countdown was the Aussie version of *Top of the Pops* and was every bit as central to popular culture in the '70s and '80s. It was then that Rik and I got reacquainted with Molly Meldrum who had interviewed us in London prior to our tour. Molly is an entertainment icon in Oz whose deep love for popular music has had a huge impact on bringing forward Aussie bands and also bringing international acts to Australia. Molly had the popularity and visibility of a figure like Noel Edmonds in the UK, but combined it with something of the music industry cred of John Peel. That's a tough balance to pull off and Molly's been doing it in Aus since the '70s.

Incidentally, that old interview Rik and I did with Molly turned up a lot on the internet after Rik's death. In it, Rik can be seen being amusingly aware of me banging on and on and on. I did that. I'm sure I still do, but I was much worse then. No wonder I pissed so many people off. Watching those old interviews (which I can't stand for long), even I find myself wanting to shout 'Just shut the fuck up for a minute!'.

When I left Australia in late May '86, I had no idea if I would ever even return, let alone make half my life there. Sophie seemed destined to be nothing more than a fond and painful memory.

Shortly after I left, Sophie's family were sat around the table at the old church which her architect/builder father Bob had converted into a home and they played a game of 'guess the future'. Everyone had to write down a prediction for everyone else. Bob wrote my name as his prediction for Sophie. I still find that amazing because I swear neither she nor I had even the remotest such expectation.

We were not to meet again for fifteen months, but it was worth the wait.

My summer of discontent

I returned from Australia to a pretty miserable summer. As I say, Kate and I were drifting apart and I think we would have broken up that year even if I hadn't developed this unexpected crush while on the other side of the world. She too had been looking outwards and the writing was on the wall. We broke up a few months later, but it was a long and painful process. We were still such great friends and it seemed strange to be throwing so much away when we still meant so much to each other. I think many separating couples feel that. You get daunted by the idea that saying you no longer want to share your life with a person somehow invalidates the love that you have previously shared. My advice to people splitting up is to go with Paul Simon in his brutally astute *Fifty Ways to Leave Your Lover*. You just have to do it, make it clean, no matter how horrible it feels at the time. If you don't, you'll be like me and Kate were, torturing each other and ourselves with guilt and regret.

Kate was certainly a big influence on me with her love of art and theatre, and her endless energy to party and live large. She had a passion for social justice and was very politically active. As a young lawyer, she involved herself professionally and personally in many of the struggles of the '80s. I did my benefits and such, but she was the real deal, turning out on picket lines on freezing mornings and getting in some pretty scary 'kettlings' with baton-wielding police, some on horses. Kate eventually rose to be a QC and then a very senior judge with responsibility for many hundreds of other judges, but she never lost her youthful passion for justice. She and I have remained close friends all our lives. We meet occasionally in London, and Sophie and I visited her and her lovely husband Richard in Cambridgeshire only last summer and spent a gloriously boozy day in their beautiful garden. I was a lucky man to have found such an extraordinary person with whom to begin my adult life.

But splitting up with Kate wasn't the only changing relationship that was making the summer of '86 a painful one. I was finding working with Rik increasingly difficult. We had agreed with Paul and the BBC that we would create a new show to star Rik, Ade and Nigel. Not a sequel to *The Young Ones*, but something new.

This was to become *Filthy Rich & Catflap*, an idea which played with the world of traditional showbiz into which we'd crashed. Rik would be Richie Rich, a D-list celebrity obsessed with fame, Ade was Eddie Catflap, his dissolute minder, and Nigel played Ralph Filthy, an old-style showbiz agent. I guess it wasn't as universal a canvas as student life had been with *The Young Ones*, but it still had plenty going for it.

Sad to say, writing *Filthy Rich & Catflap* was just horrible, the unhappiest creative period I ever went through. I was down in my personal life and Rik was not proving to be a remotely helpful co-writer. Unlike on *The*

Young Ones, he wasn't bringing stuff to the table himself, but he wasn't letting me get on with it either. When Rik got frustrated creatively, his instinct was always towards excess. He would say things like 'They should all just kill each other' or 'The sofa should explode'. Well, I don't mind the occasional exploding sofa, but you can't do too much of it. You need a situation, characters and a semblance of plot, but when I tried to concentrate on developing those things, Rik would get bored and demand that we killed another milkman.

Slowly and painfully, we assembled six scripts. Rik wrote nothing but rejected plenty. We just weren't as at ease with each other as we once had been and he was drinking a lot.

Rik was mainly sober for the final sixteen years of his life, but alcohol played a highly destructive part in the fifteen or so years before that, not least because it alienated his friends and collaborators. It fills my heart with sadness to say that it definitely drove a wedge between us. I did try to talk to him about it, of course, a number of times. When he'd come to my flat to chat about future projects, he'd ask where the Scotch was at ten in the morning. But it's very hard to reason with an alcoholic, particularly one as charming and as functioning as Rik. I remember watching him pour a four-finger measure one morning and gathering the courage to confront him about it – really confront him, telling him that he had a real problem and that if he didn't deal with it, then only disaster could follow. He just smiled his impossibly charming smile.

'Don't worry about me, Benjy. I know what I'm doing.'

He didn't, of course, or he would have stopped. The effect on his friends and, more particularly, his family was considerable. Barbara bore the brunt, of course, and tried the hardest. Rik took to secret drinking, getting mates to buy him large brandies which he pretended he wasn't having. That caused some painful soul-searching for those of us on the receiving end of the requests, I can tell you.

In the end, the accident that nearly killed him saved his life. After he hit himself over the head with the quad bike, he was on medication for life and the medical advice was that a return to alcohol would have killed him. At least that's what we all believed, including him. At the funeral, I was absolutely astonished when Barbara told me that she'd made it up.

Of course, he couldn't have drunk heavily on his drugs, but she told me that he could probably have drunk in moderation. But we all knew that Rik could rarely drink in moderation, so she invented her story and he believed it. And, as far as I know, if he did have another drink after that, he finally had it under control. Mind you, I knew him when he was a highly successful secret drinker, so you never know.

I have, of course, asked Barbara's permission to talk about Rik's drinking in this book and she said I should.

'You had to deal with Rik's drinking, as we all did,' she said. 'It's a big part of your story so you must write about it.'

We all drank a lot in the early days and loved it, but by our mid-to-late twenties, most of us were setting some limits. Rik never did. Ade and I still loved the booze and have continued to have big nights and big Sunday lunches together all our lives, but apart from Sundays and holidays, we stopped drinking during the day thirty-five years ago.

As work on *Filthy Rich & Catflap* limped along, I started to feel a bit lost and panicky. This was, after all, a sitcom commission from the BBC, a pretty public forum in which to screw up. I was exasperated and annoyed with Rik and I was breaking up with Kate. In some ways, I was sort of breaking up with both of them and, in the summer of '86, got as close to a proper emotional crisis as I think I've ever got.

And I had so much other stuff to worry about – a lot of work to do with Dick on *Blackadder the Third* for a start. Plus, there were benefit gigs and my first stand-up album *Motormouth* to record, which I was going to do live at a club called Fat Sam's in Dundee. Also, I had another Ibiza season, a week of solo gigs in Dublin and a hernia operation!

And all the while I was trying to write *Filthy*, with Rik drifting further from the writing (not least because Barbara was about to have their first baby) but not letting go. There were good days when I felt I was on to something and Rik felt so too. Then, briefly, it was like old times. Rik loved the combination of big physical laughs and increasingly erudite language.

Richie and Eddie view the corpse of the milkman.

RICHIE: Quick, grab the stiff.
EDDIE: Oo-er!

RICHIE: Eddie, a man is dead. I think that, as his immortal soul hovers over the earthly remains of his dead self, he would prefer not to be the subject of a nob gag.

Rik laughed for about five minutes over that. But there were also days when it felt like I was writing in quicksand.

This was the point at which Rik decided to drop his own writing credit, a decision about which I had mixed feelings. On the one hand, it was fair because I'd written every word, but on the other hand, he'd made writing those words bloody difficult and, as such, had seriously influenced the style of the show. We ended up billing the show by me, but with additional material by Rik.

Rik's idea of additional material was always to go bigger and sillier.

Those extra dead milkmen is a perfect example. I'd originally only had one. I think we ended up with Rik's character Richie Rich killing four or even five. I don't really know as it's been thirty-six years since I watched it. I do know that the show ceased to be anything close to recognition comedy. In *The Young Ones*, the characters had been massively exaggerated but remained recognizable as genuine student types. With *Filthy*, the writing and then the performances got so grotesque that they no longer resembled the showbiz characters they were supposed to be. The madness was no longer rooted in reality. Even as I wrote it, I could sense that I was losing any real awareness of what I was actually writing.

Anyway, somehow, I got the six scripts together and I now had to face the next hurdle.

Showing them to Ade.

He and Jennifer were on holiday in Italy with their first baby and they'd invited me out to join them for a break, so the time had clearly come to get Ade involved.

On the night before I left for Italy, I went round to Dawn's for dinner. Dawn could see that I was very tense and very unhappy, which was so totally unlike me that she insisted I stay the night. She even ran me an enormous hot bath and gave me a cold beer to have with it. That was such a lovely gesture. Len was away and we sat up late, Dawn letting me talk about my problems with Rik and guilt about Kate and being in love with some Australian bass player who I would never see again.

I was so grateful for her friendship that evening. Normally I'm absolutely fine with my own company, but that summer I was heartily sick and tired of myself.

The next day, I flew out to see Ade and Jen who offered similar comfort in the wonderful warmth of their family holiday. They'd rented a beautiful little house in some idyllic Italian town. I remember the shining red tiles on the balcony warmed by the sun and the little table laden with wine and olives awaiting my arrival. It should have been a moment to recharge, but I was definitely not myself – lonely and worried and over-emotional.

This situation was not improved by Ade's reaction to the scripts. He thought they were funny enough, but he also thought they were all about Rik. There wasn't much in it for him and, after he had read them, he told me that he didn't want to do it.

Well, we certainly couldn't do it without Ade, so I knew that I was facing another shitload of work pulling the emphasis away from Rik and working a bit more towards Ade. I was almost overwhelmed at the prospect and found myself actually crying as Ade spoke. I hadn't felt myself welling up; tears just began to flow. I think it was basically exhaustion as I almost never cry. But there was nothing for it but to start unpicking the scripts. They didn't take much unpicking because they were in such a mess anyway. But I got it done, feeling like I was writing while drowning, a process that was extra complicated by the fact I was also trying to write the material for my first full solo tour, which was already on sale and scheduled to start as *Filthy* went into studio. Obviously, I'd taken on too much, but when you're young, you think you can do anything.

But you can't. And *Filthy* just wasn't good enough.

Paul Jackson produced it and did his usual supportive and inspired job. We made it in Manchester. I wasn't there much because I was on the road, but with Paul and brilliant director Ed Bye, it was in the safest hands. *Filthy* had some very good bits and some truly grim bits. The targets were definitely a bit too niche for what our large fan base was expecting and we made them more niche by making them so grotesquely pantomimic.

Having said that, it retained and even grew its audience share. The people who watched it seemed to like it quite a lot.

Except the critics. This was my first experience of being reviewed as a writer following my new celebrity. Suddenly I was the target and it wasn't pleasant. The reviews weren't just bad, they were *angry*. It's a funny thing about comedy. With drama, if people don't like it, they shrug and say 'not for me', but with comedy they get angry. It's as if by trying to amuse someone and failing, you've insulted them. I think Harry Enfield was the first person to point out this strange phenomenon. He's an astute old bastard. Bad reviews of comedy are always more splenetic than bad reviews of drama or current affairs. And it's worse if you're perceived as currently 'hip'. Then you really get it and we got a shitload on *Filthy*. Not being as funny as your last gig is a crime that cannot be forgiven. It had its supporters. I remember I'd just got friendly with Kate Bush at the time – she's a big comedy fan and we used to meet up occasionally. I happened to be meeting her for dinner on the day we got dumped on. She personally had loved the show and I can tell you now that if you're going to get a slagging, having the extraordinary and inspiring Kate Bush be outraged on your behalf is a major consolation prize. 'Well, *I* thought it was hilarious, Ben, so fuck them.'

But it wasn't hilarious enough. This was the *Young Ones* team and it just wasn't as good. Except (and this may not have escaped your attention) it was *The Young Ones* team *minus* all the parts that I felt had diminished *The Young Ones*. That's a fact and an irony that I must own. The *Filthy* writing team was what I had wanted for *The Young Ones* – just me writing with Rik influencing. And yet *The Young Ones* was better than *Filthy*. So maybe I'm the idiot.

All I can say is that there is a time for things and 1981 and 1982 had been the time for me and Rik to shine together. We were on fire creatively and I honestly believe that had our relationship not been dislocated at the optimum moment in the way it was we could have taken *The Young Ones* and what followed to even greater heights.

The year 1986 ended on the road for me – my first solo tour and my first time doing the whole two hours. Touring was different now. Just me and a tour manager. No Rik, no lager drinkers from hell sticking Little Richard on full blast on the M1 at two in the morning. It was great to be doing a solo tour and the whole two hours, but a bit sad. There was a strange moment on the last gig of the tour, which to this day I haven't decided what I think about.

Rik and Barb had turned up in Southend to surprise me for the final show and, for some reason, Rik decided to walk on from the wings during my bows with Rosie, his little daughter, in his arms.

I'm pretty sure it was spontaneous. I don't think he planned it and I don't think he had any idea what it was that prompted him to do it. But I admit it was a bit awkward. Nobody knew what to think, including me. I remember the vibe of the applause changing and sensing something behind me and turning round to see Rik standing there with Rosie. Very strange.

We didn't discuss it afterwards and it was never mentioned again.

I get dissed by Ronnie Barker and slapped by Robin Day

At the end of that exciting and difficult year, there was the BBC Light Entertainment department Christmas party.

As far as I was concerned, these parties were just about the best night of the whole year. Such excitement! It was Christmas and we were at the BBC! Not just any old BBC, but the light entertainment bit, the bit that *was* Christmas – my two great childhood loves combined: Christmas and comedy on the telly. It was black-tie too, which I had to rent each year. A cold December day and off to Moss Bros to hire my tux to go to a party at the *BB fucking C*. The idea is still thrilling for me. Some of our alternative lot objected to the black-tie thing. They didn't want to wear the uniform of 'the establishment' and instead wore ordinary ties or even no tie at all. But I loved it. Still do. Black-tie is great. It looks good on every shape of man and it's just a very cool get-up. That's why James Bond wears it.

Anyway, back to the BBC Light Entertainment Christmas party. It was 1986 but the whole event just reeked of the 1970s, which was its great charm. The invite might have stipulated black-tie and sounded posh, but basically the party was held in an office. All right, it wasn't an office *as such*. It was the famed 'hospitality suite' on the sixth floor at Television Centre, which was basically the same as all the offices on all the other floors, but with the partition walls removed. The same '70s nylon carpet tiles, the same low ceiling, the same flouro tube lighting. There was no Champagne. It was wine or beer and curry from large tin trays with little flames under them. That was the first time I ever encountered those clever things you can clip onto your plate and hang your glass off. A fantastic bit of design and very necessary that night because there were no tables and almost no chairs – just a few scattered about for the oldies from *Last of The Summer Wine*. It was proper old-school BBC.

In the '80s, the BBC was still a relaxed, good-natured, tolerant sort of place that just seemed to bumble along producing world-class drama, cutting-edge comedy, nice and cosy variety, and extraordinary documentaries and journalism that were the benchmark for the world without really seeming to bestir itself much at all. Nobody was paid excessively, not even the stars and certainly not the upper management. It was so comfortable and solid. It felt like it would last for ever. We could never have dreamed that in California development of the internet was already advanced and an unimaginable tsunami of change would soon sweep away that world for ever.

What fun those naff old parties were. They were all there, all the light entertainment stars. Sadly I was just a few years late to see Eric and Ernie, but the Two Rons were always there, the undisputed kings of the gig. And it was at the '86 party that I first met Ronnie Barker and got roundly dissed by the captain of the old guard. He was standing there among a group of BBC execs, 'The Guvnor' as I know he liked to be called. He'd just had a little chat with Rowan and I was hovering on the edge with Stephen Fry, really just basking in the fact that we were in the same room as such a comedy colossus whom only a few years before we'd been watching from our respective sitting room sofas (well, in Stephen's case it would have been from a chair in the junior boys' common room).

Anyway, after a little while, the great man turned from Rowan and looked at Stephen and me.

'I like you,' he said, pointing at Stephen, before turning to me. 'But I don't like you.' Then he turned his back again.

It was actually a little microcosm of Stephen and my relative positions in British culture for most of the '80s and all of the '90s. In terms of the critical establishment, he seemed to be able to do no wrong whereas I could do no right. His work would always receive breathless praise while mine was routinely traduced. I don't mind admitting I was jealous, which is an awful thing to feel about such an old and dear friend, particularly one who publicly came to my defence on a number of occasions during that time, most memorably in 1989 when *The Telegraph* did a massive 'profile' piece so viciously skewed against me that it provoked Stephen, who was a columnist for them at the time, to send in his resignation. The editor persuaded him not to but *only* after he'd agreed to publish a counter piece written by Stephen in which he picked apart the flimsy hate thesis line by line.

Now that is the act of a true friend.

Anyway, back to the party and Ronnie B's lofty judgement. It was really quite a moment, Ronnie Barker telling me he didn't like me straight off the bat and out of the blue.

'I'm sorry to hear that, Mr Barker,' I said to his half-turned back. 'I'm such a big fan of yours. Might I ask why you don't like me?'

Slowly he turned back and looked me up and down.

'Because you swear too much on television. It's not necessary and it's ugly. I don't like it and I'm afraid I don't like you.'

Blimey. Who would have thought Ronnie Barker and Alexei Sayle would have so much in common?

I was really taken aback and also very hurt. This guy was a legend. I'd loved him since I was a kid. His sitcom *Porridge* was a personal fave. And it was bloody Christmas!

I struggled to keep my voice steady.

'Mr Barker, I have never sworn on television. Not once ever. Not in any of the sitcoms I've written or in my stand-up work.'

Which was true. Obviously. You couldn't in those days.

'Oh, haven't you? Well, hmmm, all right. I thought you did.'

After that, we actually had quite a long chat during which Ronnie B continued to say that he thought 'alternative' comedy was too rude, despite also claiming that he had never seen any.

Perhaps Ronnie could see the way things were heading. Because, eventually, swearing did become common for comics on TV and, in fact, it very soon got boring. It can be useful on stage. There's no doubt that the 'F' word can really push a moment of comic outrage through to its climax – and it is, after all, how most people talk. Having said that, I regret swearing *quite* so much on stage myself. It just became a habit. When my mum first saw my act, she gave me one of the wisest and most succinct bits of criticism I've ever received. She said: 'Benjy, the F word is all very well as an exclamation mark, but it's of very little use as a comma.'

Ouch.

Anyway, after a while, there were other people waiting to talk to Ronnie, so Stephen and I disengaged. But, as I left, Ronnie nodded towards me and said: 'I like you a little more now.'

I was very pleased to have partially won him over. Years later, I got to know him better. I'd become friends with Ronnie Corbett through his appearances on my TV show in '98 and Ronnie C must have told Ronnie B that I was all right, because Ronnie B and his wife Joy began inviting me to their annual 'Party at the Mill'. These were wonderful summer parties held at their old country mill house with an old-style jazz band in stripy waistcoats and straw hats providing the music. I went twice and Ronnie and Joy were so warm and welcoming. This was proper old-school showbiz. David Jason was always there, which was very cool. Ronnie had some bitterness, I think. He told me with real anguish the story about how *The Sun* had stung him over his antique shop. They went in undercover with a valuable piece to sell and caught him undervaluing it as I suppose dealers will always try to do. Ronnie was deeply hurt at the resultant front-page exposure and I can still remember him saying, 'Why would they want to do that to me? *Why* would they want to?'

Another thing which I know hurt him was in 1998 when the BBC did a big sixty years of TV bash. Part of it was a vote for the best sitcom of all time. I was invited because *The Young Ones*, *Blackadder* and *The Thin Blue Line* were all in the top ten, which was a pretty amazing result. But these votes are just a snapshot of current fashion. I imagine only *Blackadder* would make the list in such a vote today. Maybe not even that. In 1998, *Men Behaving Badly* was voted number one and while it was a good sitcom, I'm sure they wouldn't claim it was the greatest of all time. (In my view, *Steptoe and Son* probably is, with *Fawlty Towers* and *Dad's Army* joint second.)

Anyway, in 1998, *Porridge* didn't even make the top ten and Ronnie B was very upset. I met him at the bar and the first thing he said was '*Porridge*? Surely they could have found a place, if only for Dick and Ian's sake.' (Dick Clement and Ian La Frenais were the brilliant writers who also gave us the sublime *The Likely Lads*.)

Ronnie just didn't quite get that things move on. He retired early and he'd been so big for so long that I think he expected to remain 'the Guvnor' until his death. But nobody does, I'm afraid. When you're gone, you're gone. And damn quick too.

After Ronnie died, Joy Barker and I continued to exchange Christmas cards until she died too and there were no more parties at the mill.

Around this time, I did a Michael Aspel chat show. The other guest was Robin Day, the BBC's famously irascible 'grand inquisitor'. If ever there was a good example of the ephemeral nature of fame, that sentence is it. Both Aspel and Day were absolutely copper-bottomed *massive* household names for at least twenty years, but ask anybody under forty-five today and they'd never have heard of either of them. Anyway, that chat show ended up in a really weird place. Sir Robin had come along absolutely furious about me (whom he'd never met) and determined to put me in my place. He started from the word go, ignoring Aspel's questions and just turning on me and hectoring me. He'd even brought along a couple of nasty pieces on me that he'd found in the newspapers and actually got out the clippings and read bits out, demanding that I answer for it! I couldn't believe it – this man famed for confronting mendacity and demanding facts was reading out some anonymous slagging as if it was the *Dictionary of National Biography*. Michael tried to bring things back, asking us about Morecambe and Wise, of whom both me and Sir Robin (and everybody else) were fans. Sir Robin then said, 'Do you know what Eric used to do?'

and he hit me. I'm not kidding. He did the old Eric double face-slap and he did it quite hard. It actually smarted. The whole thing was just astonishing. He was clearly drunk by the way, so I guess that was part of it. Anyway, I tried to keep my cool and I think I must have done because the next day there was a review in *The Times*, which for once was positive for me. It said that the previous night on *Aspel* there had been a man they expected to behave like a yobbo and a man they'd expected to be a gentleman, and there had been, but it turned out the other way round.

'80s, '90s and '00s

Me and Neil

The moment I became a celeb, I made my support of the Labour Party public and I have argued the Labour case ever since. It's a fact which has led many reactionary bastards to call me a closet communist and many holier-than-thou lefties to pronounce me a sell-out closet Tory. Go figure.

One of the reasons I felt duty-bound to have my say was that, back in the days when the press really mattered, it was always such an uneven fight. The press barons have always supported the Conservatives, but when the Thatcher government was at its height, the absolute support of the majority of newspapers was off the scale. I felt genuinely aggrieved at the way Labour got bullied. The treatment handed out to Neil Kinnock in particular was truly terrible. Decades before Trump introduced America to the politics of the playground bully, Britain's press (and not a few Cabinet Ministers besides) had perfected the art but with an added dose of ugly class prejudice. Political commentary in the '80s seemed at times to be little more than one long catalogue of sneering inadequates loftily dismissing Kinnock as a hapless, ill-educated, working-class ginger windbag.

Only the working-class and ginger bits were true.

I knew Kinnock well. I had dinner with him many times and sat with him in the pub. I saw him make speeches, I saw him under fire and I saw him at home in his personal life. And I am here to tell you that he was (and remains) a gracious, inspiring, astute, tough, brave and *very* clever man. In fact, a great man. These qualities were not only never acknowledged in the years he led the opposition to the all-conquering Thatcher government, but they were actively denied. That's the thing with lies: the bigger they are, the more effective they are. If someone is caring, call them selfish.

If someone is inspiring, call them a windbag. If someone is strong, then say over and over and over again that they are weak.

Consider what this man achieved, this man about whom the default media presumption was that he wasn't up to the job of leadership. A genuinely working-class man, the son of an invalided coalminer and a district nurse, he rose to not only lead the Labour Party for nine years, but to bring it back after the near-annihilation of the Michael Foot-led election of '83. This would be a towering achievement even for a man born with a silver spoon, but for a man from an impoverished village in Wales, it was magnificent, which is why I suppose they hit him so hard. He was too good to mess around with, so they ganged up and sneered at him and lied about him for nine long depressing years.

And do you know what his greatest achievement was in my view? Keeping his good humour to the end. He never let them break his spirit, although God knows he had cause. He had, and continues to have, an open ear and an open heart for every single person he meets. He loves art, he loves sport, he loves people and he loves life. He represented the non-entitled Britain and entitled Britain put him through hell for it. But I had the great privilege of knowing him, having a pint with him, attending meetings with him, watching him *connect* with everyone he met. He never left an individual or a packed hall uninspired.

He was a fantastic leader and he would have made a great prime minister.

I will admit that, in one crucial element, Neil and Labour brought the fury and the spite down on themselves. They made a terrible mistake. They decided to boycott the Wapping newspapers. Does anyone remember all that now, the terrible time when Thatcher and Murdoch broke the unions? After the miners, print was the biggest battle. The print workers were powerful; they could stop the presses and they had done in the past. But they were foolish, too. Like many other unions, they stuck their heads in the sand. The traditional printing method called 'hot metal' wasn't going to last. 'Offset lytho' had been invented. Digital was coming and a lot of workers would ultimately have to go. But there could have been a compromise and the unions would have swallowed it in the end. Murdoch, however, didn't want a compromise. He wanted to destroy the print unions (all unions, in fact) and he moved all his titles to the ultra-modern, union-free printworks at Wapping to do so.

The dispute went on for a year, but Murdoch was always going to win. This was where Labour made their big mistake. During the long and sometimes violent Wapping dispute, and for some time afterwards, they would not speak to journalists who defied their own union and worked for newspapers printed at Wapping, which was more than half the national press.

It was a terrible self-defeating policy. Those journalists who, with grim face and often troubled conscience, moved to the joyless, police-ringed, alcohol-free news factory at Wapping, did not ask for the new technology to be invented. Nor did they ask for a player as ruthless and as zealous as Murdoch to buy their titles. But it had happened and they had mortgages to pay and families to feed. In the end, we all would probably have done what they did. For Labour to effectively call half the journalists in the country a bunch of contemptible scabs for the whole second half of the '80s left a legacy of hatred that never really went away.

Labour really did struggle in the '80s to get any kind of message across and, sadly, some of the party's own efforts were distinctly ill-conceived. I'm thinking principally of the 'youth' initiative known as Red Wedge.

I never thought Red Wedge was going to help. The idea that me, Billy Bragg, Paul Weller and a bunch of unknown alternatives playing town hall gigs would make any difference seemed a long shot to me. In fact, it all felt uncomfortably like my *Young Ones* 'yoof' piss-take '*Nozin' Aroun*'. I played six Red Wedge gigs in six marginals during the general election campaign of '87 and we lost the lot by about the same number of votes as there were members of our audience. Coincidence? You be the judge.

There was no Red Wedge in '92 – or at least not that I knew of – but I did plenty of campaigning. It was all much more positive than the grubby gloom of '87. Thatch was gone, John Major seemed beatable and there was a real feeling of renewal in the air. I did a couple of platforms with Barbara Castle, which were fun (she was a seriously funny, super-intelligent tough old girl from the days of Harold Wilson) and I met John and Penny Mortimer, which was also brilliant. I first met Tim Rice during that election, too. We were the left and right of a late-night talk show and we had a fantastic night together. Tim is an arch Tory (much more so than Andrew

Lloyd Webber in my view), but he is also very good company. The two of us were the last to leave the bar.

I was put up against a few other Tories on various grabs of TV. Jeffrey Archer was one. He knew how to work a room and came up to me with the opening words 'I just adore *Blackadder*' which, of course, is a great ploy. Telling someone you love their work effectively disarms you. Cecil Parkinson, who had been one of Thatcher's senior ministers, also came up to me in a TV studio all smiles and said, 'I don't agree with what you say on television, Ben, but I always laugh.' I replied: 'I feel exactly the same about you, Cecil', which was pretty good, though I say it myself.

I was with Neil and Glenys Kinnock during the last days prior to the poll. There were numerous inspiring speeches and wonderful meetings, but we could feel it slipping away. And there was a grim inevitability to it all. I was with them at a hotel in Wales on the morning of election day when the entire front page of *The Sun* was a picture of Neil's balding head in a lightbulb with the headline 'If Kinnock wins today, will the last person to leave Britain turn off the lights?'. It was brutal. The next day, after Major's win, *The Sun* ran a headline 'It's The Sun wot won it'. I certainly think it was Rupert Murdoch.

Today, with newsagents turning into vape shops and the *Evening Standard* turned into a weekly freebie, it's hard to remember just what a massive deal the press was back then. It really did set agendas and influence thinking in a way that's unimaginable in our internet-controlled culture. At the time, I hated press power with a real passion and I thought most editors were the enemies of true democracy for the way they so aggressively and disingenuously skewed their coverage of everything to support the Tories. Looking back now from our post-truth age, I mourn the destruction of a news culture which, for all its institutional bias, was relatively accountable and to a large extent fact-based. And, of course, we had the BBC to keep them honest. Now nobody watches the BBC either.

And do you know, I think that, despite the press, Neil would have beaten Thatch at that election (which, of course, was why the Tories had dumped her). I think he would have also beaten the glamorous and mega-rich Michael Heseltine who, at one point, looked like succeeding Thatch. But John Major, with his 'humble roots' equal to those of Neil and his quiet, genuine manner, was much more empathetic. He didn't *look* like the leader of the party of privilege – which is probably why the Tories choose him.

I met John Major a few times subsequently and liked him a lot. He also made by far the most intelligent, principled, passionate and articulate arguments for Remain during the EU referendum. I guess it's easier to be principled, passionate and articulate when you're no longer in the power game. Neil's great quality – and, I suppose, perhaps also his great weakness – was that he was principled, passionate and articulate when he was leader of the opposition and a prospective PM.

A pause for Pinter (geddit?)

During the 1992 election campaign, I *nearly* met Harold Pinter, far and away the most celebrated British playwright of the second half of the twentieth century, and it's because of his legendary self-importance that I didn't.

Pinter had agreed to be in one of the Labour election videos. I was in it too and we were all aware that it was being made on a tiny shoestring budget. On the day that the 'celebs' were being filmed, we were all standing round on some freezing pavement, waiting for Pinter to turn up. His 'intellectual' endorsement was considered a key juxtaposition to the various raggedy comics and ex-punk rockers who made up the rest of the celeb endorsements.

Not only did Pinter not turn up, but he also failed to send any word of explanation. Desperate phone calls were made to his office as the clock ticked. Eventually, the director decided he would have to use the sacrosanct, holier-than-holy private number he had been given but instructed never *ever* to use.

Pinter's wife, Lady Antonia Fraser, answered. When asked if she could enquire if Harold could possibly find a moment to let us know if he'd be joining the large group of people donating their time in an effort to end thirteen years of Tory rule, she replied 'We do not take messages for each other' and hung up.

So I didn't meet him, which was a sort of relief since I'd heard from a number of sources that he didn't like me. The story goes that at a birthday party the great man had been presented with a cake, which featured his portrait in icing. Someone had remarked that it looked more like me, and this caused Pinter to unleash a furious tirade objecting to being compared in any way to such an appalling figure as yours truly.

I think this story allows me some justification to 'fess up about my own views on Pinter – not the man but the writer. These views are deeply transgressive and have got me into a lot of arguments over the years, most recently a week ago at time of writing, over dinner with Stephen Fry.

Because contrary to the firm and unshakeable orthodoxy of the age, I don't think Pinter is a genius. I don't even think he's any good. I don't like slagging off other artists, but Pinter is the most lionized figure in modern English letters and a Nobel Laureate – and too dead to care – so I make him an exception.

Principally because I think the Pinter consensus is responsible for putting more people *off* going to the theatre than were ever turned on (and that by a considerable margin). And the aspect of his legend I find the most infuriating of all is the bit that says he was funny – *so* much funnier than proper funny by dint of not being actually funny at all. Enigmatic funny, strange funny, *surreal* funny. All euphemisms for not fucking funny – with bleakly self-conscious pauses that tell people when to pretend to laugh. That grimmest sound in theatre: the sound of an audience pretending to find something amusing in order to look clever or for fear of looking thick. We've all done it.

Why am I having such a go at this dead playwright? Because I think doing my little bit to debunk the all-conquering Pinter orthodoxy is important. The myth that Pinter plays are funny is symptomatic of an alienating snobbishness that bedevils British arts: eulogizing the wilfully obscure while denigrating the emotionally effective for the obvious reason that claiming to 'get' something that nobody else does makes you look clever, while laughing and crying along with the crowd doesn't. It's why I loathe the term 'guilty pleasure'. *Innocent* pleasure, certainly, but guilty? What's guilty about loving a simple tune or a well-crafted soap opera? Artistic snobbery is the worst kind of snobbery because it makes people feel ashamed of the things they enjoy and pushes them to pretend to like things which secretly they don't. The Pinter fetish is the perfect example of this. And I don't care if he did win a Nobel Prize in Literature. Henry 'Carpet Bomber' Kissinger won the Nobel Peace Prize, but it doesn't make him a man of peace. In my view Pinter's plays are also deeply misogynist – just look at the female roles. No other dead playwright would be allowed to get away with such strutting machismo. It's horrible to watch smart people continuing to tie themselves in knots trying to find excuses for the horrendous and quite ridiculous adolescent wank fantasy that is *The Homecoming*.

So there you go. I don't like Pinter. Mind you, Rik always really liked him – which, of course, is why we have that awful bit in *The Young Ones* with him and Ade talking complete bollocks in an attic. I still absolutely cringe at the memory of how shit that was. Ade agrees with me about that scene, but not about Pinter, whom he also reveres. I know I'm in the minority on this one.

Stephen said, 'For heaven's sake, Bezzah, pick another target.' But I ain't gonna.

Me and Tony

After Neil Kinnock resigned, the next Labour leader was John Smith. I only met him once, on the night before he died, in fact. I was at a big Labour do and he made a passionate speech. He seemed fine but, of course, he wasn't and he was gone the next morning. That evening was also the first time that I met Tony Blair. He actually scrounged me a fag. I was at the bar and he came up and introduced himself, a young eager shadow cabinet minister still an entire generation from a tilt at the leadership. He thanked me for all my support and asked if I needed anything. I'd had a few wines so asked if he had a cigarette (you could still smoke indoors in '94). I didn't smoke much even then, but it had been a long night and I felt like one. He said he didn't smoke but offered to find me one. I tried to say it really wasn't necessary, but he insisted. 'No problem. I'm sure Mo's got one.' He went off and scrounged one for me from future secretary of state for Northern Ireland, Mo Mowlam.

The next day, of course, everything changed. John Smith was dead and Tony and Gordon Brown were planning their generation-leaping dash for the top. So I saw Tony on the very last night he was an ordinary normal bloke. And he was very nice.

I wasn't really involved in the '97 election. Labour were on a roll towards a landslide anyway and didn't need me. And I missed the big night because I was in Brisbane on a stand-up tour of Australia. I toasted the end of eighteen years of Tory rule in a hotel bar 16,500 kilometres from home. I remember trying hard to feel exhilarated, but just felt separated and very far away.

After Blair won in '97, he had a series of celeb-packed soirées at Number 10. These were much lampooned at the time as 'luvvie' affectation, but I think they were rather well-thought-through events with the fame quota actually quite low and numerous fascinating people from all parts of society. Bishops chatting with homeless people. The idea was that Labour would be moving to a more sharing and inclusive Britain of all talents and I think those parties were a useful way of setting the tone. But I wasn't invited to the first one, or the second, and I admit I felt a bit miffed. After all, I had put in a lot of hours over the years and donated what I could. But they got round to me in the end and I had a wonderful night. As mentioned, history is my passion and I just loved being at the heart of it. Downing Street was a bit dowdy actually, which I found quite encouraging – lots of rather threadbare carpet and faded wallpaper, and a few big rooms with rather forlorn clusters of chairs in them, the kind with red velvet upholstery and gold painted legs, in this case slightly chipped. The black and white photos of previous PMs that ascend the stairs were fascinating for me and I paused at Clement Attlee and paid a moment of respect. Well, actually, I paused at all of them because there was a terribly long queue going up. At one point, looking back, I saw Robin Cook was standing waiting behind me. He'd just been named foreign secretary, one of the three great offices of state, and yet he was queuing behind a bunch of singers and social workers. Cook was one of New Labour's 'big beasts' at the time and so everyone was being a bit weird and sort of pretending he wasn't there. He looked very uncomfortable, so I called back 'Robin, I think you can skip the queue you know. After all, it's kind of your gig.' He said, 'Do you think people would mind?', to which there was a chorus of 'No, go on up and get a drink', which he did, scuttling apologetically up the stairs. Well, nobody wants to look like a queue-jumper, but there are limits. He was foreign secretary and this was 10 Downing Street, for goodness' sake.

I had a long talk with previous Labour prime minister Jim Callaghan that night. Anyone remember him? For me, that was very cool. I asked him for all the inside dirt on the great Conservative leadership battle of 1963 which had everything: a massive sex and spy scandal (Profumo), a dying leader knifing potential successors from his hospital bed (Harold Macmillan), and a great gathering of warring pretenders to the crown (The Blackpool Conference) where dark deeds were done over whisky and cigars in various smoke-filled boarding house snugs. Honestly, it sounded like 'The Red Wedding' episode of *Game of Thrones*.

Callaghan and I were chatting at the top of the stairs when a waiter came up and asked this former prime minister to move on into one of the rooms as he was blocking the way. Such is how power ends.

My next encounter with Tony Blair was shortly thereafter and was really rather strange. His office contacted me, inviting me to Downing Street to see him. Just me, no explanation given: 'just come in and have a chat'. I must admit I was quite excited; it's hard to imagine just what a superstar Tony was at this point. He seemed to embody everybody's dreams for a happier, more confident, less divided Britain. He was sort of *golden*.

The appointment was at 6 p.m. and was scheduled to last for forty-five minutes. Downing Street was as dowdy as ever and I was shown into his unremarkable office. The West Wing this wasn't. He offered me a drink and I said I'd have a beer. By his surprised expression, I realized he'd meant tea or coffee. But surely after 6 p.m. a drink means a drink? After 6 p.m., if what you're offering is tea or coffee, you should bloody well say so and not call it 'a drink'. I tried to undo my order, but he insisted and asked someone to get me one, after which we were alone. Well, we chatted away. I can't really remember about what. I do recall we talked briefly about IVF, which Sophie and I were doing at the time. I remember wondering when he'd get to the point. Then, after forty minutes my beer arrived (I'm not kidding, I honestly think they'd had to send out). Then, at 6.45 p.m., his next appointment was due and that was it.

I had three quarters of an hour of one-on-one time with an all-conquering prime minister at the height of his pomp, at *his* request, and to this day I have absolutely no idea what he wanted. All I know is that whatever it was, I definitely failed my audition. They never contacted me again.

But here's another more interesting Blair story. Sometime in 2001, I was invited to dinner by Dave Stewart, half of '80s pop colossus Eurythmics. Dave told me he was 'auditioning' a chef for a club he was hoping to open (The Hospital Club in Covent Garden). I didn't and don't know Dave well, but I knew him a bit that year because his movie had been produced by the same people as the one I had been making. Anyway, for some reason, he'd decided to invite me to his house to audition a chef. It was his country place, a large house in Surrey. Sophie was away, so I went alone, booking a car and a driver so I wouldn't have to worry about directions or drinking.

It was all very lovely and very weird. The chef was some famous bloke from Chicago and he'd flown over with his *whole team* to cook in Dave's kitchen. Blimey, eh? But it gets more 'blimey' than that. He'd flown over *the food they were going to cook* as well. And to my mind 'blimier' still, the guests at this small dinner party (about ten) included Annie Lennox, Robert Altman and Tony and Cherie Blair.

It all seemed to go very pleasantly except that I could see that Tony was pretty grey and exhausted. We were in the midst of the foot-and-mouth crisis and he was under huge pressure. I remember that, after dinner, Dave got out a couple of guitars and persuaded Tony to have a bit of a jam. It was at this point that Cherie said to me that they'd have to leave soon, which was a shame because she knew how thrilled Tony would be to be jamming with Dave Stewart and he really needed some relaxation. I asked why they had to leave and she said that he didn't, but she did as she had to pay off the babysitter at Downing Street. Now I had noticed that there were two government Jags outside with tough-looking men around them and I asked why she couldn't go home separately in one of the cars. She explained that this wasn't possible because *both* cars were Tony's – one to drive in and one for security back-up. There was no official provision for her at all. It was then I really saw the mundane part of power. There were no staff at Downing Street tasked with dealing with her babysitter either and there was no 'First Lady'-style organization to help her arrange a life which, of necessity, involved public duties. Look, nobody thinks our leaders should be showered with luxury, but whenever I see some expenses row or outcry over a taxi bill, I think back to that time, an evening when the prime minister's wife knew that he needed a bit of a break but he couldn't have it because he had to see her home in his car to pay off the babysitter who she had booked herself and had to make sure got home.

I felt really sorry for them and said that I had a car outside with a driver which she was welcome to take.

'Really? Would you?' She was genuinely grateful. 'I really do have to go and he's having such a nice time.'

'Of course. My treat. All paid for.'

'But how will you get home?'

'Dave must have a mini cab number.'

You'll never guess what she said to that.

'Oh no, Tony will give you a lift. He won't be allowed to take you home, but he can take you to Number 10 and he can call you a cab from there.'

I kid you not. That's what she said.

So I had a word with my driver and, shortly thereafter, the prime minister's wife went off in some random and unvetted car without any protection or security check whatsoever, leaving me to bum a lift with the PM and his security detail.

As the evening concluded, I could see that Tony was dead on his feet. I was absolutely sure that the last thing he wanted was somebody he scarcely knew stuck in a car with him for, at the very least, an hour. He's a polite guy and I knew he'd feel obliged to talk. Maybe I was wrong to pass up the chance of an hour alone in a car with the PM (although, after our previous encounter, maybe not), but I thought I'd do the decent thing.

'You look knackered, Tony. You don't want company. Don't worry, I'll make my own way home.'

He protested, of course, but I could see he was relieved. He clearly wanted to sleep and social obligation would have prevented him.

Well, guess what? When I asked Dave to ring a cab, Robert Altman offered me a lift home in *his* car. I may have passed up the PM, but I ended up with one of the most famous movie directors ever. He took me all the way to my door too. On the way, he asked me lots of questions about the British parliamentary system, trying to get his head around the idea of hereditary peers. I'm good on that sort of thing so, pissed though I was, I think I sang adequately for my supper.

I haven't seen Tony since, but we exchanged cards at Christmas until he left office. I didn't know where to send them after that, but he still sends me one to this day.

Tony Blair has had more hate than most. I've copped a bit myself and it's painful. It's the uncompromising totality of the hate that's so wearing. Haters don't offer nuanced arguments. They hate you totally and absolutely and present you as having no redeeming qualities whatsoever. Tony had it a thousand-fold and I think it's very unfair. He was PM for ten years. He struggled with many issues and domestically his administrations achieved some very good things – internationally too, if he'd stopped after the Balkans. I know that the Iraq invasion and its ongoing aftermath turned out to be a disaster, but it does seem rather ridiculous that a complex individual should be routinely presented as this two-dimensional moral monster because of one bad decision, no matter how bad. I think if Blair had resigned over the failure to find weapons of mass destruction in Iraq, he would be viewed completely differently. And I think he absolutely should have done. I believe he went into that war with genuinely honest and decent intentions. It was not solely to protect American oil interests, as is so often said. He and his whole cabinet trusted the intelligence and honestly believed that Saddam was a clear and present danger. I once spoke to Margaret Beckett, who served as foreign secretary under Blair, and, with tears glistening in her eyes, she said, 'Ben, we sat around that cabinet table convinced we were dealing with the real possibility of Iraqi strikes against Britain that could arrive in minutes, because that's what the secret service were telling us'.

I'm certain Blair believed it, but it wasn't true and he was prime minister. He took Britain to war for reasons which turned out to be a mirage and he should have resigned. I wish he had done with all my heart because if he had, he might have prevented a large section of the young generation losing faith in the Labour Party and even in democracy itself. He might also have ensured his own legacy.

I liked him, even if I did fail his audition.

Labour post-peak charisma

I knew Gordon Brown a bit too and I think he is a truly great man. A politician guided by fierce moral principle. Wow. Not many of them around, eh? I first met him at an evening to celebrate the legacy of the great post-war Labour firebrand Aneurin Bevan. Neil introduced us and we got on well. I won't say we had a laugh – I'm not sure I've ever seen Gordon laugh – but he did allow a warm smile to occasionally lighten those granite features. When Gordon was PM Sophie and I were invited to dinner at Downing Street, which was of course a massive thrill for me. Gordon is good company too in a serious and intellectually demanding way, as is his wife Sarah, and Sophie and I wish we could remember what we talked about but it's been more than twenty years. Gordon was in power during the terrible financial crisis of 2008 when he took such a crucial global lead at the expense of his own political capital. He still drops me an occasional line which is something I take some pride in.

I never met Jeremy Corbyn, the only Labour leader since Harold Wilson that I haven't. I did meet his shadow chancellor John McDonnell, who I found very impressive. We shared a husting together during the 2019 election and it seemed to me that he exhibited principle tempered with pragmatism and an ability to compromise that belied the 'Loony Left' label that was stuck on Labour at the time. These were qualities which people were failing to detect in Corbyn, and I wish it had been McDonnell leading the party during its most radically Left-leaning period.

And finally there is Keir Starmer. Well, I guess the jury's currently out, isn't it? I've only ever met him for a hug and a handshake, so I have no personal insight to offer. He certainly doesn't have the magnetism or charisma of Tony Blair and so of course we all hope that he'll instead display the principle and intellectual rigour of Gordon Brown. We live in an age of deeply shallow leadership, a time of government by ego not intellect – someone's got to reverse that trend, and I hope with all my heart that Starmer will get on the case. By the time you read this we'll probably know the answer.

1987. Again

Failing towards America, part one
(who won the fucking war?)

Here's a rather brilliant joke my son Bert cracked when he was eleven years old.

> BERT: We've got something in common, Dad.
> ME: What's that, mate?
> BERT: Neither of us has made it in America.

I think that's pretty good.

Just after we made the second series of *Saturday Live*, I had my first crack at America. Well, I say 'crack'. I've never been proactive in that area; I've never gone over and really had a go. My 'cracks' have all come to me, which perhaps is why it's never worked. I think unless you're very lucky, you do have to be on the ground and put the hours in. I could never do that, partly because I've always been too busy in the UK, but also because for most of my adult life, I've been commuting between two countries already: Britain and Australia.

But, *of course*, I would have loved to have made it over there. The US is the principal engine of popular culture worldwide. It's also the biggest English-speaking audience and the wealthiest country on Earth. Who wouldn't want to be successful there? And any comic or singer who claims they're indifferent to the possibility of US success is lying. America's shine has been somewhat tarnished in recent years, as it appears to have gone completely bonkers, but it remains the centre of the entertainment universe.

When I was starting out before the internet, Britain and America really were two separate cultures and while we were interested in *theirs*, they were *not* interested in ours. Of course, all that changed in music with the Beatles. But (with the exception of the Pythons) UK comedy had to wait another thirty years to be of interest to Americans; my generation of UK comedy stars was the last generation to miss out. Rik, Lenny, Dawn et al were as unknown in America as The Two Rons, Morecambe and Wise, Tommy Cooper and Bruce Forsyth had been before them. Of my generation, only Rowan and Jennifer ever made any real inroads, and that wasn't until the '90s and then solely for very specific things: *Mr Bean* and *AbFab*. Even they never made it in a more general sense.

Here's an interesting story about my first time in LA, one which brutally demonstrates my point about the general American indifference to British comedy back in the days of my pomp. I'd been invited over by Henry Winkler (yes! The Fonz of *Happy Days*). He was interested in developing a youth-focused sitcom for the US and, being a bit of an Anglophile, had heard of me. The idea came to nothing, but I had an interesting week for sure. Los Angeles is the home of the original Comedy Store and the US is without doubt the country where stand-up comedy was first developed as an art form as opposed to more of a craft.

While I was in the States, I just had to get up and throw down, as Lenny Henry would say. I couldn't come home having not done a set in LA.

So I looked up the LA Comedy Store in Yellow Pages and called them.

Now, bear in mind that, at the time, I was far and away the most talked-about comedian in Britain. What's more, a number of acts playing the Store in LA that very week had been on *Saturday Live* in the UK. Geoff Perkins had a policy of trying to present one American stand-up a week and they were all introduced by me.

I got through to a receptionist and eventually managed to persuade her to put me through to somebody in management. I explained who I was and that I had hosted some of their current talent on my show in the UK, and asked if I could possibly get up and do an unpaid ten minutes one night that week. It was something which American acts did at the London Comedy Store all the time.

The voice on the other end was surly at best.

'So, you're big in England, right?'

Americans tend to refer to the UK as England, which I find annoying and I'm not even Scottish, Welsh or Northern Irish.

'Well, yes. I don't want to boast,' I replied, adopting a self-effacing tone which, of course, doesn't exist in American showbiz, 'but yes, I can honestly say that I am big in England.'

There was a beat. Even the management had good timing.

'Yeah, well, we had a guy here last night who says he's big in Texas and he was shit. Sorry, but we book our nights in advance and there's a long queue for try-out spots. Goodbye.'

Word for word, that's a true story. Later that year, back in Britain, I would sell out seven nights at the Hammersmith Odeon, a record at the time, playing to 25,000 people in London alone. But the premiere alternative comedy club in America had *never heard* of me and had absolutely no interest in being enlightened.

That was just how it was. They simply did not give a fuck about British comedy in those days.

The story doesn't end there.

I told Henry what had happened. I wasn't angry (I have never imagined that anybody owes me a living), just a bit bemused. But Henry was furious. He's a very sweet man and could not believe that I'd been treated that way and immediately insisted that he would get me a gig.

'Not at the Store. Forget them. They don't deserve you. You need to play the LA Improv. That's way the better club.'

Of course, I'd heard of the Improv. It was even older and just as famous as The Store. Henry made the call and, being rather big in America himself, got me a slot that very night.

My first-ever gig in America was only hours away.

I set out that evening from my hotel, more nervous than I'd been for years. The place was absolutely packed and super-hip and very scary. And all these people were *Americans*! They had *Top Gun* and *Rocky*. We had *Carry On Columbus*.

I stood there alone in the crowd, wondering what to do. My name had been on the door as Henry had promised, so I got in pretty easily, but there had been no information left for me and nobody tried to find me. After speaking to a number of waitresses (not easy, those girls were there to serve drinks, not chat or give out directions), I managed to find the guy who was running the evening. He was very busy and he wanted me to know it.

'Oh yeah, yeah right. We got a call . . . *(long search of list)* Ben Elton, right? Sadly not Elton John.'

'Yes, that's right. Sadly not Elton John. Elton's my surname.'

'Okay. We have you down to do ten minutes.'

'Uhm, great. Any idea when that might be? You know, just so I can be ready.'

Honestly, you'd think I'd asked him to write my act for me. His expression was one of bored exasperation. I was a problem that someone had dumped on him.

'Christ, who fucking knows. We're squeezing you in. It's not official. Maybe around eleven.'

He made a note and turned his back on me. Not the best start.

It was only about nine, so I resigned myself to a miserable wait, sipping mineral water and trying to persuade myself that I really didn't need a crap. But then a bloke I knew came up. I forget his name after all these years, but he was a comic who had appeared on *Saturday Live*.

'Guys, guys!' he said, summoning his friends. 'This is Ben. He's huge in England. No, I mean it, like fucking huge. He has his own show.'

You'd think I'd be pleased but it just increased my embarrassment. His friends just shrugged – fame at one remove is irrelevant. Nobody cares if you're big in Japan.

Anyway, having failed to interest his mates, my friend had another thought.

'Have you met the boss, the guy running the show, Frank?'

This was the bloke who wished I was Elton John (I'm calling him Frank, I don't actually remember his name but it seems to fit). I tried to explain that I had already met Frank, but despite my pleas, my mate insisted on dragging me back into Frank's orbit.

'Frank! Frank!' he said to the harassed man with the running sheet. 'You gotta say hi to my pal Ben. He's huge in England.'

'Yeah, yeah! How many times do I got to greet the fucking limey?'

I'm not lying. I'm really not. Those were his words, verbatim. We were in LA, but he was definitely a New Yorker, either Bronx or pretending to be.

'Don't worry about Frank. He chews everybody out.'

Well, thanks for nothing.

The minutes ticked slowly by and it got closer and closer to eleven. I'd received no further information about what I was supposed to do prior to my ten minutes. I didn't even know how to get backstage, let alone get *on* stage and find a mic.

At about five to eleven, I screwed up my courage to approach Frank once more.

'Frank. Sorry, *sorry*. But I think I'm supposed to be on soon and I don't know how to get to the stage and which mic I'm supposed to use and . . .'

'Listen, pal! Who won the fucking war?'

Okay. Now you really don't believe me.

But it's true. Those were his exact words.

I'd like to report that I replied 'Well, Frank, it's complex. Britain certainly played a pretty crucial role in winning the fucking war, standing alone against Nazi might for more than a year and then sacrificing her influence and prosperity to the cause of defeating Facism. But the truth is that if any country won the fucking war, it was the Soviet Union being as how they engaged eighty per cent of German forces and sacrificed twenty million dead as opposed to 400,000 US fatalities. These are facts that America continues to conveniently ignore when claiming to have won the fucking war and saved the world single-handed.'

I'd *like* to say I said that, but I didn't actually say anything. I was too stunned. The evening had turned into a genuine nightmare.

Maybe Frank read it in my face. Maybe his grumpy schtick really was just his way of being a pussycat. Anyway, he softened. Very, very slightly.

'I'm kidding already! You can go on two acts from now.' He then called over an assistant. 'Show Elton Ben where to go.'

So I did my slot, having been introduced as somebody who was big in

England, which is worse than useless. The audience don't care, but it still sets up an expectation.

I did okay.

I got good laughs in all the right places and there was some nice back-slapping afterwards when I was finally able to get a beer.

My first and only stand-up gig in the US was over.

I take that fork in the road

In the summer of 1987, fate took a hand in my life. Actually, it clenched its hand into a fist and knocked me so far off course that I'm still reorientating to this day.

Sophie's band The Jam Tarts came to the UK to do a season at the Edinburgh Festival. The die was cast.

I'd been in very occasional contact with my Australian friends over the previous year; not with Sophie, but with the whole gang in general via mum and part-time manager Kate (she was also a full-time nurse). And now came a letter from Kate letting me know they were all coming over to do the festival. Also, that she and a couple of the boys had arranged to buy a second-hand van in London and asking if they could stay over with me. I should mention that Sophie's brother was, and is, an astonishing mandolin and fiddle player, and his band were coming too.

I hadn't stopped thinking about Sophie since the Rik and Ben tour fifteen months earlier, so I was pretty excited. I decided I had to be in Edinburgh too, so I booked myself a room at the George Hotel, that renowned media watering-hole in festival month, and started counting the days. I even got Phil to score me a bit of BBC radio reportage work which would give me a reason for going so I didn't look too like a lovesick stalker. You must remember that Sophie and I had made no romantic connection at all during the Aus tour. And apart from a slightly longer goodbye hug than I'd given the other girls on departure, I'd done my best not to reveal my aching and, at the time, impossible crush.

So August 1987. I saw Sophie again. As mentioned, I was mates with the whole gang, so it didn't look strange for me to be hanging out with them and my celebrity added an edge of credibility and even cool (although I never am) to my otherwise slightly awkward hanger-on position.

But what next? What was I there for? Sophie obviously. So why didn't I make a move?

What was holding me back were those old feelings of personal responsibility. Sophie lived in *Australia* and how the fuck was that going to work? I didn't want to just try and 'cop off' with her, as she might have put it. I knew my feelings were stronger than that and I didn't want to 'dally with a woman's affections', as P.G. Wodehouse would have said. Also, Sophie was a lot younger than me. She was twenty by this time and I was twenty-eight. She didn't have a boyfriend and, having been playing bass in bands professionally since she was fourteen, knew all about being hit on and had generally kept men at some distance.

And I had no clue as to her feelings for me. I knew she liked me, but no more than the other girls did – or the guys. We were just a fun gang, soon augmented by various mates of mine who were also in town. Sophie was extremely emotionally self-contained. Enigmatic, unlike her exuberant sister Anna, who totally wore her heart on her sleeve, be it joyful or broken. But Sophie didn't let you in on her thoughts and was therefore extremely hard to read.

I had absolutely no idea what she thought about me or if she'd even noticed what must have been my pretty obvious attraction to her. So I just hung around, staring at her on stage, going for drinks with the whole gang afterwards and trying not to make it too obvious that I was always manoeuvring to sit next to her.

I was hoping that somehow something would develop but knowing that it kind of couldn't. Sophie would be going back to Australia after Edinburgh and I had my first album coming out and a tour booked for the autumn. The only possible result of us hooking up could be a brief fling and I was pretty certain she wasn't a brief fling kind of girl.

So I dithered. Edinburgh finished and the girls came to London for a couple of final gigs prior to departure. They had lots of friends from the Australian tour, including Paul Roberts and, of course, Rik and Barbara. They met Phil and he helped them out with their Edinburgh contractual difficulties (it's always tough getting the money in Edinburgh). In fact, they made new friends wherever they went. Everybody loved Kate and the Jam Tarts. They were just infectious fun. So pretty, so down to earth and so, well, *Aussie*. And the sweetest four-part harmonies you ever heard.

And me hanging around, ogling the bass player and trying not to show it.

Lots of other guys fancied them, of course. Sophie told me later that when she rejected the advances of one of the blokes who was hitting on her, his parting shot was 'Good luck with Ben Elton'. It was that bloody obvious.

And still I did nothing, not even trying to kiss her for fear of looking either inappropriate or dishonourable. So I let her leave. They had one last night in London and we all went to the Hippodrome club in Leicester Square (it wasn't a casino then). I sat with Sophie for hours hedging around the issue, doing that pathetic thing when you try to hook up with someone but are so unsure of yourself you dismiss your own efforts before the object of your affection can even have a chance to reject them herself.

'There's no way you could stay? No, I thought not. It'd be stupid if we just decided to hang out. Yeah, of course it would.'

She must have thought me an idiot, but she didn't say. She was far too enigmatic for that.

I kept her talking and talking until finally their roadie came up and said everyone else was outside in the van and was Sophie staying or was she leaving?

Well clearly, in the absence of any obvious move from me, she was leaving.

So the Jam Tarts flew back to Australia and I was completely heartsick. Sophie tells me that she too had a little cry on the plane over what might have been, but clearly wasn't to be.

The next morning, I went up to Preston to stay with Phil because I had a TV show to do in the north. The show was called *Open to Question*, a format in which a celebrity sat among a group of youths and teens and answered their questions. If anything was calculated to feed my mood of personal despair, this was it!

It was just *awful*.

They all just seemed to dislike me. I was quite taken aback at the cynicism and hostility. They basically asked the same question over and over again for forty-five minutes.

'Are you a hypocrite? Do you really believe what you say?'

'You're successful now. How can you still believe what you say?'

'You go on about being against Thatcher, but aren't you just one of them now? Do you really believe what you say?'

I did my best, trying to think of different ways to answer the same depressing and infuriating needling. 'Yes, I do believe what I say.' 'No, I don't feel there's any contradiction between my recent modest success and supporting the Labour Party.'

Then, when the recording was over, something strange happened. They all turned into excited fan kids. They clustered round me. They all wanted autographs. So I asked them why they'd all been so negative.

It turned out the fucking producer had given them a big lecture at the start about giving me a hard time and not letting me off the hook and they should ask me if I was a hypocrite and *if I really meant what I said*.

And, of course, being nice, they did what was expected of them.

I was pretty angry. That interview was watched by millions (as was pretty much everything back then). And, for a year afterwards, taxi drivers would say 'Blimey, Ben, those kids didn't half give you a hard time on *Open to Question*.'

So there I was, sat with Phil feeling miserable about getting hated on and absolutely distraught over Sophie. Phil said, 'Look, mate. You've been talking about Sophie for a year and a half. You need to get her out of your system, one way or another.'

So I called her up.

She'd only just landed back in Perth and hadn't even got round to unpacking.

'I think I made a mistake. Can I come over and see you?'

Her reply, as ever, gave nothing away.

'If you want.'

'Great. Brilliant. Right. Amazing. When?'

'When do you want?'

'Uhm, how about now? I could get the next flight.'

'Okay. See ya.'

That was it. I told you she's laconic.

So just a couple of days after Sophie had left Britain, I got on a plane and followed her to Perth, Western Australia, where my life changed for ever.

She met me at the airport and we kissed for the very first time.

I could only stay six days. My album launch was the following week and a lot of press had been lined up.

When she wasn't on the road, Sophie still lived with her parents in the old church that her dad had converted. They never had any money so it was pretty open plan and what privacy there was was just partitions and curtains, rather than actual internal walls. This wasn't great for burgeoning romance, so we drove down to Margaret River, which back then was still a small, sleepy country town in the middle of a stunning surf and wine region. Located 300km south of Perth, it's blessed with a dramatic, rocky, wave-crashing coastline, endless deserted golden beaches, dense coastal bush and, here and there, splendid boutique vineyards. Sophie had an old Toyota with a hole in the floor, through which you could see the road, so even the ride was an adventure.

And it was an adventure. We really did hardly know each other. In fact, prior to me coming to Australia, we had never actually once been entirely alone together. Up until then, it was like a courtship out of Jane Austen!

But no longer. We stayed in a caravan for three nights and then flew to Sydney where Rowan happened to be performing the revue that Richard and I had written for him two years before. We surprised Row at the stage door. Sophie took it all in her stride. She was a penniless musician and I made the most of booking into Sydney's top rock'n'roll hotel (the much-lamented Sebel Townhouse) and ordering steaks and champagne on room service. She never cared about money, though. She didn't then and never has. She's never bought designer handbags or shoes and all that stuff. Her family had always lived from hand to mouth in a kind of hardworking, self-reliant, alternative 1960s-style manner and, apart from Champagne, which she loves, Sophie has no expensive tastes at all. As she's reminded me any number of times over the decades since, 'You're lucky I'm such a cheap root, mate.'

Very forthright, these Australians.

As my brief Aussie trip drew to a close, I rang Phil from a phone box by the Indian Ocean.

'I've never been happier.'

'Good. Now get the fuck back here. The album's out in a week and the tour starts the day after that.'

So I left Sophie behind and came home, but not before I'd asked if I could see her again as soon as it was possible.

'So are you my boyfriend then?'

'Uhm, yes. If that's what you want.'

'I do if you do.'

And that was that.

What a difference a year makes

Having returned from my Aus adventure and launched my album, I spent the rest of the autumn on another solo stand-up comedy tour. How different it was from my first one the previous year when I'd been nursing an impossible love. Now that love had come to pass, I was writing long letters to Sophie from various hotel rooms. I've just dug them out, all those old '80s letterheads. Who uses hotel stationery these days? It used to be a feature of every hotel room. Sophie and I had only spent one week together and now we were apart for three months, but finally she joined the tour at the Hammersmith Odeon for the biggest gigs of my life so far. It's a 3,600-seat venue and I did a seven-night run. Seven nights was a record at the time so, clearly, I was one of the biggest draws in the country. Once again, I look back in wonder and wish I had taken a moment to breathe and to consider the extent and the implications of my sudden and unexpected success as a performer. But I didn't, of course. I suppose on this occasion I had an excuse as I was focused largely on Sophie.

After the Hammersmith run, Sophie and I flew to Dublin for the last gigs of the tour. It was so exciting having her with me in such a romantic city and, after that, we flew back to Oz for Christmas. What a time it was!

The British press had picked up on our relationship by this time and

The Sun sent a guy to one of Sophie's Sunday band sessions at the Seaview Pub in Fremantle. The interview lasted two sentences.

SUN MAN: Ben could have any girl he wants. Why do you think he chose you?
SOPHIE: I dunno. Ask him.

In the article that followed, Sophie was 'quoted' as having 'gushed' that 'Ben could have any girl he wanted but he chose me'.

For the record, I could not have had any girl I wanted.

That *Sun* article has resulted in pretty much every single press mention of Sophie ever since calling her a saxophonist. Sophie does play the sax very well – and did so on a couple of numbers with her band – but she is absolutely first and foremost a bass player. However, 'Basey Sophie' would not have sounded as good in *Sun* speak as 'Saxy Sophie', and so *The Sun* decided she was a saxophonist.

Sofe and I were the best goss in Freo (as Fremantle is known) that Christmas '87. After all, we'd only spent a week together the previous September and now here was this Pom hanging around for the festivities. All four Jam Tarts had been much-fancied in Western Australia, as well as over in Melbourne and Sydney. They didn't have a record deal, but were big live and could regularly draw crowds of 500. The 'Which Tart do you fancy most?' was a regular game among the men in their audiences (and among their sizeable lesbian following). There was an article in a local paper that called me 'The most hated man in Freo' for having snaffled a Jam Tart. I hasten to add that the article was a humorous one.

And, of course, to add jovial insult to injury, I was a Pom. Australia is becoming more and more a multicultural society and most Australians embrace that. They certainly have the same laws against racial and cultural defamation that are in place in Britain.

Except when it comes to Poms.

Nobody would dream of scoring a point in a discussion with a Chinese Australian for instance by saying 'Ah, but you're fukn Chinese, mate', but you can still say 'But you're a fukn Pom'.

For Poms, it's open season. And by Poms they mean English. The Scots,

Welsh and Irish are embraced as fellow heroic rebels – and lots of people in Australia love to claim to be Irish or Scottish – but the Poms are given no quarter. I go to barbecues and I'm still getting blamed for Gallipoli. I should stress this is all largely affectionate by the way. Like the cricket.

In fact, I slipped very easily into my Freo life. All Sophie's friends became my friends and have been ever since. Suddenly I had a whole new social circle on the other side of the world.

What a contrast that Christmas was for me in every way, with fierce sunshine turning the pavements white, not with snow but with incredibly bright light. And the heat! Western Australia is one of the hotter Aussie states and summer can see regular forty-degree days. Drinking ice-cold beer in that kind of heat is a very different story to English real ale around the radiator. I actually think they have their beer *too* cold. It's like a fetish. One of the first gags I ever wrote in Aus was that, in Britain, you might expect to find someone's lipstick on the edge of your glass. In Aus, it was their lips.

Anyway. Christmas. In England on Christmas Day, the clouds gloom grey-black. It's dark by four in the afternoon and we all gather inside around the telly. In Freo, mid-afternoon was the time to start thinking about strolling to the beach to try to swim off the lunch, a vast cold collation of cut meats, seafoods and salads all prepared by Sophie's sister Anna, who was only eighteen at the time but was already showing off the skills that would one day make her a famous TV cook in Australia. I thought I'd miss my mum's hot turkey roast with all the trimmings and actually I did, but cracking open lobster shells and sipping Margaret River chardy under a vine-shaded terrace at Bob and Kate's converted church was some consolation.

How could I ever have imagined then, as we sat around still outside, late into the evening, hollering out the same carols I'd sung at home, that thirty-seven years later I'd still be in Freo, sitting in our Australian family home with three kids, writing about that first Christmas together? Mind you, when we do Christmas in Aus, I always do a full turkey roast just like my mum did, whatever the temperature outside.

1988, 1989 and 1990

Novelist among the cockroaches

So now I lived in two countries. A wonderful privilege and a massive headache too, although actually the first thing this new relationship gave me was a new career. It was Phil's idea. He said, since I was going to be hanging around in Fremantle for a while, I should try writing a novel.

I hadn't thought about that. Even though my first love had been P.G. Wodehouse, Noël Coward had been my first inspiration and I still dreamed of the theatrical life he'd led. But it looked as if the theatre would have to wait yet again as I was determined to spend as much time as I could in the fantastic little port town where Sophie had been born and still lived. So, in the spring (or Australian autumn) of '88, I moved in with Sophie in a little house near the Fremantle Marina. It was a pretty big adjustment; I had this massive career and wide circle of friends in Britain, and I just walked away from it all one day and started living in a run-down little cockroach-infested house (with an outside loo) in a small town on the other side of the world.

It was a bit daunting, I admit. And, with each day, I was vaguely aware that I was venturing further and further down an entirely different life path to the one I'd been on, but that's love for you. Sophie must, of course, have been feeling the same thing. One time I tried to broach it, asking her how she felt about a relationship that must inevitably lead to us living a life on two sides of the world. She replied, 'Are you trying to drop me?'. Since I wasn't, I let it go.

So I sat down at the little Formica kitchen table in Freo, living my strange new life as the boyfriend of a local musician, with a rented Apple

Mac (laptops hadn't been invented yet) and started thinking about the novel Phil had suggested I write.

It seems natural now. It wasn't then. Back in those days, writing novels was seen as a pretty specific calling. Only novelists wrote novels, not stand-up comic TV scriptwriters. Who was I to imagine that I could do this? With the exception of my stand-up routines, everything I'd ever written had been in the form of dialogue, sketches, sitcoms and plays. Now I was going to try to write descriptive prose. It was a real leap into the dark.

I decided that the novel would have an environmental theme as I'd just started getting heavily into green issues. I set it right where I was, in Western Australia, weaving a story about an uncool Pom and a cool Aussie chick (write what you know!) who have to save the world from evil billionaires. The wicked plot these villains were hatching was to continue to exploit the resources of the planet to the point of unsustainability and beyond, while also preparing a spaceship Star Ark (which they abbreviated to Stark, hence the title) in order to blast off and sit out the consequences of their selfishness in space while the world died beneath them. As I write, Bezos, Branson and Musk are all running privatized space projects, so the novel has been trending quite heavily recently, thirty-five years after publication.

It took me ten weeks to write in a highly focused blast while sitting at the little table in our kitchen (across the floor of which the occasional lizard would scuttle). Midway through, I had a crisis of confidence, thinking that the plot was just too stupid to work. 'Well, Bond plots are shit,' said Sophie, 'and everybody loves them.' As it turns out, my plot turned out to be less farfetched than those are.

I printed it out on the last Sunday before I was scheduled to return to Britain and proudly took the great wadge of paper down to the pub where Sophie's band were doing their Sunday session to show the other girls and celebrate the final full stop.

I had to get back to the UK, because Dick and I were working on *Blackadder Goes Forth* and Mad Jack was being at his most grumpy. I gave the book to the publisher that I'd signed with and was, of course, completely thrilled when he told me he loved it. It's a bloody nerve-wracking thing to hand in your first novel, particularly to somebody who's paid for it, and I'd braced myself for rejection. In fact, I had made sure that Phil had hung on to the advance and not passed it on to me. If they didn't like it, I didn't want their money.

Part of the publicity for the launch included a *South Bank Show* dedicated to me. What an amazing honour! *The South Bank Show* was *the* premier arts programme. Melvyn Bragg, the show's creator and presenter, has been at the forefront of TV culture coverage for decades and for him to dedicate an episode to me was a big thrill. They hung it on the book and even dramatized a couple of bits of it, which was pretty exciting.

Stark came out in early '89 and it was an unexpected hit – certainly to me and, I rather think, to everybody else. In fact, it went straight to number one in the bestseller charts and sold more than a million copies. I'm told it's still a regular feature in backpacker hostel book exchanges all over the world. And even some of the reviews weren't awful – although the word 'rant' did come up an awful lot. As far as critics were concerned, pretty much everything I did back then was a 'rant'. *Stark* was also a massive hit in Australia, which was validating as I was not yet known there as a comic and therefore judged solely as a novelist. I'd been wondering about how a Pommie comic 'take' on all things Aussie would go down, so it was pretty special when it went to number one there too, and also in New Zealand.

Everything looking good, right? Exciting new relationship. Number-one novel. Making *Blackadder Goes Forth* at the BBC. Last series of *Friday Night Live* just completed. Big new stand-up tour booked.

What could possibly go wrong?

What did was totally unexpected.

From Stark to stalk. Just when everything was going so well

When I arrived back in Britain, with the print-out of *Stark* in my bag, I became Terry Wogan for two weeks. Terry was on holiday from the nightly chat show he did on BBC1 and the Beeb asked me to take over. It was an interesting job, but I don't think I was very good at it. Being a really good interviewer is a very specific skill.

One thing I did do was use the opportunity, as an early champion of greater diversity on the telly, to insist on interviewing a couple of marginalized people alongside the stars. For instance, I talked to a bloke about his experience with cerebral palsy, which I think was a first for a chat show. The BBC seemed happy enough and we didn't lose any audience share, which Terry was pleased about when he got back. But one viewer who I could have done without was the one who turned into a stalker.

This is a really horrible memory.

It all began at Hammersmith when I was signing autographs at the stage door at the end of the show.

One night, a woman of about thirty was in the queue and she gave me something. I really don't know what – sweets, perhaps. I probably chatted a bit, signed her ticket and that was that. But, for whatever reason, I did remember her. And the following night, she was back and this time was more insistent about wanting to have a longer chat. Her argument was I'd accepted her present and now it was my turn to be generous to her. Some people can be like that, getting angry if they imagine you're disrespecting them. These days, we'd call it a false sense of entitlement. There have been any number of times when I've given up five or even ten minutes of my time to engage with a point a complete stranger has decided they have a right to argue with me on (always political) and when I've then tried to politely disengage, they've snarled 'Oh, so that's it, is it? I can fuck off now, can I?'

I told this chippily insistent woman that I was grateful for her gift, but that I had other people in the queue who also wanted to talk to me and she moved on.

But then it started. She started turning up at the front door of my flat. I thought then that she must somehow have contrived to follow me back from Hammersmith Odeon but much later it turned out she worked in NHS Admin so I presume she found my address there. The first time she turned up I still wasn't worried. She was rather a mousey, primly dressed woman with a slightly angry, offended expression. She was polite enough and asked if we could chat and I explained that it wasn't possible and that she shouldn't be coming to my private home. She said 'fine' and left.

Five minutes later, she was back, ringing my bell and spitting fury over the intercom. In her own mind, she believed that we had some kind of relationship and that I'd betrayed it. She was vile, aggressive and abusive. And she got worse. Over a series of random visits, sometime in the middle of the night, she'd hiss expletives down the intercom that I was gay and had AIDS and that she hoped I'd die etc. After the first few incidents, I informed the police but, of course, all they could do was make a note; my persecutor had always disappeared by the time I called. It was all pretty unpleasant, I can tell you. I began to dread the night because the bell would ring and if I didn't answer it, she'd just keep at it, ringing and ringing. After a week of trying to ignore her, I tried once more to speak to her and she said something which was horribly chilling. I asked her how long this was going to go on and she said: 'As long as I like because you don't know who I am or where I come from'.

That hit me like a sledgehammer. I realized how *clever* this woman was. She understood the peculiar menace of her anonymity. Once when she came to my door, I tried to photograph her, but she saw the camera in my hand and turned and scuttled away. Look, I'm aware that my experience was at the very lower end of the spectrum – she was a small woman and not an obvious physical threat. But her language was so violent. Even when she wasn't talking about AIDS-infected blood, her tone of moral outrage was intimidating.

'*What* did you say to me on *Wogan* last night?' she would hiss out of the shadows as I returned home. She actually believed that I'd been communicating with her through the screen.

She was turning my life into a genuine proper misery.

She started phoning my mum, who was in the phone book (as everybody was in those days). My mum is a very polite person and so had already engaged in conversation before twigging there was something wrong. Now she was getting the profane splenetic rage too.

As you can imagine, it upset Mum very much. She didn't want to change her number; she'd had the same one for decades and was fearful of losing touch with people she saw less regularly. Also, she was upset at being forced to adjust her life due to this foul-mouthed stranger.

I remember Dawn tried to reason with the woman. Dawn is so kind and protective of her friends and she was at my flat one evening when we'd been having a drink together and I'd poured my heart out about the awful situation, a situation that was now on my mind *all the time*. Then, as I was speaking, the doorbell rang with the familiar intolerant intensity. Dawn insisted on going out to speak to the woman. Dawn had been a school-teacher and I could hear her using her best teacher voice to speak very firmly to this unbalanced woman. It was a good effort and I loved Dawn for trying. Dawn could put any sane person in their place, but I knew it wouldn't do any good with my tormentor. You can't reason with paranoid delusion.

Then the woman found out Sophie's number in Australia. Directory Enquiries could do that for you in those days. So now Sophie and anyone living in her house was getting harassed too, with the added misery of there being an eight-hour time difference. In the early years of our rela-tionship, Sophie and I spent quite long periods apart out of necessity, an absence not made any easier by her being woken up in the middle of the night, after playing an exhausting gig, by a spiteful, foul-mouthed lunatic.

Of course, I reported all this to the police and they were sympathetic, but without knowing who she was there was nothing they could do. I was actually getting pretty desperate. So was my mum.

Then we got a bit of luck.

The woman had been around abusing me over my intercom in her usual outraged and furious manner. She had an idea that me and Dick Curtis were having an affair and she made some pretty pornographic observations about its supposed physical aspects. She had also phoned the papers about her theory because Phil's office had been contacted by *The Daily Mail* and *The Sun* about a tip-off they'd received about Richard and me.

It was strange. She looked so prim and proper, and yet her sexual delu-sions were so vivid and explicit.

Anyway, having vented her spleen at me over the intercom for a few minutes, she went away as usual. The cops had said to call them when it happened so I did and a couple of constables came around, although it seemed pretty pointless. We'd been through it all before. They came and we were in my sitting room chatting about it when the doorbell rang.

I knew at once it was her. The usual, forceful, outraged anger. *BUUUUUZZZZZZZZ.* I can hear it now.

The cops and I exchanged glances. Then one of them raised his finger to his lips for silence from me and they went out into the communal hallway. The moment she saw them through the glass of the front door she turned and ran. But gawd bless the long arm of the law because they ran after her, demanding that she stop. And she did.

I couldn't hear their conversation, but when the cops came back, the first chink of sunshine had appeared. We had her name. She'd actually offered a false one but the cops demanded ID and now, incredibly, they had her name and address. She'd lost her superpower.

At first, it didn't seem to have made much difference. She kept on coming and, despite knowing her identity, the police could do nothing to stop her. Believe it or not, she wasn't breaking the law. There was no 'stalking' law in those days. Ringing door bells in the night, abuse on the doorstep, endless phone calls at all hours . . . These were not crimes and she appeared to know it. My lawyer explained to me that the only way we could get a court to act against her was to demonstrate that she was doing us 'material harm'. In the absence of violence or damage to property, he told me we would have to prove that she was affecting my ability to earn, that her actions had financial implications for me. That was the law in those days. Aggressively making someone's life a misery wasn't enough. You had to be out of pocket.

So my lawyer instructed me to write an essay, describing how this woman's actions were disrupting my life and making it difficult for me to earn my living.

My mum had to write a similar essay. She had returned to teaching and had to explain that the nocturnal harassment was impacting her professional life.

And, on that basis, a civil court summons was issued. A court summons is a matter of public record and, of course, the press keep an eye on them. So when it was listed that Ben Elton was taking a woman to court, you can bet it caused a hell of a stir. My tormentor now got a taste of harassment herself as her address was listed in the filing and she found herself besieged with journalists shouting stuff like 'Has Ben got you pregnant?'.

You're not going to believe this, but this caused her to ring *my* lawyer, complaining that we had caused her to be harassed and asking what we intended to do about it!

Well, that put an end to it. She attended the hearing and the court found against her (fortunately neither I nor my mum were required to attend). A court order was made banning her from making any contact whatsoever with either me or my family and associates. With that, thank God, she disappeared from my life just as suddenly as she'd entered it. But it was months before I began to remotely trust that she was gone and, for literally years afterwards, I jumped at the sound of the doorbell.

I become a roadie

Sometime in 1989, Sophie's band moved from Fremantle to Melbourne – going 'over east', as we say in WA. They had really done as much as they could on the Perth scene – building a big live following and releasing an independent album – but if they wanted to get any further, they needed to be in Sydney or Melbourne. These days, the internet has shattered the confines of physical geography and a WA artist like Tame Impala has been able to conquer the world from his studio in Fremantle. But back in the '80s, any band with half a shot eventually considered trying their luck in the eastern states.

It's hard for us Brits to get our heads around just how big Australia is. Western Australia alone is larger than Western Europe and when I first visited, it still had only just over two million inhabitants. The East Coast is a five-hour flight away. So not only is Australia a very long way from Britain, but the bit of Australia I ended up in is a very long way from most of Australia!

Perth and WA have a vibrant and distinct culture (both post-colonial and indigenous), and also a huge economy, but we 'Sandgropers' are still viewed as distant country cousins in Melbourne and Sydney.

So the Jam Tarts moved to Melbourne and Sophie and her sister found a house to rent with some local musicians in the suburb of St Kilda, a very cool if rather grubby and run-down area of the city where the sex industry and artistic community lived side by side.

What a double life I had begun to live! It was quite a contrast for me when I was with Sophie, in her little room in that rock'n'roll shared house – plastic chairs and torn couches and an itinerant community of friends and bandmates who dropped regularly in and out. It was kind of like being a student again.

I absolutely loved Melbourne and I still do. It's a multi-cultural city with an amazing array of great food and a fantastic live music and arts scene. In those days at least, it felt like Melbourne went to bed at about the same time Sydney was getting up for work; the bars stayed open until dawn. Perhaps the night scene developed more because, unlike Sydney, Melbourne doesn't have a beach culture. It's colder and wetter and, in the early '90s, it was very goth. The first song Sophie and Anna wrote when they got there started 'In a town where no one's wearing white / It's gonna rain down on me tonight.' I think they were missing Freo!

But they soon got used to it and Sophie and the girls became a part of the vibrant pub rock scene and life was fun. Sophie had permanently shifted her focus from double bass to electric bass and I carried her big bass amp into some dark and gloomy, sticky-floored basement club or pub many times. Mine was an unusual double life. Back home in the UK, I had a million-selling novel on the charts and *Blackadder Goes Forth* on the telly. In Aus, I was my girlfriend's roadie.

I finally get there. A West End play

Remember how I used to be a playwright? I'd been a bit side-tracked since leaving uni, but that youthful dream had never left me. Ever since reading Sheridan Morley's biography of Noël Coward in 1973, my most passionate ambition had been to have a play of mine staged in a West End theatre and, in 1989, it happened. The play was called *Gasping* and I had written it at that rock'n'roll house in Melbourne, in Sophie's bedroom, sitting at a desk made out of milk crates and planks.

It was a political satire concerning a world in which air is privatized. You'll perhaps recall I first encountered this basic conceit while reading *The Ragged Trousered Philanthropists* on a student holiday in 1977. That book was written before the First World War, but the theme is timeless and was particularly appropriate at the end of a decade marked by the wholesale privatization of public services in Britain. I wrote it as a wild farce as much reminiscent of Dario Fo as Noël Coward. An energetic Yuppy venture capitalist identifies a machine (used by hayfever sufferers) that stores and cleans air. He sees the potential for 'designer air', Perrier water for the nostrils, with high-end bars and restaurants wafting differ-ent bespoke atmospheres to suit their menus – Tuscan air with the pasta, Highland air with the Scottish beef.

Pretty soon, events start to spiral out of control. Companies begin to store air in order to control the price (the EU butter mountain and wine lakes were much discussed at the time) and the air in general starts to get thin. The play ends with all the air in private hands being eked out in tiny amounts to a gasping population, while the Big Air companies struggle to maintain a maximum 'gulp price' which they see as the right thing to do as their first duty is to protect the interests of their shareholders and not the breathing public.

Very much 'a little bit of politics'.

When I returned to England, I offered the play to Phil to produce. It felt like an obvious and fun way to approach the challenge. It would be my first time as a professional playwright and his as a West End thea-tre producer. Most creatives (as we are known in the business part of showbusiness) compartmentalize their representation. In fact, I think I am genuinely the only one who doesn't. The model is to have separate UK agents and US agents, separate literary and acting agents, agencies to handle appearances, publicists and often managers too who will negotiate for them to work with many different producers. Phil has basically been all those things for me. He and his team negotiate all my deals, promote all my live work, have produced all my plays, two of my musicals, the first of my two films and some of my TV. It's been that way since 1984. Perhaps I've missed out on some diversity of advice and opportunity, but I think I've also had a lot more fun.

Finding a theatre for *Gasping* wasn't easy. A TV stand-up comic trying to open his first play cold in the West End is not an attractive prospect to theatre owners. It was actually about my twentieth play, but they weren't to know that and had they done, I don't think they would have cared. *Blackadder* was already a hit and I'd had a number-one novel, so you might have imagined that would be seen as evidence that I could write, but as I mentioned, demarcation lines were much firmer in those days. Playwrights wrote plays. TV writers wrote TV.

But Phil overcame the odds and found a theatre for *Gasping* and not just any theatre: The Theatre Royal in Haymarket (established 1720) no less. With Phil and me both being very much the outsiders, there were definitely some raised eyebrows in the arts media about these two upstarts checking into such a posh gig, but the Haymarket made us welcome.

I had written the lead role of the eager-to-please but inventive young yuppie for Hugh Laurie and, to my great joy and relief, he loved it. In the role of his tyrannical boss, we cast Bernard Hill, who had become famous in Alan Bleasdale's game-changing *The Boys From The Blackstuff*. Rounding off the cast were Jaye Griffiths and Simon Mattacks. It was a fantastic company of actors centred around Hugh's simply brilliant and properly moving comic lead performance, which was everything that I'd hoped for from the role and more. The play opened in London in June 1990. The night I'd been dreaming of since reading Sheridan Morley's *A Talent to Amuse* at the age of thirteen had come to pass.

And it was a hit! It ran for a year and a half, with John Gordon Sinclair and Jim Carter taking over from Hugh and Bernard after six months. Even the reviews were pretty good on the whole; they took a wary tone, but conceded it wasn't a bad effort. A couple of them made reference to Swiftian satire and the play was even nominated for an Olivier for best comedy.

For me, the highlight was Hugh's amazing bit of physical comedy in the massage scene. The writing of this scene, such as it was, required a lot from any actor, in that there was to be no actual masseur present and the actor was required to hurl themselves about the massage table at the hands of an invisible but clearly massive and aggressive sumo wrestler of a tormentor. There were some pretty good gags in that play, but Hugh's non-verbal comedy was the showstopper. Not everybody knows he can do that. I think Charlie Chaplin would have given him a pat on the back and a thumbs-up.

Gasping ended up being translated into a number of languages and playing all over the world, most notably for me in Germany. I was so happy to go there with my father to see it, fifty years after his escape in those darkest of all times.

The play was written in Australia, but it actually took many years to be performed there. It might have made it much sooner. Australian readers won't need telling what a big star Daryl Somers was back then. He fronted a show called *Hey Hey It's Saturday*, an Australian Saturday-night institution for decades. Daryl and I had talks about him bringing *Gasping* to Australia, with him in the lead, but it all collapsed. The play ends with the whole world suffocating, which Daryl thought was a bit bleak so he wanted to give it a happy ending! You can take the man out of Saturday night TV but you can't take Saturday night TV out of the man.

The Man from Auntie

While we were discussing how best to approach getting *Gasping* into the West End, I went back on the road for my last stand-up tour of the 1980s, a two-month trawl round the country culminating in another week's run at the legendary Hammersmith Odeon.

Those tours were hard work, but the real effort was put in before getting in the van. For every tour I did (and do), I have to write a new show. Material is a real a tyranny for comics. Musicians can play their greatest hits. In fact, that's what fans *want*. Comics can't do that. Most comics employ other writers, but that would defeat the object for me. As I explained earlier, I'm in it for the material.

One of the great advantages of having such a big turnover of live gear was that it always meant that I had plenty of new material to service the extraordinary access to TV that I had in my years of being a big thing. It's hard to believe, looking back, but in those days I could basically get on the TV whenever I wanted. No wonder I caused resentment. I'd have resented me. In hindsight I can understand and also sympathize with how much jealousy my extraordinary ubiquity must have been causing.

Saturday Live and *Friday Night Live* were over and its two break-out stars (me and Harry) were both now ready to do our own shows. I asked Geoff Perkins to produce mine and so did Harry. That's how good Geoff was. I called my show *The Man from Auntie*. The title was actually suggested by my ex-girlfriend Kate. Younger readers (if there are any) will perhaps not know that the BBC was once known as Auntie BBC due to its high moral tone. Older readers may even remember that there was a hugely successful spy show in the '60s called *The Man from Uncle*. Hence Kate's title, which I still think is very good.

The show was mainly stand-up, but we also did some sketch stuff, which was kind of physical representations of the stage monologues. And there was an element called 'The Chins'. These were developed out of a habit I had in my live work of doing a sort of running commentary on my act as I delivered it, adopting various character voices to represent the various critiques that were made of me. In an effort to visualize this element for TV, we created little characters by putting miniature wigs, eyes and makeup on my chin and then filming just my lips and chin. I had to lie on my back with a camera suspended over my chin doing a Mary Whitehouse figure, a 'Sun' TV critic, an unimpressed left-wing zealot. The 'chins', with my inverted mouth pretty much filling the screen, were then dropped into the stand-up in the studio. I'm not sure it really worked frankly, but it was visually quite striking and the makeup department had fun making all the tiny wigs and props.

The Man from Auntie was a big hit for BBC1, getting between seven and eight million viewers. The Royal Television Society even gave me their writers award that year. I owe that entirely to Paul Jackson, who was on the committee. The award had always gone exclusively to a drama writer (and has done ever since), but Paul argued that I had written six half-hours of monologues and sketches, which covered any number of topics and observations, and that it was time comedy writing was acknowledged as a serious art form. He won the argument and I got the award. I wish Paul was on more award panels.

A play too far

Sophie and I flew straight back to Melbourne after *Gasping* opened. I returned to my retro student rock'n'roll life, sitting back straight down at the plank-and-milk-crate desk and writing another play.

I'd had what I believed was a pretty good idea. There had been a recent court case where an actress had sued a columnist for defamation. The columnist hadn't just insulted the actress personally. She'd said that the actress couldn't act, which the actress claimed was demonstrably untrue and damaging to her career. It struck me that this would make a great theme for revenge comedy. I wanted to write what they call a well-made play. *Gasping* had been rather a linear farce, exclusively pursuing the grand conceit of its big central idea. There was no room for any real character development or much sub-plot, beyond a comedy love story drawn in similar broad farcical terms. Since this new play was about personal emotion and not political satire, I moved away from Dario Fo and closer to another hero, Alan Ayckbourn. The result was *Silly Cow* (a name which I rather regret), a comedy about a larger-than-life newspaper columnist being stalked by a vengeful actress.

I had another reason for wanting to write that play.

Dawn French.

She had recently asked me in no uncertain terms why I had never written a play for her. In fact, that had been the subject of our dinner on the night she confronted my stalker.

Dawn tells a funny story about this, very much against herself. It seems we were at a party and I had been telling her about *Gasping* and I said 'I've written a play and I'm hoping you will star in it'. Of course, what I'd actually said was 'I'm hoping *Hugh* will star in it'. Dawn recalls she then had a wonderful few days thinking I'd written her a play. I imagine it was probably more like a few minutes, but the story has grown and now even features hilariously in her current stage show 'Dawn French is a Twat'.

Anyway. I wrote *Silly Cow* for Dawn and this time I decided to direct it as well. Dawn and I had been bantering together for years and I reckoned I was best placed to work on the comic chemistry of the play. My decision to direct caused more raised eyebrows (me being a sparkly suited stand-up, after all). But fuck 'em. I've got a degree in drama.

By this time, *Gasping* was approaching the end of its eighteen-month run and we'd been such a hit that Phil was able to persuade the Haymarket owners to follow on with the second of my plays. With a star like Dawn in the lead, it looked like a very good bet and the deal was struck. Patrick Barlow was cast in the role of a conniving tabloid editor.

From the first read-through, the play seemed to be really flying. I loved working with Dawn, of course; we'd been friends for ten years by then. We only had one bust-up in the whole rehearsal period and it won't surprise you to learn that it was over chocolate. Dawn is an evangelist for the joys of chocolate and she had ensured that chocolate treats were provided at easily accessible points of the rehearsal space and, later, the stage at all times for anyone who felt peckish. One day, we were working away and as I was giving my notes, I absentmindedly picked up a Twix from one of the numerous bowls (not fun size by the way – full strength) and wolfed both barrels.

'Bloody hell, I wish I hadn't done that,' I said as I pocketed the wrapper.

Dawn put down her script.

'Why do you wish you hadn't done that?' she demanded quite sharply. Believe me, Dawn can do sharp.

'Well,' I replied, 'because I didn't actually want it.'

'Of course you wanted it, otherwise you wouldn't have eaten it, Ben! You're a grown man with free will. Nobody forced that Twix down your neck so clearly you wanted it and now you feel the need to sub-ject yourself to a guilt trip over having eaten it. Just admit you wanted it and enjoyed it.'

'No, Dawn. I just really wish I hadn't eaten it.'

Let me tell you the barney went on for twenty minutes. I wasn't giving ground and nor was she. It got quite heated, with her maintaining I was a lily-livered hypocrite denying my true self in order to conform to an oppressive social norm and me saying that actually it had made me feel a bit sick.

Eventually, we both just started laughing and agreed to differ. The next time Sophie and I went to lunch at Dawn and Len's, she made ice cream with a melted Mars bar sauce which I certainly did *not* regret eating. Back in the '90s, we saw quite a bit of Dawn and Len. Lenny had a beloved side hustle – a fantastic soul band called Poor White Trash, in which Sophie was the bass player. (One night, Jeff Beck asked Lenny about her, saying he loved 'how that chick plays bass!'. Pretty cool, eh?) Hugh Laurie used to play keyboards and I was a groupie always at the front of the crowd, watching Sophie and doing my exuberant dancing. I *always* dance like there's no one watching.

We all thought *Silly Cow* was going to be a hit. That was the vibe around it, the view of various theatre pros who dropped in to see how we were going. It felt like a good night out at the theatre, mainly fun but with a bit of edge. The preview performances were simply rocking. Every gag landed (they tend to with Dawn) and the twists and turns received rounds of applause.

But we got absolutely panned. A universal, savage, world-class, bol-locking of the highest order.

I put at least the tone of vitriol down to a stupid mistake I made. I think a pretty big mistake.

Phil and I were still new to the West End and it's a complicated world filled with weird archaic practices and fragile egos, particularly back then. There were ways of doing things which the theatres expected you to comply with. One of these was that you engaged the services of one particular press liaison bloke.

He was a louche, supercilious, boozy-looking old ligger whom I shall call Ronald. Ronald was a fixture of the theatre scene and his 'job' was to deal with the first-night press. This shambling, posh old chap with a pleasant way about him was a sort of archaic version of a modern publi-cist. He would invite the critics, make sure they got their favourite seats and ensure they knew where the little roped-off area was in the interval so they could get their free drinks (I don't think that happens any more either).

You had to have Ronald, or one of a couple like him. That was just the way it was then. Theatre press agents were a different breed.

Well, *Silly Cow* has a big twist in the second half. And it was an effective one. I had watched the show through every preview and no one had ever spotted it. There was always a gasp, a huge laugh and then a round of applause when the penny dropped. Well, I was worried about my twist getting out. I'd recently been to see *The Mousetrap*, which ends with an appeal not to give away the twist. For some insane reason, I suggested to louche old Ronald that perhaps we might politely ask the critics not to give my twist away.

Now I can tell you what Mr Fucking Supercilious, who Phil was *paying* to advise us on press matters, *should* have said to that.

'Ben, are you out of your mind? If we tell them there's a twist, they're going to be *looking* for it throughout the play and if they know it's coming, they're going to work it out. But, worse, they will shit on you from a very great height for having had the sheer arrogance, the rudeness and the cocksure naivety to tell experienced and respected arts journalists how to do their fucking job. So NO! We do NOT tell them there is a big twist in act two and we do NOT make suggestions about what they should put or not put in their reviews.'

That's what he *should* have said. The snooty, soupy fuckwit.

Instead, he just smiled a little smile.

'You want me to warn them not to give away the twist?' he asked.

'Well, uhm, yeah. I just really don't want it to be given away.'

I was STUPID. Idiotic. I absolutely admit that.

They never would have given it away. Of *course* they wouldn't have. Critics do some dark things but they don't give twists away. I can't think why I imagined they might. I was clearly nervous and strung-out and I just wasn't thinking straight.

Yes, I was stupid. But our PR colleague was an absolute bastard. Of course he felt he owed more to the group of regular reviewers whom he'd been sharing free wine with at least twice a week for decades than he did to a couple of cocky arrivistes like me and Phil (who, after all, were only paying him).

'Mr Elton, our *esteemed* young playwright, wishes you to know that there is a *terribly* clever twist in act two and he begs that in your enthusiasm you restrain yourselves from giving it away.'

I didn't hear him actually say it and he may not have been quite so sarcastic. But he told them there was a big twist and he told them I'd asked them not to give it away.

Just as I'd asked him to.

And just as he ABSOLUTELY should have declined to do since it was his job to advise me. I still shiver to think how stupid I was.

They didn't give my twist away. But that was the single positive aspect to one of the truly grim mornings of my career.

The reviews weren't just bad, they were savage. And much attention was given to the fact that there was a twist. Some even mentioned that they had been *asked* that it should not be revealed, which, of course, they would never have dreamed of doing. But readers needn't worry because it was so glaringly obvious, they would work it out in five minutes. I think that Michael Coveney in *The Observer* spoke for them all when he enquired why Ben Elton didn't just pack up his 'tawdry Punch and Judy show and get the hell out of London's most beautiful theatre'.

Now I know what you're thinking.

Maybe the play *was* shit and the twist obvious. Did I ever think of that?

All I can tell you is it's been played successfully many times since. The Stockholm production won a Swedish Theatre Award for best foreign play and, in the Noughties, it had a very successful six-month run in Paris in French translation. Phil and I went to see it and the audience were still applauding that twist more than twenty years since it was first revealed. What's more, it got fantastic French reviews.

There was one absolutely brilliant thing which came out of that critical London drubbing: a public tribute from the great Ray Cooney.

Cooney is a writer who had been delighting theatre-goers for decades with hugely successful comedies and that year he finally received an Olivier award for best comedy. In his speech, having wryly first thanked Tom

Stoppard and Alan Bennett for *not* writing a play that year, which gave him a shot at a prize, he went on to thank *me*.

I wasn't there and I'd never met him. *Silly Cow* had, of course, not been nominated and I was sitting at home on the couch with Sophie watching the ceremony on the telly.

'Finally,' Ray said clutching his Olivier, 'I'd like to thank Ben Elton for writing *two* wonderful funny new plays and giving us all hope for commercial theatre in the West End.'

I was completely stunned.

Can you believe it? How incredibly, wonderfully generous was that? On *his* night, picking up *his* award, he chose to finish his speech by speaking up for a man he'd never met and taking a dig at the hatchet job that had just been done on me. I was so touched I could have cried.

That first London production ran for a respectable eight months, but it was always a struggle, even with Dawn's stellar leading performance. No matter how hard everybody assures each other that bad press doesn't matter, in the theatre it really does.

A proper full bore pasting is almost impossible to get past, particularly back in the days when people actually read the papers.

1990 to 1992

City of Rock

Sophie and I had been going out for three years by this time, although 'going out' mainly meant criss-crossing the globe. I'm just so glad that this period of our lives preceded awareness of climate change. I feel guilty enough about leading an international life now when we do at least live in the same country, but before we got married the amount of travelling I did was insane. But nobody considered the environmental impact. Carbon hadn't yet been recognized as the threat it is – or, at least if it had, I wasn't aware of it. I was a member of Greenpeace, but we were all about CFCs, the ozone layer and the rainforests. Nobody was swearing off flying.

By this time, Sophie and I were steady enough for her to feel she could accept sharing a little more in my good fortune and so agreed that I could rent a house for us in Melbourne. Charming though it had been to revisit my student house-share days, I'd had enough of accommodation choices based on what she could afford. So we rented a nice little terraced house in the pub-filled, bustling inner city suburb of Richmond which she lived in for the next four years, with me commuting back and forth to the UK. It was a funky little two-up two-down terraced house with a patio out the back and huge old-fashioned sash windows at the front that rattled massively in the winter storms. I can remember getting out of bed in the small hours and climbing up onto the inner sill, standing spreadeagled between the blind and the window pane, struggling to stick little folded wedges of paper into the cracks. And I was stark naked because I couldn't be bothered pulling my pants on. Any reveller returning home in the small hours would have copped an eyeful of the full moonlit meat and potatoes, which could have given them nightmares for weeks.

It was a wonderful time for me, a writer living with a cool beautiful bass player in a cool beautiful foreign city. As mentioned, Melbourne is a great place to play at being a bohemian artist. Sophie's band never quite made the step-up to a recording contract, but they got great crowds and were part of a vibrant music scene. I followed all the bands in Sophie's circle of mates: The Catalinas, The Hooley Dooleys, The Neptunes, The Breadmakers, Vika and Linda Bull, and Sophie's own new band The Boom Babies. So many great nights, so much talent.

There was lots of cross fertilization, jamming and hybrid collaborations. Jodie and Sophie played in a country outfit called Shonky Tonk and had a regular gig down in the docklands at a pub called Mulcahy's. It was here that my singing career picked up again after the twenty-year hiatus that had followed my performance as the Artful Dodger. I'd get up with the band each week and do my three numbers: *Teenager in Love*, *Me and Bobby McGee* and *Guitar Man*. I'd never have got through it without the tender loving care offered by my dear friend, guitarist supremo Sam 'The Doctor' Lemann.

All those mates from our Melbourne days are still mates and, even now, a party can get wild. Occasionally I'll look at Sophie and realize she's about to hit the piano Jerry Lee Lewis-style. After that, only one more drink and she's spinning round and doing those long slides down the keys with her bum.

I got pretty into the Melbourne art scene in general. Without really noticing it, I was starting to build an Australian life. I did a TV gig there in '91, similar to my *Wogan* residency, sitting in for a Melbourne producer and performer called Steve Vizard who was having his moment with a show called *Tonight Live*. I did the show half-stand-up and half-interviews. I remember interviewing the Australian novelist Colleen McCullough (who wrote *The Thorn Birds*) and we really got on. The next day, she sent me her complete works signed and invited Sophie and me to stay at her home on Norfolk Island.

I also interviewed my friend Andrew Denton, thus turning the tables on him. British readers won't be aware, but Andrew is a colossus in Australian broadcasting, an enormously talented and innovative radio and television original who changed the rules of the game as both producer and presenter on several occasions over the years. I first met him in 1989 when he interviewed me on his Sydney radio show when I was flogging my first novel *Stark*. We locked horns over Kylie, who Australians were a bit embarrassed about at the time and were calling 'The Singing Budgie'. Ever faithful to my commitment to the value of popular art, I called Andrew out on his gentle derision and got him to concede the merits of highly catchy pop music sung by extremely attractive and talented young people. In return, he introduced me to Midnight Oil, one of Australia's greatest rock bands in my view, second only to AC/DC – although Cold Chisel are vying with them. If British readers don't know either Chisel or the Oils (as the bands are known in Aus), I suggest you check them out.

Andrew Denton and I are friends to this day and we usually try to have dinner together whenever I'm in Sydney. Back then, we were also squash buddies. I kept a racket at his house in Sydney and we'd always play when I was in town.

I also got to know Midnight Oil's charismatic frontman, highly politicized environmental activist and Australian icon Peter Garrett. Peter is six foot four, skinny but muscular and entirely bald. He is an inspiring and deeply principled man and has an aura of timeless spiritual wisdom about him. It's like hanging out with a shamen or a buddha. And despite being a wild-man rocker on stage, he's very temperate off it. One time he asked me to do a Greenpeace benefit he was organizing at the legendary Harold Park Hotel in Sydney, which was a celebrated pub rock gig. (Sadly, the Harold Park Hotel doesn't rock any more, another victim of noise restrictions in changing neighbourhoods which has also bedevilled the UK pub rock scene.) I was top of a very rowdy bill and had to wait all evening to do a half-hour set at past midnight. It was a long grim wait with the audience getting drunker, but me staying sober and feeling like I'd gone back in time to my Comedy Store days. The gig was fine but high-octane, and when I came off, sweating, hoarse and desperate for my first beer of the night, Peter met me with a cup of tea! He said, 'That was great, mate. I got you a cuppa. You look like you could really use one.' I guess even rock gods can't be rock'n'roll *all* the time.

In 2004, Peter surprised everyone by becoming a Labour (Aussies spell it Labor) MP and did a couple of terms as a federal government minister for the environment. Quite something, eh? Imagine Noel Gallagher or Stormzy having a seat in the UK cabinet.

Another person I got to know back then in Melbourne was John Clarke, who was Australia and New Zealand's foremost satirist, a man with a wit so dry it makes the Nullarbor Desert look like a water park. John was the genius behind the Sydney Olympic satire *The Games*, which was to inspire the British show *2012*. With his partner Bryan Dawe, he also came up with the inspired idea of doing satirical topical 'interviews' in which each week John would play a different public figure but always in his own voice and deadpan style, making no concession whatsoever to the character he was supposed to be playing. This idea also resurfaced in the UK as the highly popular 'Two Johns' on Rory Bremner's TV show. I have to say John always felt somewhat embittered by this, but he approached those disappointments with the same good-humoured, if somewhat weary, tolerance that he viewed all human foibles with, including his own. He and I shared a Thai meal and a couple of bottles of wine together on many evenings in Melbourne. He was as wise and astute a comic wit as I've ever known, and also a great and caring humanist. He died quite young and, like all Australians and Kiwis (he was actually from New Zealand) who love comedy, I miss him greatly. A giant of Antipodean comic arts.

I wrote my second novel *Gridlock* while Sophie and I lived in our Richmond rental. It was inspired by an article I'd read in *The Guardian* about how a handful of individual car accidents in key locations in London could create a city-wide gridlock. This got me thinking about an eco-themed action thriller based around a plot to paralyze a city.

There was another inspiration for that book, one much more important to me. This was an encounter I'd had at a stage door on my '87 stand-up tour. One of the people waiting for an autograph was a young man with severe cerebral palsy. He was small and twisted with shaking limbs, and forming words was a tense and laborious process for him. When I asked him what he did, he told me that he was studying for a maths PhD. It took me just a second or two to type that, but it took him about a minute to say it. At the time, I was somewhat ashamed to have to admit to myself that I had been looking at this bloke only through the prism of his disability. I started thinking about how, in my traffic-jam adventure, a brilliant person who was always ignored and underestimated due to their disability and problems with communication might be a great alternative action hero.

Coincidentally, it was around the time that I began working on *Gridlock* that I was forced to accept that I was dealing with a pretty intrusive health condition of my own.

Shedding my skin. Literally

I had psoriasis, an incurable skin condition. It manifests itself in patches of thick, silvery dry skin with red raw flesh underneath it. You'll know that if you saw Dennis Potter's seminal TV drama *The Singing Detective*, which quite frankly scared the living shit out of me and every other red-raw, flaky skinned psoriasis sufferer in the country back in the '80s.

I first noticed it when I was in my early-to-mid-twenties and, for a while, it only appeared on my scalp. Poor Sophie would have to regularly rub this horrible coal-tar gunk into all the patches and then comb out the softened build-up of skin. If we didn't do that, then my dandruff became appalling and I couldn't wear black T-shirts or it would look like it was always snowing heavily.

In the early '90s, however, the condition spread down from my head and onto my body and started to be a real problem. It was very itchy and very unsightly, and the endless smearing of creams that didn't work was a clammy, greasy intrusion on every day. My skin fell off me in flakes and powder, like washing detergent. Sophie used to joke that it didn't matter when I went away because she could pretty much rebuild me from all the skin I'd left behind.

One comfort I took was to always remind myself that it had only got really bad in my late twenties. I'd had over a decade of being able to take my shirt off in front of girls without embarrassment (about my skin anyway!). And when it did start to develop into a serious problem, I already had a girl who fortunately loved me enough not to be disgusted by my nasty scaly skin which, in bad periods, covered more than half my body. I could scarcely imagine what it would be like to develop it as an adolescent, just when you're summoning up courage to try to date and when you're dealing with a million other embarrassments of growing up. Many young people have to deal with this and as a man who (as my Aussie dermo says) 'has seriously shitty psoriasis', my heart goes out to them and I have taken trouble to involve myself in charities that deal with skin conditions.

One burden you might not have guessed to having an incurable condition is that everyone knows a bloody cure. Once science has produced the right drug, all other bets are off, but as long as science can't help, then every alternative healer, new age mystic, granny-quoter and dopey crystal waver has a free ride. I know people mean well, but you very soon get sick of them telling you that their cousin tried hamster spunk and it cleared up overnight, or to keep a rune stone clenched between the arse cheeks. The three big ones in the '90s were Chinese medicine, Dead Sea mud and acupuncture. I tried them all at some length: boiling up great saucepans full of evil-smelling bark and toxic-looking mushrooms in my kitchen; keeping huge sacks of Middle Eastern salt and mud by the bath; and lying on slabs as some bastard told me to relax while sticking needles in me. Look, it might work for some people. All I can say is that none of it helped me in the slightest, although the noxious Chinese brews, which I had to force down my throat, did make putting up with psoriasis seem almost preferable.

The brilliant Tim Minchin (he's from Western Australia as it happens; as a teenager, Sophie used to play regularly in his uncle's band) once said: 'There's a word for alternative medicine that works. It's called medicine.' Go, Tim.

I even tried detox.

God, that was miserable, three months without a drink on a macrobiotic diet. So many people were going on about all the toxins in my skin, I thought I had to give it a go. It always sounded convincing – 'Your skin's so *angry*. It's because you're poisoning it.' So I gave up booze, tea, coffee, sugar, white flour, meat, chocolate, sweets . . . In fact, anything remotely tasty at all. Phil suggested we do it while I was on tour to make it containable, so we had a cook on the road with us and she'd cook meals in the dressing room and then give me packed breakfasts and lunch for the next day. My big treat was a cup of *acorn* coffee in bed at night. After a fucking *gig*! The funny thing is, I actually started looking forward to that acorn coffee. Small pleasures, as they say.

Not only did all this diet have no effect on the psoriasis, but I also didn't even feel better or healthier. I remember Emma Thompson trying to convince me that at least I must be feeling the *internal* benefits of detox, if not on my skin. But I wasn't and that's the truth. Bollox to detox as far as I'm concerned.

The other thing people go on and on and on and ON about, if you've got psoriasis, is stress. You're *working* too hard. You need to *calm down*. You wrote a novel and a play and did a tour last year. No wonder 50 per cent of your skin looks like something out of a horror movie.

Nothing is more stressful than people telling you that you need to be less stressed.

And, anyway, I think it's crap.

Trappist monks get psoriasis. Zen Buddhists get psoriasis. It's a genetic condition, not a symptom of a busy life. Besides which, if I worked less, I'd be more stressed because I like to work. It's hanging about that makes me tense. I'm no good on beaches at all. I always have to go for a run.

Anyway, through the '90s, the condition got steadily worse and I admit it was starting to get me down a bit. But I'm fortunate in that I'm not at all prone to depression and, like Chumbawamba, when I get knocked down, I get back up again. But the terrible itching in the night, the skin falling out of the bottom of my trousers and the fact that I was embarrassed to take off my shirt in a park were draining and sometimes upsetting. I remember saying to some dermo that I'd be prepared to consider giving up a couple of fingers to be rid of it for good and he said that it was quite common for people to try to quantify their discomfort in that way.

Then medicine threw me some sort of lifeline. Not a cure, not even remotely a cure, but a chance at remission. It's called PUVA and it uses ultraviolet light. When I first started doing it, you had to have a bath in some solution that made you light-sensitive before the treatment. So twice a week I'd go into this clinic and lie in a bath of treatment for an hour, then I'd spend a few minutes in the UV chamber, naked save for goggles and a sock on my nob and balls – like an early Red Hot Chilli Peppers band shoot. Apparently it was to protect the sperm from being fried. Not that my sperm seemed to be up to much chop anyway (but I'll get to that).

Anyway, amazingly, stunningly, ecstatically it worked. After a couple of months, my psoriasis had *completely* gone. It was the most amazing feeling in the world. Of course, within three months it was all back as I'd been warned it would be. But at least I knew there was a chance of remission. The bummer was that each treatment was less effective than the last as your skin builds up resistance, so they have to increase your UV exposure, which will eventually give you skin cancer, which is definitely even worse than psoriasis. Ain't life a bitch?

Nonetheless, I relied on PUVA for years to give me a month of release here and there. At some point, the treatment got more sophisticated and I didn't have to sit in the bath any more. But I've been surrounded by fluoro tubes with a sock on my nob more times than I care to mention.

Dermos tried other cures, a couple of the injecting kind. That was grim, having to stick a needle in my stomach three times a day. And the treatment was a disaster. The psoriasis actually erupted aggressively and I could almost see it advancing over my remaining good skin in real time. I thought I'd have to go into hospital. They say that if it covers you completely, your skin suffocates, like that Bond girl covered in gold paint (this may be an urban myth). So I stopped the injections and it went back to normal, which sometimes was 50 or 60 per cent coverage, but I'd say it was more usually closer to 30 per cent. But it was still really shitty psoriasis.

In the end, I gave up treatments and just got used to it. I'd moisturize all over at least once a day, which gets rid of the silver flaking and just leaves you with smooth patches of red – a somewhat better look. My kids got totally used to me spending hours of every day in only my underpants, my red patched body glistening with gunk, trying not to get it on books and furniture. It was a drag when they had friends round, particularly my daughter's. You don't want to be walking into the kitchen oiled up in your underpants if there's a bunch of fourteen-year-old girls in there making milkshakes. I used to hide in my study. Maybe that's why I wrote so many novels.

I used to get as much sunshine as I could, which was a lot easier during the periods I was living in Australia. In the UK, it was always much worse.

And sometimes it really was fucking awful. I remember going for a two-hour run in the middle of the night just to distract myself from the itching. Sometimes I'd stand in a cold shower for as long as twenty minutes before going to bed, numbing my skin. In some ways, I got used to it. The whole family did too. The kids didn't know anything else; it had begun long before they were born and they used to say I wouldn't be Dad without it.

But it turned out I was. Because it's gone and I'm still Dad.

Ever since around 2015, my brilliant and celebrated Aussie dermo Kurt Gebauer had been pressing me to try new injections. He assured me that the medical technology had improved vastly since my first disastrous try, that the treatment specifically targeted the one gene that caused the condition and that no collateral damage had been detected in all the trials. What's more, you only had to inject four times a year. But Sophie was always against it. Earlier injections had been all about suppressing the immune system and she just didn't think it was worth the risk. However, in 2019, I had decided to return to stand-up touring after a gap of fifteen years. I knew that three months on the road during a British autumn and winter would provoke a possibly unmanageable outbreak. Getting in and out of hotels and driving every day would make regular effective moisturizing almost impossible and, with no sunlight and underneath winter clothes, I knew from bitter experience on previous tours that my skin would creep and crawl and then explode in fury. I honestly believed that if I did not do something, that tour would put me in hospital.

So Sophie and I decided I would try the new injections.

And the result was a genuine, bolted-on, copper-bottomed life changing miracle. I was saved. Almost overnight, too. I had pretty bad coverage at the time (it was winter in Aus) and yet it cleared up within a week. That was five years ago and it has never returned. My family and friends still can't believe it. Nor can I. There are various versions of the treatment; the one I use is known in Aus as Ilumya and I'm afraid as yet I don't think the NHS has caught up with it. I get my needles in Australia.

So that's the story of my thirty-year miserable time with psoriasis. It could have been worse, but it was fucking horrible all the same. And it's gone now, not cured. Apparently, if I stopped injecting, it would come back, but – oh, my goodness – the relief.

I save Stephen Fry's life

If I hadn't been with Stephen the night he nearly died, he would have actually died and then where would everybody's fantasy dinner parties be? As his parents wrote to me in a lovely note after the event, 'Thank goodness you were there'.

It happened in '92 or '93, I can't quite remember. I have many 'dinner with Bing' entries in my appointment diaries for those years and I never annotated them retrospectively to note the ones that ended in near-death experiences.

Stephen was housesitting for the late and hugely missed Douglas Adams at the time while Doug was on a US book tour. We'd been having one of our evenings – just the two of us for dinner in town – and had ended up back at Douglas's house in Islington. It was that time of the night when you know that it's time to pull the pin but you don't and instead you open another couple of bottles. We were drinking beer, which Stephen very rarely did, and for some reason he had some weird organic Belgian stuff which he thought we should try.

We were smoking fags pretty copiously as we did in those days and, on top of that, Stephen was whacking cocaine up his nose. I can say this because he's been entirely forthright about it in his own memoir and, having admitted to doing it at Buck House, doing it with me is hardly a scandal.

I have never been interested in hard drugs myself. I was a member of the Groucho through the notorious days of the late '80s and used to sit with my beer while everybody else was in the toilets. I just thought everybody had a weak bladder.

After a couple of these cloudy Belgian beers, I called it a night and Stephen ordered me a taxi. Had I decided to have another beer, Stephen almost certainly would have been dead in an hour because shortly after he'd called for the cab, he started to wheeze. At first (while he was still able to talk), he tried to brush it off.

'Oh, it's nothing [wheeze]. Just a smidgeon of asthma.'

Stephen suffers a bit from asthma and he was working away at his puffer. I was pretty drunk so it took a minute to sink in that it didn't seem to be helping much. As the wheezing turned to throaty gasping, I realized that something was wrong.

'Bing? Is this serious?'

'Yes.'

His head was rolling a bit and his breathing suddenly sounded alarmingly hollow. It happened in a minute.

'Do you want me to call an ambulance?'

'Yes.'

He was beginning to slump in his chair.

Stephen pushed his mobile phone towards me. He had one, of course, but I believe they were so new that I didn't know how to work it. I grabbed the landline and was in the process of dialling 999 when I realized I had absolutely no idea what the address of the house was. I knew we were in Islington but 'There's a bloke dying in a nice house somewhere in Islington' wasn't going to get me the result I needed.

ME: What's the address, Stephen?

HIM: Wheeze. Gasp.

ME: Focus mate, please. What's the address?

HIM: Wheeze. Gasp. Gurgle.

He couldn't answer. He tried but the words were just empty air. Resolving not to panic, I started to search Doug's kitchen for an envelope or something with the address on. There was nothing pinned to any pinboards or stuck to the fridge with jolly magnets. This was a very large posh kitchen/eating area, no doubt very efficiently maintained by an army of cleaners. I'd just begun pulling open random cutlery drawers when the doorbell rang.

The taxi! I'd forgotten we'd ordered one!

Thank one million types of fuck.

I started to get Stephen onto his feet. He's a very big bloke and I'm not, so it wasn't easy. I got his arm over my shoulders and together we staggered out of the kitchen and down the hall. I even had the presence of mind to grab Stephen's keys off the table. Otherwise, if he survived, he'd be locked out of the house.

He wasn't even trying to speak now. I could see that he needed every possible ounce of strength to get oxygen into his blood. A black taxi was at the door and I asked the driver to take us straight to the nearest hospital, which I guessed would be University College. I say 'guessed' because I was drunk and disorientated and I've never been great on geography. I sat opposite Stephen in the cab on one of the flap seats while he slumped on the main bench. I kept talking to him but his eyes were rolling and the sounds he was making were truly horrible. The driver drove fast and pretty soon we'd arrived at our destination. I can't even tell if you if it was an A & E. I don't think it can have been because the steps and doorway we'd arrived at were very quiet and empty. It must have been at least two in the morning, which I imagine would be a busy time at A & E. Anyway, the driver asked if this would do me.

'Is it a hospital?'

'Yes.'

'Okay.'

I got Stephen out of the cab and virtually dragged him up the steps to the front entrance. I don't know where either of us found the strength because he was pretty much a dead weight (literally). His breath sounded like a death rattle and I couldn't imagine he was getting any oxygen into his lungs at all. At the top of the stairs, I found a wheelchair. My memory is that the chair was outside the front door, which seems a bit strange. Perhaps some poor old dodderer in his pyjamas came back after a sneaky fag to find his wheelchair gone. Anyway, I got Stephen into the chair and through the doors. Inside was a long corridor which was also completely deserted. It was all eerily quiet. Stephen was slumped like a sack, almost falling out of the chair. His long legs were splayed out and I couldn't get his feet onto the foot plates. And the only way I could move the chair was by turning it round and dragging it backwards. I remember as I turned it in the corridor, Stephen lolled further and I bashed his head against the wall. He didn't seem to notice but I felt absolutely sick about it as I dragged the chair and Stephen into what was clearly a reception.

I recall a large echoing chamber with polished stone (marble?) floors and a desk in the middle. This too was deserted. I know it sounds strange that it was just so quiet and empty, which is why I guess the place couldn't have been an A & E.

Anyway, I had to shout – an awful thing to have to do in a large empty room in a hospital at past two in the morning, but I didn't need to be a doctor to be able to see that Stephen was in extreme danger.

'Hello! . . . 'HELLO! IS ANYBODY THERE? PLEASE, I HAVE AN EMERGENCY!'

My voice rang round the cavernous cathedral of polished stone. And then, blessed relief, a nurse appeared from somewhere. She ran in, took one look at Stephen and called for help. A doctor came running and, a minute later, they'd spirited him away and I was left absolutely alone. I don't even recall that there was anywhere to sit down. I just stood there, wishing I hadn't drunk so much because I knew I had to concentrate. It had occurred to me that I needed to tell them something. Urgently. Fortunately, the nurse reappeared with a doctor who told me that Stephen was in the emergency room.

'Has he had much alcohol?' the doctor asked.

'Yes, a lot,' I said, 'and many cigarettes.'

I took a deep breath.

'Also, I need to tell you that I think it's possible – quite *probable*, in fact *certain* – that he has had cocaine.'

Have you any idea how hard that was? This was the early '90s and Stephen was years and years away from his drug confessions. Since those long-gone innocent days, he and Kate Moss and a host of other white-nostrilled celebrities have established a culture where talking to Jonathan Ross about how much illegal powder you've ingested is commonplace. Spun properly, cocaine can even be cited as the protagonist in a heroic narrative struggle with personal demons, which has resulted in a greater understanding of the need to focus on mental health. But, back then, cocaine was a scarily illegal Class A drug and I was grassing up my old mate to an authority figure.

I hated doing it but absolutely I felt I had to. I didn't know what was wrong with him or what drugs they were giving him. Who knew what one drug did to another drug?

The doctor nodded and made a note.

'I don't bother with it myself,' I added rather weakly.

While true, that sounded so pathetic. It seemed to me that, at best, an entire hospital would now be telling all their friends that I did cocaine and, at worst, I was going to be spending a night in a police station while Stephen died and avoided all the unpleasantness.

Anyway, they left me alone again for about half an hour. I was worried sick about Stephen and also vaguely expecting the police to turn up and arrest me. But it seems doctors don't feel obligated to pass on all the things they know about people that come their way because when they returned, it was just to say that Stephen was going to be okay and that I could go in and see him.

I was shown into the emergency room and he certainly didn't *look* okay. He looked like a corpse – grey, translucent skin, seemingly no life left in his eyes, numerous tubes and wires attached to every part of him.

It was then that the doctor told me that Stephen had been *minutes* away from suffering permanent brain damage. And not many more minutes away from death. I said I was quite sure that, given the choice, Stephen would have preferred the latter.

So there you go. I saved the most celebrated brain in showbiz. The throbbing, cerebral epicentre of national treasure-dom has throbbed on these last three decades 'cos of me.

The doctor said Stephen was absolutely fine now but that they were going to keep him in overnight and I asked if I could go with them as they wheeled him to a room. I wanted to stay with him because I wanted to tell him what I'd told the doctor. I was still really worried. I imagined that the big 'coke' word was all over Stephen's notes and I felt he needed to know. Let me remind you once more, reader, that Stephen taking coke would have been very big and entirely surprising and probably career-destroying news to the public in '92. Plus, it could have led to his arrest and even imprisonment.

They left me with him. I know that might seem surprising in our para-noid post-9/11 times, but they let me go with him to the room and then left me with him in a hospital in the small hours of the morning. They were busy and their job was done. They just said, 'Say your goodbyes and then let yourself out'. Unbelievable really.

Stephen was pretty woozy and nodding off, but he was conscious enough to hear me.

'Bing, mate,' I whispered. 'I'm sorry but I told them you'd been doing coke. I felt I had to because they were medicating you.' He squeezed my hand and whispered that it was fine.

'Don't worry,' he added between mercifully longer breaths. 'I'll be writing an entire book about it in twenty years.'

Actually, that last bit's not true. He just said it was fine.

Then he started to nod off, so I put the keys to Doug's house on his bedside table and crept away.

So that was it. Adventure over.

Or so I thought. But there was a final twist.

I couldn't find my way out.

I am not kidding. I had taken no notice of where I was going and I was now alone and there were no signs to be found. I wandered those silent empty corridors in increasing panic. I didn't want to wake up any patients but I could not find a member of staff. Again, I know it sounds strange but it's bloody true. Perhaps the part of the hospital they'd taken Stephen to wasn't the main public bit, I don't know. All I can tell you is that I was on my own in an institutional labyrinth, still pissed and I couldn't find an exit.

Until . . .

I escaped out of a window. I was wandering around the first floor looking for stairs when I saw a slightly opened window through which I could make out a kind of inner courtyard with many large bins. Beyond the bins was a wall with a gate. If I could get into that yard, I could climb over that gate.

UCH (if it was UCH and I'm pretty sure it was) in those days was an old Victorian building and the window was a sash one which, as I say, was already an inch or two open. Remember buildings that had windows you could open? God, I loved them. I climbed through the window, out onto the sill and then, taking my courage in my hands, dropped a couple of feet down onto the bins from where I was able to scramble to the ground.

I don't think I could have pulled it off if I'd been sober. I wasn't so lucky with the gate that was firmly locked – the first thing that had been – but by dragging over one of those very useful enormous wheely bins and climbing up onto that, I was able to hoick myself over the wall.

There was a bit of old Victorian defensive metalwork on the top of the wall, but it wasn't exactly razor wire – although I suppose it's lucky that, having saved Stephen, I didn't end up dead myself, impaled on Dickensian ironmongery. But I'm pretty athletic and managed to get over it and I then hung down from the wall on the other side and dropped to the street below. Clearly there was no CCTV back then – or, if there was, no one was watching, because as the first cracks of light appeared in the sky, I was free and looking for a taxi.

1990 to 1996

Failing towards America (again), a camel in the desert, Montreal, another flipping eco novel and Harry Enfield nails me bang to rights

As previously mentioned, I wasn't overly focused on 'cracking' America but I sure wouldn't have minded either, and another promising chance came my way in 1990 while I was directing *Silly Cow*. An American called Larry Brezner got in contact. Larry was a proper player, a big agent and film producer who, among other things, looked after Robin Williams and Billy Crystal. And he wanted me to come up with an idea for a movie that we could develop together.

It was a proper break in the States from a big Hollywood beast. And I blew it.

It started well, as my screw-ups often do. I came up with a screenplay about a dysfunctional group of misfit scientists on an Antarctic exhibition who discover a secret plot to mine for oil in the pristine wilderness. I called it *Dirty Snow* and Larry Brezner thought it had real promise.

He wanted me to spend time with him and his team in Hollywood, but I was already leading a two-country life. I had no time to add a third, even for America. I could only drop in. And I mean that – drop in. I started going to Melbourne via LA and stopping for a couple of days to work with Larry. One time, I stopped for just eight hours. Totally mad. Larry had arranged a meeting for us at 20th Century Fox and I attended it between flights. It sounds exciting and it was (sort of), but it's not the way for an unknown writer (as I was in America) to impress the big bosses who expect 100 per cent commitment. Nor was it the way for a writer to write a movie.

Turns out you need to focus. Who'da thunk?

I should have been pausing for thought, probing Larry's experience, thinking hard about the art of story-telling. Instead, as usual, I threw more dialogue and gags at every problem. My development process was 'you don't like that? No problem, I'll write some other stuff on the plane!' Eventually, over dinner in LA Larry told me it wasn't working and maybe we should stop. That 'maybe' was all the encouragement I needed! So of course I sent another set of pages, but I don't think he read them and I don't blame him. I'd exhausted him. One day I'll read the first draft of *Dirty Snow* again. I'm sure that first draft was the closest it ever got to being a movie.

It wouldn't be my last failure in the US, but it was my most pointlessly self-inflicted.

Anyway, no regrets. At LA airport on my way out for the final time, I spoke to Phil and heard *Gridlock* had sold 750,000 copies. Those long nights in Melbourne thinking about petrol engines and disability had paid off. Perhaps, if I hadn't been doing so well in the UK, I would have made a better job of trying in the States. Win some, lose some.

Another reason I wasn't fully focused on *Dirty Snow* was because at the time I was also trying to adapt my novel *Stark* for TV. I know. I'm getting exhausted even remembering it.

The BBC approached me in '91 with the idea of doing a mini-series and, since almost the entire story is set in Australia, they set up a co-production with the ABC in Australia to get it made.

Note to writers! Never adapt your own novels for the screen. It's HELL. My book was actually quite cinematic, in that it had a broad sweep, big ideas and great Aussie locations. But that doesn't make it a screenplay. To make an effective movie out of a book, you need to be able to step outside the book and think afresh. That's pretty hard if you're doing your own adaptation. I did many drafts and got very frustrated. It was a gruelling writing experience and I came to believe that the author of a novel is generally the *last* person who should be adapting it (that didn't stop me later trying again, of course!).

In the end, I produced the required three one-hour episodes for *Stark*. Super-talented Aussie movie director Nadia Tass made a wonderful mini-series, filming it not in WA but in Victoria and South Australia. She and cinematographer David Parker did such a beautiful job, making a budget of about three million Aus dollars look like thirty. It really is quite something. Take a look – it's somewhere on YouTube. The script may have aged slightly, and creakily, but the direction and cinematography are stunning. And guess what? I starred in it! A three-hour mini-series! Amazing, really. I've never pushed myself forward as an actor because I know I'm not a very good one, but Nadia insisted I was right for the lead character of the terminally uncool pom. Ha, why on earth would she think that?

The rest of the cast were absolutely stellar, in particular the other two leads. There was Colin Friels, a tough, hard-drinking Scottish-born Aussie who was already a senior figure in Australian film and theatre. I remember during a chilly break in one long, frustrating night shoot (deserts are cold at night), Colin did the 'Tomorrow and tomorrow and tomorrow' speech from *Macbeth* for us. It was breathtaking, just his rich beautiful voice in the velvety stillness. And our leading lady was the mesmerizing Jacqueline McKenzie who played the ball-busting, thrill-seeking principal eco warrior and the object of my character's unrequited love. Jacqui was right at the start of her career then, but she has gone on to achieve considerable success both in Australia and Hollywood. I recently saw her starring in *Orlando* at the Sydney Theatre Company and we had a wonderful catch-up dinner thirty years after we'd worked together.

Making *Stark* was a hell of a lot more fun that adapting it had been and it was actually pretty well-received in both Britain and Australia. A couple of years after we made it, Sophie and I were having a weekend visiting friends in Amsterdam and when we turned on the TV in our hotel room. There I was in the desert on a camel speaking Dutch.

Ninety-two was a busy year in lots of other ways too. I was working on material for my next tour and I also played the Montreal Comedy Festival. This used to be almost as big a part of the UK comedy circuit as Edinburgh. All us Brits went over at some point in the unashamed hope that, because Canada was closer to America than Britain, it might prove a better jumping-off point. It never did, of course. If you want to crack the States, don't try doing it via a French-speaking city in another country, even a neighbouring one. Most Americans are pretty mean about Canada in general, but they scarcely know the French bit exists. Believe me, showbiz-wise, London is a lot closer to the US than Montreal.

During this time, I was also writing my third novel – the third of what might be called my 'eco trilogy' – that is, the last one before I decided it was time to stop writing novels about eco warriors for a while.

This Other Eden was set slightly in the future where the consumer 'must-have' was an eco-fall-out shelter. I called them 'Claustropheres' – mini eco systems that were tiny, clean worlds into which the population could retreat to avoid the great big dirty real one. The main element of the thriller was that a maniacal green zealot (I was trying not to make all my environmentalists total goodie-goodies) was plotting to trick the world into thinking it was time to enter the Claustropheres. His idea was that, with humanity spending a couple of hundred years in their eco shelters, the planet would have time to recover its health, free from human activity.

Thirty-five years later, as preppers fill their cellars with guns and cans of baked beans and billionaires buy up New Zealand in an effort to sit out the coming apocalypse, I think the plot was quite prescient.

Most fun of all that year was the day I spent working on *Harry Enfield's Television Programme*. Harry had written a sketch called 'Benny Elton' and it was, I think, the only truly funny thing anybody has ever done about my image of earnest uncompromising political correctness. His idea was very simple, as good ideas usually are: he wanted to do a spoof of the way Benny Hill used to end his show. As I mentioned earlier, Hill would always end up in a park in a sped-up series of incidents with mini-skirted and bikini-wearing girls. There would be snogging couples and dresses torn off and all sorts of saucy high jinks. It ended with Benny being chased by mobs of irate, scantily clad girls and the whole thing was done to a tune called 'Yakety Sax', which all Britain was familiar with. Harry decided to put 'Benny Elton' (sparkly suit and all) into a park full of gorgeous girls, but have him react very differently. At high speed and to the same tune, I ran around like a maniac, *covering up* sun-bathing girls and tut-tutting at the length of their skirts. I pass two snogging couples on a park bench, tut-tut and then, at high speed, swap the couples round so it ends up with the two boys snogging each other and the two girls snogging each other, possibly the first 'queering' joke (as opposed to the ubiquitous homophobic ones) ever to be shown on UK television.

It was really brilliant, beautifully conceived and made, and I was thrilled with it. Harry possesses one of the most original comedy minds of anyone I have ever met. He constantly surprises, thrills and sometimes offends with the spin he puts on common experiences and presumptions. He is a deeply good and caring man, but there is a streak of the reactionary in his work, which is what makes it dangerous and edgy. These days, comedy, which used to be censored from the right, is now also being censored from the left and some of Harry's work has come under a critical spotlight (like his wearing blackface to play Mandela). But context is everything; criticism without context is less than nothing. In my view, Harry is always on the side of the angels. Mind you, perhaps Benny Hill's fans would use the same argument in his defence against me.

'Don't fucking act, love!' (Tuscan adventures with Denzel, Keanu and Keaton)

Sometime in early 1992, I was sitting in our rented house in Melbourne late one night, faxing reams and reams of doomed *Dirty Snow* pages to Los Angeles, when the phone rang.

'Ben, it's Ken. You've been engaged for fucking hours, darling. Faxing a script? Thought so. Get a second fucking line, love.'

Kenneth Branagh does 'actor speak' in the way most actors do as a fun and ironic 'in' joke – a kind of deliberate, erudite, foul-mouthed excess. Ken is one of the funniest proponents of it I've ever met. Richard Briars was, in fact, his only equal ('Darling, call me Dicky. Fuck knows every cunt does'). Ken had something very nice to suggest although I can't say he put if very flatteringly.

'Ben, mate, love,' he said. 'I'm directing *Much Ado About Nothing* in Tuscany in four weeks' time and there's a part that's perfect for you. You're not my first choice, I'm not going to lie about that. Neither are you the second or indeed the third. The simple truth is, darling, no fucking American will do it because it's too small so I'm asking you, love.'

How could I refuse?

I'd met Ken through Emma, of course. Ken and Em were the golden couple of British theatre arts at the time and Ken, having been Oscar-nominated for his first movie (*Henry V*), was the hottest young director around. He was also the person who really opened up Shakespeare for me. I remember seeing him in *Much Ado About Nothing* on stage and being absolutely convinced that he was paraphrasing and re-wording the text. It just sounded like natural modern dialogue to me, like a genuinely funny sitcom. When I checked, I found that, of course, Shakespeare had written every single word. I couldn't believe it. Ken had made it flow like genuine chat. His passion for Shakespeare is so absolute that he seems to be able to physically morph his own extraordinary understanding into the minds of the audience.

And now I was going to do some Shakespeare with him. Off I went to Italy. Ken had taken his film unit to a villa near a village in Tuscany called Greve in order to shoot his gloriously sun-tanned, crowd-pleasing adaptation of *Much Ado About Nothing*. And what a cast he assembled there – Denzel Washington, Michael Keaton and Keanu Reeves from the States and Em and Ken leading a fantastic British contingent, including Richard (sorry, Dicky) Briars, Imelda Staunton, Brian Blessed and the ridiculously beautiful Kate Beckinsale, at that time an absolute newbie ingénue fresh out of college. We were all billeted around the Tuscan countryside and, for my week on location, I shared a house with Imelda and her husband Jim Carter who was visiting and who I knew already from his lead role in *Gasping*. It was a proper luvvie holiday camp, with the emphasis on camp. When the pinot grigio flowed, the camp bantz was off the scale.

It was a very interesting mix on that set. The director and crew were British, as were the vast majority of the cast, but we also had these big American stars with us who tended to have their 'people' with them, so there were quite a few Americans hanging about too. It was a real clash of cultures, so much so that it might have made a movie in itself. All movie units take their tone from the director and Ken is the most inclusive and considerate of men, so it was a very happy and convivial set, but there were definitely two cultures nonetheless. For instance, there is a real status thing about American showbusiness. What we in Britain might see as petty requirements, Americans see as important indicators of due respect. American stars have a lot of people round them saying 'You should have this. I will make sure you get that.'

British stars always make a self-conscious effort to look like 'one of the gang', making a point of being seen to muck in. The opposite is the case with American stars who don't *want* to look like one of the gang at all. They want to look like stars. I have to say there is a certain refreshing honesty to it.

Denzel, Michael and Keanu were all very nice people, but there was definitely a distance between us and them. For instance, at the end of the day's shooting, the crew and most of the British cast used to go for a drink, a 'bevvy in Greve' as inevitably it was called. The beer and the pizzas were excellent, and it was a very jolly way to unwind for an hour or two. The Americans never came. Again, I don't say this remotely as a criticism. There was no reason why they should spend their free time with a lot of people whom they scarcely knew, particularly since all those people mainly knew each other. Brian Blessed and Dicky Briars firing volcanic and comically vitriolic barbs at each other about long-forgotten British soaps and sitcoms isn't everybody's cup of tea (although it was certainly mine!).

'Did you ever work with *so and so*, Dicky?' Brian would roar across the plates of antipasti.

'Shared a dressing room with the poisonous bastard, darling,' Dicky would reply. 'Stole my custard cream biscuits. I kid you not. I saw him dunking them in his tea. Turned the stomach, I tell you. Revolting fucker. And *never* knew his fucking lines'.

Anyway, one day, to everybody's surprise, Michael Keaton decided he'd come. He was on set with his girlfriend, who was only Courtney fucking Cox! It was still a couple of years before her *Friends* super-stardom. She was just a nice and incredibly beautiful girl who at the time was only known as the gorgeous young woman Bruce Springsteen plucks from the audience to dance with in the 'Dancing in the Dark' video.

I worked quite closely with Michael that week because my part, Verges, is a sidekick to his more important role of Dogberry. As usual, I'd asked him if he and Courtney would like to join us for a drink and I can still remember him thinking hard before saying, 'Okay, we'll try a bevvy in Greve', almost seeming to surprise himself with the audacity of the idea. And that's exactly what they did. They tried it. He and Courtney came down to the village with us, squeezed in on one of the benches crowded with actors and crew and tried a bevvy in Greve.

One beer each. Which neither of them finished.

'Okay,' he said, putting down his glass. 'We did that, it was nice. Thanks.'

And they left after fifteen minutes. It really wasn't standoffish or rude. It was just not their scene. I think, for them, it was almost like a kind of cultural visit, the way a tourist might sit in on a Japanese tea ceremony and, after ten minutes, thinks he's got the gist of it and moves on.

My Keanu Reeves story is another one of culture clash. Keanu is a very thoughtful actor and a very thoughtful man. He was quiet and said little on set. This again was very much in contrast to the loud, jokey, gossipy manner of the Brits who, led by Dicky Briars and Brian Blessed, gagged away pretty much non-stop. One night, there was a bit of a cast dinner on the balcony of some lovely vine-dripping country trattoria. There were about twenty of us, but Keanu was the only American who attended. The table was loud and boisterous, as you'd expect, with many tales told and Ken letting himself really relax and join in the fun. Keanu, however, said almost nothing, just glancing about occasionally – mysterious and quietly amused. Eventually, Brian Blessed – who, as most people know, has a huge voice, which he uses often and to considerable effect – decided it was time to stir Keanu up a bit. Suddenly Brian's voice BOOMED above the babble 'TELL ME, KEANU!'

The table fell silent. Brian was just so *loud*.

And the object of his attention was just so quiet.

Brian fixed Keanu with his flashing-eyed stare, eyes famously topped with massive demonic-looking brows. He left it a beat and then asked his question, his bright-toothed mouth in a friendly snarl.

'What do you know of God?'

It was clearly a gauntlet thrown down, a good-natured one but a gauntlet nonetheless.

The question hung in the air.

It may be that Brian had been discussing theological matters but, to Keanu and most of us, the question came absolutely out of the blue. It was quite obvious that Brian was testing Keanu's resistance under fire.

Keanu was sitting pretty much opposite Brian across a large wide table laden with booze and food. Ken was at the head of the table and his face wore an indulgent smile, but I could sense tension. Keanu was already a massive star. The Americans were most definitely a group apart. They were all doing favours for Ken, the usual fee for any one of them being more than his entire budget. If Keanu took umbrage at being put on the spot by this massive-bodied, massive-bearded, Everest-climbing British luvvie, the delicate ego-balancing diplomacy of Ken's entire production might just fall apart.

Keanu waited a moment. He had been previously concentrating on the contents of his plate and he gave himself a long beat before raising his head slowly and looking Brian in the eye. There was a proper pause, this handsome, super-cool young American facing down the vast bearded bulk of the quintessential British actor opposite whose great pointed bushy eyebrows were raised in amused expectation.

'I don't know much about God,' Keanu said almost in a whisper, like Clint Eastwood facing down Lee Van Cleef. 'But I know you're the devil man.'

Believe me, after that pregnant pause under the Tuscan stars, it landed brilliantly – perhaps because, in the flickering light of the hanging lanterns, with his flashing eyes and those massive eyebrows Brian Blessed really did look like the devil. Anyway, there was a huge laugh and cheer which Brian Blessed joined in with. Keanu, allowing himself a half-smile, returned to the contemplation of his food. He didn't speak again. And nobody challenged him either.

My Denzel story is, you guessed it, yet another one of culture clash. One day, he was sitting alone on set, studying his lines, and since I had nothing to do, I asked him if he would like me to test him on them. He looked up in surprise; clearly unknown bit part players didn't normally approach him on set. But after quite a long pause for thought, he said 'Okay, sure' and handed me his text.

I sat down opposite him, this impossibly handsome man with a natural intensity of delivery that mesmerized even in a simple line reading. We began to read together. We read for about twenty minutes while set construction work went on around us, with me correcting Denzel's occasional errors. When he felt he had got it down, he nodded, reached over, took the script back, got up and left.

Without a word.

Not the smallest thank you, not even a muttered goodbye. Again, I tell this story without judgement or rancour. Denzel was always nice and polite on set, and, frankly, doing a line reading with such a fine actor and great star was my privilege. Also, I imagine that many times in his work there would be people who were there to read for him. Maybe he thought it was my job. Even so, it was a little strange, not even to say thanks. It was indicative, I think, of a general social wariness felt by all the Americans. They really kept themselves at a distance. As I say, it seemed to me that this was because they always appeared to have people around them whose jobs were dependent on encouraging them to feel separate and special.

Status means absolutely everything in the American entertainment industry. I'm sure it does in ours too, but they are definitely more openly invested in it and it goes right down to bell hops and valet parkers. Americans *revere* status, whereas we Brits affect indifference to it (ha!). And in the American industry, without status, *American* status, you're nothing. It wasn't to be the last time I felt the cold consequence of this brutal reality.

But enough with the big American stars! What about me? How did I fare as an actor among all this talent? Well, it was a very small role. Verges is a low-life clown who exists exclusively as foil to Dogberry, leader of the night watch. I think the end result was okay. The film was wonderful and I don't think I ruined it. Ken gave me just one piece of direction, a single note, but for a performer like me, it is the truest and best advice possible. We were on set in a group scene – Denzel, Robert Sean Leonard, Emma, Imelda and others. After the first take, Ken called cut and hurried in among us. He engaged Denzel in an intense, whispered exchange; arms were waved, gestures made. Denzel nodded. Ken moved on to Robert and clearly another artistic meeting of minds was being conducted in urgent whispers and nods. Next was Emma as Ken made his way around the group, delivering a series of focused, detailed directorial beats. Then he began to make his way back to the camera before, almost as an afterthought, turning back and pointing at me.

'Don't act,' he said.

And that was it. A single sentence and a bloody short one at that. But brilliant advice for a hopeless mugger like me. Sadly, in the thirty-two years since Ken said that to me, I've scarcely been offered another acting job, so I haven't had much chance to put it into practice.

In fact, it would be thirty-one years before I'd do a proper acting part again.

And then I had to cast myself.

Dinner with Bob

And since we're on the subject of massive American stars . . .

Because of our mutual love of Queen, I've ended up seeing quite a bit of Robert De Niro (or Bob as he likes to be called) over the years, but I first met him when he was in London making *Frankenstein* with Ken.

I was invited to a couple of dinners that Ken organized for Bob which took place at Julie's Restaurant in Notting Hill. Helena Bonham Carter, who was also in *Frankenstein* and who I knew a little and liked a lot, was there, and Bob, of course, came with a couple of people; I won't call it an entourage, but as I'd noticed when filming *Much Ado . . .*, big American stars always have their 'people' with them. Bob turned out to be a sweet bloke who told some fascinating stories about his days as a young solo backpacker in the UK and Europe, sharing evocative impressions of exploring ancient cities and treading lonely roads in the Scottish Highlands. But the conversation was nonetheless a little stilted because through nobody's fault (and certainly not his), there was never a moment when we weren't all aware that this was Robert De fucking Niro. Of course, Ken and Helena were very big stars themselves but, you know, Robert De fucking

Niro. Not only was he a ridiculously famous movie star but also one of the most respected and you just never quite shake that. It's like having dinner with royalty.

So, despite everyone's best efforts, that sort of dinner is never entirely natural. In this case, it was part Bob, part us and a lot his 'people', who constantly referred and deferred to him and kind of encouraged him to hold the floor to a point where he ran out of steam. Anybody would have.

Another thing was that Bob stole food. I imagine he was hungry because he scarcely ordered any himself.

In fact, Bob ordering was a story all on its own.

Our server was a nice, eager young woman who efficiently took every-body's order before finally arriving at Bob. Bob picked up the menu for the first time at this point and took a lo-o-ng look at it, his face doing that De Niro thing, which was kind of shrugging, if a face can shrug. We all waited in silent expectation before finally he handed the menu back to the young woman and said 'Just bring me something good'.

He put it perfectly pleasantly, but the waitress clearly had no idea what to make of it.

'Uhm . . . it's all good, I believe,' she replied. 'There's some lovely dishes.'

Bob frowned a little. 'That's okay. Just tell the chef to send out some-thing he thinks is good.'

Another moment of confusion for the poor girl.

'Uhm . . . I think he thinks it's all good.'

It was a culture clash. It was pretty obvious that Bob was used to having every chef in New York falling over themselves to suggest dishes to him. I doubt he'd actually made an order in years as clearly it was always 'Bob, you have to try this' or 'Mr De Niro, do I have something special for you tonight!'. He is, of course, a celebrated foodie and I imagine he rarely eats out in his hometown without the chef coming out to greet him and rec-ommending dishes. But London isn't like that, or at least it wasn't then. The poor girl didn't know what to do.

'I think you have to make a choice, Bob,' Ken said finally, to which Bob shrugged philosophically and said, 'Okay, just bring me some steamed vegetables.'

He didn't eat his vegetables. He just ate other people's food. Again, I imagine it's a New York thing, a New York Italian thing. Food is convivial and dining is a sharing, group experience. In Bob's case, though, the sharing only went one way. All his people pressed their own food on him, waxing lyrical about the dishes they had ordered. Bob also took an interest in all our food. 'Is that good?' he'd say before reaching over and sticking his fork into our plates. It was very much not how we Brits dine but, hey, it was Robert De fucking Niro.

However, he pushed his luck too far with Helena. She'd gone off to the loo and, while she was away, Bob literally demolished the remaining food on her plate, even reaching over with a big piece of bread and mopping up the sauce, as if we were all in a private version of one of the numerous eating scenes in his gangster movies. But Helena was not happy when she returned and told him so in no uncertain terms. This was culture clashing to the max. For all the fact that Helena is as nice and down-to-earth a person as you could meet, she is also pretty much an actual aristocrat; there are earls and prime ministers in her direct lineage. I imagine that Helena's upbringing did not involve eating off other people's plates, while Bob's Irish/Italian New York culture clearly did. So Helena ticked Bob off, not meanly but firmly, like Mary Poppins addressing some minor and slightly disappointing misdemeanour.

'Bob! Have you eaten all my food while I was having a pee? That is simply not acceptable.'

For a moment, poor Bob looked like a scolded little boy.

Not a lot of people get to see that.

Best day of my life

By 1993, Sophie and I had been together for six years – although, due to the tyranny of distance, only *actually* together for about half that time – and I asked her to marry me. Fortunately for me, she accepted. When we told her dad, his first words were 'About bloody time'. I suppose it had been a while since he'd made his famous prediction about Sophie's future.

I admit that I had procrastinated about asking. It was the global relationship thing. Marriage is a big decision for any couple, but for us, it involved more than the usual complications. Which side of the world to live on? How to maintain relations between two families who meant so much to both of us but who lived in different hemispheres? In the end, it was the kids thing that forced my hand. Sophie had always made it clear that she definitely wanted to have children. I, on the other hand, had never wanted children in the abstract sense. I'm not a clucky or broody kind of bloke at all. If handed a baby by a harassed mum who needs a pee, I will take it out of sympathy for her, but I'm never going to pretend it's a joyful experience. Anyway, Sophie was twenty-six by this time and I knew it had always been in her mind to have kids before she was thirty. I wasn't *against* the idea if it was with the woman I loved and I did love Sophie, so it looked like decision time.

So I got down on one knee in time-honoured fashion and our life's course was set.

We were married on 14 May 1994 and I can honestly say it was the best day of my life.

We did the official bit in the morning at Chelsea Register Office with just family, plus all the Aussie friends. Phil was with me as best man and also Ade and Jen, and Rik and Barbara. After that, it was off to the best party ever.

We did it in full champagne socialist style at Claridge's – champagne reception, public ceremony of commitment, dinner, then rock'n'roll. Sophie and I waited until everyone had arrived and then we made our entrance for our public committal. The other three Jam Tarts and various Aussie boys played as we entered to the Nick Lowe song 'I Knew the Bride When She Used to Rock'n'Roll'. The roof nearly came off and they followed that with 'Concrete and Clay'. Then we had a little ceremony, which was led by my father as a sort of secular MC. We actually used the vows from the Church of England wedding service because they are so beautiful. Sophie and I just spoke them to each other in front of most of the people we loved. Then Ken Branagh did a couple of readings, which was pretty magical as you can imagine. We chose the obvious ones because there's a reason they're the obvious ones, Sonnet 116 ('Let me not to the marriage of true minds') and the bit from 'The Prophet' about marriage being two pillars that hold up a single building. There were a few old ladies dabbing their eyes at that one, let me tell you. My only regret was that Emma couldn't be there to also read as she was away filming. It's always been a sadness that she isn't in our wedding album. The 'ceremony' ended with Sophie and me singing 'Love Me Tender' to each other. Sophie is a fantastic singer and did the harmonies while I bumbled along with the tune, the ever-helpful Melbourne guitar maestro (and one of our dearest friends) Dr Sam Lemann nodding me in with a very big 'start singing now' nod.

After that there was an amazing feast – at least I think there was. Both Sophie and I were so excited and busy that we never really took a moment to appreciate the food and wine (although we drank plenty of the latter).

One of the most memorable moments of the day was the realization that Jennifer and Kate Bush had come in the same dress! And this wasn't from bleeding Top Shop either; this was a proper full-length designer number. Of all the dresses in London, what are the odds of that? But wait. It gets more unlikely. We had *sat them next to each other* with only Ken Branagh between them! Needless to say, both ladies totally owned the moment.

After dinner and speeches, the Bootleg Beatles played. It was an amazing moment – the curtains parted and there they were in the full 1963 regalia, looking *so* like the real thing (except 'Paul' played bass right-handed). They opened with 'I Wanna Hold Your Hand'. Sophie and I got up to dance and everybody leaped in after us. It's such a feelgood song.

After the Bootleg show, the Australian musicians took over with Sophie on bass, with a fag in her mouth and the beautiful train of her wedding dress stuffed into the top of her tights behind her. It all got very rock'n'roll from then on. The Aussie musicians led by Sam were so good that they could accommodate any request. Ade (who is a very talented musician) did a lengthy turn on guitar and vocals, Hugh played keyboards for a while, Robbie Coltrane sang some fab old school rock'n'roll, Vic Reeves got up and did 'Born Free' and Lenny did half an hour of soul classics, which absolutely rocked the house.

It really was the best day of my life and for the first week of our honeymoon, which we spent in Italy, I insisted on going over every minute of it at dinner each evening.

The honeymoon itinerary was all recommended by Joanna Lumley! She was a guest one day at the regular Sunday lunches which Sophie and I used to attend at Ade and Jennifer's house in Richmond. We were talking about where to go for our honeymoon and Joanna just launched. 'Darlings, you must begin at Positano! The most romantic place on Earth.' We'd never heard of it but she was right. Over lunch, Joanna then pretty much mapped out our whole itinerary, which took us down the leg of Italy and over to Sicily. Pretty cool, I'd say. Not everybody gets someone as tasteful and experienced as Joanna Lumley to plan their honeymoon for them. We had simply the best possible time and we will for ever be grateful to Joanna for her wonderful, joyful advice.

Becoming a sitcom writer again

After our wedding, Sophie and I embarked on a sort of extended working honeymoon. I did a big stand-up tour of Australia and New Zealand and took Sophie's band The BoomBabies in support. We pretty much knew it would be the last hurrah for the band. Anna was married and pregnant, and Sophie was married and hoping to get pregnant, and we were going to live in England anyway, so this was the end of an era.

The proceeds of that tour left a big and happy mark on our lives, in that they went a long way towards financing our little house and block of land near Margaret River, the beautiful wine, cattle and surf region 300 kilometres from Perth in Australia's glorious south-western corner. It was the place where Sophie's family had always camped when she was a girl. That little spread remains our Aussie heaven to this day.

Also on that tour, I began to ponder another sitcom.

I'd been trying to think of an idea for Rowan. He is, after all, an inspiration for any writer and I very much wanted to work with him again. The Adder was definitely over. Dick had just taken a mega step up in his career by writing *Four Weddings and a Funeral* and, anyway, immensely proud of it though we were, *Blackadder* had got less and less fun for Dick and me. And, I think, probably the rest of them too. Despite it having ended on a career high for all of us, neither Dick nor I had any desire to get back on to that gruelling treadmill of sucked cheeks, angry frowns and endless passive-aggressive debates about the comic potential of the word 'wibble'.

But I wanted to write another sitcom. For me, a hit sitcom is the holy grail of British entertainment. The '90s era of knowing, laddish comedy was in full swing and I wanted to write a *good-natured* family sitcom, one that celebrated human silliness and weakness rather than laughing at it, one which revelled in the idea of community rather than chippy isolation. Like *Dad's Army* which I loved so much. Like Brit sitcoms used to do.

And I came up with *The Thin Blue Line*, a comedy about a big-hearted but largely incompetent little police force led by Rowan's Inspector Raymond Fowler, a man of deep moral conviction and crippling British reticence struggling to come to terms with policing a modern town in which all his core values were being challenged. I wrote out a pretty detailed character and situation synopsis while I was on the road and sent it to Rowan. You can imagine how thrilled I was when he expressed 'qualified enthusiasm'. For Row, this is the equivalent of anybody else jumping up and down and screaming that they'll club a seal pup to do it. As anyone from my generation of the comedy business knows, it is extremely difficult to get Row to do *anything*. If he is against something, then nothing will sway him. I share a little phrase with Row's agent Peter Bennett-Jones. We say, 'You can't buck The Adder'. And you can't.

But by some miracle, Rowan decided he wanted to do *The Thin Blue Line*. He was immediately drawn to the character of Inspector Fowler, possibly because they shared so many characteristics. Fowler was a traditionalist and a stickler for getting things right, a conservative (with a small c), a monarchist and a deeply moral man. But he was also sharp and extremely articulate when he chose to be. I'm not saying Fowler *was* Rowan; Row is far more culturally astute and sophisticated a spirit, but there were real elements of similarity. Mind you, I can be a bit like Inspector Fowler myself.

For me, there was no doubt about who I wanted to produce it. Geoff Perkins and I had been a team since '87 and I valued his advice and guidance enormously. Row loved Geoff too, so the three of us took the project to the

BBC who, unsurprisingly, were happy to commission a new Rowan Atkinson sitcom. Although *TTBL* was undoubtedly a star vehicle, Rowan and I also wanted it to be an ensemble piece in the way *Dad's Army* had been. When James Dreyfus walked into our audition room, we knew we had found our PC Goody, the frantic, over-enthusiastic boy/man of slightly confused sexuality who was secretly in love with sensible PC Maggie Habib. Constable Habib was played by the brilliant Mina Anwar, another obvious choice the moment we met her. Mina is a subtle and convincing actress who can also deliver assured broad comedy, which is not such a common combination. She had the toughest job in the show in that she often had to play straight, particularly to James's non-stop crazy. She managed it to perfection while maintaining a sparkling comic charm of her own and became a popular favourite overnight. Serena Evans was perfect as Sergeant Dawkins, Fowler's long-suffering girlfriend, and we were so lucky to be able to get Rudolph Walker as PC Gladstone, the philosophical old West Indian whose ambition in life was to take things easy.

I also featured the non-uniform detective side of the station. Once more, casting-wise we struck comic gold. As the wiseacre, jack-the-lad detective constable, I cast my old mate from *Silly Cow*, Kevin Allen. Mark Addy took over the role in the second series and they were both fantastic. The real triumph, however, was Detective Inspector Grim. This endlessly furious, massively deluded character was played by David Haig, truly one of Britain's finest actors. I invented a whole new language for Grim and gave him some of the best lines I think I've ever written. In fact, quite frankly, *the* best line.

If you mess this up, Fowler, it's me that'll get the blame. Your cock up. My arse.

From day one of rehearsals, it felt really good. Led by Row, the whole cast was on absolute fire. This was one occasion when my 'relentless pursuit of the one-line gag' was paying off, probably because I was pursuing character gags and plot gags, along with a degree of heart and soul that made the characters genuinely lovable.

We knew we were on to something and were approaching the live studios with nervous glee. In my case, there was also at least some trepidation because I knew Row. No studio recording with Row is ever what you'd call *easy*. His intensity and focus are absolute and I have to say a tiny bit joyless. He *looks* like he's hating every minute of it and I'm pretty sure that he is. This can rather confuse the audience and it certainly makes them nervous. Frankly, he scares them a bit, particularly if his very slight stutter kicks in. Row does sometimes take a moment to get a word out which he can deploy to great comic effect, but not if it takes too long. The audience laugh, of course – nervously, supportively – and then they laugh again. Slowly, they sense Row's anger (with himself not them, but they don't know that) and so they try to stop laughing. Then he'll do a perfect take to cowed silence.

That's okay. We can lift a laugh from an earlier take, which incidentally is the *only* 'canned' part of what otherwise is always an entirely honest and organic live audience track (and that's the case for all studio sitcoms I've ever known, whatever cynics might claim). However, the mood in the studio may not recover.

Row has another habit in studio, which was pretty maddening for Geoff and me. He's always kind of half outside the take, wondering if it's good enough. So if the opposite actor delivers a line he thinks is less than their best work, you can see him thinking 'Blimey, if they use that one, it isn't good enough.' We'd be in the control box watching this process going through his mind and knowing exactly what was coming next: Row would himself then blow the take to make sure it was unusable. But in the box, we *knew* we had a perfect take in the can from the other player from a few minutes before and it was only Row's reaction we were doing the bloody take for at all! I have to tell you that used to drive me and Geoff Perkins bonkers.

But Row's tendency towards professional agonizing aside, we wrapped all six episodes in a spirit of joy and good fellowship. The BBC adored it and commissioned a Christmas special before the show had even been broadcast. Sophie and I gave a drinks-and-nibbles do at our house on the night of the first broadcast and the whole cast came to watch. I remember making a speech afterwards saying 'Well, they might not all love it, but I can't see how anyone would *hate* it.'

Got that wrong.

The press reaction was universally vitriolic. Outraged contempt was heaped on the show and, as ever, most particularly on me. All the qualities which we had thought were the glory of the piece – its silly characters, its lack of cynicism, it's high gag count and its traditional production values – were used to beat it with a passion which I'm afraid I must insist was grotesquely disproportionate, even if it had been total shit. Which it really wasn't. The thing about a good joke is that, after the event, it appears simple, obvious even. I have spent my entire life being accused by critics of going for 'easy laughs'. Cheap laughs, even.

But the truth is that *genuinely* easy laughs are rarely proper funny, but proper *funny* laughs by their nature generally *look* easy, as if they were always waiting to be written.

The morning after the first broadcast of *TTBL* was absolutely horrible. Ever since *Silly Cow*, I've tried not to read reviews, but Geoff let me know the gist and I remember walking for hours on Hampstead Heath trying to manage my emotions which were a combination of righteous fury and mawkish, soul-sapping self-pity.

Rowan read them all.

That was where the damage was really done. I think his dedication and focus to his work made him think it was his duty, that perhaps there were lessons to be learned. But I'm afraid the only lesson to be learned was 'Don't fucking work with me because that's what you're going to get'.

Anyway, it turned out that the audience loved it. This was still in those halcyon days when bad press really was tomorrow's fish-and-chip wrappers. They could kill you in theatre but did infinitely less damage in TV. We were on BBC1 and one of only four channel choices. Some people might have been put off by the savagery of the criticism, but enough people were going to watch it anyway to give it a shot. And the shot turned out to be a bullseye. Our audience started big and then grew. *The Thin Blue Line* became, in numbers at least, by far the most successful TV show I ever did, peaking at a record-breaking thirteen and a half million viewers (far more than *Blackadder* ever got). So a lot of people loved it. I'm sure plenty of people didn't love it. But as far as I know, only about a dozen people actively *despised* it. Unfortunately, they all worked for national newspapers. I was starting to get vaguely used to this. Except, of course, you never do.

And despite our ratings success, that morning of hate had done its damage and that feeling of pure goodwill was never quite the same again. It never is after a true savaging. You never really fully recover, even if you succeed despite them.

We did two series and two Christmas specials of *TTBL* and the BBC were eager to go on for ever, but I'm afraid Row never quite got over that first morning. It worried him and I think really hurt his pride. It had never happened to him before and I don't think has since (fuck, I wish I could say the same thing). That's why you have to try not to read reviews. You can't let them live in your head rent-free. I really think Row only did the second series out of stubbornness and respect for me. He still loved the show but the joy had been bludgeoned out of it.

And for the record, once again we did get recognized abroad, winning both the audience *and* the jury awards for best comedy at the European Television Awards at Reims. And *TTBL* was regularly repeated for years on the various gold channels. Geoff always deeply regretted that we didn't do at least three series, if not more. With a piece like that, you have to really bed in. *Only Fools and Horses* was a hit after two series, but nothing like the colossus it became. It was in fact Geoff Perkins who brought *Only Fools and Horses* back, which was when it truly went stratospheric.

One day, I'd love to think Row might agree to do the third series. Sadly, if he does, Geoff Perkins won't be there to do it with us.

Mary Whitehouse loves me

It was 1995 and Sophie and I had been married for a year. We lived in England but visited Australia when we could and that summer had a couple of months back in WA. It was on this trip that I had what I think was one of my better ideas. I was chopping wood at our new property in Margaret River and it just dropped into my head. I don't recall having even been concentrating; the thought was just suddenly there, a whole concept in a single moment. I put down the axe and went for a stroll to try to fix it in my mind, working it through while circumnavigating our red dust firebreak, fringed with strange, many-mouthed banksia trees, sap-oozing red gums and ancient grass trees with their gnarled, knobbly, fire-blackened trunks topped with great fringes of spiky fronds, like skinny, black-clad, green-haired '80s rock stars. The bush was alive with noise: buzzing, chirping, chirruping and the sudden swish of unseen lizards (and snakes!) getting out of your way. It's a nice place to ponder, that's for sure – except when you thoughtlessly walk into a vast spider web stretched three metres across the fire break and have to disentangle yourself from the strong, sticky threads with half an eye on the furious-looking beastie at the centre.

So, my idea. I was excited. There had been a lot of 'designer' violence in the cinemas of late: bloody murder depicted as pop art, sadistic mayhem perpetrated by attractively hip people in a sardonic manner to a cutting-edge soundtrack. Quentin Tarantino was the most successful artist working in this genre with his ground-breaking *Reservoir Dogs* and then the smash hit *Pulp Fiction*. He had many impersonators; even a senior industry figure like Oliver Stone dipped his toe in the genre with *Natural Born Killers.*

Unsurprisingly, all this highly seductive screen violence had sparked a revival of the old copycat killing debate. Did movie violence provoke actual violence?

Leaving aside the deeply questionable relationship between cause and effect, the robust confidence of the anti-screen violence lobby struck me as presenting the most fascinating moral dilemmas. Because if, as many respected voices were saying, the movie-makers were responsible for crimes that they had not personally committed, did that mean that the *actual* perpetrators of the crime were innocent?

How's that for a moral and legal can of worms?

So I wandered around my 'block' – as they call a person's bit of land down south in WA – and started putting together a story. It concerned two witty, canny psychopaths (modelled loosely on Stone's hip killers in *NBK)* who take a famous movie director hostage in his home on the night he wins an Oscar for his super-violent flick *Ordinary Americans.* Their plan is to invite a news team into the siege and force the director to accept responsibility for their crimes on national TV. It all ends when, as the siege is about to be stormed on live TV with the inevitable bloodbath that must follow, my killer punk turns to the news camera and offers the millions watching a choice. He says that if they all stop watching and he sees the ratings fall on his monitor, then he and his accomplice will turn themselves in. If, however, the viewing millions continue to watch, then there will be a spectacular gun battle which will end with him killing everybody in the room including himself.

'Not a bad show, huh?' he says. 'And all you have to do to see it is keep on watching. Well? Are you gonna turn off your TVs?'

And there the story ends, leaving the audience considering the same question.

I pretty much had the bones of the whole thing down on that walk and, over the next few months (on breaks from *The Thin Blue Line*), I wrote it. In fact, I wrote it twice because I couldn't decide whether it was a play or a novel. It started off as a novel, but because I was writing some of the novel as a 'movie' – that is, with dialogue and stage directions – I began to wonder if it might make a better play, particularly as the action of the story moved into the director's house and became a tense claustrophobic siege. In the end, I wrote a novel and a play in tandem, side by side; a scene here, a chapter there. The novel has a lot more characters and a much broader canvas, although its core remains the siege. The play is just the siege. I'd written both play and novel before I settled on a title. I called them *Popcorn* because having failed to come up with any options which suitably summed up the theme, I opted for a vaguer more atmospheric title resonant of the movies and of popular culture. I wasn't entirely happy with it then and I'm still not but, it's too late to change it now.

I took the play to Stephen Daldry at the Royal Court.

I've tried a few times in my life to get the gatekeepers of the great subsidized centres of so-called theatrical excellence to take an interest in me. This was one of them. I've also had a couple of goes at the National Theatre, with the idea that, maybe with their help, I might have something to offer them as a writer, but I've never got anywhere. One time, a few years ago, I got a meeting with the then director of the NT and he said 'But you're so successful. Why would you want to come to us?' I had a hundred reasons why it would be a dream come true to work with the National on developing new writing. What was very clear, though, was that he could think of zero reasons why the National would want to develop a play with me.

Anyway, Stephen Daldry was very nice about *Popcorn*, but he said he had another project with a lot of violence and swearing in it (I think it was a play called *Shopping and Fucking*) and he didn't feel he could do two, so thanks but no thanks.

It was a big disappointment. I really thought I was on to something and I would have absolutely loved to have developed *Popcorn* at the Royal Court, but it wasn't to be.

As ever, it looked like Phil and I would have to row our own boat, which meant finding a director. I didn't want to do it myself; I could see that it would be a very good thing to bring a whole new perspective to such a challenging project – which, of course, was why I'd taken it to Daldry.

I didn't know a lot of theatre directors, but there was one I knew and liked: Laurence Boswell, who'd been a year below me at university. He'd done a production of Steven Berkoff's *East* in the Stephen Joseph Studio that had really stunned me and we'd been sort of mates ever since. Laurence did a great job with *Popcorn*, not least in casting Paddy O'Kane and Dena Davis as the brilliant leads. Phil managed to get the Apollo on Shaftesbury Avenue and Laurence's production turned into a big hit. It ran for eighteen months and won me an Olivier Award for best comedy.

Popcorn the play has proved an enduring success and has been performed all over the world. Particularly exciting was a French-language production which ran for a year in Paris and was nominated for seven Molière Awards (their Oliviers). Phil and I went over for the ceremony, which was hugely glamorous and ridiculously French. The audience were all beautiful and sophisticated, while the hosts were two gurning, wrinkled old clowns who were dressed as tramps. There was much pushing and mugging and at one point they brought a live donkey onto the stage to present an award. Euro comedy is a different world.

Popcorn didn't actually win anything, but it was great to be nominated and I had a very exciting champagne-drenched night with our glamorously French cast feeling very glad that I wasn't a French comic.

Meanwhile, there was *Popcorn* the novel, which actually came first and which was also a big success. I remember it reached number one in the bestsellers chart during the first week of work on series two of the *The Thin Blue Line* and Rowan led a round of applause. The book actually remained at number one for the whole six weeks of rehearsal and production, but Row politely declined my suggestion that I should have a round of applause *every* week. The novel also won the British Crime Writers' Association Gold Dagger Award for Crime Writer of the Year. I never expected to win one of those. I was on tour when they had their awards dinner, so Sophie went with a friend to collect it – a lovely award in the shape of a dagger and also a case of Macallan, one of my favourite whiskies. They know how to do things, those crime writers. *Popcorn* also won the Swedish Kaliber Award for International Crime Novel. This was in the form of a mounted shotgun cartridge. Not as elegant as a dagger, I think.

Something very interesting happened to that novel on its way to number one. It became briefly a *cause célèbre* for some of the more conservative members of the press and establishment. This was because it was seen as an attack on screen violence. It wasn't any such thing, although it did definitely debate the responsibilities of artists who sexualize and glamourize violence. The 'anti-smut' campaigner Mary Whitehouse was said to have expressed her support for me (because she was *told* that I'd 'attacked' screen violence; she hadn't read the book and did not claim to have done). For a year or two after that, I had to deal with every interviewer saying 'So, Mary Whitehouse is a fan of yours. How do you feel about that?' as if she was sat at home watching old vids of *The Young Ones*.

The most surprising and one of the most exciting developments of this misunderstanding was that it led *Evening Standard* editor Max Hastings to read the book and get very excited about it. He made *Popcorn* the subject of an editorial headed 'The Importance of Elton'. An editorial in the *Standard*! For a novel! I was completely astonished.

In fact, for a little while, it really looked like *Popcorn* was going to be the thing that got me away from the sparkly-suit Ben and would allow me to be viewed as a proper writer. Believe it or not, the novel was long listed for the Booker Prize. Sadly, I didn't make the final shortlist. Gosh, I would have loved that. I was told afterwards (by a member of the panel) that the novelist A.S. Byatt, who was also on the judging panel, had pronounced that if such 'populist' fare was on the shortlist, she would resign. It was another depressing example of those self-appointed arbiters of taste who confuse the word popul*ist* with popular.

1996 to 1999

Failing towards America again. First, Nicolas Cage stops me in my tracks, then a Black Hawk brings me down

Popcorn was nearly my break in America. Twice.

One day I got a call from Joel Schumacher's office. Joel died a few years ago, but back in the late '90s, he was a very famous and successful Hollywood director. He'd had huge hits with *St Elmo's Fire*, *Falling Down* and *Batman Forever*, and he wanted to option *Popcorn*. He had no idea who I was, but he'd come across the novel at a Heathrow bookshop and now he wanted to make a movie.

Pretty exciting, right? This was in the days before I realized that every major movie player – be they producer, director or star – has a number of projects in development, all of which they want to make but only some of which they do. Nonetheless, Joel's enthusiasm was very real and, for a while, I think we both thought this film would happen. We met up first in London and got on so well that Joel pitched my novel (with me as screenwriter; his choice not mine) to the big studio with whom he had a production deal. The next thing was the studio wanted to fly me to Hollywood for further development discussions.

Brilliant! So exciting. That's a thrill you never get over.

I took Joel a present. We'd already discovered a mutual fascination with Winston Churchill and I gave him one of my treasured possessions, a first edition of the two-volume *The World Crisis*, Churchill's history of the First World War. Even though the movie never got made, I'm glad I made that gesture because I could see how much he appreciated it.

313

We had a couple of great meetings in LA. Joel was the most tremendous company, waspish in a jolly, highly camp LA way, but also clever and kind, at least he was in my experience. The thing I remember best about our chats was his hilarious summation of the Oscar nomination process as it was back then. You have to imagine him leaning back on one of his vast couches in his exquisite home (with armed security at the gate), drink in hand, like I imagine a kind of less pompous, more impish Gore Vidal might be. Screamingly camp and also massively erudite.

'Oh *please*. You Brits with your dusty little period-piece movies. You think we vote for them because we *like* them? Because we think they're *the best*? Give me a *break*. We vote for them because we *don't fucking care* if they win! Because they are *no threat*. This is a *movie* town. Everybody in this town is filled with hatred and jealousy for *everyone* else. All we care about is that none of our fucking *rivals* win. I make hit movies–' (he pronounced it moofiz) '–in a town that makes hit moofiz. I do *not* want my fucking competition to win an Oscar and they don't want me to. Brits in costume with upper-class accents are *not* my competition, okay? Don't you *get it*? You guys win because you're not important enough to vote against. Mind you, I *love* Emma Thompson. She *so* deserved it. Oh my God, I can't believe you *know* her! Tell me she's as lovely as she seems, *please*.'

For years after that, every time another British costume drama won, I thought back to Joel. Obviously, I'm not saying those movies didn't deserve it; who knows what deserves a prize? I'm just reporting what Joel said. These days, it seems almost quaint that such a dusty old habit even existed. The idea of all-white eulogies to upper-class lives – and colonialism in general – ever winning again seems pretty unlikely, particularly now Harvey Weinstein has stopped funding them.

Anyway, as I worked on various drafts of my *Popcorn* screenplay, it really looked like I might finally be getting somewhere in America.

Then Nicolas Cage ruined everything.

I'd known that Joel had other projects in development, of course. There was one in particular he had talked about called *8mm*. He'd told me it was a small movie and he had it in mind to do after *Popcorn*.

Then one day I got a call.

'Ben, Ben, *Ben*. I have good news and I have bad news. I'll get the bad news done right off because I love you so much. Okay, I can't make your *moofie*. The thing is Nicolas Cage read *8mm* and he wants to do it, which means now it's not a small moofie. It's a big moofie because Cage just won an Oscar and you do know that I can't walk away from an Oscar winner, don't you?'

He was right, of course. In movies, casting is everything. If you can attach a name to a project, then it gets made and Joel had attached Nicolas Cage to his, thus turning on a big green light.

'Maybe we can revisit *Popcorn* later,' Joel went on, 'but right now you need to get on with your life.'

In a way, it was good of him to be so brutal. He could have kept me hanging on, but he knew that, two years down the track, he'd have numerous other things he wanted to make. Souffles never rise twice and, once you get moved to the back burner, you have basically fallen off the whole cooker and down into the murky grease and crumbs behind where no one ever goes.

Well, I've never been one to cry about setbacks, so I was about to say thanks and goodbye when I remembered something.

'Hey, Joel? What was the good news?'

'What? Oh, didn't I say? I *think* I said. That I still *love* you, of course. Unless you wanna to *divorce me*.'

That's what he said and that last line is verbatim. I can hear it now in my mind and no doubt always will with that camp lisping lilt: 'unless you wanna *divorth me*'.

I will say that it's testimony to the fun we had that Joel rang me himself to kiss me off. That's not so common, you know. Usually the phone simply stops ringing. I really think I was close on that one. Bugger Nicolas Cage.

But *Popcorn's* movie prospects weren't dead yet. An even bigger name was about to enter the picture. The following year, I got a call from Ridley Scott! Yes, he of *Alien*, *Blade Runner*, *Thelma and Louise* and the about-to-be-released *Gladiator*. Ridley owned Shepperton Studios, where I was working on my own film *Maybe Baby*, and one lunchtime he invited me over to his office for a cuppa. Ridley is exactly what you'd expect by the way: a tough, grizzled, whisky-drinking, cigar-smoking. working-class man's man – quite scary but with buckets of charm and a real twinkle in his eye. He and Russell Crowe working together must have been like two poetically inclined bears having a man-off. Ridley worked his way up from an army background in South Shields to become one of the most successful directors in Hollywood. And he wanted to meet!

Surprisingly, what Ridley actually wanted to talk about was a light romantic comic movie he was planning to make about an English wine-maker in France (it eventually became *A Good Year* and starred Russell Crowe). At that point, Ridley was thinking about asking me to write it. It probably would have been best if I'd focused on that, but Ridley's right-hand lady had read *Popcorn* and I bounced off her enthusiasm to pitch the project to Ridley. He went off and read the book and loved it. Suddenly, having been dumped by Joel, I was in development with Ridley.

This was big stuff indeed. And, like all the other chances, it was good until it wasn't. We met in London and then he flew me out to spend a week in Italy with him where he was location spotting for *Hannibal*, the sequel to *Silence of the Lambs*. Hanging out with Ridley in Italy. Pretty cool, eh? In fact, to be honest, I didn't see a lot of him. Well, how could I? He was working on another movie. Having said that, things seemed to be moving along. After the Italy trip, I wrote maybe three drafts of a screen-play, working off great notes which he gave at long range. We seemed to be getting close.

Then I became a victim of another Oscar-winning success, in this case Ridley's own. He had been huge for decades, but the release of *Gladiator* in 2000 put him back at the absolute top of the pile, which led directly to him deciding to accept the mega-budget *Black Hawk Down*, right in the period he'd pencilled for *Popcorn*. It's just the way the game goes. Ridley and I never formally called it a day; the phone just stopped ringing. Of course, by this time it had been six years since *Pulp Fiction*, so the whole subject was beginning to feel a little tired anyway.

The rather frustrating story has an equally frustrating sequel – a true tale of Hollywood woe in which I lost the movie rights to my own novel.

I just gave them away.

That's right. When Ridley decided to do *Popcorn*, he was locked into a picture deal with Warners and, in order for us to proceed, Warners had to quickly acquire the rights. Obviously, I was not going to cause any delays to what was just about the biggest break of my career, so I just told Phil to hand them over. A quick contract was drawn up which contained no 'turn around' clause. These are the clauses that cause a project to revert to the original owner if, after a certain time, no movie is made. They are in every single rights contract. Except mine.

Warners took the rights and *they've still got them.*

Ridley has been off the project for nearly twenty-five years and his Warner deal is ancient history.

Nobody who was around at Warners then is around now.

Nobody who is around at Warners now has ever heard of me or *Popcorn.* But they still own it.

A few years ago, a French movie-maker wanted to make the *Popcorn* movie. We met twice in London and once in Paris and he actually paid me a decent amount of money for my commitment, even though we explained that we didn't have the rights. He wasted his money because, despite trying, we couldn't get them back. I offered to pay and asked Warners to name a price for this thing that had cost them nothing and which had been gathering dust for many years.

Absolutely no interest.

It's not that anybody at Warners has any intention of making the movie. Or reading the book. Or the various ancient and dusty drafts that I wrote for Ridley either. The reason they won't give the rights up is because of Hollywood's paranoid 'dog in the manger' mentality. Supposing the current head of acquisitions let it go and somebody else made it *and it was a hit*? Then the person who let the project go would be finished in the industry. That's why I can't get my story back.

It's a tough game this biz called show.

Me and the Spice Girls

I hosted the BRIT Awards twice – in '97 and '98.

From where I sit now, it seems almost impossible to imagine that I was ever that hip. The choice of BRITs host used to be a very big thing and, in

'97, it was of particular media interest because that year marked the end of Chris Evans' era-defining turn. Chris had really made the Brit Awards the massive deal that it was during the glorious decade when it genuinely held the nation's focus, before the internet started spreading everybody's attention so thinly.

And I was chosen to follow him, which is something I'm pretty proud of. I'm certainly the only novelist who's ever hosted the BRITs. Also the only playwright. And the only sitcom writer, librettist or movie director.

What a great gig! You know already how much I love pop music and here I was, slap-bang in the middle of it. And what a year to start! It was the year of the Spice Girls. It's extremely hard now to give people any idea of just how huge the Spice Girls were in the spring of '97. They'd broken through the previous autumn with their wonderfully catchy debut 'Wannabe' and, in a few short months, had become a genuine global phenomenon. They were in the papers *every single day*. All the papers, all over the world. *Everybody* was interested in them, from kids to grannies. They were just such a fun breath of fresh air. Beatles comparisons are *always* ridiculous, but in their cross-generational 'everyman' appeal, the Spice Girls did have a tiny touch of the community-unifying magic of the four and only Fabs.

When I met the five girls at rehearsal, they were as open and fun and entirely without affectation as they always appeared to be. They said that they would make me an honorary Spice Girl and we decided my name should be Farty Spice, in honour of my ongoing campaign against people trying to be cool. They themselves were never 'cool' and they knew it. They were far too much fun for that.

Introducing them later that evening was an amazing feeling. The arena was going berserk and my main fear was blanking on one of their famous nicknames. There was no autocue and it would have been so awful. Fortunately, I got it right. 'Sporty, Ginger, Scary, Baby and Posh – the fabulous Spice Girls!'

I was the last thing the world saw before Geri strutted forward in her Union Jack micro-dress and big boots, instantly becoming the defining image of an era and making the front page of just about every newspaper in the world.

The whole brilliant night is a bit of a blur, but I must have done okay because they invited me back the following year. The Spice Girls were on again doing 'Stop', draped all over five Mini Coopers. They were still the biggest thing on the show and almost as exciting as in '97. Not long after that, they went on tour and Sophie and I went to see them with Jennifer and Ade and their three young daughters (all of whom we are very close to). Everything seemed great with the band and, at the drinks party afterwards, Geri gave me her mobile number.

'Ring me when we finish the arena tour. I want to talk to you about something.'

What she wanted to talk about was a Spice Girl sitcom. They'd just made their movie and Geri said that they wanted me to write them a sitcom. They'd need it fast because they wanted to make it between their current arena tour and their planned stadium tour.

Great. Fast is what I do.

It might have been quite exciting. I think all the girls would have been fantastic in a madcap weekly comedy. But it wasn't to be. A couple of days later, I turned on the news and the top story was that Geri had left the Spice Girls.

Weird, eh? From planning the next two years to leaving the band within forty-eight hours. That's rock'n'roll, eh? Having been able to observe the girls a bit, I have an idea of what I think was the emotional impetus for this sudden crisis in pop. But I ain't saying. Sorry.

Blasts from the past (a novel and also a legendary comedian)

In 1996 I changed my publisher. That's a big thing for a novelist and it wasn't easy. I'm a very loyal person and I always end up being friends with the people I work with. Nick Webb who published my first four books was a good man and a good editor – we parted ways with sadness but as friends, and I went to Larry Finlay at Transworld. Larry and I forged a great partnership and worked on twelve novels together.

The first novel I produced for Larry was called *Blast from the Past* about a US Air Force general who is going to run for the Republican nomination as an arch conservative and who, years before, had had a relationship with a young anti-American peace protester at Greenham Common (yes, shades of that old idea I'd had back in the '80s) and needs to prevent this ever coming out – by any means!

Blast was also the novel in which I addressed my own experience of being stalked. It seemed to strike a chord because it went to number one and, as with *Popcorn*, I also wrote a play which took place entirely in the attic bedsit of the woman whom my ruthless presidential candidate needs to silence. It was presented at West Yorkshire Playhouse. Imogen Stubbs played the ex-Greenham girl at the centre of the web of intrigue and gave a truly mesmerizing performance. My favourite memory was doing an audience Q&A one night. Among the many Leeds voices came a rich deep American one. A big middle-aged guy introduced himself as – guess what? – a real US Air Force general who'd been a young man at Greenham! He politely corrected a couple of points of minor military detail and then said 'I don't agree with your politics, sir, but I sure loved the hell out of your play.'

Through '97 and '98 I was as busy as ever – quite a number of gigs, *Blast* in Leeds, a book tour, recasting *Popcorn* etc. Also that year, I did what was to prove to be my last TV series as a solo performer. It was basically another series of *The Man From Auntie*, but since Geoff Perkins couldn't do it, we changed the name to *The Ben Elton Show*. It was a boring name but I liked it because it reminded me of my love of '70s light entertainment. They used to call the shows after the stars in those days and I loved being part of a BBC1 light entertainment tradition.

The Ben Elton Show was, once again, mainly stand-up with some sketches. This time, however, I had a musical act each week. My idea was to get bands to cover stuff they weren't associated with. Boy George did a searing 'Suffragette City' and, as a big Clash fan, I asked Kylie to cover 'Should I Stay or Should I Go' which, for a while, became a staple of her live act. Quite cool, don't you think? Not everybody gets to put a song into Kylie's setlist. Sophie played bass in the hot band music maestro Simon Brint assembled to back all our fab guest stars.

I also had a regular guest star: entertainment legend Ronnie Corbett. This was a little dream project of mine which, to my delight, found favour with its subject. My friend Paul Jackson knew Ronnie C from his days producing *The Two Ronnies* and arranged a meeting for us. Ronnie wanted tea at Claridge's and, over the cakes and sandwiches, I asked if he'd revive his famous 'chair' monologues for my show. Now, with the passing of time, Ronnie quite rightly achieved the legend status he deserves, but back in '98, he was still in that period post-major success where you are seriously out of fashion (tell me about it!). Ronnie Barker had retired and Ronnie Corbett didn't really have a gig.

Ronnie and I got on very well at our Claridge's tea and he agreed to do the show, which I took as the most tremendous honour.

'No, *no*, Ben. The honour is all mine,' Ronnie said with a twinkle while slathering clotted cream on a scone as if his forty years in showbiz had been but a preparation for this hour. I knew he was teasing me, but it was very friendly teasing.

And he was in! What was more was that I even got to write some of his monologues. Imagine that? The square-eyed '70s teenage TV comedy fanatic was *writing* Ronnie Corbett's chair pieces! If only my gran could have seen that. Ronnie loved the material I gave him and later admitted to me that he'd put some of it into his after-dinner speaker routine. He loved the little family I invented for him – his daughter Kylie and granddaughter Beyoncé. I'm also thrilled to report I may have given him the first Viagra gag ever delivered on the TV: 'at least now when I do the washing-up, I've something to hang the tea towel on'.

We got quite close actually and Sophie and I, and Ronnie and his wife Anne, had dinner together a number of times. I remember once we went to a party at their Croydon home, which was a really wonderful old showbiz occasion. Ronnie and Joy Barker were there, along with Danny La Rue and Jimmy Tarbuck. They all entertained round the piano; Tarby really knows how to work a room. Harry Hill was also there and Tarby invited us to get up too, but neither of us had the guts to have a go in such legendary showbiz company.

There was another regular guest slot on *The Ben Elton Show*, which, as with Ronnie C, was about me being a fan. One of my favourite Australian acts of all time is Roy and HG, two loud and opinionated characters who became an Australian comedy institution with their frank and fearless improvisations at various sporting events, riffing off each other into spiralling peaks of insane logic. They are much-loved in Australia and I had hoped that perhaps my show might break them in Britain, but sadly the three-minute slot didn't give time for a new audience to pick up on their unique rhythm and slow-build to outrage. It was a great shame as Roy and HG are true originals.

That TV series was bigger than either of the *Auntie* series had been, getting between six and eight million viewers. Nonetheless, the clock was ticking for me. Pretty soon I would find the door at Television Centre firmly closed to me as a stand-up and it's remained so ever since. Fair enough. I had an amazing run.

IVF gets me a stand-up routine, a book and a movie. Oh yes, and twins

After we got married, Sophie and I bought a house in Primrose Hill, a beautiful family home in a beautiful area. Now it just needed the family. One of the reasons Primrose Hill is so popular is there's no through traffic, which is almost unique in London. The arteries go around the edge leaving a real little village in the middle. It's great for kids and, for the adult in you, dirty, sweaty, rock'n'roll Camden is just over the canal. So the two of us moved into this four-bedroom house and we confidently expected it would soon be home to the children that Sophie had always wanted and I now wanted because she wanted them.

It was to be rather a long wait. They say that 90 per cent of couples trying for a baby conceive within a year and that 90 per cent of the remaining 10 per cent conceive in the second year. That means by the time you get to year three, you are either very unlucky or you have a problem.

We started doing the tests and nothing showed up, but that's pretty normal. It's called 'nonspecific infertility', which really doesn't help much.

Of course, the whole infertility process is much more horribly intrusive for the woman than a man, so I'm not going to dwell much on it here. Save to say that it's not much fun. Having to masturbate in a municipal building does count as one of the worst social experiences of my life. You sit in a grim waiting room, along with a bunch of other wankers (literally), avoiding each other's eye. Your name gets called and you are summoned to the nurse at a desk who gives you a little pot and sends you into the wanking room. Of course, once you're in there, you know that all the blokes in the queue are sitting there thinking 'Come ON! For fuck's sake! How long does it take to knock one out?' just as you had been thinking yourself moments before. It's intimidating, I can tell you, and stroking up a fat (as we say in Australia) is not easy under those circumstances. The NHS were thoughtful enough to leave a couple of items of what they politely called 'reading material' in the wank chamber. I'm not sure that ancient dog-eared copies of *Penthouse*, with all the relevant pages stuck together, helped much but it was a kind thought. Eventually, you eke one out on a semi, emerge sheepishly, trying to make your body language say 'Sorry I took so long' and then deliver your little pot with its pathetic, sad-looking deposit in it to the nurse at the desk. I'm sure she didn't actually sneer, but it's hard not to presume that all the other blokes' pots were overflowing.

On our third attempt, we went private and they had a different system, which allowed me to wank at home as long as I got the sperm back before it died (about an hour apparently). It had to be kept warm and the clinic's advice was to keep the pot down the back of your pants between your bum cheeks.

I explored these experiences and other sperm- and egg-related fertility comedy at length on my 1998 stand-up tour. Well, what was I to do? Even if we didn't end up conceiving, at least I'd got a shedload of nob gags out of it.

We did our first two rounds of IVF in the very public sector. I don't deny I was expecting to be front-paged (or at least page seven'd) with a 'We always said he was a wanker'-type headline. I wouldn't have minded, a small price to pay. But it never happened. I imagine that this is because I don't think, in the whole history of municipal masturbation, anybody had ever met anybody else's eye.

Besides the stand-up gear, I also started thinking about an IVF novel.

I wanted to get beyond the broad comedy (yes, I know that seems out of character) and put down something of what I and Sophie were really thinking and feeling during a period which, levity aside, was quite an emotionally challenging time. I wanted to make the case that having children is not *necessarily* a prerequisite for happiness or for a successful marriage. At the time, it seemed very possible that we might never have children and I believed that while a couple wanting children and not getting them is sad, that doesn't make *them* sad or their relationship a failure. I think this (obvious) fact is much better understood these days than it was twenty-five years ago. So many more couples choose not to have children now that the phrase 'childless couple' (which inherently suggests something's missing) is much less common. Some couples without children choose not to have them; some simply can't. Either way, their relationship is every bit as valid as a couple with a family.

I called the novel *Inconceivable*, which was a slightly better title than its punning nature suggests because it was about creative fertility as well as physical fertility. In the story, the husband, who is a writer, is suffering from terrible writer's block. That is, until it occurs to him to turn the IVF experience he is going through with his wife into a screenplay. Unfortunately for him, when he tells his wife his plan, she absolutely bans him from using their private sorrow (and physical intimacy) as source material for a comedy. But he can't stop himself and begins to write in secret, leading to professional success and massive personal failure. A lot of interviewers asked me if this was based on truth: had Sophie objected to my writing the novel? Well, obviously not. Firstly, I don't tend to suffer from writer's block and, secondly, if Sophie had objected, of course I wouldn't have done it. But, in fact, Sophie was perfectly happy that I fictionalized our experience. She said at the time that she thought it might actually be helpful to other couples going through the same thing as us because it normalized it, as well as allowing for a bit of humour instead of the tones of empathetic sadness which people used to adopt when talking about our fertility 'struggle'. And so it was to prove. I have had many letters over the years from people who have experienced IVF thanking me for that book, which is a lovely thing.

We did two cycles of IVF in '98. My diary is filled with entries like 'deliver sperm', 'Sophie starts arse injections' (which I had to administer by the way, a horribly nerve-wracking experience) and 'eggs harvested'. Both cycles failed, which was pretty sad. Fertilized eggs were reinstated but did not make the grade. We made the mistake of investing emotionally on the first occasion – you know, naming it and all that. The second time around we knew better.

I am not a remotely superstitious person and I am pretty immune to all invitations to spirituality, but Sophie is more normal in that respect. She worries about stuff she thinks is bad luck (hats on beds, for instance – weird, arbitrary shit like that) and I'll occasionally see her spitting over her left shoulder to recorrect the balance of her fortune. It's complete bollocks if you ask me, but Sophie, while far from being a dippy hippy, was happy to take what help she could get. Barbara Mayall was very big on the positive energy of crystals and she had Sophie gripping one in earnest. Sophie's family have always had friends among the indigenous community and hold traditional Aboriginal culture and spiritual life in great respect. So Sophie and her mum Kate decided to visit a women-only cave in Western Australia. I can't tell you what they did there because, as a man, I cannot be party to that knowledge, but I think they just mainly thought positive thoughts! One rather more comical effort she and her mum made at spiritual fertility treatment concerned the apparent convergence of ley lines on Primrose Hill. I don't really know what a ley line is supposed to be or why various of them are said to cross in this particular bit of north-west London, but Sophie was always threatening to make me sally forth in the middle of the night and do the business with her on top of one. She never took it that far, but one slightly drizzly, chilly autumn night, she and her mum ascended the hill and did a dance for the Druids. I think wine may have been involved. Basically, I think she was trying anything and it wasn't much weirder than her having to drop her knickers while I hovered behind her ready to stab her in the arse with a hypodermic needle full of God knows what.

One way or another (and I'm pretty clear it was the scientific way), things turned out okay in the end because by the time *Inconceivable* was published in 1999, we had conceived our twins on the third cycle of IVF. This time they'd 'taken' and were on their way.

Two kids and a movie

The novel was a success and being me, of course, I'd already turned it into a screenplay – not so much an adaptation, more of a parallel project like with *Popcorn*. I thought that the whole story was perfect for a little British romcom with a bit of extra edge.

Movies are incredibly difficult things to fund and getting *Maybe Baby* (as I called the screenplay) financed was no exception – although in fact, while it seemed like a very tough slog at the time, Phil performed a miracle and we got from first draft to first day of shooting in under two years.

It might have been even quicker if I hadn't decided very firmly on who I wanted for the male lead. I'd written the whole script with Hugh Laurie in mind and I was certain he'd be brilliant. The thing is, you don't cast a movie before you try to get it funded because the first thing any movie-funder will want to do is discuss the casting. It's their favourite game and I've witnessed it many times, a series of wonderful fantasy meetings where people say things like 'We have a contact at Fox who can certainly get this across Clooney's desk. Apparently he loves working in the UK' or 'I believe Meryl Streep is looking for a low-budget British comedy by a first-time writer she's never heard of'. The discussions tend to get more realistic quite quickly, but casting remains crucial. It is the key to whether your movie will be made. From day one, the only thing anybody *ever* wants to know is who's in it.

And what they didn't want to hear was Hugh Laurie.

Nobody wanted to develop a movie with him attached as romantic lead. Funny, eh? These days, he's a mega star, a massive name in the US. He's hosted *Saturday Night Live* several times, conducted prestigious acting masterclasses on American arts channels and has a stack of A-list scripts on his desk that reaches the ceiling. These days, everybody knows that Hugh is a sexy, charismatic, intense and masculine screen presence whom the ladies die for. After his massive success in *House* he was voted sexiest TV doctor *ever* in the US.

Oh yes. We all know he's a leading man *now*.

But back in 1998, it was rather different. Phil had got me a development deal with Fine Line Cinema, a big important company. They liked the script and they were very happy for me to be a first-time director, but they didn't want Hugh. I remember Ileen Maisel, their head of development, shouting at me: 'He's not sexy, okay? He's a TV comedian! He is *not* a fucking movie leading man.'

Fine Line made it very clear that they could not raise the budget required with Hugh in the lead and that I needed to embrace looking elsewhere. I wouldn't. I knew Hugh would be brilliant – intense and moving and sexy and most important of all, very, very funny. So that was it. I had a script and a leading man but no movie.

The whole thing was in imminent danger of fading away when Phil worked a miracle. I still don't know how he did it, but he eventually found funding in Paris with some sort of sub division of Pathé. Out of the blue the movie was funded, modestly at £3,500,000, but definitely enough.

And suddenly I was a movie director in pre-production!

As leading lady, we were fortunate to cast Joely Richardson. She really loved the part and that shone through at the read she did with Hugh. Joely told me afterwards that, on the walk home, she'd been skipping with excitement and jumping up and high-fiving leaves on branches of trees.

And what a cast we assembled for all the other roles! Emma agreed to do a small part as a crystal-waving hippy guru, while Rowan played an insensitive gynaecologist (the scene where he assembles his equipment before Joely's horrified eyes is still a YouTube hit). Joanna Lumley played Joely's boss and Matthew Macfadyen played Hugh's. Adrian Lester was Hugh's best mate, James Purefoy played the handsome actor who nearly seduces Joely, Dawn played the IVF nurse and Tom Hollander played the crazed Scottish film director who takes on Hugh's script. Adrian, Matthew, James and Tom were not well known at all then, but have, of course, since become massively successful and respected actors. I take some pride in the fact that I gave them all some of their earliest big movie roles. In Matthew's case, it was his very first. Blimey, look at him now!

Because the film was always going to be 'about IVF', I wanted it to look beautiful and fun and also sexy. I was definitely going for a light romantic comedy feel as part of my ongoing commitment to not feeding the myth that infertility was irredeemably grim and draining (it pretty much is but that doesn't mean the people going through it also have to be).

The film was brilliantly produced by Phil and Lucy Ansboro and it was a very happy unit. Paul McCartney even recorded the title track for me (well, he did own Buddy Holly's publishing) and it was produced by Jeff Lynne, which was something of a thrill to say the least. The portents for the movie were very good. When we previewed it in the UK, the scores were really strong, getting 75 per cent and above on the audience reaction cards, which are numbers that generally translate into a hit. I remember a wonderful night after a screening in Leeds when our French producer's stat-cruncher looked up from his calculations and said that we were perfectly placed for success. Neither Phil nor I were stupid enough to expect good reviews, but I did make the mistake I'd made on *The Thin Blue Line* five years earlier and imagined that the film was so goodhearted and fun that nobody could actually hate it!

I must stop making that mistake.

The critics really, truly, deeply hated it. And as with *The Thin Blue Line* there was an element of furious irritation, kind of like 'For God's sake, can Ben Elton *please* just fuck off'. Poor old Phil got it in the neck too this time. He'd produced two movies that year (an extraordinary achievement); the other one was Rik and Ade's *Guest House Paradiso*, which had also been savaged. The general tone was the same one that Michael Coveny had struck when reviewing *Silly Cow* in *The Observer* ten years before – that we should pack up our tawdry Punch and Judy show and get the hell out of the elevated world of British film and theatre arts.

There was one positive review for *Maybe Baby* – from Barry Norman, a film critic of such authority that, back in the '70s, it would have been enough to change the direction of our fortunes. But, sadly, Barry Norman was not the force he had been and was no longer at the helm of his once-mighty BBC movie review show. The BBC had dropped him in favour of Jonathan Ross as their sole movie critic and presenter of their venerable and hitherto highly respected film review show.

And Jonathan gave my movie a nationally televized stinker. In fact, so dismissive was he that you might not have thought he could get any meaner, but a month or two later, when presenting the dispiriting, drunken

Above: With Rik during our Ibiza stand-up season in 1986. This is how I like to remember him – he did so love to laugh.

Solo tour in 1987, seven sold-out nights at the Hammersmith Odeon. I had absolutely no real understanding of how big I'd suddenly got. Still just trying to keep one syllable ahead of the gong.

'My name's Ben Elton. Goodnight!'

Above: The 1987 election campaign with Red Wedge and Neil and Glenys Kinnock. Red Wedge was a bit crap quite frankly, but Neil and Glenys were an inspiring political powerhouse – a beacon of decency in a dirty game. That's Robbie at the back, by the way.

Left: Hosting *Saturday Live* in 1987. This is my second 'sparkly suit'. The first one was stolen from a dressing room. Fortunately in the 1980s shiny suits were easily found. I called it my Sizewell B suit 'cos I did a gig near the nuclear plant and it's been glowing ever since'. Little bit of politics.

Right: At the launch of *Stark*, my debut novel. Billionaires in private space rockets escaping a planet they've helped to devastate felt like science fiction in 1989.

Below: With Ken and Em after a long day filming *Much Ado About Nothing* in Italy. That summer of '92 felt as golden as the movie Ken made.

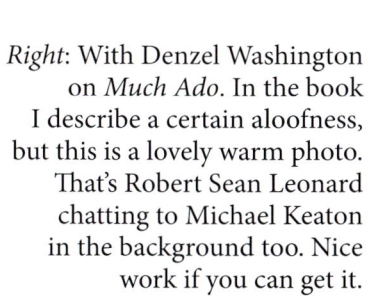

Right: With Denzel Washington on *Much Ado*. In the book I describe a certain aloofness, but this is a lovely warm photo. That's Robert Sean Leonard chatting to Michael Keaton in the background too. Nice work if you can get it.

Sophie and me on our wedding day in 1994.
Best day of my life.

A very special night in 1994. George and Olivia Harrison come for dinner at ours. Harry and Ade and Jen came too. Note The Beatles figures behind George's head.

'Yes. It needs work.' Mid-90s at my flat, and another grim script-marking session with Rowan, this time working on *The Thin Blue Line*.

Farty Spice. My second Brits-hosting gig in 1998.
Tough job, but somebody's gotta do it.

Me and Tony at a Labour do in '98.
A superstar at his absolute zenith.
Him not me, obvs.

1998. Me and Andrew enjoying the
media reaction to the announcement
of our collaboration on a musical.

1999. Emma and Hugh were staying with us for a combined fortieth birthday family celebration weekend (me, Em and Hugh were born only weeks apart).
Both Sophie and Em were pregnant at the time.

At Hugh's for his fiftieth. We decided to recreate our old *Saturday Live* photo together. It looks like I'm having a flashback to the bowel-clenching trepidation of twenty-five years before.

I'm with the band. One of many *WWRY* script sessions with Brian and Roger,
going through my work (2001 to present). Roger is looking a bit fierce,
but I'm sure it all got sorted out over dinner.

In studio for the first *Upstart Crow* Christmas special with Gareth Edwards (producer)
and Richard Boden (director). I think it's my best work for television, and working with
David was an unalloyed joy. Emma graced our first Christmas special as Elizabeth I.
What a studio night that was.

hooligan fest that was the god-awful British Comedy Awards in the '90s (again, nationally televised) he described it as *the worst British movie ever made*. Wow. Why don't you tell us what you *really* think, mate?

I will never forget the utter horror and amazement of our French producers from Pathé. On the morning after the onslaught, we sat together in a cafe in Soho and one of them was actually crying. 'Why?' they asked. It seemed like a reasonable question, even if the movie had been shit, the kind of offended fury of the notices was out of proportion. 'It's a British movie,' the Frenchman said. 'These are British newspapers. Why are they doing this?'

I thought about trying to explain about the long shadow of the bloke in the sparkly suit, but I didn't bother. What was the point? Hosting those comedy awards, Jonathan Ross (I'm afraid he had a bit of a thing about me) made a public appeal to me to throw away my typewriter to give everyone a relief.

I am aware of what you might be thinking by the way.

Same as you may have thought with *Filthy Rich*, *Silly Cow* and *The Thin Blue Line*.

Maybe it *was* shit. Did I ever think of that?

Well, firstly, a film would have to work very hard to *be* as shit as they said it was. And, in fact, I *know* it wasn't shit. It wasn't a work of genius, but it couldn't have been shit because I'd sat through the preview audiences (anonymously, they hide you behind a screen so you can hear the reactions) and I'd heard the laughter. Also, I'd read the comment cards and been there when the cruncher totted up the scores. It wasn't *Citizen Kane*, but it wasn't a bad little romcom which managed to be a bit sexy and quite fun while also taking on a very serious subject. What's more, nobody could deny the quality of the stellar cast (the reviews, as ever, had got round that one by mainly ignoring them to focus on me).

Incredibly, despite the trashing and Ross's best efforts at sabotage, the movie did okay-ish. It wasn't a smash, but it was in the top five in the UK for a couple of weeks and 'washed its face' as they say – which means that my French saviours didn't lose their money. It was distributed globally, reaching number three in Italy and even being nominated for a prize at the Emden Film Festival in Germany. It got an excellent review in the

Hollywood Reporter, had a decent life on DVD and has been well-received on television in the years since.

So, no. As it happens, it *wasn't* total, reprehensible shit.

And hey, I got to make a movie!

And I loved it. All eight months of ultra-intense, all-consuming work, all day, every day and long into the night. I loved it. I worked with incredible people and fulfilled a dream many people have but few are so lucky as to achieve.

I really, truly can't complain, even though I suppose it must look like I am a bit.

A matter of life and death

I've saved the best part of the *Inconceivable/Maybe Baby* story until last.

To our great joy, Sophie was finally pregnant. Our third cycle of IVF had been successful and, by the time I began shooting the movie, she was just over five months gone. Our twins arrived in the middle of principal photography, nine weeks premature. Sophie had actually been scheduled to make a brief appearance as an extra the day they arrived, playing a pregnant lady in a park at whom Joely was to have stared wistfully, but her cameo was not to be.

What a morning that was.

I was on location in some park directing a film about *not* being able to have babies while my wife was hurtling across town in an ambulance about to have two. You can't shut down a movie even for babies (not a small budget one anyway), so I asked Hugh Laurie to take over as director for the morning while I rushed off to join Sophie at the hospital. When I arrived, they'd just got her settled and given her some drug or other to delay the birth and speed the development of the baby's lungs, which apparently is the main thing with prems. Then the specialist took one last look at the business end of things and shouted 'Whoops! Incoming!'

I swear that's what he said.

An emergency caesarean was required and, in seconds, there were ten extra medical staff in the room – a whole separate crew for each baby.

We've got very used to acknowledging the debt we all owe the National Health Service these days. Everybody does it, even those who have spent their political lives trying to undermine and underfund it. But as the COVID consensus starts to fade, I recommend anyone who needs reminding how incredibly fortunate and privileged we are in Britain to have the NHS to try having premature twins. Sophie and I will be for ever grateful.

George Michael sent us an enormous bunch of flowers.

It was amazingly nice of him because I scarcely knew the guy. We'd met a couple of times a decade earlier during the '80s. Maybe he'd heard that his album *Faith* had been a favourite of mine when I first courted Sophie; I mentioned it on *Desert Island Discs*. Anyway, for whatever reason, he decided to send us a stunning bouquet, which was deeply touching. And, let me tell you, the nurses were extremely impressed. They thought it was even better than the cards from two Beatles and the Prince of Wales. But now I'm just name-dropping again.

Of course I am. I owe it to my publisher.

So our twins Bert and Lottie were born nine weeks early and thus began a period of our lives of heart-stopping emotional intensity. For a while, it really was touch and go, particularly for Bert. Both babies were unimaginably tiny, the size of your hand. And scrawny. So scrawny. They were just skin and bone, and scarcely an ounce of that – only half-cooked, as Dawn French remarked when she came to visit.

Bert, Lottie and Sophie entered the prem unit at Chelsea and Westminster Hospital (and, later, the one at University College), where they remained for many weeks. It was the strangest of worlds: a room filled with cots, each containing a tiny creature that represented the entire world to the anxious parent or parents hovering over it, and each cot barely a metre from the next. The room was full of twenty or more individual and all-encompassing life-or-death dramas. Literally. Some babies lived, some died. Some survived, but with lives fraught with the challenges of their early births ahead of them.

I would only visit once a day, just a half-hour focused on our own story. But Sophie lived in that world 24/7. She was part of a community which existed entirely on hope and despair. Were the babies gaining or fading? Ours began to grow; Lottie more robustly, Bert more slowly. A transfusion was required – the heart-breaking, heart-stopping, seemingly impossible task of finding veins no thicker than a thread in limbs no thicker than a little finger must somehow be achieved. But when it was and the blood was deemed to be finding its mark, how to celebrate? When, a metre away, people Sophie now knew, with whom she was sharing an experience so rare and so all-consuming, gathered round the next cot, were losing the battle to will their baby through.

The tragedies were overwhelming. The heroin-addicted mother who now had a heroin-addicted baby being treated for withdrawal. The couple next to us whose baby looked to be the healthiest and most perfect of them all and yet who had been basically born without a brain. Surely this was an occasion in which further care was not the ethical option. And yet how to turn off the life support of a baby that looks as if it has its whole life ahead?

And what of me in all this? Well, I went back to work. I had to finish the movie. Is that callous?

We didn't think so. Sophie was very clear: there was no advantage in me hovering about all day every day for what was clearly going to be an open-ended period. I had responsibilities and, frankly, had we been dependent on my weekly wage, I'd have had no choice but to go back to work, as all men used to do. More than a hundred people were relying on me. Our modest movie budget could not possibly have borne the strain of standing down the unit for a day, let alone an indefinite period. We'd have lost key cast and crew and painfully negotiated locations and studio time. The movie would have collapsed with the investment lost taking those 100-plus jobs with it. Neither Sophie nor I were in any doubt what I had to do. But it was quite hard, playing make believe while only miles away, Sophie and our babies were living the reality of life and death.

I used to unburden myself to my driver at the end of a long day of filming, saying how useless and helpless I felt. He had recently arrived from Africa and I've never forgotten what his reply was.

'You want to kill a bison so the family will eat.'

And he was right.

Late '90s / Early '00s

Long time ago when we was Fab

I mentioned getting cards from Beatles. This fabbest of fab things came about because during the '90s Sophie and I had become friends first with George and Olivia Harrison. I still have to pinch myself even writing that sentence.

Like a number of the best things in my life, it actually came about through my friendship with Rik Mayall. I think I've made it pretty clear how much we loved early rock'n'roll. Well, in the summer of 1992, Rik rang me to say that he'd had a 'celeb' invite to a Hard Rock Cafe anniversary party and that Carl Perkins – the legendary '50s rocker and writer of 'Blue Suede Shoes' – was playing. I didn't need telling twice. I jumped in a cab, picked up Rik at his place in Ladbroke Grove and the two of us hurried down to Piccadilly for a night of beer, burgers and rock'n'roll bliss.

And what a night it was. Just seeing Perkins live would have been enough, but imagine our excitement when we walked into the Hard Rock and realized that GEORGE HARRISON was guesting on guitar. I reckon we were as excited as two kids at the height of Beatlemania. He was only about twenty feet from us and, unlike those kids back then, we could actually hear his guitar breaks.

Afterwards, Rik had to get home (he had small kids), and I was happy to hang around (Sophie was in Aus), standing at the bar drinking beer and thinking that the night couldn't get any better. Then there was a bit of a kerfuffle in the crowd and I realized that George was making his way through the throng towards me. A Beatle was seeking me out!

'Thanks for keeping us amused in the 1980s.'

That's what he said.

Those were the first words he said to me and I will never forget them. I can still hear that famous dry, laconic Liverpudlian voice, very slightly Americanized over the years but utterly recognizable.

'Thanks for keeping us amuuused in the nineteen eightieees.'

After that first meeting at the Hard Rock, we saw George and Olivia quite a lot in the '90s. The Christmas parties at Friar Park, their incredible home and garden, were very special treats. I remember the first time we went to visit them. The Beatles' *Live at the BBC* compilation had just gone to number one and George was so pleased; 'Not bad for a bunch of live one-take wonders from thirty years ago.' I can remember sitting on a couch transfixed as I watched Joe Brown, Jeff Lynne and George busking together on ukuleles. George was a massive fan of the instrument all his life and a proud member of the George Formby Society. That was, of course, one of the unique elements that made the Beatles so entirely extraordinary: all of them drew not just on their fascination with the roots of American rock'n'roll but also on a deep love of traditional British popular culture.

At one of George and Olivia's parties Sophie and I had an experience to treasure all our lives. We *played* with two of the Beatles. The party was in full swing and George came up to us looking a bit furtive and invited us to go upstairs to his studio. He said that he wanted to have a 'ciggie', but his aunt was at the party and he didn't want to smoke in front of her! Nice to know that, even in his early fifties, the man who wrote 'Something' and 'Here Comes the Sun' and who, with his mates, kickstarted the counterculture and the entire social revolution of the 1960s was still concerned about what his elderly aunt might think of him smoking tobacco! Anyway, Sophie and I followed George upstairs into his wonderful recording studio. We stood there looking at the huge, old-fashioned mixing desk, with what seemed like a million coloured knobs on it, and the many, many instruments that stood on stands and hung from walls. I don't suppose we thought at that point that things could get any better. But they did. George picked up a guitar and started to play.

'Come on, Sophie,' he said. 'Pick up that bass.'

And so she did, kicking in with the effortless, matter-of-fact aplomb that is her trademark. So now George and my wife are jamming and I'm in heaven, but also wishing as much as I ever have that I could play an instrument too. Well, guess what happens next? Ringo strolls in!

'Oh, so this is where the party's at, is it?'

And he sits down at the drum kit.

I *know*.

George starts playing 'I Saw Her Standing There'.

'Come on, Ben,' George says. 'I'm guessing you know the words.' He always seemed vaguely surprised at what a massive Beatles fan I was.

So there you have it. George on guitar, Ringo on drums, Sophie on bass and me on lead vocals with George harmonizing. How many millions, *tens* of millions, *hundreds of millions* of people over the years would have given anything to be in my shoes?

It was a short set. We just did two numbers. The other was Elvis's 'All Shook Up', which I'd known since I was eleven. After that, we re-joined the party. As we went back down the stairs, I couldn't help gushing to Ringo, whom I'd never met before.

'Mate, please just allow me to say I can now die happy, that I can tell my kids I jammed with Ringo Starr.'

'Hey, I'm going to ring mine now and tell them I jammed with Ben Elton.'

Of course, he was just being polite and frankly a bit wry (well, he is a Beatle), but he *said* it (in those deep nasal permanently sardonic-sounding tones) and it made me very happy.

We had some wonderful evenings at George and Olivia's. But on our first evening together, they actually came to us. We invited Jen and Ade and Harry (who was single at that point) and it turned into a great night. Sophie nearly severely scalded one of the world's best-loved artists when a coffee plunger shot a geyser of boiling coffee across the table. Fortunately, it all went over me.

George, of course, noticed my psoriasis. Everybody did in those days, my ears and hairline being red and flaky. And he decided he needed to help. Now, I know that earlier in this book I was railing against people forcing 'alternative' cures on me, but for George Harrison, I was of course delighted to listen. George was very sure that what I needed to do was drink my own piss and he sent me several handwritten faxes describing ayurvedic medicine and encouraging me to try it, mentioning that even if it didn't help my psoriasis, he'd heard that the effects were still generally health-giving. I didn't try it. There are some things you don't do even for a Beatle.

George was also very kind on keeping me abreast with Beatles developments – 'because I know you're into all that stuff'. (Like *that's* a rare thing).

They had remastered the movie *Yellow Submarine* and were having a private screening in Soho. None of the band had seen it in thirty years and all three surviving Beatles attended with just members of their families.

And us!

There were maybe twenty people in all and George had invited us. What a sublimely intimate experience. I remember Ringo heckling the screen from the darkness when the band make their appearance at the very end of the film. 'Get off! You're not funny.'

In fact, the Beatles had an ulterior motive for asking me that night. They had been wondering about the possibility of using the *Yellow Submarine* characters (*not* the Beatles characters) to base a cartoon series on, which would feature one actual Beatles track each episode. In the bar afterwards, George asked if I thought there was anything in the idea and if I'd be interested in perhaps writing it. Wow. That was truly something let me tell you. But in all honesty, I didn't think the idea would fly. Without the Beatles themselves, I wasn't confident the other characters in the film – Old Fred, Jeremy Hillary Boob and the Chief Blue Meanie – were strong enough to base decent storylines on. Besides, the film was so special and of its time I'd have been extremely loath to tinker with such a perfect bit of '60s surrealism. So, with infinite regret, I told them I didn't think the idea would work. They never did it so I presume they came to the same conclusion.

George's early death saddened the whole world. We had lost an artist for the ages, a uniquely original spirit and a deeply beautiful man. Olivia and I remain in touch – always a Christmas card with a lovely note. And, quite recently, she sent us a beautiful private edition of her own poetry, which is very lovely. She's even kind enough to continue to occasionally keep me informed about Beatles stuff. I was so touched to be invited to the screening of Martin Scorsese's documentary *George Harrison: Living in the Material World*, at which, once again, all the Beatles family were gathered, this time including Yoko Ono.

I do think it's wonderful how, for all their many disagreements over the years, all the elements of the Beatles family remain truly connected. It's a great testimony to their power to create love.

One of the last times I saw George was at a party in Friar Park. Sophie and I were leaving and George came out with us to see us into our car. Being in a mellow, late-night mood with glass in hand, he chatted matters spiritual for a moment. He was saying how friendship transcended distance and that we all occupy the same place and every place in space and time. I couldn't resist it. I said, 'George, it's happening'. He asked what. I said 'We're talking about the space between us all', which, for those (few) who don't know, is a quote from George's song 'Within You Without You' on the *Sgt. Pepper* album. I'll never forget the beautiful smile he gave me and the warm hug that followed.

'Hey, Linda. We're doing it. We're talking about the press again'

Sophie and I also became friendly with Paul and Linda. We met them at George and Olivia's.

I actually think that might be the craziest thing I've ever written.

Paul and Linda were also open and warm and, as with the Harrisons, family was the core of their life. Sophie and I were thrilled to attend Stella McCartney's graduation show and the small party afterwards. Linda photographed me in one of the funky little hats Stella had designed for the show. So I modelled one of Stella McCartney's very earliest creations! Also at that same party was Twiggy, whom I was chatting to when Kate Moss approached, anxious to meet Twiggy for the first time. So there I was – the lucky witness to a truly cosmic convergence of cross-generational beauty and unknowable, indefinable charisma – standing bang in the middle of the ultimate Olympian supermodel summit! Both women are working-class Londoners (actually, Kate's from Croydon) and got on at once. Before long, they found common ground on which they could both express equal frustration. People standing nearby all stopped and listened as these two wonderful London girls engaged in animated agreement.

'Did you get blamed for anorexia? I get blamed for anorexia!'

'I certainly did get blamed for anorexia! Do *you* get blamed for anorexia?'

'I'm *always* getting blamed for anorexia.'

'And I eat *so* much. I'm a total pig!'

'*I'm* a total pig!'

As if to prove the point, they conducted the conversation through mouthfuls of canapes. I haven't met Kate since, but Twiggy and I have been friends since the '80s, a friendship which eventually resulted in a wonderful collaboration when I embraced the fabulous project of writing a jukebox musical about her life.

Sophie and I spent one of our most memorable days ever with Paul and Linda at their home. It was just us and the McCartney family. They invited us to spend the day with them in their small, unassuming but beautiful little farmhouse in East Sussex. Linda was experimenting at the time with what would become her famous and hugely successful range of vegetarian sausages and burgers. Paul cooked them on the barbie and there was much debate over their strength and consistency.

'They've got to act like a proper hamburgers, Linda, or people won't take to them. They're breaking up.'

'Well, don't flip them so hard.'

'You've got to be able to flip them, love.'

They certainly got them right in the end. I'm here to tell you that Linda's veggie range of pies, sausages and burgers are bloody delicious and absolutely *do* act like their flesh-and-blood equivalents. I know, I eat both.

It was a glorious day. Paul and Linda lived so simply and without any domestic staff. Linda told a story of how hurt she'd been by a recent newspaper profile which confidently stated that this was all a PR sham. A female journalist had come into the McCartney home to interview Linda at her kitchen table and had eaten sandwiches and drunk many cups of tea which Linda of course prepared and served. The journo had engaged in what had seemed like a sympathetic conversation, only to write the hatchet piece she'd been preparing all along, scathingly sneering at the multi-multi-millionairess 'pretending' she was just an ordinary housewife and mother, making her own tea when no doubt an army of staff were lurking in the background. It was a horrid story and, not surprisingly, Linda had felt very used. But Paul stopped her mid-anecdote.

'Hey, Linda,' he said. 'We're doing it. We're talking about the press again. Gotta stop.'

That has become a family phrase in the Elton household. It's almost impossible not to get hurt and uptight when people are mean about you in the press, particularly when they state with such confidence that they are portraying the real you. And, of course, you only feed that hurt by talking about it. Nobody had better cause to feel hurt than beautiful, gentle, genuine, caring, creative, utterly kind and considerate Linda McCartney, who suffered twenty years of bullying spite. You may have forgotten about it because, since her death, it all changed but, oh God, people used to be mean about Linda.

So Paul's warning – 'Hey, Linda. We're doing it again. We're talking about the press' – is a good one for us all. And not just the famous these days as the internet makes hating a mass-participation sport. You can't feed it. You can't let it live in your head rent-free.

But it ain't easy.

Rik dies and is reborn

One day in the summer of '98, I got a horrible phone call from Barbara Mayall.

'Rik's had an accident. He's in a coma. He'll probably die. You'd better come.'

Rik had decided to go for a ride on his quad bike at his home in Devon. It had flipped over and landed on him.

I went straight down. Ade was already there. He was there for the whole initial life-teetering crisis, which lasted nearly a week. Barbara was magnificent – a strong, passionate woman who kept her children positive while seeming almost physically to *will* Rik back from the nearly dead. For quite a while, he was in a strange half-consciousness, not really here but not quite gone either. When I was sitting with him, he came round a little and recognized me from what seemed like a great distance.

'Hello, Benjy. I fucked up.'

He asked me to lie on the bed with him and put my arms round him. This wasn't so easy. He was a big bloke and there were a lot of tubes and wires, but I managed it. I'm not the most huggy or tactile person, but Rik is. He was huggy even before his brush with death and got more so after.

Years later, at Rik's funeral, when Pete Richardson spoke, he mentioned how the accident had given Rik sixteen good years, because it had caused him to stop drinking.

In my view, Rik's drinking reached its absolute crisis in 1995. And it coincided with the crisis of another close friend – Stephen Fry's disappearance from the play *Cell Mates* and his subsequent reappearance in Bruges. I remember that phone call too, when Jo Laurie rang up to say that Stephen had disappeared and that neither his family nor she and Hugh (his best friends) knew where he was.

Much has been written about Stephen's agony in that period, which was very real. He subsequently discovered his bipolar condition and has spoken a great deal about mental health, using his own experience to help others recognize their problems. What's less known is how badly that dreadful couple of weeks affected Rik. They were in *Cell Mates* together – virtually a two-hander – and were at the beginning of a presumed West End run. I'd been out to see the two of them in a Richmond preview a couple of weeks before and everything had been fine. Stephen and Rik were friends. They'd worked together lots. They always had a laugh and they were having a laugh that night.

Then the play came into town and, on the morning after the opening night, Stephen disappeared. Rik was devastated. There was no explanation and he didn't know where Stephen was. Nonetheless, he had to go on that evening with the understudy. That was very brave of Rik. The whole of London was talking about Stephen (it really was massive news), but Rik still had to do the show in front of an audience who would have been thinking about nothing but Stephen from start to finish. Such was the media distraction that I think Rik could have legitimately refused. But he didn't. He continued the run, despite the fact that the papers were now stating as fact that Stephen's departure would without doubt mean the play must close. This was very hard. Rik and Stephen were equal stars at the time. If anything, Rik was bigger but the story was much better if it played around Stephen and the press went with that line for days and days, on *the front page* and prominently on radio and TV news with Rik virtually ignored. He was a small footnote in the great mystery of Stephen's sudden disappearance, his whereabouts (still unknown) and speculation about his mental health.

Eventually, Stephen's agent tracked him (via his credit card) to Bruges from where he agreed to move to her house in France and Hugh rode off on his motorbike to go and see him. In the meantime, Rik was desperately unhappy. I visited him in his dressing room a number of times and of course, being Rik, he showed this in terms of a 'fuck everyone' bravado, but it was a thin veneer. He was deeply on edge. The audiences were dwindling (how could they not be with front-page stories saying the play was nothing without its 'star') and yet Rik was doing the show with the understudy, while also having to rehearse all day with Simon Ward, who had been cast as Stephen's replacement. It was a horrible situation, particularly for a proud man. And Rik was a very proud man.

He started to drink more than ever, getting drunk and angry. One night after a performance, he took the show's prop reproduction gun with him for his usual night of drinking. At some point later, he produced it in the streets of Soho and started waving it around. Unsurprisingly, he was very soon surrounded by armed police and was lucky not to have been shot. They arrested him and he spent the night in the station, from which Barbara collected him in the morning when he was released. He got off with a very serious warning and had to make a contrite public apology.

I think that incident was a sort of cry – not for help, but for *attention*. There was just so much focus on Stephen's crisis that I think Rik felt invisible.

And then the play did close. I'm not even sure if poor Simon Ward, with whom Rik had been working all day every day, ever even made it onto the stage.

It was a bitter double blow for Rik – a financial one and a personal one because it looked like he couldn't headline a play, which he absolutely could, but not under those circumstances. Rik always valued his star power highly and, of course, had he been the sole headliner in that Simon Gray play, it would have been fine. But the story had become about Stephen *not* being there and the play just couldn't survive. It left Rik looking sidelined and unimportant, things that he simply couldn't bear to be.

I've chosen to tell this story because to have two very close friends going through a kind of mutual but entirely separate parallel agony is an unusual experience. Also, because as I have described, Rik's pain was kind of invisible at the time and I wanted to show how this was very much a shared crisis of mental health. Utterly devastating for them both.

A musical about terrorism. Can't think why nobody thought of it before

In 1998, I got a call from the office of Andrew Lloyd Webber.

'Andrew would like to have dinner with you.'

Well, I knew what to say to that. The very *idea*.

Struggling to contain my fury as my knuckles turned white around the receiver, I replied in as calm a voice as I could muster.

'Excuse me? Are you crazy? Andrew Lloyd Webber is a TORY. I vote LABOUR. Do you really think I would have dinner with someone who didn't agree with me politically? What would Toby Young say? No, I haven't heard of him either, but I suspect at some point in the future, he'll turn up on my Wikipedia page calling me the worst sell-out of my generation. So, no, I won't have dinner with Andrew. I suggest you invite Adolf Hitler and Genghis Khan. He'll find them much more convivial company.'

That's what I said.

Except. No . . .

I *didn't* say that.

Crazily, madly, illogically and, above all, *hypocritically* I said:

'How interesting. I'd be happy to.'

Why did I do it? Why did I say to the world 'Here is my arse, please kick it', thus beginning a relationship that would allow my many detractors to imagine that they now had the proof that they'd been seeking with which to condemn and demean every word I'd ever said or written?

I did it because I wanted to. I'd loved Andrew's work all my life. That's why. I'd known every word of the pharaoh's song from *Joseph and the Amazing Technicolor Dreamcoat* since I was eleven. I listened to the album of *Jesus Christ Superstar* when I was twelve and thought it a work of true greatness. I still do.

I love musical theatre and Britain's (in fact, the world's) preeminent artist in the field wanted to have dinner with me.

Fuck, yeah!

Andrew's reason for wanting to meet me was to ask if I would like to write a few new gags for *Starlight Express*. He felt that it was getting a bit tired and wanted to give it a polish. *Starlight* had already been running for fourteen years, making it one of the most successful musicals of all time. I did not want to go down in showbiz history as the guy who broke its winning streak, so I declined the gig. Instead, as a very convivial dinner progressed, we started talking about working on an original music-al together. All of Andrew's previous musicals had been based on known source material – and pretty ground-breaking stuff, too: The Bible (Old and New Testaments), the life of a South American dictator's wife, T.S. Eliot's poems, an old French novel about a physically and mentally dam-aged composer. Even *Starlight* was inspired by *Thomas the Tank Engine*. I don't think Andrew gets remotely enough credit for the originality of his choices of source material. But now Andrew was excited to originate an original and contemporary musical, a new story addressing current issues. He hadn't done a piece with any kind of political or societal edge since *Evita* and that had been an historical story.

There and then, he decided that if we could find the right idea, he wanted to do it with me. Andrew was well aware of our conflicting views on numerous issues and it was that which attracted him. He wanted to be challenged. Don't you think that was kind of interesting of him?

Of all the people in the world whom he could have worked with who were *queuing up* to work with him, of all the soft subjects he could have pursued in theatre or taken to Disney, he chose to ask me to write an original libretto for him. And he didn't want this show to be 'sung through', as all his previous hits had been. He wanted dialogue and standalone scenes set in a relevant and challenging contemporary setting.

As background subject matter, we very soon decided on the conflict in Northern Ireland. 'The Troubles', as they were known, had exploded into violence in 1969 and had been the dominant story of our times ever since. By the late 1990s, sectarian civil war was still tearing the province apart and the IRA were also highly active on the British mainland. They had recently, and spectacularly, staged a mortar attack on Downing Street itself.

We resolved to write a musical drama set in Belfast in 1969, which would take as its theme the radicalization of young people that turns some to terrorism.

The story would explore the lives of a group of young people centred round a local football team, young people unfortunate enough to be born into terrible times, kids whose ordinary lives would be devastated and corrupted by the boiling hatred surfacing around them. Some would succumb to hatred; others would find a way to rise above it. But there would be no clear heroes or villains. Our story ended extremely bleakly, with the leading man leaving his wife and child to join an IRA active service unit in England. He was a young man who had begun with such promise wanting only to play football and marry his girlfriend but, having been interned without trial in 'Long Kesh' prison (the famous 'university' of the IRA), he had been radicalized and was now set on a life of murder and possible martyrdom.

We both knew that such a story was scarcely a commercial prospect. Even though we intended to thread it with humanity and humour – and, of course, wonderful music – we knew that the subject matter was, on the surface at least, unsuited for the commercial stage. Nonetheless, Andrew was determined this was to be his next musical.

When the project was announced, the media reaction was really actually rather wonderful and the excitement within the arts community was genuinely warm and encouraging. Here's an example of one leading arts editorial:

'How surprising and how fascinating. The most successful theatre composer in the world, a man long identified with Conservative politics, has chosen to collaborate with a writer of known left-of-centre views. The man who composed *The Phantom of the Opera* and *Cats* has reached out to the politically vocal comedian, playwright and novelist whose hits include *The Young Ones*, *Popcorn* and *Blackadder*. Together they are to create an entirely new and original musical. What's more, a musical on the most difficult and intractable of themes: how young people become terrorists. Even more impressively, this project is to be developed in the commercial theatre. Surely there is something for the National to learn here. Shouldn't publicly funded arts houses be encouraging such bold collaborations between popular artists on such challenging political and social themes?'

There were loads of articles like that. In *The Guardian*, *The Times* and *The Telegraph*. Everybody was fascinated. Andrew Lloyd Webber and Ben Elton? Now *that* is bloody interesting. *Newsnight* did a whole thing about how Andrew Lloyd Webber could have been writing *Aladdin* for Disney, but instead he'd chosen to write (and fund) a musical about sectarian violence and the genesis of a terrorist with Ben Elton.

Except, hang on . . .

Nothing like that was said at all.

Instead, when our project became public knowledge, it was universally and comprehensively vomited on. Scarcely anyone even *considered* the thought that this might actually be a *good* thing, an interesting thing, a brave initiative. No. There was just one long scream of horror at the very idea. From all sides.

Later on, when we were much further down the track, good old Melvyn Bragg became a lone but important supportive voice. He thought it was a fascinating collaboration and did a whole *South Bank Show* on us. But the rest was pure contempt.

And I'm so bloody naive, I genuinely didn't see it coming. I really didn't anticipate the anger that my decision to work with Andrew would provoke – more so for me than him, of course. As I think I've mentioned, the left is far more gleeful at decrying its own than the right. On Andrew's side, there was just spiteful amusement. On my side, it was much more vicious. It kind of became open season on me.

I really had dealt myself a massive blow. But, reader, let me assure you. Even if I *had* seen it coming (and, of course, I should have done), it wouldn't have made any difference because I'd have done it anyway. I thought our collaboration and the project we settled upon were brilliant things and I still do.

And, for what it's worth, I might point out that while Andrew is certainly a Conservative, he lives and has always lived in England and, unlike many much 'cooler' figures in our cultural elite, he pays and has always paid his tax here. Also, on social issues he's as liberated as any man I know. He's passionate about racial and sexual equality, and when the Tories were still against gay marriage, he defied the party whip in the Lords and made a major speech in its favour, likewise on gay adoption. He and I disagree fundamentally on many political issues, but we also have plenty in common in terms of our interests and, believe it or not, our principles.

Working with Andrew was a joy. He's brilliant and generous company, fiercely intelligent and perceptive on any subject and with a wicked and highly original sense of humour. We became and remain close friends, still corresponding and meeting up for occasional dinners (generally with Madeleine, his wife, also now an old friend) fully twenty years after our professional collaboration.

And what a collaboration it was. We'd sit together in his music room, him at the piano and me with all the story and lyric pages scattered around me, and he'd just *play*. Andrew needs to compose like he needs to breathe; he just *has* to do it. He'll sit at the piano, his face in ecstasy, excited beyond words for you to hear the latest tunes he's been working on. Sometimes I had to pinch myself. I was in Andrew Lloyd Webber's music room, *writing songs* with him!

And Andrew is always up for the craic. One evening after work, he said 'Let's go out' and I took him to the Dublin Castle in Camden where I sometimes go with Ade. There are always a few bands on, usually goth or grunge or thrash or punk, and that night didn't disappoint. Andrew and I stood with our drinks among a dozen or so teenaged emos and watched a couple of bands thrash it out at volume eleven. I'd love to be able to report that Andrew and I pogoed the night away and ended up in the band room drinking their rider, but the volume defeated us and we wandered up the road for a nasty lasty at the Jazz Cafe. It was a fun night.

I remember another time we were in Ireland. Andrew has a castle there (as you do) and having finished work one day, we went down to the village pub. We were having our drinks and a wedding party arrived. A young couple had just got married in the church around the corner and many of the guests had come into the pub while the bridal party did the photos. They were all very pleased to see Andrew and me, and wanted us to meet the bride and groom. The next thing you know they insist we're in a photograph. And then another. Then another. We were photographed with the happy couple. With the families. With the bridesmaids, the groomsmen, the priest and the ushers and God knows what other groupings. We tried to politely withdraw but they wouldn't have it and so, somewhere in a drawer in Ireland, there's a wedding album which, along with the happy couple and their families, features me and Andrew Lloyd Webber in every single photograph. It was a very long and very boozy day.

Writing *The Beautiful Game* was hard work. We knew how sensitive the subject was and were determined not to shy away from its difficult nature. I'm pretty sure it's the only West End musical that features a kneecapping scene. If you're going to work with that kind of terrible and confrontational subject matter, you are duty-bound to do your research and get it right.

Incidentally, I received many letters of support from both sides of the sectarian divide for the way we handled that scene. On one occasion after the show, I was sought out by the family of a man who *had* been kneecapped. They were so generously positive about the scene and the exposition of its causes and the way it had been portrayed.

We opened at the Cambridge Theatre in London in September 2000.

The reviews were pretty grim. Well, grim for me. They were *sort of* okay for Andrew in a grudging kind of way. But, sadly, they were *definitely* not ticket-selling reviews. There was absolutely no suggestion that this was an *event*. The story and lyrics to which I'd devoted so much passion and thought were pretty much dismissed out of hand.

Once again, the experience was made bearable by the audience reaction, which delivered tears, laughter and a hugely emotional nightly standing ovation, particularly for the incomparable Josie Walker who was funny, moving, super-intelligent and inspiring in the massive leading role. Actually, the woman in the second lead wasn't bad either. The now globally famous Hannah Waddingham delivered a wonderful and hilarious performance as the lapsed Catholic girl dating a Protestant. She stopped the show with her number *Our Kind of Love*.

But as I say, the reviews were medium to poor, and grim for me, and for a while it looked like we were dead in the water, but then things suddenly turned around. There was a late, very long and very comprehensive review by John Peter in *The Sunday Times*. I am going to trespass on your patience by quoting a paragraph from it. I'm putting it in italics so you can skip if you like.

'Andrew Lloyd Webber romps home with his finest piece of musical theatre ever. With this show, Webber and his librettist, Ben Elton, have taken on a huge subject: real life, real death, real history, humanity at war with itself. The subject brings the best out of Andrew Lloyd Webber. His music has great sophistication as well as cunning theatricality and deep feeling. Elton's book and lyrics burst with energy, indignation and intelligence. Brave and bitterly truthful, this show need not fear comparison with West Side Story. *Offhand, I cannot think of greater praise.'*

I can't tell you how grateful we were to get that notice. Finally, somebody seemed to get us and was prepared to say so publicly.

After that, things picked up a bit and we actually ended up getting the Critics' Circle Award for Musical of the Year, which was frankly astonishing considering the initial reviews. The show ran for a year, which is a pretty respectable run – particularly for a musical about the routes of terrorism – but it still lost a lot of money, as Andrew had always suspected it would.

We were all set for a Broadway run, too. The theatre had been agreed on, the backers ready. But then 9/11 hit and nobody in New York wanted to back a musical that took a sympathetic view on the genesis of a terrorist.

The Beautiful Game has since been revived several times, most notably by the Hungarian State Theatre Company. Using public money, they were able to feature a full symphony orchestra and the football ballet in the middle boasted twenty-two players and a proper crowd! Andrew and I saw it together. It was simply mind-blowing.

I directed a new production in Canada under the title *The Boys in the Photograph* with an inspired young cast led by Erica Peck in the role originally created by Josie. It was produced in Winnipeg by the Manitoba State Theatre Company. Winnipeg is a town with many social problems and the best moment was when a group of youth workers brought members of warring street gangs to see a show about a town ripped apart by tribal hatred.

The show has also been presented in Northern Ireland by cross theatre community groups. I worked with them and am grateful for the detailed feedback they gave me on linguistic nuance. The script is better for it.

But the happiest moment of all with *The Beautiful Game* was when the South African State Theatre Company put it on in Johannesburg as the principal theatrical event of the 2010 World Cup (again titled *The Boys in the Photograph*). I attended the premiere and was so moved to hear the speech made by Danny Jordaan, who was the head of the South African Football Association at the time. Jordaan had been a senior anti-apartheid activist during the years of struggle. He told the audience that the story and lyrics had spoken directly to him and his own experience.

That was pretty special. I wish Andrew had been there to share that moment with me.

Sleepover at Elton's

Looking back, it's hard for me to even understand just how culturally visible I was back at the end of the last century. In early 1999, I got a call from an unfamiliar but strangely very familiar voice that said 'Elton, it's Elton. I've always wanted to say that.'

Yes. Elton John cold-called me.

I would never have even presumed that such a global icon would have even heard of me, but it seemed he had and we had a bit of a laugh at how his decision to adopt a surname as a first name had condemned a world of real Eltons to a lifetime of Elton John gags (Richard and I did a similar thing to the real-life Blackadders). He then explained the reason for his call: he and his partner (now husband) David Furnish would like to meet me with a mind to collaboration.

I *know*.

Sadly, yet again I fucked it up, but it was lovely while it lasted.

I met them somewhere in town. I guess I must have been blinded by fame because I don't remember where and my diary doesn't say. They were (as I hope you will have presumed) as kind and lovely as they seem and explained that they had formed a film production company called Rocket Pictures and had acquired a play about a flawed lawman in cowboy gold-rush times that they thought might make a movie. Their idea was for a kind of lyrical, music-driven (possibly even fully sung) saga of the Old West. I resisted the urge to say that this sounded like a perfect project for Elton's famed lyricist Bernie Taupin who, despite being from Lincolnshire, is a natural-born cowboy. What I didn't resist, I regret to say, was the urge to edge our chat towards the possibility of Rocket Pictures perhaps being interested in an original screenplay.

Jesus, I can be stupid. I do that kind of thing all the time – getting asked to consider one thing and ending up talking about something else, something which I would originate. Remember when Ridley Scott wanted me to write a romantic comedy about vineyards and we ended up looking at *Popcorn*?

In my defence, Elton and David seemed very open to the idea of me pitching my own moral saga of the West and we agreed that I should go away, think about it and pitch something back at them. What was more, they suggested that I come out to their house in Cannes for their annual movie festival party which was the following month and discuss it then! And since they would be hosting various friends that evening, why didn't I stay over?

Exciting? Just a bit.

But I did what I always do. I threw as many words at the challenge as quickly I could. Instead of hanging cool and offering an enigmatic paragraph or two developed out of their source material and with lots of possibility for their creative input, I did too much too soon. I sent a densely typed, highly detailed fifteen-page synopsis of a completely original story plus token 'guide' lyrics.

I say 'completely original'. It was based on the biblical story of Cain and Abel, so frankly it wasn't even that original.

Why didn't I just read the play they had asked me to read and work on that? Because I'm me and I can be really stupid.

I doubt they ever got through my pages. I just reopened the document for the first time in twenty-five years and I couldn't. If any young writers are reading this and you're ever asked by highly creative people to share in an idea, keep your first response brief and focused on what they have suggested.

Anyway, I went to Cannes and attended Elton and David's festival gala dinner *and* the private house party that followed *and* stayed over. And at no point during the whole time I was with them was there any mention of the pages that I had sent them. Impeccable manners, I guess. You don't invite a bloke to your party and then tell him he is a fucking idiot who has massively over-reached himself.

But what an amazing thing, eh? The gala dinner was as fascinating and as glamorous as you'd expect. I sat next to Mike Myers and opposite Sean Connery. And, afterwards, I was a house guest in Elton and David's beautiful French home. Apart from me, they were entertaining close friends and David told me that the tradition was that people who were staying took a moment after the gala to get out of their glamorous party wear and reassemble in something comfortable or dressing gowns to compare notes on their evening. It was without doubt a lovely thing. Elton, of course, doesn't drink, but there was lots more champagne and I remember chatting to Janet Street-Porter, who is always great fun, and meeting the brilliant (and dryly witty) Neil Tennant of Pet Shop Boys. At one point, there was a brief commotion when a gatecrasher arrived – a young woman not yet as famous as she would become and so beautiful that she literally stopped the conversation dead. Photos simply do not do justice to the extraordinary loveliness and radiant presence of Salma Hayek. She apologized happily for bursting in uninvited, explaining that because of the value of the jewels that had been loaned to her for the night she had been given her own car plus two bodyguards. Check out the photos of Salma Hayek Cannes 1999: her necklace is indeed stunning but, frankly, if I were Cartier or Tiffany hoping to showcase my wares, I wouldn't use Salma Hayek. *Nobody* was looking at the jewels. Anyway, Ms Hayek told us that the car and the bodyguards were not for her *but for the necklace* and, as long as she wore it, they would stay with her. So she was making the most of it and doing the late-night rounds! Elton and David were, of course, utterly gracious and the vision hovered with us for a few minutes before continuing on her tour.

The next morning, I had to leave long before anyone else was up and that was that. I never heard another word from Elton and David about our Western project. They had been nothing but kind and generous to me, but I had not surprisingly failed my audition. I never bother regretting anything in retrospect, but I think this story is the perfect example of a side of my creative personality which could do with a bit of work.

For those about to rock

And, so, from a failed collaboration to a very successful one, one which would come to loom larger in my professional life than perhaps any other project I have ever written, one which would consume me for years – decades, in fact. It would bring me immense joy and some pain, and cause the forming of friendships which I treasure deeply to this day, and no doubt always will.

It happened this way. One day, while I was still deep in *Maybe Baby* and *The Beautiful Game*, I got a call from Paul Roberts.

'Queen are big fans, they want to do a musical with you.'

In fact, Paul had previously rung Queen's manager Jim Beach and said 'Ben's a big fan, would you fancy doing a musical with him?' It seems Jim had replied something along the lines of 'Well, who knows. Maybe. Let's talk.'

Not quite 'Queen want to do a musical with you', but, still, not flipping nothing either.

And as it turned out, Jim Beach *was* interested. It seemed he'd been working on a Queen musical for a number of years. Robert De Niro has a production company in NYC called Tribeca. It's primarily a movie-making concern, but they'd wanted to try a theatrical venture and had fixed on a Queen musical. Bob is a big Queen fan and, for both he and Jim, the Queen musical was a passion project. The idea was to make it a biography of Freddie, and they had progressed as far as staging a full-scale workshop production in New York.

Unfortunately, the idea had then hit a wall. Having gone over to see it, Brian May and Roger Taylor had not liked it at all.

Which was why, when Paul Roberts phoned Jim about me, Jim was interested particularly because one of the principal objections Brian and Roger had about the workshop was its lack of humour. I believe that, even before Paul's call to Jim, my name had come up in their discussions on how to fix things. A bit of synchronicity was in play.

I first met Jim in Notting Hill I think. I do remember the meeting being in the most ridiculously minimalist hotel I have ever experienced, a place of hospitality so pure in its design concept that furniture was considered unnecessary clutter. We sat on large cold polished stones around a water feature. I'm not quite sure why this ridiculous venue was chosen. Jim is a man who knows how to enjoy life and I never again met him in anything other than the most pleasantly indulgent and comfortable surroundings. It must have been Paul; he likes a bit of design.

Anyway, as we perched on our polished stones, Jim told me about the Freddie project and asked me if I would like to take a look at it. He explained that Brian and Roger's principal objection to the workshop production had been that it was very, very *serious*, the emotional engine of it being Freddie's diagnosis and death from AIDS. Brian and Roger felt that any show reflecting Queen had to feature some lightness and comedy, and Jim wanted to know if I'd take a pass at the script with a view to putting in some laughs.

Yet again (as with Elton and David's idea a few months earlier), I didn't want to do the thing that was being suggested. But this time, it honestly had nothing to do with ego or ambition. I just didn't think that Freddie's life was the right subject for a Queen musical. Queen's music doesn't belong to Freddie. It doesn't even belong to Queen any more. It belongs to the world. It's been part of everyone's lives for two whole generations. It's played whenever people come together to celebrate anything. From wedding discos to mega sports stadiums, Queen's uniquely engaging and uplifting music is always with us. When I left home at sixteen and went into those awful digs, 'Bohemian Rhapsody' had just gone to number one. I think it was still there when I went home for Christmas.

Besides which, Queen themselves weren't *about* Freddie. They were a band, a miraculously successful four-piece collective. All four members of Queen wrote number one records. That is an incredible testimony to the diversity of their talent. Freddie wrote 'Bohemian Rhapsody', 'Somebody to Love' and 'Don't Stop Me Now'. But Brian wrote 'We Will Rock You', 'Fat Bottomed Girls' and 'Who Wants to Live Forever', Roger wrote 'A Kind of Magic' and 'Radio Ga Ga', and John Deacon wrote 'Another One Bites the Dust' and 'You're My Best Friend'. Queen were a *band* in every sense of the word.

So, with regret, I passed, the regret being obvious. The Queen songbook? What writer on earth wouldn't want to get their hands on such a crowning jewel of popular culture?

Jim, however, is a man who combines pragmatism and optimism in equal degrees. His reply was: 'Well, if you don't think that's the story, then tell us what you think it should be and we'll see if we like it.'

What a challenge. What an opportunity. I wanted to grab it and run with it.

But I couldn't. I didn't have an idea and I didn't have time to try to work on one either. I was in post-production on *Maybe Baby* and writing the book and lyrics for *The Beautiful Game*.

Also, we had two babies in the house. I've always been a fully connected dad and while Sophie certainly did a lot *more* on the home front, I did my bit too. If you write for a living, you're only ever in the next room when a nappy needs changing or a bottle needs mixing. So, frankly, besides being busy, I was completely exhausted.

The matter rested for a whole year, constantly niggling at me – a wonderful opportunity which I presumed I'd missed.

But I guess I must have been turning it over in my subconscious because, one day in 2000, the idea came to me. I was pushing the twins round Regent's Park in their double buggy – half-dead with that tiredness that only new parents understand, trying to keep the babies out for as long as possible to give Sophie an hour or two's sleep – when an idea occurred to me.

I'd already told Jim that, in my view, whatever the story for this musical was it needed to be epic.

Huge. Like the band.

A legend. Like the band.

That was the key and I'd known it at the first meeting. While I didn't think the story should be *about* the band, not Freddie and not any of them, I thought it should reflect their *spirit* and that spirit was rock! It had to be an anthemic story worthy of rock gods!

So I needed a legend. But what legend? I'd toyed with the Greeks and the Norse Gods, but that seemed too cliched and overblown. The story also had to be witty and satirical and modern – because Queen are all those things too.

I'd recently seen *The Matrix* and hadn't really understood it. I'd loved the style and the vibe, but the story was murky. I couldn't quite work out why everybody was being kept enslaved inside the computer dream. Where was the profit for the enslaver in that? A lot of these modern dystopian visions in movies imagine a world enslaved by a corporate machine, but it's always a bit confused as to why. Capitalism doesn't need sleeping slaves. It needs pliant consumers. If people are asleep, enslaved or dead, they can't *buy* things.

So, with these thoughts in my head as I was pushing the twins past London Zoo, I was thinking that what a computer-controlled society would really want would be to generate more product consumption, hence more profit. I started thinking about a world lived online where humanity wasn't enslaved or asleep but endlessly *distracted*, a world in which sanitized, computer-generated pop culture was downloaded directly to them via hand-held devices, homogenized pop and TV entertainment delivered directly to the consumer from the vast corporate entity that generated it.

Don't forget this was early 2000, seven years before the first smartphone was even announced.

I imagined an endless stream of corporately generated cyber pop stars delivering guaranteed number ones to a public who were no longer part of their own loop. This was a year before *Pop Idol* and four years before *The X Factor*, so again it was quite prescient. In my opening timeline, I set 2040 as the year that the first entirely computer-generated pop star would go to number one. It's 2024 as I write and AI-generated 'influencers' are already gaining millions of followers, and there are K-pop bands that are already a combination of human and computer-generated members. Clearly, I put my date for virtual bands powered by AI twenty years too late.

And, don't forget, I was imagining a story for a band that, above all, believed in live, human, guitar, bass, piano and drum-driven rock, a band that had proudly announced 'no synthesizers' on all their early albums. Again, I don't think, in all the shit that was subsequently to be thrown at my story, a single commentator ever thought about that.

So I had my political and satirical vision. Now I needed my jeopardy. What was the story? What was the *legend*?

If a vast Sony/Apple/Disney-style machine is bent on owning every aspect of the entertainment cycle, then the last thing they want is for the kids to make their own music. Because if you've got your next Christmas number one teed up, the last thing you want is punk coming along and ruining your carefully prepared marketing cycle. You don't want the kids choosing or making music for themselves.

That was my jeopardy. In my dystopian vision, the kids would no longer be *allowed* to make their own music. Electric guitars, that ultimate weapon of youth empowerment, would be banned by law. All *live* music of any kind would be outlawed.

But somewhere in this cultural wasteland, one guitar would remain, buried in stone by an ancient, long-dead collective of Hairy Rock Gods. Buried in ROCK, waiting for an Arthurian hero to rise up and draw forth the mighty axe and once more the kids would be free and The Rhapsody would be upon the planet.

I absolutely *knew* it was the right idea for Queen. I can't remember ever being more certain about any idea in my whole life. I pushed the twins home double-quick, rushed to my study and wrote out a treatment that evening, detailing the story of my two teenage outsiders, Galileo and Scaramouche, the Ga Ga world they were fighting and the Bohemian Rebel gang who would join them in their struggle against the Killer Queen's brutal Globalsoft corporation. I mapped out the whole story, right through to the discovery of the guitar buried in the rubble at Wembley Stadium, where once Queen had delivered their legendary Live Aid set. I even had much of the song sequence down.

I was very excited but also scared that, in the intervening year, Queen would have moved on. I'd had no contact with them at all and imagined that they'd commissioned another writer. But rock stars don't hurry themselves. Jim assured Paul that they were still open to ideas and would be interested to read my document.

So off it went. The treatment for *We Will Rock You*. To be read by Queen. Amazing.

I'd met Brian before, but only briefly when he worked with the Comic Strip on Ade's very funny spoof band Bad News. We'd played Pop Quiz together in their bus at Donnington Monsters of Rock. But I didn't know him well and I'd never met Roger at all. John Deacon, I would soon learn, was out of the picture, having retired from direct physical involvement with the band, but Jim told me that he too had read my document and approved. Queen only ever do anything if they're unanimous. With Queen, it's all or nothing.

So Brian, Roger, Jim and I met up one day for lunch at Roger's house and, sometime later, Jim and I met John and, after that, I joined the band. That's how Brian put it and that's kind of how it felt. They work on stuff together and that meant me too. Freddie may get the full writing credit for 'Bohemian Rhapsody' but Brian wrote those giddily brilliant guitar breaks. And Brian in particular was all over my script from day one, down to every comma. He was always respectful and generous with his praise but also clear with criticism and generous with ideas. Back in those days his many thoughts would arrive by fax, often pages long and in the small hours of the morning (Brian's brain never stops buzzing).

Hearing the distant beep and whirr of my study fax in the small hours of the morning, I had no idea that I was beginning an intense and at times all-consuming association that would dominate my life for the next *fifteen years.*

Murder in the dark

Meanwhile, another miracle was occurring in my life, a major new production which under the circumstances seemed even less likely than me ending up working with Queen.

Our son Fred was on his way.

And, this time, not via a small plastic pot of sperm.

Sophie and I presumed that, after Bert and Lottie were born, family-wise we were done. We'd been delivered a perfect result in boy and girl twins and that was good enough for us. We certainly didn't consider any more IVF treatment. Nor did we consider contraception either. After six years of non-fertility, you wouldn't, would you? But, one day in July 2000, Sophie and I got the biggest surprise of our lives. After all those years, we'd finally conceived naturally – the last thing on Earth we'd expected, although apparently more common than you'd imagine. The day we found out we'd been at Jennifer's birthday lunch at the Riverside Cafe. It had turned into a long afternoon (obviously) and, when we finally got home, I was in the back garden having a drunken final fag when Sophie came out. 'You'd better have another drink. I think I'm pregnant.' She had started to have her suspicions and so had done a test, but it was an ancient kit from the very back of the bathroom cupboard and dating back to before our IVF times, years past its use-by date, so I ran into Camden to get more. I made her wee on three of them.

Fred was born on the day of our workshop production for *We Will Rock You.*

So now there were five of us and, leaving Phil and Jim to get on with the mammoth task of bringing *We Will Rock You* to the stage, our little family left Britain to spend a happy but exhausting year of babies in Fremantle.

Incidentally, I have a bit of advice for people travelling long-haul with babies. Admit that you're the elephant in the room. Every parent knows the feeling as you walk along the aisle looking for your seats, babies and toddlers probably already screaming. You can feel the hate, every traveller thinking 'Oh Christ, we've got to put up with THAT for the next God-knows-how-many hours'. Acknowledge it. Honestly, it really helps. As with so many smouldering resentments, they are at least partially alleviated by a bit of human contact. As we got strapped in, I'd say to the people behind and in front, 'Look, I know it's a pain and we really promise we'll do everything we can to keep them calm. But, frankly, if they go off, there won't be a whole lot we can do about it.' A bit of polite connection with the problem goes a long way.

Kids are hard work. The hardest. Nothing prepares you for how tired you'll be. In the first few months, Sophie was pretty much fully occupied with brand-new Fred, particularly at night, so it was down to me to deal with the terrible two who were going through, well, their 'terrible twos'. Bert, in particular, really put me through it. The twins had been pretty reasonable with us after the first very tough few months, but now they unleashed. I imagine it was Fred's arrival that triggered it. It can't be much fun to have all the world you've ever known colonized by some new guy. So there were a lot of lo-o-o-ng nights. I've done quite a lengthy routine, and also a sitcom, about the pressures of living with small children. I'm not gonna lie – wine o'clock was bath time, plastic flutes of fizz next to the baby shampoo. They'd just started putting wine in screw-top bottles, a particular advantage of which meant you could open one while holding a baby. A mild anaesthetic was essential to avoid infanticide – although, of course, babies and toddlers have their own evolutionary protection mechanism. They drive you to the point of insanity but just when you're ready to drop-kick them out of the window, they give you a little smile or a cute gurgle or say 'Love 'oo Dadda' and they're safe for another day.

There is nothing more emotionally powerful or physiologically challenging than early-years childcare and, in 2001, with three babies under two, we were right in the middle of it.

On many a night, I beat a weary path, carrying Bert in particular round the house, jiggling him for hours. Our house in Freo is pretty big and I had a three-room-and-hallway circuit. Some nights I kept a glass of Scotch on Sophie's piano and I'd have a sip on every twenty-fifth perambulation. And as I walked, I started pondering a murder mystery. The *Big Brother* phenomenon had just begun and I found it fascinating. I'd come to it via the first *Celebrity Big Brother*, which Richard Curtis did for Comic Relief in early 2001. I'll never forget the look on Anthea Turner's face when she was nominated for eviction. She had recently trodden that well-worn path from tabloid darling to tabloid whipping girl due to a decision to allow a chocolate bar to sponsor her wedding, and she had clearly gone on the show with hope of setting things right. Believing as so many have believed since that if people could only see the 'real her', then all the negative stuff would go away.

But what Anthea was learning in front of the nation, I understood instantly from the safety of my couch. That there is no 'reality' on *Big Brother*, only the fiction that the editor creates. It was so obvious to me: twenty-four cameras, 24/7, the hundreds of hours of tape that had to be edited into fifty-minute packages. There could be no *possibility* of covering the situation objectively. The only option would be to do what most documentary makers do and 'shoot the script', to decide broadly on the story you want to tell and edit towards it. If *Big Brother* wanted to have a contestant falling in love with a bit of furniture, they need only to grab a shot of the victim looking winsome and pensive and then cut to an empty sofa. Bang – you've built yourself a furniture fetishist and your victim will never escape the innuendo.

These days, the world is savvy to the manipulations of 'reality' TV, which is why we see endless postmodern refinements to the form which factor in that awareness. But, back then, the world was innocent. People believed that *Big Brother* was a genuine observation of reality. A valid social experiment even. And it occurred to me that the format offered an opportunity for a really interesting comedy thriller.

A locked and bolted mansion where nobody could enter or leave, the perfect modern environment for the old country house murder mystery where Agatha Christie would give us a snowbound house in which the lights flicker and a corpse is revealed.

The *Big Brother* house was not only locked but it had the intriguing challenge that it was entirely covered by cameras. Could I invent a plausible murder plot that took place under the relentless gaze of all those cameras and the production team watching in the control room?

That was what I pondered in the still watches of the night as I padded round our house in Fremantle with a toddler (who would wake up if I even *thought* about sitting down) in my arms – imagining the contestants locked in while cloaked and hooded camera operators glided along the outer perimeter, watching through the one-way glass. It occurred to me that it wouldn't be just the housemates who would be forming relationships. What would it be like for all the observers, watching these nubile young people over whom they held such power, manipulating them, *creating* them as their subjects endlessly dressed and undressed? Surely some strange and fascinating psychological bonds would form between the watchers and the watched.

The result of all this was *Dead Famous*, which came out in late 2001 and was my biggest hit as a novelist since *Gridlock*. And after the book had been sitting at number one for a couple of weeks, I got some interesting validation from the Big Bro' himself. Endemol (who make *Big Brother*) got in contact with me and asked who my spy was! They thought the novel was so close to the dark reality of their production process (murders aside, obviously) that they presumed I must have an inside informer. They suspected Richard Curtis, but it wasn't true. I had worked it out simply from watching the show and knowing a bit about TV. Endemol told me that, for a few series, my book was often mentioned in the house. They always edited those conversations out, though, which I thought was a bit mean of them.

There were various talks and efforts made to turn *Dead Famous* into a movie or TV series and I produced more screenplays for my pile of broken crockery. Endemol themselves looked at making it using the real house, which sounded rather exciting. We had several meetings but to no avail. You know why? They just couldn't stop being Endemol. Suddenly they wanted to *cast* the show in a *Big Brother*-style reality show, with groups of actors living in the house (as themselves) and then assuming the roles in various theatre sport games for the audience to vote on who should play the parts in the real drama. By the time we'd discussed this idea for an hour or two, my head had spun all the way up my ironic, postmodern arse and I decided to leave *Dead Famous* on the page.

2001 and 2002

(And Ever Since)

Triumph and disaster (fortunately not in that order): *We Will Rock You* from page to stage

Eventually it came time for us to return to Britain and for me to reconnect with the *We Will Rock You* production process. The story of the show's survival and eventual triumph is perhaps the most intense of my professional life.

Queen and Phil were planning a production on a massive scale and Jim had chosen, as director, a guy who had a Tony Award-winning Broadway show to his credit. I'd met him with Jim and liked him well enough. Besides, it was the producer's choice. I was just the writer and, having written the story and script, my work was done.

I did take part in final casting. Comedy isn't easy and spotting funny bones in a ten-minute audition isn't easy either. Probably the most contentious of the casting decisions was that of the female lead Scaramouche, the chippy, angry, sarky rock chick who constantly pricks the pretentions of wannabe rock god Galileo. Whoever played it had to be able to deliver huge rock songs, but also had to be a very good actress and, above all, have great, natural funny bones. After a number of false starts, the director brought in Hannah Jane Fox, who had a small role in another of his shows. It turned out to be an inspired choice and the Scaramouche Hannah created set the bar for all that would follow.

With a wonderful cast assembled (which included my old friend Nigel Planer as mad old rock guru Pop and Sharon D. Clarke as the Killer Queen), the show was ready for rehearsal and I left them to it, returning to Oz and life with screaming infants.

The next time I visited wasn't until final week in the rehearsal room when the director was to show us the first full run-through. Robert De Niro (who had decided to remain a producer) flew in from New York to attend and we all trouped down to the Alford House rehearsal rooms south of the river to check it out. It was a beyond-exciting day for the cast and, of course, I was pretty excited myself, impatient to see the story I'd dreamed up in Regent's Park 'on its legs' for the first time.

It turned out to be a disappointing afternoon. I guess – almost inevitably with all the nerves and excitement – the run-through of the show that day was going to be a bit of a damp squib, lumbering and slow and lacking comic sparkle. But, hey, it was a first full run after all and the cast were petrified with Robert De Niro and Queen sitting just a metre or two away from them, separated only by coffee cups and water bottles.

Afterwards, we 'key creatives', plus the producers, went to a restaurant for a post-run discussion. It started off low-key positive and got gloomier and gloomier. There was certainly some cause for concern. The run had been very slow and lacking in spirit, and the show was definitely too long. But first runs are almost always like that. For me, the solution was simple: I would make a few trims to the script while the director would give his production a good kick in the arse. He needed to inspire his troops and get them to pick up the pace.

But then Bob, who had said very little up to this point, started talking about the casting.

I should have seen it coming. In movies (and sadly increasingly in TV), all anybody *ever* talks about is the casting. It's rarely the script and never whatever it is that's supposed to make the sodding director so special. Just the casting. Who's in it? Are they hot? Can we do better? Everything in movies is about casting. And Bob was a movie guy to his toenails. Faced with an apparent problem, his instinct was to recast.

But this was theatre and recasting simply wasn't a physical option. We were only a week from beginning technical rehearsals. The numbers and routines were complex and could not be re-taught. Everybody had been contracted for a year and sacked people would still have to be paid. It is an absolute stone-cold practical impossibility to recast a massive musical six weeks into rehearsal, one week prior to tech and a month before the first preview.

And, anyway, the cast was not the problem. The cast were great. The problem was pace and spirit. But, true to his movie instincts, Bob was prey to the siren voice that all solutions lay in casting and started musing on alternatives. Now that was the point for the director to robustly stand up for his actors and choices, but possibly cowed by the presence of such a massive star, he went along with it, ramping up the despair by nodding sadly and saying things like 'Well, personally, I always wanted Debbie Harry for the Killer Queen', thus provoking expressions of enthusiastic interest from the movie contingent.

I mean, what the actual fuck?

Suddenly we were actually seriously talking about starting all over with the casting process on the strength of a slow run-through!

It was utter madness.

I suppose this type of star whim can be indulged in movies because everything about movie development is mad and the reason they cost insane amounts of money. But this was theatre and we had more than a hundred people under contract and the tickets had been on sale for many months. Also, having secured London's largest stage venue (the Dominion), if we failed to start generating revenue for its owners on the day that had been agreed, they would assuredly be seeing us in court.

I'm not a producer, but I'm not an idiot and I knew I had to stop this before we all talked ourselves into chucking out a *very* large baby with a teaspoon of bathwater. It wasn't down to Brian and Roger, I could see that. The music was, of course, not any kind of problem. It was the storytelling that they were trying to fix.

I told Bob that the cast was fine. Better than fine; they were great. They needed work, but that was what we had a director for. In the theatre in the meantime, work had been completed on installing our massive, multi-million-pound production and technical rehearsals were about to begin. All the costumes had been fitted and made, and the choreography and the songs had been taught. There was no point even discussing recasting one single ensemble member, let alone the leads. And there was definitely no point in fantasy discussions about casting superstars, which was where the talk was heading. Cher was not a realistic option. She was not going to take on a year's work in London for money she could make in a single hour in Las Vegas.

Bob's people sucked their cheeks and took a firm line.

Bob's people: Bob's *name* is on this thing.

I took a firm line back.

Me: All our names are on this thing – Queen's, above all.

Bob spoke.

Bob: But you know . . . If there are other casting options, we should look at them . . . delay production. Okay, not Cher but we talked about Debbie Harry . . .

Bob was still talking like a film-maker.

You can delay films. In fact, in my experience, they are *always* delayed, often indefinitely. But this wasn't a movie and there could be no delay. Besides which, there was no possibility of simply conjuring up a better cast than the one we'd arrived at after months of the most exhaustive auditioning. Massive stars were not an option because it wasn't a movie. Stars don't commit to eight shows a week for a year, which was what we required. We needed trained, talented musical theatre professionals (who could *sing* those songs eight shows a week) and those we already had. You might get a major star to do a week in an arena, but not a year in a theatre.

After I'd finished, Bob shrugged.

'Well okay, Ben. I guess we need to let the director do his work.'

The meeting soon broke up and Bob headed for the airport, but not before giving me a hug, which I thought was a very nice gesture.

I went back to Fremantle one more time, leaving the director to take his company into the theatre for the required month of technical hell. I didn't return until the very day of the first dress rehearsal, four days before the first public preview.

Why would I? It wasn't my production. We had an award-winning professional in charge. I was just the guy who wrote the book.

Sophie's parents Bob and Kate were with us when we returned to the UK and, after we'd landed, I went straight to the Dominion Theatre to watch a dress rehearsal that was scheduled to begin at 2 p.m. and end at 5 p.m. I was jet-lagged but super-excited. I had absolutely no reason to believe anything was wrong. My first warning came when I found Paul Roberts waiting for me outside the great doors of the Dominion as I emerged from the Tube entrance on the corner of Tottenham Court Road and New Oxford Street. His smile was nervous.

'I've told them "Don't panic yet. Let's see what Ben has to say."'

Ouch.

Then I walked into the Dominion where, unbeknown to me, I would be spending pretty much every waking hour for months to come.

The dress rehearsal was an absolute train wreck. The allotted time came and went. As did the evening session. And we hadn't got through Act One.

We were less than a week away from our first preview audience and the show was clearly absolutely unpresentable. In fact, the director had whispered to me during the opening bars of 'Innuendo', which begins the show, 'We'll have to postpone by at least a month. I've told Phil but he won't listen. *You* have to talk to him.'

Phil told me later that his view was if the guy couldn't get it on in the six months he'd had, then another month wouldn't make any difference, so we might as well get the car crash over with.

For me, it was absolutely devastating, a beautiful dream turned into a nightmare. In an instant. Well, a very long, very horrible ten-hour instant.

There must have been nearly a hundred people in that massive auditorium and every single one of them knew that we were facing what looked like certain catastrophe. My story and, more importantly, Queen's extraordinary music had been buried under the corpse of a lifeless, joyless £7m production that just couldn't move.

Basically, there had been a complete communication breakdown. The design had gone one way and the directing another and now they simply didn't fit in the same building, let alone on the same stage.

The one thing directors need to do is lead. Our choreographer, the endlessly energetic and inventive Arlene Phillips (who is also a massively talented director), could have sorted it all out, but she had been left alone in a dance rehearsal room, totally marginalized. Now she was horrified to find herself delivering her fabulous ensemble of dancers to a stage which had no room for them and, even more importantly, nowhere for them to go when they left it.

Much of the technical artistry involved in presenting a big-scale music-al, both in terms of design and choreography, is in the 'backstage tracks', the mind-bogglingly complex human traffic involved in delivering large companies of dancers regularly to the stage in different wigs and cos-tumes and from different parts of the set. Sadly, our stalled production allowed no room for such small details. The Dominion is an old cinema and so its wings are not generous. They're certainly not generous enough to accommodate the automated sets and Arlene's human ensemble at the same time.

At the end of ten hours, during which every aspect of the production (or the first third of it anyway) had either collapsed or ground to a halt, it suddenly became clear that it was to fall on me to address the exhausted cast and crew. I did not put myself forward, but nobody else appeared to be in a position to take the lead. They'd all been in that building for a month. I was the only new face. The director was actually lying down in the bar with his eyes closed and his fingers on his temples saying 'It's a calamity, it's a calamity'. I am not making this up.

Paul Roberts whispered, 'It's up to you. You need to say something.'

I can still feel that awful moment in that vast auditorium, facing the gloomiest-looking bunch of theatre professionals I've ever stood in front of. I thanked them all for their hard work, told them they were wonder-ful, that, clearly, we were in some difficulties and action would have to be taken, and that I and all key creatives needed time to think.

'See you at ten tomorrow morning.'

I went home that night, numb with horror and foreboding. I knew that everybody was looking to me to find a way out of the mess. I needed to take control of a design and a production that I hadn't originated, which I had yet to remotely get my head around and which was in the largest theatre in the West End, the workings of which I had no knowledge of whatsoever. It was a horrifying prospect.

Explaining what had happened to Sophie at about 1 a.m. that night, I was suddenly completely overwhelmed with despair. Maybe it was the jet lag, but I found myself tearing up. I think that this, and the time when Ade nearly dropped out of *Filthy, Rich & Catflap*, are the only times I've ever done that over work.

There was a lot to do. The show clearly needed cutting. The set had to be streamlined and the only way to do that was to edit and rearrange the action. Clearly that was my job as writer. But besides that, I knew I had to breathe some life into the complete lack of heart, soul and any vestige of *humour* that currently existed in the performances. The whole thing felt like it had already died and was waiting to be buried in what would be an extremely public funeral.

So, the next morning I took over as director. I didn't do it officially until long after we'd opened. Roger and Brian had wanted to make it official there and then but I said no. It wasn't my mess and I didn't want the media saying I'd barged in and fucked it up. It was a very difficult situation and I did my best to act respectfully and to make my sudden and unlooked-for authority appear a cooperative project.

I must add that the one aspect of the show which was already close to perfect was the sound production and the music. Brian and Roger had seen to that, assembling and rehearsing the band, creating the orchestrations and working on the sound design. Up until then, however, like everybody else on the show they'd been compartmentalized, operating in their own little bubble, passengers on their own musical. The director had even discouraged them from attending rehearsals, which astonished me. I mean, who bans Queen from Queen? Brian and Roger are both absolutely inspired creatives – not just musically but theatrically in every sense. It was obvious to me that the more they involved themselves in the production, the better it would be. From that moment on, we worked together 24/7 to shape a cohesive vision for our show. Brian in particular was as ever across every detail of script and production. I found him an invaluable creative resource. They both were and the three of us have been working on *We Will Rock You* together ever since.

Anyway, I cut and I slashed and I rearranged. Nigel Planer told me that I was known among the company as the Ninja. I worked sixteen hours a day, every day. I had just a few days left before the first official preview and Nigel also told me a book had been opened backstage on how many shows I'd have to cancel. The most optimistic punt was fifteen. We cancelled only two. Admittedly, the first few shows we got on were pretty slow and a bit stop-start, but we worked on it all day every day over the full month of previews. Slowly but surely, it began to come together. I cut and cut and wrote new dialogue and even changed the plot to cover the gaps. With Brian and Roger, I redistributed songs and chucked large and horribly costly chunks of our lovely set into a skip. The day that the Killer Queen's massive foam-filled bath – and the golden stairway down which she descended into it – got chucked was a sad one. But it was too big to get on and too big to get off, and when it was backstage, there was no room for more plot-driven bits of set, so out it went.

Alongside the technical challenges, I worked constantly with the human element. First and foremost, the story of We Will Rock You is a comic satire. It needs lightness of touch, glee, confidence, joie de vivre. Scaramouche is a wise-cracking cynic, Galileo a pompous, preening wannabee rock star, the Killer Queen a half-pixellated escapee from a video game. The rebel Bohemians are so confused about the lost history of rock that they revere the Wombles as much as the Beatles. Amidst the industrial warzone that was our tech work, I needed to rediscover the show's humanity.

About a week and a half before opening night, we got our first standing ovation and from that moment on, no We Will Rock You performance anywhere in the world has failed to get one. These days, standing ovations for musicals have become almost an obligatory ritual, but they certainly weren't back in 2002. In fact, I think We Will Rock You started the trend.

And so the crisis had passed. Contrary to our fearful expectations, we had our show ready for opening night.

And what a brilliant, wonderful, exciting night it was.

I had so many friends there and all my family. De Niro was there, of course, the biggest among a host of guest celebs (although I was more excited about Noddy Holder of Slade). Sophie and I sat next to Bob and it went just great. The standing ovation was genuine and the cheers loud and long. Bob turned to me and said, 'Well, I guess we got a hit.'

He was standing in the middle of 2,500 cheering punters, having heard a barrelful of laughs, a few tears and large swathes of some of the best-loved rock music in the world delivered live and thrillingly. Why wouldn't he think it was a hit, particularly since he wasn't British and came from a country where popular success wasn't a term of abuse?

As far as he could see, everybody seemed to love us.

And almost everybody did. But, sadly, not *quite* everybody.

We would find out who didn't the following morning.

We Are The Champions – eventually

Queen and I had prepared ourselves. We didn't expect an easy ride.

There had been portents. Jonathan Ross (yes, him again) had set a nasty tone on his BBC chat show a few days before. His production office had contacted Phil asking for two first-night tickets for Jonathan, which, of course, had been supplied. He was, after all, the biggest broadcaster in the country at that time and the BBC's entertainment department seemed to be his and his coke-snorting rottweiler agent Addison Creswell's personal fiefdom.

Anyway, guess what Jonathan did with those tickets? In his opening monologue to his studio audience, he claimed to have been 'sent' two first-night gala tix, but wouldn't dream of attending such a god-awful horror as a Queen jukebox musical by Ben Elton and so was offering them to anyone who wanted them. These were actually the hottest tickets in London that week, but the audience had been fully briefed and so no one put their hand up, after which he threw them away live on air.

Yes, it wasn't as if both Queen and I weren't used to haters. The *NME*, when reviewing their 1977 album *News of the World*, had famously dismissed two tracks in particular, stating that, on a generally awful album, 'We Will Rock You' and 'We are the Champions' stood out as among the worst songs ever written. But the level of hate we got on the morning of 15 May 2002 was beyond anything even either I or Queen had experienced before. The reviews were so bad that their savagery made the TV news and our closure was confidently and gleefully predicted in all media outlets.

Queen got it bad. I got it worse. After all, being world-conquering hits already, their songs were harder to dismiss as crimes against music, but my criminally awful script was theirs to misunderstand and misrepresent to their heart's content. The absolute universal critical consensus was that I should be publicly pilloried for the childish banality, the cheap humour, the pathetic, lazy, ridiculous and predictable plot and, above all, the CYNICISM of this new low in my irredeemably compromised career.

This was the justification for the fury of the tone. 'Don't give them your money,' *Time Out* screamed. It was a common theme. Reviewing for Radio 4, comedian Stewart Lee made a public appeal to all artists and journalists to unite in their efforts to shut down this cultural abomination. Apparently, it was nothing but a disgustingly grubby money-making venture by a couple of multi-millionaire dinosaur rock stars and a sordid little champagne socialist. The *Daily Mirror* reviewer called for me to be shot.

It was interesting the way money kept coming up in all the commentary. Critics don't normally object to the possibility that a show might make a profit.

And, for what it's worth, we weren't doing it for the money. The investors were taking enormous financial risks in order to ensure that our audience got better *value* for money than any other show in the West End. *We Will Rock You* cost seven million pounds to mount. That was very hard to raise, but Queen had said from day one that our show had to be bigger and more spectacular than any other and everyone involved risked a very great deal to ensure that happened.

And for the record, apart from in my earliest days, I have never done a job for the money. I've been lucky, I never had to. But I would be a great deal richer if I *had* gone after the money. I alone among my entire generation of alternative stars never did an advert. And I was offered plenty. To be clear, I don't *object* to adverts, or stars doing them. Ads fund programmes. Anyone who works for ITV and Channel 4 (as I have done many times) is being paid with advertising revenue. I just personally didn't do them. I was famous for being a comedian with opinions and attitude. I figured that if my attitude to a product could be seen to be bought, I would undermine the very reason anyone was interested in my opinions in the first place.

So, no. *We Will Rock You* wasn't made for the money. Indeed, it didn't *make* any money for a couple of years. Its weekly running costs were astronomical and so chipping away to pay back the original investment was a very long haul. *We Will Rock You* was made for love – the love of live music and of live theatre.

Another theme common to many of the reviews was the certainty that Freddie would have hated it. They were quite sure about that and were very angry on his behalf.

Well, here's what Freddie's mum had to say about that. His family came to the opening night. The following morning (after the reviews), his mum sent a beautiful note to us all at the theatre. This is what she said.

Freddie would have loved this show.

It's a comedy and he loved to laugh and it looks to the future where Freddie always looked.

If music be the food of love – Rock On!

Robert De Niro rang me. I was back working in the theatre (there was still much to do, besides which, once a show opens, you have to get the understudies up to speed asap) and there was no caller ID on mobiles back then, so I didn't pick up. He left a nice message. I quote his very words: 'Ben, it's Bob. I'm so sorry. You didn't deserve this. You really didn't.'

The whole company assembled on stage for a meeting. We had to say *something*. Everybody tried to be brave and Jim read out that old *NME* verdict on the original 'We Will Rock You' song, but there was no disguising the fact that more than a hundred people were staring down the barrel of immediate unemployment. They'd all thought they had a guaranteed year. Rent had been paid on the strength of it. Loans taken out. Theatre arts is a very precarious business. In no other industry is it possible for a tiny group of completely disassociated strangers to make large groups of workers redundant on a whim. Even if theatre artists are working (which they aren't most of the time), they're mostly on bare minimum. Our show was a big employer, perhaps the West End's biggest at that moment. We represented a considerable percentage of the current work available to the many dedicated musical theatre professionals. We were also occupying the Dominion, a notorious barn of a gig which is almost impossible to make pay. If we had closed in a sudden and shocking collapse, it certainly would not have been easy for its owners to find another show of sufficient scale to fill it. The building would have been 'dark' for many months, maybe a year, representing a massive dent in the fragile viability of London commercial theatre.

I'm not saying any of this obligates critics to give good reviews, but I do think it might make them think twice before actively trying to close something. Yet the *joy* provoked by our presumed certain closure was palpable and deeply dispiriting. Talk about fucking schadenfreude! *The Stage* newspaper actually front paged the news 'Queen musical to close'. Most arts pages were giving us a month tops, with a very sincere fuck off and good riddance, another tawdry Punch and Judy show that should get the hell out of London's West End.

People often say to me, 'But you got the last laugh, didn't you?'

Not really. There was nothing to laugh about in that dreadful mugging and there never will be. It was just awful. And, at the time, brutally effective.

Because reviews do matter. In theatre, they matter above all. They still do even in our internet age, but much more so back then when print was king and newspapers set agendas.

On the day after we opened, our box office take was cut *in half*. The day after a star-studded opening night, traditionally a production's biggest day ever, was our worst. Such a collapse was unprecedented and it was desperate. The only comfort were the wonderful reactions of the half-full audiences who were attending the show and the ovation they gave us each night.

And somehow, over many months, things slowly began to turn around.

Hannah Jane Fox and the company did a brilliant 'Somebody to Love' on *Parkinson* with Brian and Roger playing. That helped. Parky had seen the show and loved it and was kind enough to make that clear on his show, saying it 'lights up London'. We put that on the front of our theatre.

And we also got a very nice boost from the actual Queen. Well, not directly, I admit. But we played at her Royal Golden Jubilee concert.

Queen were there with our whole cast delivering a blistering set on what was a wonderful, happy afternoon. I was doing some compering duties and, of course, the highlight of the whole thing was Brian playing the national anthem 100 per cent live on the roof of Buckingham

Palace – utterly alone save for a lone camera operator, in considerable wind and synched via ear pieces to a full orchestra and a flipping military band hundreds of metres below. Imagine the pressure, knowing that a billion eyes are on you. But he pulled it off to perfection, playing with haunting beauty and, of course, adding the sort of impossibly inventive power riffing that makes him one of the greatest guitar heroes in the whole rock pantheon.

But Queen and *the* Queen notwithstanding, what really saved WWRY was word of mouth. Frankly, that's all that can ever save a show. It was touch and go, though. For many months, we had 'the curtains in', a terribly depressing theatre ruse which involves hanging massive drapes in the auditorium to reduce its size. We cut off many hundreds of seats in the stalls every night. Audiences had to walk down half the length of the centre aisle past row after row of empty seats before being directed through a slash in the vast black cloth wall in order to enter the half of the stalls we were selling. Many nights we didn't open the balcony at all.

Then, all of a sudden, we were a smash.

We had survived just long enough to hit the critical mass where word of mouth begins to build an advance. A trickle became a flood. At first, we'd been playing largely to people who particularly liked Queen (and who didn't read theatre reviews), but eventually we crossed every demographic. The year after we opened, the show won the Theatregoers' Choice Award for best new musical. Eight years into its run, it won an Olivier for most popular musical.

Roger threw a party for the cast at his home in Surrey. What a day. The sun shone and there was a swimming pool, endless wine and food. Queen chartered a bus to bring everyone down so that they could really enjoy themselves. There was even a hypnotist show. I didn't watch, but Sophie was in there with the children and she looked down to find Bert (who was three) completely mesmerized! She had to take him out and gently bring him round. A number of other adults and kids had a similar experience. I've never really believed in any of that stuff, but I did a bit after that.

We Will Rock You ran for twelve years in London and also in numerous productions around the world. In the end, it played to more than twenty million people (and counting), all enjoying the real fellowship of live theatre. I've stood among them many times, waving my arms with the rest. It's a great feeling.

For more than a decade, while our enormous, beautiful Freddie statue stood at the foot of Tottenham Court Road, *We Will Rock You* was the central feature of my professional life. I rehearsed every new London cast and supervised shows all over the world. Andrew Lloyd Webber warned me very firmly not to continue to direct it. 'You cannot nurse this show around the world, Ben. It will take over your life.' He was right. It did. And I have loved every minute (almost).

Generally, West End and Broadway hits are subsequently ignored by the original creatives. They are boxed up with what is called 'The Bible', the annotated script that describes every breath and move and twitch of the first incarnation, and then reproduced abroad by associate directors in ever diminishingly scaled productions. In fact, originating directors don't normally even return to the original shows much. There's a famous showbiz joke about *Starlight Express*, which was directed by Trevor Nunn. Apparently, the cast wrote to *Jim'll Fix It* asking for him to fix it for them to meet their director.

Brian, Roger and I haven't been like that. We have personally supervised the casting, the band and the production of all the major originating productions of *WWRY* worldwide. We have to do it; our show depends on the individual creativity of the artists in it. Rock bones and funny bones are very individual things.

It's been hard work but also fascinating, and a wonderful privilege to get the chance to immerse myself in musical theatre worldwide. Most notably, I've directed productions in Las Vegas, New York, Melbourne, Toronto (twice), the Netherlands and Sweden – and, most successfully, all our wonderful German-language productions in Switzerland, Austria and Germany, all produced by the late Michael Brenner, a dear friend and champion of popular art.

And the best part of all of my many years working on *We Will Rock You* has been the friendship I forged with Brian and Roger. Brian and I have even called it a kind of brotherhood. We have been collaborators and dreamers together.

Brian is a true Renaissance man. Besides his globally celebrated brilliance as a song writer, maestro guitarist and general Queen visionary he holds a Physics PhD in interplanetary dust and is a friend and colleague of NASA. He has a thousand different interests, ranging from animal welfare to stereo daguerreotypes (an early photographic process). He is the most fascinating of men and ours has been a wonderful friendship and creative collaboration. We have exchanged many hundreds of emails over the years digging ever deeper into our mutual passion for our show, discussing every tweak and rewrite. And also, thrillingly, Brian has regularly *appeared* in the show! He has performed on all of the major first nights. I have stood in many packed and roaring auditoriums watching Brian May emerge from a stage trap to join the company for 'Bohemian Rhapsody', tearing off those mighty riffs, his arm slashing in the smoke and the lights. Let me tell you, the love and energy in the room on those very special nights is unique and overwhelming. *We Will Rock You* has been a bumpy road at times for me, but Bri's loyalty and support has never wavered. And of course our friendship exists outside of the show. We've enjoyed many dinners together, occasionally in the company of his wife Anita. Anita is a very busy and successful actress so I don't often see her, but when I do it's a treat. She loves a champ and a giggle! Bri reads my novels and has attended all my stand-up shows, very publicly supporting my work outside of Queen on his social media, which is always such a boost.

And I truly treasure my friendship with Roger also. We have enjoyed many wonderful times together, both working on our show and socially, sharing many a 'nasty lasty' as Roger brilliantly named that unwise final round. Aside from his fearsome creative talents as songwriter, drummer and visionary rock original, Roger is also ridiculously well-read, well-informed and forensically astute on pretty much any subject under the sun. This makes him one of the world's great dining companions. It's impossible not to be enthused by his sheer love of life and there are few things I look forward to more than joining Roger and his lovely wife Sarina to enjoy one of his favourite things: 'a lovely long lunch'. Like Bri, Rog is also hugely supportive of my life outside of Queen – he too reads my novels, and he and Sarina always come to my stand-up shows, which means so much to me.

I believe those bonds with Brian and Roger, which are set not in stone but in ROCK, will be a part of my life for as long as I live.

So that's me and Queen, one of the great boons of my life. I know I talk quite a lot in this book about the crap I've copped over the years, but I really do know how lucky I've been!

2002

Failing towards America, part four.
Taken prisoner by DreamWorks

As the intensity surrounding the birth, near-death and triumphant resur-
rection of *We Will Rock You* began to lessen, I started to think about other
stuff. I wrote a screenplay for Rowan. It was my effort at the spy spoof
he was after, which would eventually produce *Johnny English*. Row was
enthusiastic for a while, but my first draft was a mad gag fest and I had
too many commitments to put in the required number of rewrites, so it
withered on the vine. I also did a TV screenplay of *Silly Cow*, which Dawn
and I got quite excited about for a while, but yet again I didn't have time to
focus properly and we both moved on to other things.

Two more piles of broken crockery. My own fault again. Either do
something properly or don't do it at all. It's taken me a lifetime to learn
that lesson. In fact, writing this book has helped a lot with that process.
Better late than never, I suppose.

A more successful writing project was another novel. I'd written it in
late 2001 and early 2002, again mainly in Fremantle. By this time, Bert
no longer needed walking round the house at 2 a.m., but all three kids
often woke us up and when that happened, instead of going back to sleep,
I'd find my mind racing and have to go to my desk. There were so many
nights when I watched the dawn through the window of my study, writing
away and waiting for the first baby/toddler to stir and the day's mayhem
to begin again.

The novel was called *High Society* and it was a passionate denunciation
of the so-called war on drugs, which had clearly been lost decades ago. It

won the WH Smith People's Choice Award for Fiction and, rather surreally, I was asked to address the Drug and Alcohol Committee of the Scottish Parliament in Holyrood. The assembled MSPs all strenuously condemned my call for legalization during the session and then, in the bar afterwards, admitted that it was the only way and that the current zero tolerance 'war' was a madness of which the only beneficiary was organized crime – 'but, of course, we can't say so *publicly*, Ben. The press would kill us.'

Then, towards the end of 2002, I got a call which would lead to what was perhaps my best chance yet at a career in the US industry.

And yet again, I blew it. Although, on balance, I think I was right.

The man on the phone was a New Zealander called Andrew Adamson, who had directed the smash hit DreamWorks movie *Shrek*. Being a Kiwi, he knew my stuff right back to *The Young Ones* and he liked it (NZ used to show a lot of British TV). Now he was working on the sequel to *Shrek* and wanted to know if I'd take a look at how far he'd got and maybe muck in a bit.

What a lovely call to get.

Andrew turned out to be a very nice and interesting bloke – as you would imagine the co-creator of *Shrek* would be. He was a really cool, long-haired, laid-back friendly Kiwi with a touch of surf and mountain about him. When we met in London, we hit it off immediately. All he wanted me to do was come over to DreamWorks in LA and take a look at work in progress on *Shrek 2* and offer my thoughts. Exciting stuff.

So, I was brought to DreamWorks, the fiefdom of the legendary studio executive Jeffrey Katzenberg who, for decades, has been one of the two or three most powerful people in Hollywood.

It was a very strange day. The whole place was a kind of benign fortress, a sort of hippy ethic on the surface with lots of beards and T-shirts amongst the suits, but underneath it was clear there lurked a stupendously efficient corporate machine. It's gleaming and shiny and there is free food and drink everywhere. No booze, but lots of everything else. Whatever you want – good food and health drinks, candy and soda. Just pick it up and consume it.

'That's so people don't have to leave,' I was told. 'They feed you so they can keep you working.'

The place did sort of have the feel of a prison: a very, very comfortable one, but still a kind of place of incarceration. There was a lot of security hoo-hah to get in and, as I was to discover later, it wasn't so blinking easy to get out either.

On the morning I was invited, they were having a full screening of the assemblage created so far and many people had gathered to see it: animators, storyboarders, music people, techno wizzes . . . It was very much a work-in-progress screening, very interesting for me, of course – not everyone gets to drop in on a DreamWorks mega movie halfway through production.

After coffee, during which nobody spoke to me, we were all invited into the plush screening room with a notepad and torch pen on every seat. We'd been told the screening was about to start but it wasn't. Jeffrey hadn't arrived yet. So we all sat in near-silence as the minutes ticked by. There was a definite tinge of nervousness about the place. In my very limited experience, Hollywood is pretty feudal. The bosses really are all-powerful barons and their studios are their castles. Richard Curtis takes a more positive view of the place, but then he makes smash hit movies and, in Hollywood (which is no longer a single town but a global US production archipelago), power and status are everything.

Eventually the great man arrived. The room fell completely silent as he swept in, speaking on the phone as he bustled to his seat, accompanied by his assistants.

He sat down beside Andrew and, after a cursory nod of greeting and without acknowledging anybody else, he continued his phone call. It was fascinating. Here was a man, at whose command we had all assembled and for whom we'd all been waiting now for some time, sitting amongst us but ignoring us entirely while speaking to someone who wasn't even in the room while we sat in on Katzenberg's side of the conversation. A textbook exercise in passive-aggressive power.

I'm actually not dissing him. I respect him. Hollywood is a different culture and perhaps a more realistic one. There may have been no time for manners, but there was equally no time for *false* manners. It was Jeffrey's gig and his rules. At least you knew where you were. I've been love-bombed by plenty of people who didn't really give a fuck about me.

At work if people don't give a fuck about me, I'd prefer it if they don't pretend that they do.

Anyway, eventually Jeffrey finished his call. He nodded briefly to Andrew and waved at the screen.

The movie was half-made. Most of the voicing had been done (including Jennifer as the Fairy Godmother – so strange to suddenly hear her voice so far from home. The last time I'd heard her she'd been slurring slightly over the cheese at the end of one of Ade's monumental Sunday lunches), but only about 50 per cent of the computer-generated animation was in place. The rest was storyboarded with wonderful still line-drawings, which reminded me of documentaries about Disney making *Snow White*. Sometimes there was nothing on screen at all and we listened to Mike Myers and Eddie Murphy in darkness.

When it was over, the lights came up and Jeffrey got up and left. Andrew rose and nodded to me to follow. A smaller group of about fifteen was assembling around a table in a conference room for the big chat. I'd been at DreamWorks now (at their invitation) for about three and a half hours and, with the exception of a friendly 'hello' from Andrew, not a single person had said a word to me since I cleared security.

I took a seat among this large group of strangers with Jeffrey and Andrew at the head of it and we all sat there while they began an intense, whispered conversation without so much as a nod to the rest of us. I was starting to get a bit irritated now. I'm really not someone who expects status in any shape or form, but I was beginning to wonder why I was even there. I had been told that I was being brought in as some kind of comedy sounding board and, now, I was very much an anonymous part of an anonymous crowd of DreamWorkers watching the big boss whisper to his main man.

Also, I was feeling uncomfortable because – I'll have to say it although it sounds so *wrong* – I hadn't thought much of the movie. I found the plot inconsistent, the gags too few (with too many opportunities missed) and, above all, the characters were starting to irritate, particularly Shrek whose single dimensional grumpiness was wearing thin with me.

Clearly, I know NOTHING. *Shrek 2* took almost a billion dollars and, after more than twenty years, remains a beloved part of popular culture.

After Jeffrey and Andrew had sat and whispered for about ten minutes, they began to open it up a bit. Jeffrey started firing questions at various figures round the table. They were getting into detail when personally I thought they needed to address some bigger issues, like pace, plot holes and sometimes irritating characters. But nobody asked me. My very presence had still not been even acknowledged.

So, when a tiny gap appeared in Jeffrey's interrogations, I decided to take my moment and spoke up – uninvited. I think it was probably the first time it had ever happened in that conference room but, fuck it, I hadn't asked to be there. They came to me. I was certainly the only person in the room who wasn't getting paid.

Jeffrey was talking to an animator or a production supervisor or something about some small detail he'd picked up on and I said, 'Excuse me but I'd like to make a couple of general points, if that's okay.'

I said it nicely and I didn't cut over anyone. I waited for a pause but I did say it.

The room fell silent and Jeffrey turned to me. It seemed that he had been aware of my presence after all, because he said: 'And what does our English friend have to say for himself?'

I'd flown half round the world at their invitation and those were the first words anybody said to me. Mind you, I should be so lucky. This was Katzenberg. People in Hollywood would kill to be patronized by him.

Andrew nodded to me. He's a very decent man and had made it clear when we met in London that he wanted me to be honest about what I felt and so I began to list the areas I thought needed work. After about a minute, Katzenberg stopped me. Literally, mid-sentence.

'Stop! Don't say another word. Not one.'

Well, I thought, that's it. Game over. It looked like I was about to be slung out of DreamWorks on my arse. But I wasn't. Quite the opposite in fact. They took me prisoner.

'We have a lot to do here,' Jeffrey went on, 'detail that you don't care about nor can help us with. Also, it's corrupting. We've been on this two years already. You've done two hours. I don't want you a party to our discussions. I want you fresh and honest. Go away now and write down all your impressions, every single one. Take the rest of the day. All night if you need it. You'll be given an office.'

That's a leader of men for you. He hadn't said hello or referred to me by name. I didn't work for him and he certainly wasn't offering to pay me, but he absolutely *ordered* me to start working for DreamWorks until I'd done what he wanted.

And I did. I suppose I *could* have said no and asked them to call me a cab, but it didn't feel that way. There was already a smiling staffer standing behind me. She'd gathered up my bag. Another stood at the door which she'd already opened. I got up and went with them. Not another word was said. Jeffrey had already re-focused on the conversation I'd interrupted before the door closed behind me.

They took me down by lift into a subterranean world of little rooms filled with many screens and found me an empty one. I was given a computer, offered food and coffee, and left on my own. It felt so weird, sitting alone, deep in the bowels of DreamWorks, on the orders of a mogul who had yet to even address me by name. It really did seem like I might never actually get out.

I worked for about four hours and, when I'd finished, I handed in my essay to one of the numerous PAs and was allowed to leave.

'Jeffrey would like to see you here at 9 a.m. to discuss this.'

Not 'could you please' but 'Jeffrey wants'. When you're at DreamWorks, employee or not, that's an order.

Andrew called me later and arranged for us to have coffee at 8 a.m. When we met, he had a copy of my notes.

'Wow, you don't pull punches, do you?'

For a minute, I thought he was angry but he wasn't. He could take criticism. Of course, he didn't necessarily agree with it (and no doubt with good reason) but he could take it. I'm the same. If you're getting notes from somebody you respect, no matter how critical they may be, it's *always* useful. Even if you don't see eye to eye, you can learn simply from hearing what worried them.

'Of course, I didn't say all the good stuff,' I replied nervously.

'Quite right,' Andrew said with a big smile. 'We don't have time for nice at DreamWorks'.

The meeting with Jeffrey was as cold and distant as the first had been. Again, there were a number of people attending, eight or nine, and again

Jeffrey spoke mainly to Andrew and in hushed tones. He had my notes in his hand and kept referring to me across the table but in the third person.

'He's right about this . . . He's wrong about that . . . This is interesting but we're past that point.'

Two things came out of the meeting. Andrew wanted me to do a bit of work on the script of *Shrek 2*. What they call 'hood and fender' stuff, gagging things up. There wasn't a lot of room to manoeuvre. Most of the dialogue was 'locked' because the animation was already being created, which meant that even raising one of Donkey's eyebrows would cost tens of thousands of dollars. But the early part of the movie was still under review and I was welcome to offer up suggestions in that area. I ended up doing a bit of work on the scenes when Shrek is summoned to Far Far Away in as much as I threw a thousand lines at it and I think Andrew may have used one or two.

The second thing that was discussed at that meeting was that, out of the blue, Jeffrey Katzenberg announced he wanted me to make *my own* movie at DreamWorks.

Yes, you read that right. It was that sudden.

It wouldn't be *quite* my own. They already had a basic idea, but it was in its very earliest stages, and I could take it in any direction I wanted. I was to write it and also, hard to believe even now, direct it.

Wow. This was unprecedented, the sort of break that every writer in the US dreamed of: to be *personally* commissioned by Jeffrey Katzenberg to write and direct a DreamWorks animated comedy on just an hour's acquaintance. It was the *personal* thing that stunned people most when I told them. People queued all their lives to get face time with Katzenberg and I'd lucked into it via a Kiwi *Young Ones* fan. And been given my own movie the following day.

And the idea was great, too. Really great.

They wanted to make a movie about a bunch of animals putting on a show in Las Vegas.

That was it: the whole thing in one line. The rest was up to me. What was more, while I was on the West Coast, they wanted me to *go* to Vegas, at once – tomorrow, in fact – and spend a few days checking out all the shows. You think I'm making it up? I promise I'm not.

So, I said 'O-o-oh, all right then' and DreamWorks put together an itinerary that afternoon. There was no problem getting into all the sold-out shows when Katzenberg's office was asking. I was to leave the following morning with a couple of DreamWorks producers who had been assigned to development. First-class flights, first-class hotels. The best seats in the house for all the shows. All this had come on the strength of my less-than-positive *Shrek* notes. When Sophie says to me 'Treat 'em mean, keep 'em keen', she's talking about her attitude to me. But it had worked just as well between me and DreamWorks.

But I didn't go to Vegas.

Because while this rather exciting conversation was being conducted in LA, back in London, Bert was having an asthma attack. As it turned out, he's not very asthmatic at all, just moderately, as many kids are these days. Every now and then, he needs a puffer, but not often. However, this was the first time it had manifested itself. Sophie had been alone in the night in London with two three-year-olds and a one-year-old and, out of the blue, one of them had started wheezing and gasping and seeming to struggle for breath. She'd been up all night on the edge of taking him to casualty, which would have meant waking up the other two and taking all three of them. When I spoke to her, she'd seen a doctor and knew that Bert was asthmatic but not yet how badly. What with Fred and Lottie sensing tension and going off as well, she was understandably pretty frazzled and very worried about Bert.

'I think you should come home,' she said.

This is I think the only time Sophie has ever asked me to put family before work. I *have* done, many times incidentally, but she's never asked me to.

So, an hour after it had been agreed, I told Jeffrey that I couldn't do the Vegas trip. It didn't go down well. Tickets had been reserved and flights booked. Also, I could see that he was excited about his animal idea and wanted to get on with it. But it had to be.

Looking back, I wonder if that trip might have bonded me closer to DreamWorks and made it harder to make the decision I eventually made. If it did, then it's a good thing because I know I was right. Who knows, but for Bert's wheezing in the night, we could all have moved to LA and the kids would have American accents.

Anyway, Vegas trip or not, I promised to think hard about their animal show idea and I did. Back in Britain, I prepared a set of notes on some animal characters and the semblance of a plot and sent them back to DreamWorks. Jeffrey had them before I would have even got back from the Vegas trip, if I'd gone. I've always worked very quickly; sometimes it's a good thing, sometimes not. This time it was. They were thrilled at the quick turnaround and loved my material.

Within hours, my development colleagues were back on the phone saying Jeffrey wanted to get on a call and giving me the time he expected me to be available. Not asking me, telling me. *This is when Jeffrey wants to talk to you.*

As it happened, I couldn't do it. I was minding the babies; Sophie had to take one to a doctor or something and I needed to be there for the other two. What's more, the time Jeffrey wanted was *feeding time* in the UK – 5.30 p.m. – the hell hour when the kids were at their most tired and I'd have been on my second glass of wine, just before their bath. I suppose I could have held off on the booze, but frankly there was no way I could do a serious call with two out of three of our mini-terrorists demanding my attentions. I told them that I couldn't make that time and I explained why.

Here's what the bloke said. 'What are you? Pussy-whipped?'

Not kidding.

Anyway, they found a different time. Jeffrey Katzenberg rearranged a call, possibly another first for DreamWorks. And he did it because he liked what I'd written. He's not an effusive guy – you'd get more man-love from a Dalek – but within the boundaries of his inscrutable reserve, he was gushing.

'I enjoyed and approve of your exploratory notes.'

Honestly, it was like working with Rowan.

'We're going to make this movie,' Jeffrey went on '*You're* going to make your movie.'

At this point, I should mention that, while I was briefly in LA, I'd learned a little bit about what it meant to make a movie for DreamWorks – and, I imagine, every other studio.

'It's basically indentured slavery,' I'd been told. 'They pay you not particularly much and you work until Jeffrey is satisfied. It's open ended. You get your deal but there's no time frame. It takes as long as it takes but there's no more money'.

This is, of course, the kind of deal you get *before* you have a hit. After you've had one, things improve, but for the first movie it's pretty harsh. It's just the way the system works. A first-time writer/director might get maybe $300,000 upfront, which might seem like a lot, but after three years maybe not so much, particularly if you've had all the huge expense of relocation. Because that's the other thing: you *have* to be at DreamWorks. Their movies are made on computers in their fortress. That's where the director needs to be – or, at least, they did then. CGI movies take at least three years and you spend all day, every day in the prison full of free food. But, on the outside (if you're not from LA) there's a second home, a second set of taxes, new schools, new furnishings and a car – all of which has to be covered by your initial advance. And, at the end of it, they might not even finish or release your movie.

Anyway, there I was with these words of warning in my ears, but also with one of the three most important people in global entertainment expressing muted enthusiasm for my notes.

And they were fun notes, because it was a fun idea: an all-animal musical troupe struggling to put on a show in human-dominated Las Vegas. I still love it now. The character I'd written, which everybody liked most, was the gay sheepdog. There's a TV show in Australia where sheep-rearing jackaroos and their sheepdogs show off their skills. Gnarled, taciturn Crocodile Dundees growl indiscernible commands at their dogs, which then drill the sheep into perfect lines and fascist rally-style formations. My idea was that one of these dogs, trapped in a world of grim, rural regimentation, was in fact a Priscilla Queen of the Desert-style character who kept trying to choreograph the sheep into fabulous show numbers instead of making them march into pens. Eventually he's thrown out of the outback sheep station and makes his way to Vegas. He, of course, would end up choreographing the show. There were lots of other characters but that gives you an idea.

And Jeffrey loved it.

By happy circumstance, he and his development team were going to be in the UK talking to Aardman (the *Wallace and Gromit* people) on what would eventually become *Flushed Away*, so he suggested that I spend some time with his two top development guys and then present it all to him while he himself was in Britain. So that's what we did and great fun it was too. I got on very well with my new colleagues, despite the fact that we'd missed out on our Vegas bonding session. We figured we'd get to go in the end and it would be all the more useful for us having real story targets to location hunt for. So we discussed my plot and characters and we laughed a lot and then I went away and constructed a new treatment in fuller detail with a few bits of dialogue thrown in. Armed with this, the three of us went to see Jeffrey at some swanky hotel in London. I'm pretty sure it was Claridge's, but I can't be certain as my diary doesn't say.

We went up to his suite and I handed over my pages, pages my two new colleagues and I loved, pages they'd been very pleased with.

It was like me and Richard taking those sketches to Rowan for *The New Review.* Except this time, as it turned out, I was on my own.

Jeffrey and I sat opposite each other in old-fashioned leather armchairs. The two guys from DreamWorks flanked me. After all, we were pitching this together. Or so I thought. As Jeffrey read, he started to make verbal notes – very critical verbal notes. 'This is no good . . . 'You can't do that' . . . 'I didn't see this going in that direction at all'. As he spoke, I sensed movement around me. Slowly, discreetly, my guys were shifting across the thick carpet until, by the time Jeffrey looked up from my pages, they were flanking *him* not me. Clearly Jeffrey's reaction hadn't been as positive as they'd hoped it would be and they were making sure they didn't get caught up in the fall-out.

Actually, the let-down was really just a symptom of my previous success. Jeffrey had been so positive about finding a new talent that he'd been slightly less dour than usual. All he was doing now was getting back to business. The honeymoon was over. Now we were starting work in earnest, which was, of course, fair enough.

But, as Jeffrey spoke, I began to realize that this wasn't for me. Perhaps if I hadn't been warned about how the system worked, I might have felt differently. But I could see exactly what was happening; the open-ended years of working towards Jeffrey had begun. He was pretty much throwing out everything I'd written, stuff which previously I was under the impression he'd loved.

I asked him why.

'I loved it because it told me what you were capable of,' he snapped impatiently. 'Now you need to justify my faith.'

Like I say, if hadn't known what I knew about the business side of things . . .

If I hadn't been so busy (I was actually leaving for Australia that very night to direct *We Will Rock You* in Melbourne for its Australian premiere) . . .

If Phil hadn't just struck a two-novel book deal for me that would pay a very great deal more than DreamWorks were offering . . .

If I wasn't in pre-production of my Rod Stewart musical (I'll get to that) . . .

If I'd had the next three years spare to devote my *entire* energies to Jeffrey (that's what writing/directing requires) without any guarantee of success at the end (most movies fail if they're even made) . . .

Above all, if I'd felt comfortable about relocating my young family to a suburb of Los Angeles and then not seeing them for twelve hours every day while Sophie went quietly crazy as, to all intents and purposes, she became a single mum (mom!) alone in California . . .

If I didn't already have a life, personally and professionally . . .

If I'd been twenty-one-years old and single, instead of forty-four and married with children . . .

If all those things had been or not been the case, I'd have grabbed the biggest break of my life with both hands and never let go.

But it had come twenty years too late and I knew I had to be brave.

'Jeffrey, I'd love to do this but I just don't think it will work.'

'Ben,' he said. 'I am giving you the chance to make your own movie.'

But, you see, he wasn't. He was giving me the chance to make *his* movie. My job was to keep working and keep trying until I arrived at something he recognized as what he wanted, no matter how long it took. It was fair enough – the bloke was behind some of the biggest commercial hits in movie history. I damn well should work towards him, if that was how I wanted my life to go, but I didn't.

'I just don't feel this process is for me.'

I'm proud to say he tried briefly to dissuade me.

'Why? Tell me the problem.'

I couldn't tell him all the stuff I've listed here. One thing I'd learned on all my trips to LA was that they absolutely do not give a fuck about anything you're doing in Britain. If it hasn't crossed over, it's irrelevant. I remember Dawn telling me how she'd been over there with Lenny when he made his movie. There'd been a dinner and she'd been charming all the execs with her funny chat, but the moment she began to tell them about her work, about how she played a vicar in one of the biggest sitcoms in Britain *ever*, they turned off. Instantly. To the American industry, if you ain't big in America, you don't really exist. That may have changed a bit now, with the streaming channels' insatiable lust for content driving big Americans like Netflix and Apple to seriously check out the international scene – which has led to previously unimaginable phenomena, like the world going crazy for Norwegian murder procedurals and Korean weird shit. But, back then, Katz could not give one solitary toss how many opportunities I had in the UK. His view was 'This is an opportunity in *America* so grow the fuck up.'

So I tried to offer an explanation that I thought might make sense to an American movie mogul.

'Well, for one thing you don't pay very much.'

I didn't like saying it. It's really not me at all. I never ask about the money and actually prefer to work for nothing until something's really rolling. I always feel a bit guilty being paid for development that doesn't bear fruit.

And Jeffrey didn't like hearing it either.

'You get paid on the next movie,' he said bluntly.

It hadn't been about the money anyway, but I didn't try to explain further. He was losing interest. If I was crazy enough to turn him down, then we were done talking.

It was clearly time to leave. I started putting away my notes.

Then Jeffrey Katzenberg did the strangest thing. There was an occasional table between us, on which was a large glass bowl full of rose petals.

He gathered some up in his cupped hands, took a step or two across the thick carpet to stand over me and opened his hands over my head, showering me with petals. How fucking weird was that? I was left sitting there, covered in a hundred rose petals. They were in my hair, in my shirt, in my lap. A couple were wedged in my glasses. Then he retreated to another part of his enormous suite without a word.

He'd assaulted me with petals. It worked, too. I felt stupid, which I presume had been the intention, although it was such a strange gesture that I still don't really get it. I think that basically he was saying that he had offered me the world and, fool that I was, I had rejected him.

And, of course, a part of me still regrets it. The chances are small to non-existent that I will ever be offered such an incredible opportunity again.

The Noughties

Yes, I think ya sexy

I did another musical in 2003.

This was *Tonight's the Night*, my musical based on Rod Stewart's greatest hits. Phil had been in negotiation with Rod's management since before *We Will Rock You* opened. It had been part of the same management strategy that led him and Paul to approach Queen.

So now it was happening and, just as I'd done with Queen, I tried to write a story that I felt reflected Rod's *vibe*, which was and remains that of the larrikin troubadour. I wanted to have fun with his reputation as a ladies' man without portraying him directly or being biographical. I came up with a Faustian pact story about a sweet, shy, reserved guy who is in love with a girl, but doesn't have the guts to declare it. One night, the shy guy makes the old mistake of saying he'd sell his soul to be like his hero Rod, who never had any trouble talking to girls. Of course, the devil turns up and my hero gets his wish, with many comic and romantic complications.

I met Rod for the first time when he came to the workshop presentation that Phil produced and I directed. We'd invited twenty or thirty people to watch and he walked in last with Penny Lancaster on his arm, all seventeen feet of her. The ultimate rock star and rock chick. It was a nerve-wracking moment as my script was absolutely full of gags which had fun with Rod's reputation as a shagger. Here's an example, my hero Stu (who has been granted Rod's soul) is speaking with Rod's manager Baby Jane.

Stu: I can be a star! I have the best part of Rod Stewart right here inside me.

Jane: Kid, I've *had* the best part of Rod Stewart inside *me*. And I'm telling you now, you ain't no Rod.

401

And there he was listening to this for the first time sitting next to his brand-new wife!

I needn't have worried. They are both great sports and roared with laughter from start to finish.

'You've made me a legend' was Rod's first comment to me, the twinkle in his eye making it very clear that he knew very well that he *was* a legend and had been for forty years.

Sophie and I got to know Rod and Penny quite well working on that show. We had dinner a couple of times and even went to a pub-rock gig together. That was a good night. Rod is a genuinely funny man, still the same geezer in the pub he was when he was leading the Faces. His favourite trick in a restaurant is to peruse the wine menu with lofty intensity, turning the pages with an air of slight derision while the sommelier hovers nervously. Then, just when it's getting uncomfortable, he slaps the menu back in the poor bloke's hands and says 'Bring me the cheapest'.

It was just as well that Rod was up for a laugh because the gig we went to was a real down-and-dirty one. I wanted Rod to check out Tim Howar, a brilliant Canadian musical theatre artist I had in mind for our lead. I wanted Rod to be confident that the man who was borrowing his soul would have rock bones and Tim was playing a gig that night with his band.

I didn't tell Tim or anyone else that I was bringing Rod. You can never be sure if rock stars are going to turn up and I didn't want to freak Tim out, only to disappoint him. But Rod and Penny were as good as their word. Let me tell you, there's nothing like walking into a packed and sweaty pub-rock boozer with Rod Stewart and Penny Lancaster. The shock followed by the sheer delight, followed by the collective effort to try to be cool was wonderful to behold. Mouths dropped, then turned into huge smiles before resetting with attempted indifference in a matter of seconds. Rod and Penny are just so *golden*. You could not meet a better turned-out couple. They just look great. You'd expect Penny to make the effort, but Rod too was always immaculate. I never saw him when he wasn't perfectly groomed: the closest of shaves, the best-pressed shirts, faultless tailoring. In some people, it would look like vanity or preciousness, but with Rod it's just *right*. He once sang about some guys having all the luck and that's just how he walks, like the guy who's had all the luck. The funny thing is nobody minds it with Rod. Even the British forgive him his success. In fact, we love him for having it all and having the style to pull it off. Some people have a twinkle in their eye and Rod is a walking human twinkle.

And as for Penny! Well, as I say, the pub was packed, three-deep at the bar, and I'd just begun the horrendous task of trying to penetrate the throng when a strange light seemed to fall upon me. I looked up and found myself blinking in the glare of a flashing smile and a great mass of perfectly tousled blonde tresses swinging above me. It was Penny. Despite standing at the back, she seemed to have been able to extend herself by a metre or two and now she was leaning over the petty throng like some great golden flamingo. No barman could have failed to catch her eye and, of course, she was served instantly.

'What are you and Sophie having?' she said, looking down at me from the Olympian heights in which she lived. Now that's the way to get served in a pub.

Rod was very excited about *Tonight's the Night*, particularly about the fact that the common presumption was that we would have a hit. The reviewers thought this too and it drove them crazy with anger. They panned the show mercilessly, as ever focusing very personally on me. *The Telegraph*'s headline summed up the mood ('How does Ben Elton get away with it?'), but having been so wrong in their certain predictions that *WWRY* would close, they were careful to add the caveat that it would no doubt sell hugely and run for ever, making its unworthy creator billions – as if I was some kind of strange magician who could make people pay for shit.

One of the things they found most objectionable was the very concept of so called 'jukebox musicals'. Many arts writers were quite certain that somehow catalogue shows were stifling the creation of 'legitimate' musicals – that is, ones with original scores. I really don't get this at all. Most musicals are based on some form of non-original source material. Why should it be considered more legitimate to take an old story and add new music (as happens with almost all musicals) than it is to take a *new* story and add old songs? Many musicals are now verbatim reproductions of movie animations and nobody says that's killing musical theatre. I love *The Lion King* stage musical, but in truth the only original contributing artist to the stage version was the designer. In every other aspect, it's a carbon copy of the cartoon.

Personally, I think the term jukebox musicals is a compliment. Jukeboxes are fantastic, magical things, icons of popular culture packed full of memories and shared emotions. They're fun. They make you want to dance and punch the air, cry sometimes and reach out to the people you love. Theatre can do that, particularly musical theatre, and when it does – it's a kind of magic!

As it happens, the Rod musical wasn't a huge hit. It did okay, running for a year at the Victoria Palace before making room for *Billy Elliot*. It wasn't a bad run, but wasn't remotely enough to recoup the investment on a big-scale production like the one Phil had mounted. The reviews hurt us badly and, unlike with *We Will Rock You*, the show just didn't have the legs to overcome them.

You win some, you lose some. There is no such thing as a guaranteed hit.

My home is girt by sea

After *Tonight's the Night*, Sophie and I took the children to spend a few months in Fremantle with our Aussie family. The kids started school at North Freo Infants and I wrote another novel, another murder mystery called *Past Mortem*, the French translation of which won a rather nice prize, the Prix Polar at the Cognac Literary Festival for Best International Crime Thriller. They had the ceremony in Cognac and I went down for it with my French publisher, which was a great trip as you'd imagine. I got a nice new gong for my shelf and also an expensive bottle of vintage cognac, which I asked them to send to my translator, who I never met but with whom I clearly shared the award.

And while I was writing *Past Mortem*, I became an Australian, meaning my home was 'girt by sea'.

'Girt by sea' is a line from the Australian national anthem.

Yes, the word is 'girt'; 'girt by sea' means surrounded by sea.

Sophie always thought 'girt' was an abbreviation of 'got to', as in 'our home is got to by sea', which frankly would be no less crap a line. I think the lyricist probably used the perplexingly arcane term as a way of distracting from the banality of the observation. The surface of the Earth is 70 per cent water. Everybody's home is girt by sea. It's not a terrible anthem – no worse than 'God Save The King' – but they should have used 'Waltzing Matilda'.

I say 'they' but, of course, I should say 'we', because in 2004 I was granted Australian citizenship. I'd held a permanent resident's visa for years, but with us being based in Freo that year, it seemed the right time to make a formal commitment to my unexpected double life and become a dual citizen.

My citizenship ceremony took place at the beautiful old Arts Centre in Fremantle, the town in which I'd written (and set) my first novel sixteen years earlier. It was a wonderful day. There was a respectful and moving acknowledgement of the Traditional Owners of Australia, then a dignified but upbeat formal ceremony followed by a true-blue Aussie picnic with free pies and lamingtons while a rocking little bush band played! It couldn't have been more Australian if Paul Hogan had turned up wrestling a crocodile. Lamingtons, by the way, are a peculiarly boring Aussie cake that for some reason has gained status as a bit of an Antipodean bakery icon. It's basically just a small block of dull sponge, *very* lightly covered in chocolate (a thin veneer rather than an actual coating, like it was painted on) and then sprinkled with coconut. When challenged on why, in a world filled with ever richer and more luxurious chocolate and cake-based indulgence, the lamington still exists, Australians will tend to say, 'perfect with a cup of tea'. Like a chocolate Hobnob wouldn't be?

Still, dull cakes aside, it was a brilliant day and I was interested to note that, of the forty or so excited new Australians getting sworn in that day, I was the only white one. Western Australia has always been the whitest Aussie state, but that is now changing with invigorating pace.

Incidentally, I had the opportunity to contrast citizenship ceremonies when Sophie finally got her 'pomdom', gaining British citizenship in 2009 having sat the exam which asked her who Churchill was and did he burn any cakes. With the greatest of respect, the Australian ceremony was better than the UK one. In the UK, it was just the straight business. No music, scarcely a speech, really – and certainly no picnic. Just a brief handshake with the mayoress and the county sheriff. Both ladies conducting were absolutely lovely, but it was a peculiarly uninspiring event for what is, after all, a massive thing. I think that a bit more dignity and reflection, followed by some form of thanks and celebration, would have been appropriate. We five Eltons had gone as a family and we all dressed in our Sunday best. I was in a suit and tie and felt slightly silly among the general casualness.

I think maybe the fact that, when my father got British citizenship, it was the final liberating act in a terrible and terrifying odyssey has made me more aware of what a privilege finding safe haven in a stable and prosperous democracy is.

Toddlers, the Great War and other catastrophes

Towards the end of 2004, I started work on a new sitcom, my first since *The Thin Blue Line* almost ten years earlier. It was about a frazzled couple bringing up babies and originally was going to be called *The Stockholm Syndrome* because of the way babies hold you captive and torment you – and yet you love them. Less interestingly, it ended up being called *Blessed*.

As ever, it all began with high hopes. I assembled a brilliant cast. The leading roles of the two frazzled parents were played by Ardal O'Hanlan and Mel Giedroyc, who were absolutely perfect.

I directed *Blessed*, shooting the series on a single camera like a movie. That's a hard job on a small budget in the streets of London. You spend 90 per cent of your time waiting for planes to pass over and when they've finally faded and you're about to call 'action', the sound guy says 'Sorry, police siren'. Until you've shot TV or film in an urban environment, you have no conception of the number of police sirens and car alarms that go off all day every day. It drives you truly crazy knowing that the 'take' you're going to end up using in the edit won't be the best one. It'll be the one without the low-flying jumbo blotting out the dialogue and making it impossible to cut to the reverse. If it hadn't been for the incredible patience and humour of Ardal, Mel and the rest of the brilliant BBC team, I believe

I'd still be lying in a road in north London, manically chewing the tarmac while waiting for planes to pass over to this day.

Blessed did okay, but it wasn't commissioned for a second series. It just didn't quite do the numbers. Maybe it was a bit grim, focusing on every aspect of the hard part of raising babies and toddlers with none of the joy. This wasn't *Outnumbered*. It wasn't about the kids at all. In fact, I deliberately hid the kids; the toddler boy spent the whole series in a Power Rangers mask. It was about the parents so, basically, it was a sitcom about exhaustion where two people who love each other fight over who has had less sleep.

The only people who would have gone 'Yes, Ben! I so know what you mean. That is *my life*' weren't watching. Nobody with babies is watching telly at 9.30 p.m. in the evening. I know Sophie and I didn't. For at least five years, our idea of a BBC comedy was *Postman Pat*.

We didn't even watch *Blessed*. Too knackered.

A more successful project that autumn of 2005 was the publication of my next novel. This was called *The First Casualty*, my first historical novel. Set in the First World War, it was an idea I'd been mulling for years. The hero is a police detective with a brilliant analytical mind who, having been a hero before the war, becomes a pariah during it because he refuses to serve, not out of moral conscience but because he believes that this particular war is 'illogical' on every level. After conscription is introduced, he is imprisoned. Then the authorities find they need him. A scandalous murder has occurred at the front and it must be solved. He has to conduct his investigation with the evidence and witnesses being blown apart, whilst pursuing a culprit who will probably be killed before he can be hanged. The novel looks at the notions of crime, punishment and justice in the midst of the legalized murder of millions of men.

It was published that autumn and has proved to have real 'legs', as they say, selling well ever since. It seemed that while my TV career was definitely not what it once had been, and my theatre career had become an unmitigated critical shit-storm, my novels were still approved of by public and even reviewers (mostly). Years later, Russell Crowe even tried to develop a screenplay of it.

I'd known Russell for a while. We'd had a couple of goes at adapting my stuff before, with *Gridlock* and *Gasping*, but with *The First Casualty*, he really got the bit between his teeth and we ended up spending five days working pretty much alone together at his home in New South Wales. It was all very convivial. I'd write in the mornings while he did his other stuff, then we'd spend the afternoon together going over what I'd done. Then, perhaps unwisely, we'd repair to the pub for the evening. His pub. Many blokes build their own bar, but Russell being Russell, he had built a whole pub, a standalone building next to his recording studio, beautifully done out with all sorts of sporting, drinking and movie paraphernalia and real beer pumps. You could have entertained a footy team plus supporters but those nights it was just us, me on a bar stool, him behind the bar, and it got pretty bleary.

Despite the hangovers, we did a lot of work in those five days and got quite excited over *Douglas and Rose*, which was what we were calling *The First Casualty*, but we didn't nail it. The thing about an intense period of work like that is that it's very hard to continue over email. Still, it was good fun while it lasted. For two or three years afterwards, I'd get the occasional enigmatic email saying something like 'Douglas needs to pass Rose in France but be unaware'.

Midlife crisis? What midlife crisis?

In the late summer of 2005, we moved out of London and relocated to Sussex, where I spent the autumn writing and rehearsing material for the new tour, wandering round our garden, swearing at the trees.

That tour took me through to the early summer of 2006, meaning that I had effectively missed six months of the kids' young lives. So I decided that I'd slow down for a bit.

I've always loved chopping and sawing wood and have done a very great deal of it in my time. Ever since we bought our house near Margaret River in 1994, I've had land on which to manage fallen trees and, once we moved from London to a house in East Sussex with its three acres in the

Ashdown Forest, I've had the privilege of owning playgrounds on both sides of the globe.

Sometime in the autumn of 2006, I decided to build a little climbing frame in my back field for the children. There was already a good swinging rope hung from the branch of a tree which Greg Wise, Emma's husband (who is a proper man's man and could build a rowing boat out of two hedges and an apple core), had installed on a family visit. I decided to build a structure from which the kids could swing off. There were two old country gates leaned up behind a shed and I used them to build an upturned V-shaped arrangement on the top of which I built a platform. At that point, Lottie, who was seven, ran out to ask what I was building. 'A structure,' I replied. She ran back and told Sophie 'Daddy's building a structure'. 'The Structure' is how what it grew into would always be known.

The Structure became a very time-consuming but hugely satisfying part of my life for the next three years. I worked on it on and off for many months. Sometimes I'd spend whole weeks in my back paddock; the moment the kids had left for school, I'd be out there, chopping, sawing, nailing and bolting away until they returned. They loved it too and climbed on it a lot, but there can be no doubt who got most fun out of it. The reason it all began really was because of all the holly wood I had (ha! The one time that Holly-wood has been good to me). When the house had been built in the 1910s (around a very ancient cottage, at least 300 years old), the grounds had been fringed with holly hedges. In the intervening years, the pruned bushes had been left unattended and grown into large holly trees. Sophie and I decided we'd try to bring the hedges back to life, which meant cutting back many mature hollies and forcing them to sprout sideways rather than upwards. This left me with many brilliant holly trunks, some straight, some twisted, some wide as a football, some thin as a forearm. It's wonderful wood, hardy and long lasting, and I started making bridges and wobbly walkways and even constructions that could sustain a flying fox zipwire. I raised a great three-sided pyramid frame from which to hang a swing. I constructed supports for a long, upwardly thrusting holly trunk with a pommel rope suspended from its end and a commando climbing net hanging off it. I built a raised walkway which extended forty metres down a slope from the main structure. The walkway started at ground level, but the other end was four metres high and ended in a lovely two-storey treehouse. Inside the house, there was a little table and three chairs, all made from fallen wood. I bought a huge, twisting tubular slide and built a massive frame to support it. Doing that was an exercise in logistics, I can tell you.

And I did all this entirely alone. I'm funny like that. I love company but I work alone. It's why I'm not attracted to the idea of writers' rooms. I know writers who love the collegiate atmosphere of mutual riffing, but it isn't for me. Be it a script or a climbing frame, I like to make it on my own and do my socializing afterwards. I was sometimes offered help by friends or neighbours, but I always politely refused. For me, the challenge of working out how to do things single-handed was fascinating. I used to say to Sophie, when she brought me out a cup of tea, that I spent as much time thinking as I did working (her eyes would glaze over, there's no bore like a wood bore). But, let me tell you, raising two four-metre holly trunks, binding them at the apex and then swinging in a third to form a standing frame from which to hang a swing all on your own, is not easy.

See, I'm doing it now. Once I get talking about my structure . . .

I swung ropes from the boughs of trees overhead and I developed fulcrums and levers to raise each heavy trunk or branch bit by bit. I was nearly killed a number of times, which was bloody stupid but exciting. I recall trying to shoulder a long piece into position while standing high on a pile of tree-trunk discs that I'd raised for the purpose. I slipped and fell a few feet to the ground, but the real issue was the trunk I'd been manhandling. Fortunately, I'd secured it with ropes to a tree above, a precaution which definitely saved my life. I recall lying on my back in the field, the wind knocked out of me, staring up at a few hundred kilograms of wood swinging directly above me. Luckily, my granny knots held.

Lots of friends saw the structure over the years and, although they thought it was impressive, I think most also thought it was weird. Ade was the only one to actually *say* it, suggesting that it might represent some sort of midlife crisis. I remember we were sitting up high on one of the platforms with a beer as the sun set over Sussex and Ade said that he thought I'd gone slightly mad. If I had, it was a very pleasant and benign kind of madness.

The structure gave me some of the happiest days of my life and memories I believe my children will treasure for ever. I can still remember the shared joy when Sophie brought the three of them back from primary school and they'd tumble out of the car and rush around to see what new bit of madness Dad was working on.

Simon says

It isn't that I stopped work altogether during the years of The Structure, just that I did a bit less.

In 2006, I wrote a novel called *Chart Throb*. This, like *Dead Famous*, was inspired by a TV show, in this case *The X Factor*. Watching the show, I was astonished at the blindingly obvious story-building (which was clearly done in the edit), the blatantly cynical manipulation of innocent and vulnerable contestants, and the utterly shameless deceitfulness of the entire judging process.

We all know that now, of course, but back in 2006, there was still a genuine pretence that Simon's sudden afterthoughts ('Why don't you try a different song' or 'I'd like to hear you without the others') were not meticulously planned, that the jokes and the tantrums weren't storyboarded in pre-production, that the contestants weren't goaded and schooled into being cute, angry, rude, tearful, desperate and insane ('I really, really, really want this 'cos it's my dream and I'm better than Beyoncé').

Back then, nobody was quite asking themselves if – as the voiceover claimed over and over again – 100,000 people were being given auditions, how was it that the geriatric, tone-deaf, substance-abused, deluded psychopath with no teeth was making it through to meet Simon, Sharon and Louis? Back then, nobody was asking how it was that film crews had very early footage and interviews from the finalists at their *first* auditions. Were they interviewing the whole 100,000? Or was it not slightly more likely that the finalists had been selected from the beginning? All this occurred to me watching the show on the TV with my family and the kids complaining 'Why do you have to *think* about it, Dad? Why can't you just *enjoy it*?'.

It's all been out in the open for years now and, as with *Big Brother*, the show changed accordingly, then slowly died. Simon and the production team became so counter-intuitively, knowingly postmodern and self-aware that the term 'disappeared up their own arseholes' doesn't do remote justice to the whole camp, in-on-the-joke mess that *The X Factor* eventually became.

But, at the beginning, it sure was great TV, a compelling mix of the 'people' show and the talent show, combining elements of Michael Barrymore's *My Kind of People*, *Candid Camera* and *Noel's Gotchas* with *New Faces* and *Opportunity Knocks*. While I was on the road in 2005 and 2006, I absolutely loved it. We called ahead to hotels to ensure they taped it for us.

And that's why I wrote *Chart Throb*.

Because I could see that it was a light entertainment show and not a singing competition a bit earlier than most and thought it would make a really good and quite illuminating comic novel. And, for once, not a flipping murder mystery.

It turned out pretty well, although it might have been better (certainly different) if my publisher hadn't insisted on showing it to a lawyer.

The novel as published is quite broad in its satire with highly exaggerated comic characters. But the first draft was much closer to reality. I drew the judges Sharon Osborne, Louis Walsh and Simon Cowell as more direct parody and inevitably the issue was raised that one of them might sue. Personally I couldn't see on what grounds – after all, I was only portraying them as cynical, manipulative and exploitative, which I felt they'd have a hard job denying given the nature of the show – but, as I think I've mentioned before, common sense doesn't apply when dealing with lawyers.

So I had to re-write the whole book in a more heightened satirical style. For instance, in the original draft, the person whom my 'Simon' character tries to make into a star (having claimed he can manipulate anyone into winning) is a fire-brand left-wing politician and media hate figure – basically George Galloway, who had just made a complete arsehole of himself on *Celebrity Big Brother*. I'd written a pretty good character story about the weird delusional madness that leads previously serious-minded people to go on reality TV shows. Of course, the lawyers said it was too close to Galloway (who actually gets hard over *any* publicity) and made me change it. I ended up using the Prince of Wales, which was allowable because the lawyer deemed that the idea of the heir to the throne winning *The X Factor* was so crazy it could not be seen as libellous.

Just wait a generation, I say.

The Prince Charles thing was actually a pretty good joke, but I didn't want to offend him (because, unlike George Galloway, I didn't think he deserved it), so I wrote to him and asked if he'd mind if I drew him as a decent, but bemused, earnest old fogey/hippy who allows himself to be persuaded to go on the *Chart Throb* show in an effort to make the monarchy more accessible.

He wrote back a single line. 'Fame at last!'

Pretty classy, eh? And funny.

So the novel was a lot broader than I had wanted it to be, but it was still pretty close to the truth and I know that for a fact.

How do I know?

Because Simon told me so.

I was at home in Sussex when my mobile rang.

'Ben, it's Simon Cowell. Got your number from Richard Curtis.'

I thought he was going to unleash on me, but he didn't.

'The novel's brilliant. I love, love, LOVE it.'

I told him that I was half-delighted and half-disappointed because if he loved it that much, I couldn't have been hitting hard enough. But, actually, that's not really fair on him. It was a pretty savage satire, but he absolutely didn't mind. That's his amazing strength. He *gets* the joke about himself; he's always got it. That's why he's such an attractive screen presence. Self-confidence, when combined with a bit of self-awareness, is attractive. As for criticism, as long as he's making money and staying famous, he's incredibly relaxed about it. Once, when he was the subject of a sort of *This Is Your Life*-style programme, he asked if I'd appear and do a bit of a roast to avoid it all getting too sycophantic. One joke I wrote was 'Simon is so vain he considers masturbation to be an act of fidelity'. He loved it.

Anyway, back to that first phone call.

'I thought you'd hate it,' I said.

'Why would I hate it? I'm the star and I win. I read a chapter on the loo each night.'

So there's an image for you.

He really did love it, too. He gave out copies to the crew and it was the talk of the *X Factor* team for a while. Louis rang me and demanded a copy and I heard Sharon's voice in the background shouting that she wanted one too. I sent them over and, having spoken to Louis since, I think he was cool about it. I never heard from Sharon Osborne. My guess is she didn't read it. Otherwise, I would have got a turd delivered by courier, which showbiz lore says is her preferred method of payback.

Anyway, Simon loved the book enough to want to work with me and I was summoned to his office. He is just the same off-screen as he is on, which is, of course, his greatest talent. People sense an honest original, which is what he is. Vain but funny too. We met at his office (where, in defiance of the law, he chain-smoked) to discuss the possibility of an *X Factor* musical.

We got on great and had a very productive chat, so productive in fact that pretty soon he brought up a second project.

That's one of Simon's problems. He gets bored easily.

It's an advantage on TV when we can all enjoy his eyes rolling in frustration at yet another murdering of Robbie Williams's 'Angels', but in script development it's a problem. On our third meeting, rather than discuss the musical again, we started talking about an *X Factor* movie. Suddenly, we were developing two separate projects and the focus was lost. It ended with a friendly confrontation. I'd written some detailed notes on the movie idea and Simon said he just wanted a couple of sentences. He said that if an idea's good, you should be able to get it all in a single phrase or two. I suggested that while *ideas* can be short, plots to service those ideas needed a bit more detail.

He sucked sagely at his cigarette and suggested we meet when he next got back from LA. I've never heard from him since.

A Rose and an It Girl and a bleak novel

As The Structure spread across my field in Sussex through 2007, I did a TV show called *Get a Grip*. Although it was based on my stand-up material from the 2005 tour, I performed it as a double act. With a girl who was half my age.

Pretty strange right? But I couldn't get a gig on TV as a lone stand-up any more. Like I say, you have your time. It had been true for Benny Hill, so it was for Benny Elton.

My old friend Paul Jackson had become head of entertainment at ITV and he still thought I had something to offer, but such was my unsaleability by this time that he didn't think he could sell the show to his controller as just a version of *The Man From Auntie*. It had to have a real new hook and, essentially, a youthful one. The idea I came up with was probably pretty stupid, but it felt good at the time. I suggested to Paul that maybe I should do my material as a double act with a young person who would represent a more youthful perspective.

ME: Good evening. I'm Ben Elton.
SHE: And I prefer younger comedians.

Paul liked it and we were away. The young woman we cast was quite fantastic – witty, opinionated and original, and she made a very good job of making the stuff I wrote for her sound genuine and organic. Nonetheless, the idea was flawed from the start, purporting to be two edgily opposite ways of looking at the same subject but with me writing both sides. It was never going to convince.

Although, in my defence, it had worked for Plato.

If I'd also cast somebody else in my own role, it might have worked but with me in it, it was fundamentally confusing. Not dishonestly so. I actually often am in two minds about things, but it just didn't ring true.

As I say, this was no fault of the amazing star-in-waiting we cast opposite me – who was none other than Alexa Chung! Bloody hell, we got that right if nothing else! We were looking for a cool, edgy, fascinating and quirky 'voice of youth' and we chose the girl who would soon go on to become an international style icon with just that vibe.

Get a Grip came and went. It had its points: Alexa mainly and an excellent team of actors for the sketch work. The problem was me, really, and what role I should have (if any) as a performer in my middle age. Leastways we don't seem to have done Alexa's career any harm!

And my past glories still meant something because I won a nice prize that year: the Golden Rose (Rose D'Or) at the International Television Festival in Lucerne in Switzerland. This was for my services to TV arts, which I must say was pleasing. Love an award. Everybody does. Fact.

After *Get a Grip*, I wrote another novel, without doubt my bleakest and most satirically bitter. It was called *Blind Faith* and the inspiration was unashamedly Orwellian. In his masterpiece *1984*, Orwell wrote of a nightmare world in which the ultimate horror was to be constantly under video observation, the famous 'Big Brother' who was watching you. It struck me that we now lived in a world where this Orwellian nightmare had been embraced as the ultimate *ambition*. People now actively sought and subjected themselves to video surveillance, seeking ways to confess, share and generally expose themselves and their most private thoughts and emotions at all times.

In my own dystopian vision, I imagined a world in which the desire for privacy was viewed with deep and angry suspicion. People lived their lives publicly online via their personal computers, so much so that the government is forced to mandate days when people are required to physically attend the office. This was before social media and 'work from home'. Perhaps back in 2007 it all seemed a bit far-fetched.

The Tens and the Teens

Failing towards America again. Another nice dream while it lasted

As the first decade of the twenty-first century came to an end, I was as restless as ever writing-wise. I pitched a history-based idea to the BBC but got nowhere. I pitched a play to Nick Hytner at the National but got nowhere. Then, in late 2008 I got another break in the US and, for once, I don't think it was me who screwed it up. Phil was old mates with a bloke called Ben Silverman, a dynamic American TV producer who had introduced *The Office* to the US. Silverman was now a huge player as the CEO of the American network NBC.

And he wanted a light comic detective series.

Phil had pointed out to him that I was a winner of the Crime Writers' Association Golden Dagger Award for crime fiction and also the Prix Polar for the same subject. The next thing I knew, Ben S was asking me to pitch some ideas for a comedy detective series.

After five or six rejected suggestions, I came up with one that he loved. I remember the exact moment it came to me; I was doing the washing-up and absolutely knew it was good. It was about an English actor in New York – a real super-luvvie, uncompromising and vain, too grand to take daytime TV work, adverts, etc. and hence usually out of work. But instead of serving in bars and waiting tables, which is what most actors do when unemployed, Garrick (as I called him) decides to hone his skills further by playing to the toughest audience of all – criminals and cops – becoming a part-time private detective who uses his brilliant actor's insight into human nature and his ability to assume a multitude of roles to solve crimes. So, plenty of drama and plenty of comedy. Making him English in

New York helped with that, playing on his arrogance and vaguely endearing self-confidence.

I was really excited writing out the idea and even more so when, the very next morning, Ben emailed back a single line. 'Love it. We are going to make this.'

Can you imagine? I remember taking Sophie her morning cup of tea and telling her that NBC were commissioning me to write a comedy drama for the US! Wow.

One of the things about being commissioned by the big boss is that he's not actually going to be there with you on the ground. So, suddenly, I was in script development with various people from NBC's production process. That's fine, I didn't mind that. I never mind notes and new drafts. But Ben is a very instinctive guy; he goes off at tangents and then delivers his thoughts from on high in ten-word emails written at four in the morning. For instance, I'd written the character aged in his late twenties, but one day Ben emailed me to say he'd told Kevin Spacey about the idea who had shown real interest. Spacey was without doubt one of the great American actors, but he was nearly fifty and lived in London. Ben's view of that was 'Okay, so instead of a young Englishman in New York, he's a middle-aged New Yorker in England.'

Ben actually arranged a meeting and I spent a very interesting couple of hours with Spacey, who not surprisingly was fascinating company. But he was also running the Old Vic and so not exactly available to hop into what was being planned as a long-running, prime-time series. The Spacey idea went away as quickly as it had emerged.

But development on *Garrick* went on for another couple of drafts. I went to LA to see Ben, which was a particularly nice trip because I got to visit Hugh and Jo Laurie. Hugh was over there making his mega-hit medical drama *House*. It was so amazing to see how far he had come as an actor, one of the biggest stars on global TV in his Hollywood home.

The meeting at NBC the next day was great too. I kind of felt we were getting close.

Then, bam. The old enemy of all ideas in development.

Regime change.

Kills ya every time.

Ben Silverman got knocked of his perch as head of NBC and that was it. The end of *Garrick* overnight. That's how it happens. A new boss came in and she cancelled all of Ben's development projects, including mine.

Why wouldn't she? If she keeps them and they're a hit, Ben gets the credit. If they flop, she gets the blame.

Maybe someone else could do it, I hear you say. It is, after all, quite a promising idea.

Are you crazy? *Of course* somebody else can't do it!

NBC own it. They paid for it and it belongs to them. And, no, they wouldn't sell it back to me because if they did that and it's a hit, they'll be fired for selling it. The same story as *Popcorn*. As explained before, such deals usually contain 'turnaround' clauses, which means eventually they revert to the originator, but NBC saw itself as the originator and hadn't offered that and so it's still sitting there. Nobody remotely connected with it is at NBC any more but it remains a good idea locked up for ever.

One more pile of crockery round my ankles.

A very nice rock star and making a novel out of a crisis

While I was in Canada working on *The Boys in the Photograph* (the alternative title for my Lloyd Webber musical *The Beautiful Game*), I had a brief but very nice experience with U2 and, in particular, Bono.

The show had arrived in Toronto by this time and U2 were also in town and I was invited to their after-party. The Edge and Bono were in development with their own musical at the time (*Spider-Man: Turn Off the Dark*) and so we had a common interest. Of course, the fact that my show was about the struggles in Northern Ireland was of particular interest to them. Bono himself is the son of a Protestant and a Catholic, so he knows a thing or two about the sectarian divide and asked if he could drop in on rehearsal the next day!

Could he? Uhm, YES!

Bono arrived eating an ice cream, which kind of broke the 'God is in the room' tension. We did a couple of scenes for him and he spoke to my young Canadian cast about his own experiences as a youth in a divided country. It was an amazing thing for him to give up his very brief period of free time and I'll always be grateful.

While I was in Canada, I also completed the first draft of my thirteenth novel. It was set during the great financial crisis through which (in the spring of 2009) we were still going. I called it *Meltdown* and it was about four couples whose lives were irrevocably changed by the crisis. Looking back the drama of that time still surprises me; the financial news was the number-one story for weeks and weeks. I suppose we're more used to that now, but up until then, money always came at the end of the news, which was the signal to get up and make a cup of tea.

Times have changed so much on that score. When I was growing up, if you were to have asked anyone what the two most boring professions were, one of them would almost certainly have been accountant and the other might well have been working in a bank. Both were symbols of solidity and prudence. Imagine! Anyone under forty would find that hard to believe, but when I was young, people who worked in money were seen as a bit dull but also steady and trustworthy. Remember that famous Monty Python line 'I'm an accountant and consequently too boring to be of interest to anyone'? I wonder if Captain Mainwaring (of *Dad's Army*), who was the steady, prudent manager of the Warmington-on-Sea bank, came back now, what he'd make of a banking industry that lent so much money it would have brought down the world had the taxpayer not stepped in to bail it out.

Dodging a bullet and dropping a bomb Down Under

On 30 December 2009, in the chilly pre-dawn dark, Sophie and I and the children left Sussex for Australia. That was a big moment. The kids were leaving all their friends, Sophie too had built up a life in Sussex and I was facing the prospect of a very great deal more travel and the estrangement of distance from my career and friends and family.

But it had to be done. Many people have presumed it was some kind of lifestyle choice, that we chose to relocate to Australia for the kids' high-school years as a sunny alternative to drab old Britain. That's not the case at all. We moved because of family. Had we not relocated, at least for a while, our kids would only have known their Australian family as a distant thing and we were determined that shouldn't be the case. Sophie and I had long held the plan to do the children's primary years in Britain and their high-school years in Australia. Sophie had lived in Britain for sixteen years and it was time to flip the coin.

Or the globe, in this case.

It was quite hard on my mum, but the same had previously been the case for Sophie's. If you can avoid it, I'd say try not to fall in love with someone from the other side of the world. But, then, who was ever able to avoid falling in love?

The Daily Mail gave me a nice, jolly send-off, building a narrative that having been vaguely responsible for imposing a Labour government on the UK, I was now selfishly avoiding the consequences by sneaking away to enjoy a sun-drenched 'champagne lifestyle' on the beaches of Australia.

They dug up some gags I'd done on an Aus chat show about the royals, claiming my 'vile rant' had been designed to ingratiate myself with my new country folk, but that 'monarchy-loving Aussies' were having none of it. The fact that I'd actually done the same 'vile rant' in front of Prince Charles at a Prince's Trust gig went unreported. You get used to it but my daughter, who was ten, was visiting a retirement home with her school, serving tea and cakes for the residents, and an old lady refused to take one from her, saying 'Your dad hates our queen'.

The *Mail* hadn't finished yet either. Just prior to our leaving, posh snob columnist A. N. Wilson did an *entire page* celebrating the departure of a no-talent hypocrite, a piece which was so splenetic in its relentless spite it was actually funny. Poor old A. N. had to do some serious double-think to skew the piece the way his editor had clearly demanded. It was obvious that his brief was to loftily establish that I was self-evidently irre-deemably worthless both as an artist and as a man. Unfortunately, he couldn't get round the fact that he'd previously been rather a fan. He once reviewed my stand-up act saying there was literally no one to beat me live (Phil still puts that on my posters sometimes) and had given my novel *Popcorn* an absolutely glowing review. We'd even met very agreeably on more than one occasion. But while A. N. might see himself as an eminent historian and essayist, he earns rather more as Paul Dacre's posh snob attack dog. He dismissed the stand-up review by claiming to have been momentarily seduced by the crowd of braying sycophants around him and as for his previous unstinting praise of *Popcorn*, he claimed to have since discovered that Beryl Bainbridge had written something very similar before me, implying that I'd *plagiarized the whole plot*. I can only hope that as he banked his cheque from Mr Dacre, he experienced the tiniest twinge of conscience for what really was an extraordinary episode of duplicitous spite. I wrote to him (the only time I've ever done that) more in sorrow than in anger, but he didn't have the guts to reply . . . I suppose there wasn't much he could say. But, feelings of personal betrayal aside, I don't really mind getting it in the neck from *The Mail*. It's kind of a sport for them and sometimes they even go the other way and are very nice to me. It's all so OTT as to almost be fun (well, at least kind of shruggable offable). When *Guardian* critics and columnists have had a go over the years, it's always harder. I guess because that's my tribe, as people now say. I'd rather have had Bernard Manning hating me than Alexei. You don't get to choose your haters although, among the fractured fraternity of the left, there's always plenty to choose from!

Anyway, there I was, once again living in Fremantle as I had first done in '87, but this time our house had inside dunnies. The kids were happily ensconced at the same local school that their mum and auntie had gone to and I thought I would have a crack at working in Australian TV. If I was hoping for a warm welcome, I was going to be sorely disappointed.

I'd been talking to my good friend Andrew Denton about maybe doing something together (which would still be an exciting prospect, he's a unique broadcaster and I can't think of an obvious Brit equivalent). Then, out of the blue, Fremantle Media (the huge international media company and nothing to do with my West Australian hometown) got in touch and asked if I had any programme ideas.

I pitched them two. The bullet and the bomb.

The bullet (which I dodged) was to have been a sitcom.

I really thought it was a brilliant idea (I always do I'm afraid) and I tried hard to get some interest. My pitch was a Christopher Guest-style mockumentary chronicling the trials and tribulations of the development of a new Australian musical. Australia, for all its gritty 'Crocodile Dundee' international reputation, has a massive camp side and loves a musical. This is the country which produced *Priscilla Queen of the Desert* and *Strictly Ballroom*, after all. There's a lot more glitter and sequins than khaki shorts (it was Abba's biggest market) and Sydney was pink and dancing when Soho was still grey and grumpy. I thought a comedy about the search for the next great Australian musical would be something an Australian audience would warm to. And I reckoned it needed to be an Australian jukebox musical featuring a great Australian songbook with which much fun could be had.

Back in 2011, the answer was obvious.

Rolf Harris.

I even had the shout line.

It's not just a musical. It's a Kangaroosical!

Honestly, I was so excited. Rolf had just the right slightly alternative vibe of being so naff he was actually cool. He'd done Glastonbury and, prior to that, a career-rebooting version of 'Stairway To Heaven' (wobble board and all) on Andrew Denton's brilliantly eclectic Aus TV show *The Money or the Gun*. Clearly Rolf Harris got the joke about himself. Also, he had written some wonderful songs (and not just the funny ones; 'Sun Arise', for instance, is really quite haunting). My vision was to get Rolf on board playing himself in the mockumentary but, of course as is the way with these spoofs, he would be playing against his mega-friendly persona and instead assuming the character of a manipulative, self-important, abusive bastard.

Ironic, eh?

Fortunately, Fremantle Media Australia were never as keen on the idea as I was and eventually passed. I thought they were mad at the time. But, blimey, thank goodness for unadventurous execs! If they had gone with it, the show would have been about to air at the exact point that Rolf Harris was arrested for sex crimes. A joke on Rolf Harris would most definitely have not been funny any more.

Unfortunately, having dodged that bullet, I then walked into an entire fucking firing squad.

The bomb that would end up exploding in my face was for a sketch/stand-up/music show with me as host. *Saturday Live*, really. I had a lot of road-tested stand-up gear that I'd never done on TV and a lot of sketches that I'd written on and off over the years. Australia has a fantastic tradition of sketch shows, running from Paul Hogan's early TV work through *The D Generation*, *The Comedy Company* and *Fast Forward* but, by 2011, there hadn't been anything for a long while. I thought it was high time there was.

And I wanted to do it live. Streaming hadn't started yet, but TV was already changing from the old model and I thought a live variety show would make a real impact with the all-important topical stuff to go alongside the more generic material – just as I'd done back in the old days.

There was a lot of excitement around the idea and I was hoping it might go to the ABC (the publicly funded Australian version of the BBC). The commercial channels in Australia are fiercely competitive and dominated by ratings analysis and American product. They also have far more ad breaks than are allowed in Britain, which makes them pretty hard to focus on. The ABC would have been the natural home for a live, locally produced comedy night, but unfortunately the ABC is permanently broke. They are not funded by a licence fee like the BBC, but instead are directly funded by government grant, which means it's in constant fear of dying the death of a thousand cuts. Fremantle insisted that to make the show pay, *Live From Planet Earth* (as we were calling it) needed to be on a commercial channel which could afford to give it the production values we thought it needed.

It was good fun while it lasted.

Fremantle and I took enormous trouble assembling a brilliant young performance team, which was as talented as it was diverse. I admit I wrote all the sketches for the first show, which was perhaps asking for trouble, but the absolute plan was for all the performers to start developing their own characters and material, and we also fully planned to seek other material in the vibrant Australian comedy scene. The strategy was for me as a reliable and established older name to provide a platform from which a whole lot of great new talent could be launched.

We never got that far with the plan.

We started our first absolutely live broadcast at 9.30 in the evening and, although we didn't know it, we were dead by the first ad break.

And it had felt so *good* in the studio. We actually thought we had a hit. It was a massively complicated show featuring three separate stage set-ups, costume changes, special guests and a chat show with a spectacularly rude female host played by Genevieve Morris (Ruby Rose was a great sport as first guest). There were also a couple of stand-up slots from me and one from a guest comic and numerous live sketches, including a ridiculously ambitious one called Girl Flat, which was designed to be a regular mini sitcom – a show within a show. It required the four young women in our already super-busy cast going into costume and makeup mid-show with about five minutes to be turned into Beyoncé, Lady Ga Ga, Amy Winehouse and Lily Allen, all of whom, in the grand conceit of the idea, were living together as flatmates. There was live music too and Tim Minchin delivered a stunning number live at his piano.

I fucking loved it. Still do. And I still believe it could have been huge, given a moment to find its feet.

Anyway, we went merrily through our show, breathlessly hugging in the ad breaks, sublimely unaware that our obituaries had already been written. We found out at the after-show party, which had been planned as a celebration but turned into a wake.

Twitter was in its first 'new democracy of the internet' bloom at the time and tweets were still being viewed as considered opinion rather than the trolling and heckling that they mainly were. Within five minutes of us going on air, we were being absolutely twit-twatted. The Twatterati had scarcely let us run our opening credits before gleefully pronouncing it utter shit. It was like a national version of *The Gong Show*. 'Good evening, ladies and gentlemen . . .' GONG!

Another problem, which had nothing to do with the quality of the show, was that in their effort to go for broke, the network had scheduled us to follow its number-one programme, *Top Gear*. Unsurprisingly by the end of the first show, we'd lost a large slab of the *Top Gear* audience.

I had kind of presumed the network would be expecting this, but it seemed they thought that the male, petrol-head, Jeremy Clarkson fans of Australia would warm instantly to a gobby lefty pom and a highly diverse group of young Australians doing edgy live comedy. Of course, we needed the chance to build our own audience. In Australian commercial television, that was no longer an option. Maybe it isn't anywhere any more.

The next morning, the drop in audience figures, plus the Twitter trolling, was *the* story. The media 'pile-on' was absolutely fucking shocking.

Radio morning shows, of which there are many in Australia, devoted their whole TV coverage to it, gleefully reporting that I was a sad flop who should have stayed in Britain. In a larger market, we'd have been one of many stories, but in a market that produces less and less local content, the birth pains of the *only* piece of commercially produced, all-Australian sketch comedy that *decade* was an exquisite and irresistible pleasure.

Nothing like shitting on your own – particularly if your own is led by an interloping pom. I think had I been a *visiting* celebrity gracing Australian TV with my presence, there might not have been the same level of cultural cringe-fuelled venom. But I was a local now. I'd tried to join their gang and, human nature being what it is, that increased the glee at putting in the boot.

Channel 9 hastily organized a round of media in an effort at damage control. I walked into the eye of the storm. Each radio confrontation was basically the same (and I mean 'confrontation').

'So, mate. Your show's shit. Didn't see it myself but I've read the flack you're copping on the socials. When are Channel 9 going to put you out of your misery, mate?'.

It kind of spiralled into a sort of madness. The total flop story was just too good to let go. There were articles and jokes and morning DJs organizing public bets on how soon we'd be axed. In a relatively small industry (that was rapidly being outsourced to American interests), the utter and complete public shaming of a locally produced show (and one fronted by a pretty big name) brought out the worst in quite a lot of people, many of whom really should have known better. Richard Kingsmill, the top honcho at Triple J, the ABC's generally superb youth music station, tweeted: 'Missed Ben Elton's show last night. Looking forward to missing it again next week.'

Bit weird. A grown adult man and an executive producer in public service broadcasting publicly boasting about hating something he hadn't bothered to watch. It was one thing for the commercial jocks to be having a big laugh at my expense, you have to take that in your stride. But bullying from champion of local talent Triple J was painful proof of how bad things were. I think it was a symptom of the newness of Twitter. Everybody was just so excited about the chance to be clever.

Look, that first show was a mixed bag for sure. We definitely tried a bit too hard and it was all rather frantic. The test audience on the night before had been excellent and we were over-excited and scared. But for heaven's sake, it was a whole hour of *live* comedy and music! Two out of the seven performers in our team had never even been on TV before. In a commercial environment utterly swamped with American imports, what we were attempting was actually an amazing thing. But in that first week, nobody gave either me or Channel 9 one single iota of credit for the scale and danger of what we were trying to do. No one wanted to admit the obvious, which was that a brand-new hour from a brand-new team doing it *live* was going to take a minute to find its feet. No one wanted to give the show even a split second's benefit of the doubt. The biggest Melbourne tabloid *front-paged* me with a gleeful slagging and a smiling picture of me taken at the launch titled: 'HE'S NOT SMILING NOW!'

It was pretty tough facing the company as we started prepping the second show (very like the morning after *We Will Rock You* opened). They were shell-shocked. Nobody had ever experienced anything remotely like it. Even for me, the intensity of the pile-on was kind of new because it went beyond arts media and the critics and into a kind of general public shaming (this was before my UK nadir getting roasted on *Newsnight* for *The Wright Way*). But we soldiered on, bloody but unbowed (just), and the second show was actually really good. *The Melbourne Age* and the *Sydney Morning Herald* admitted as much in thoughtful and supportive pieces, which also began to ask the question: 'Hang on. What just happened?'

But it was too late. Channel 9, no doubt under huge pressure from their shell-shocked advertisers, lost their nerve. They decided to kill it. Week three's show went ahead. but was buried after 11 p.m. and after that we were gone, like we'd never existed at all.

And at such a cost, both short and long term.

Channel 9 had been extremely brave to commission the show, but completely potty to axe it after three weeks. They might as well have simply flushed their money down the toilet. If I'd even dreamed that such a development was a possibility, I never *ever* would have gone into it.

No comedy show can click that fast. *The Young Ones* didn't (certainly not in Australia where it tanked horribly on its first outing) while *Blackadder* didn't click until the *second series*! New comedy is always dismissed at first and Twitter has turned that into a public sport. But the people who are tweeting *while it's on* by definition can't be listening, so you are getting barracked and bollocked by people who aren't even pretending to understand what you're trying to do. Anyone who watches five minutes of anything and then starts tweeting that they hate it is nothing more than a heckler, yet these days they are requoted the next day on the news as if they represent the whole audience.

After the frenzy and the pieces in *The Age* and the *Herald*, there were the beginnings of a turnaround. The very excellent Adam Hills (who later became huge in the UK) expressed his support and invited me on to his ABC show to reflect on the absurdity of it all, but I didn't do it. The idea of having to say 'Actually it was quite funny if it had just been given a minute' was just too dispiriting. Still, it was very nice of him. A few others were equally supportive and I'll always be grateful to Jim Schembri in *The Age* for being the first to call the whole pile-on thing out.

And it's never been mentioned in Aus again. I've done numerous PR and media since for my novels, stand-up tours, musicals and a film but my one and only Australian-made TV show has not come up once.

And as to what happened to the idea of anybody trying locally produced scripted comedy on the commercial networks?

Take a guess.

An opportunity I'd been waiting for

In many ways, I should be grateful to Channel 9. If they'd have stuck with it, I'd have spent the following nine weeks in that studio working towards a hit.

And had we made it, Channel 9 would have commissioned a second season. I'd have been writing and producing for a whole year and then another and probably another. I always put 100 per cent into what I do and my intention going in had been to devote the next few years to trying to make comedy for Australian TV.

Had that been the case, it is unlikely that *Upstart Crow* – which I think is the best thing I ever did for TV – would have happened. Nor would I have written a movie for Ken Branagh to star Judi Dench and Ian McKellen. And a novel that I had wanted to write all my life would not have been written.

With *Live From Planet Earth* having firmly closed the door for me to Australian TV, I suddenly found myself without a gig. I was free of a gruelling TV schedule and also free of the nagging feeling that I should try to build a proper TV career in my second home. I'd made my bid, been very firmly rebuffed and I needed to find something else to do.

What I did was begin a novel I'd been planning in my mind for a long time. It was a fictional version of a unique element of my own family history: the interesting circumstance of my father and uncle having a cousin who was adopted and not of Jewish descent and who had remained in Nazi Germany when his cousins fled. From this came the most heavily researched and heartfelt novel I have written – a saga of a Berlin family from the 1920s to the 1950s, a Jewish family with one natural son and one adopted non-Jewish son. Any writer seeking to depict such a nightmare period needs to give themselves the time and space to dig deep. Channel 9 had given me that time.

I worked on *Two Brothers* at home in Fremantle through 2011 and 2012. It was a very big undertaking. Half of the book takes place in the culturally glorious Weimar years when Germany, and Berlin in particular, were the epicentre of creative thinking in the Western world. It was the time of

Cabaret. But then came the Nazis, crushing everything beautiful beneath their steel-clad boots. Delving so deeply into such a dark and darkening time was quite draining and I remember many nights being 'woken' up by the book and going to my study in the small hours. There were no tiny children now to bring me to my desk; just the gloomy shadows cast by history, a history which for me, of course, was personal. My father and my beloved grandparents, whom I had known well as a boy, had lived it. *Two Brothers* was a labour of love and I'm very proud of it. My only regret was that, by the time it was published, my father's Alzheimer's was too far progressed for him to have been able to read it. It was my fourteenth novel and the first he didn't read.

A major consolation prize was a heartfelt and touching reaction from Uncle Heinz in Germany, he being the non-Jewish adoptee who had inspired the story. At 100 years old, he still remembered very clearly the murder or displacement of all his family by a regime which he had been required to spend six years in arms defending.

Wiggles, Yorkshire puddings, time travel and dancing under the stars

So the teen years of what was no longer a new century played out. After publishing *Two Brothers*, I did *The Wright Way* sitcom, which you already know was pretty much as deep a nadir for me in the UK as *Planet Earth* had been in Aus. I mentioned that *Planet Earth* was never spoken of in Aus media again. But, in the UK, a *Guardian* columnist happily told the story as part of his thesis that I should never be allowed near a TV show again as long as I lived.

Personally, these were very happy years. Years usually are for me. I know I've focused on a lot of negative commentary, but that is because I am writing my life as a writer. As a man, my glass is always half-full. In fact, quite frankly, my cup is overflowing. I am never down for long and the love of my family and the company of my friends is where my true emotional barometer is set.

When the kids were young and then also in their teen years, I focused a lot on family life. I'd done it in Sussex and now I did it in Freo. I tended to do the family cooking while Sophie did all the other house stuff and all of the *endless* fucking driving that our boys' football playing required. I'm very good with family meals, stews, casseroles, pies, toad in the hole and onion gravy – stuff kids like to eat and that mine frankly still do. When they come home now, the family WhatsApp always focuses on which of my half-dozen signature meals they want to have cooked for them on the night they arrive. I make my own fruit mincemeat at Christmas and start baking pies (my own pastry, *of course*) on the first day of December and keep going until New Year. My family-and-friends Sunday roasts are big events for us. Many times, in the days when there were still lots of kids, I did seventy-two Yorkshire puddings (in two shifts using a double oven). My school packed lunches were also much envied by the kids' friends: cornflake chicken burgers and beef and onion pasties. My pies and pasties were always too big for the sandwich boxes, so I used to make containers for them out of cut-up cereal boxes. Sophie used to say my school lunch constructions were my new 'structure'. I do like to keep busy.

But, of course, I kept working. I directed various productions of *We Will Rock You*, including one in Berlin which was very special for me. I had never been to Berlin before. It's a very cool town. And the Holocaust memorial is almost overwhelming emotionally. I think Germany has confronted its cataclysmic past in a truly inspiring way and it is a joy to me that I now have so many great colleagues and friends in Germany through *We Will Rock You*. I admit I do feel a special connection to Germany and at the time of writing I am considering applying for the citizenship which my father's displacement as a boy may entitle me to. Principally this would be to allow our children the privilege of a post-Brexit Euro passport but also because for me it would represent the closing of a circle which began when my father hurried through Germany in the night, a terrified fifteen-year-old in fear of his life. A small belated victory for one German Jewish family over Hitler and a celebration of Germany's reckoning with its darkest history.

A fun bit of broken crockery from the early 2010s was a screenplay I wrote for the inspired and inspiring Aussie children's group The Wiggles.

I wrote a script imagining the gang emerging from Wiggle World with no knowledge of the real world which they encounter with naive and trusting good nature (if you saw the *Barbie* movie, I was there first). We got close to a green light, but never quite over the line. We're still all friends, though. They asked me to write a lyric for one of their tunes, which I did, called 'Wiggle Town', where everything is the reverse of normal. Google it – it's very catchy! And it's on an ARIA (Aussie Grammys) award-winning album! The cheque which I still get for that lyric each year buys a very nice wiggly dinner out for me and Sophie.

In 2014, I wrote my novel *Time and Time Again*, a time-travelling alternative history adventure yarn about a plot to avoid the First World War orchestrated from the future. I had enormous fun with that book and the research into pre-apocalypse Germany and central Europe was rather less harrowing than research for *Two Brothers* had been.

Meanwhile, I'd been tinkering with another idea for an Aussie movie, one that would allow me to pretty much work from home which, with the kids still at school, was a very attractive idea. Indeed, the whole thing would turn out to be something of a family project.

There used to be a wonderful folk festival held near the WA town of Pinjarra. It was called the Fairbridge Festival after its location, a heritage site in the sun-burned bush, centred round a little colonial-era chapel. Every year, hundreds of families would pack up their tents or dust off their caravans for a weekend of beer, barbies and music. It was a great place to take kids as they could all go completely feral. There was a pretty secure outer perimeter, lots of stewards and lots of organized activities.

We went several years with various friends and loved it. One year Emma Thompson and Greg Wise were holidaying with us with their daughter Gaia and we took them along. It was quite a shock for the dressing-gowned ladies in the morning queue for their ablutions to discover a double Oscar winner with her sponge bag under her arm among them.

One evening, we were all sitting in the bar tent and I started talking about what a great location it would be for a movie, with a highly photogenic Aussie country bush setting and ready-made facilities on site. Emma and Greg were suitably enthusiastic over the Margaret River chardonnay and the idea for my film *Three Summers* was born. So many people were Fairbridge regulars (including many of the musicians) that I got to wondering about a multi-character story across three consecutive festivals concerning people who met only once a year.

The movie was a real labour of love involving lots of local people and many friends. And, best of all, family. The core story was between an uptight and aloof techno-orientated, theremin-playing boy and a happy-go-lucky fiddle-playing girl, who was the leading member of an Irish folk band. Sophie's brother Adam played both the fiddle and the theremin for the soundtrack, and he and Sophie wrote and scored the music which Sophie produced. Sophie also played the bass for the traditional folk tracks and acted as musical director.

And what a cast we assembled! The absolute cream of Aussie talent – Magda Szubanski, Michael Caton, Deborah Mailman, John Waters, Jacqui McKenzie and Kelton Pell in an inspiring ensemble cast led by wonderful actors Robert Sheehan and Rebecca Breeds as the mismatched romantic leads. All of us were together on a campsite in rural WA for five glorious, if frantic, weeks.

One particular joy was a chance to get involved with some of the Noongar mob – as the local indigenous Australians call themselves – around Pinjarra. Part of the story featured a First Australian (Aboriginal) youth dance company and our indigenous advisor Kudda (my brother from another mother, as he was kind enough to call me) made me feel very at home in Noongar country. One treasured memory is the dance and smoking ceremony the local mob put on for our cast and crew on the night before we began principal photography. There were didgeridoos and rhythm sticks, and we made fire in the traditional wood-on-wood friction method, which takes an exhaustingly long time. Rebecca and I were invited to join the Willy Wagtale dance in the thick smoke that was being created. The Willy Wagtale is a funny and charming little bush bird that really shakes its tail feathers and you dance it by putting your hands behind your back just above your bum, splaying out your fingers and wiggling about. It's not very dignified but good fun and soon the young indigenous dancers joined us in the smoke and lithe, elegant human emus pecked at us. It was very communal and bonding, dancing together in the smoke underneath a vast blanket of stars. I remember thinking about my father. He had gone from Germany to Czechoslovakia and then to Britain. And now, here was his son dancing an ancient traditional dance under Australian stars with the descendants of people who came to Australia at least 60,000 years ago. Human beings have always moved around the Earth, sometimes happily, sometimes tragically. I'm not a very spiritual person, but I can't deny I was pretty moved.

I think we made a lovely film and it was extremely well-received by audiences in Aus and it did okay commercially – critically less so (whod'a thunk). As ever, I'd put in my 'little bit of politics', touching on racism and the refugee crisis which was polarizing Australia at the time – the ruling Liberal Party (which weirdly is the name of the Conservatives in Aus) was running a brutal immigrant scare campaign with the slogan 'stop the boats'. This wound up some columnists, particularly the ones writing for the more right-wing papers who clearly viewed me as a foreigner trying to tell them their business. The Murdoch-owned *Melbourne Herald Sun* gave it zero stars, which is pretty harsh, eh? But the audience ratings at test screenings were north of 80 per cent positive, which was nice, and it ended up being seen by many happy punters. The BBC screened it too, which was great, and it won its slot, as they say.

Oh, and it won the Jury Prize at the Cannes Film Festival.

Yes, you read that right.

But perhaps I should say it won the Jury Prize at *a* Cannes film festival. The Cannes Ecrans Seniors Festival of Film, to be precise. This is a local festival organized by the senior citizens of Cannes which runs concurrently with the major festival and *Three Summers* won the OAPs' Prix Du Jury for best foreign film. I have a nice little award in the shape of a movie clapperboard to prove it, so many thanks to the pensioners of the Alpes-Maritimes region. They can keep their Palme D'Or; I've got the Oldie Prix. And I've danced the Willy Wagtale in the oldest country on Earth. When Kudda and I parted ways at the wrap he gave me the fire sticks we'd used together and a kangaroo pelt.

Why does everybody hate you?

So, as you can see, I had a lot of fun in the 2000s and the early 2010s – doing some interesting gigs, finding lots of time for family and occasionally even combining the two. But I certainly was no longer the success I had once been. My novels aside, the only real hit I'd had in the twenty-first century was *We Will Rock You*. That was okay. If you're gonna have a hit, that ain't a bad one to have and it alone kept me pretty busy. I felt lucky to be still working at all. And I had plenty else to occupy my time with: school-age kids, a large extended family, friends to meet, wine to drink, big roasts to cook, and also a lot of fire hazards to clear on our bush block.

I guess there was the occasional, somewhat dispiriting reminder that my name remained for many a source of bitter amusement – as one comedy buff asked on Twitter, 'When did Ben Elton become the punch-line?' I remember Sophie and I were watching an episode of *Never Mind the Buzzcocks*, a show which we enjoyed, when suddenly my name came up and the host and a couple of guests just started piling in on what a sad and compromised old prick I was. The same thing happened on *Mock the Week*. In fact, that sort of thing happened all the time. I love BBC Radio 2, but I had to stop listening to it because I'd turn it on and, surprisingly often, somebody would be having a pop. It was weird, like a malign universe was willing me to turn on at the wrong moment. Jonathan Ross would be heaping derision on his otherwise very listenable Saturday morning show, and one time when I turned on during a late-night drive, a DJ called Mark Radcliffe was venting his spleen about me in general and my appalling musicals in particular like they were self-evidently a crime against culture. I even made it onto Ricky Gervais's *Extras* with Ricky's character smashing his face repeatedly into his plate of spaghetti at the prospect of being forced to attend '*Ben Elton's* We Will Rock You'. I put my name in italics because that was clearly loaded. I don't think I'd ever heard it referred to as such without so much as a mention of Queen. I was actually kind of flattered; Ricky was, by then, a global star, so my name was very fleetingly big in America!

Sometimes the aggression was quite amusing. I was publicly savaged by winking gameshow host Anne Robinson. She put me in *Room 101*. I am, in fact, the only person to have been put in *Room 101* twice. You know *Room 101*? The '90s show where grumpy old Paul Merton invited people to hate things? Anne Robinson explained that her reason for despising me was that I had betrayed every left-wing value I had ever stood for, a stance which Merton saw no reason to challenge. You have to laugh when it comes from a self-serving, tax-avoiding monster of vanity like Robinson. But when Mark Steel, whom I respect a lot, also put me in *Room 101* (again with Merton gleefully agreeing and pulling the lever), it did hurt a bit.

Guardian darling Stewart Lee guaranteed himself a question in pretty much every interview I have done since by claiming (at some length) that I was worse than Osama Bin Laden. As far as I can glean, the reason he thought I was worse than a mass-murdering terrorist was that at least Bin Laden's actions were consistent with his beliefs.

I know a lot of this mainly because some dick or other has found the time to put it in my Wiki page and therefore it is constantly brought up whenever I do promotional media.

After Rik died, when I first thought about writing an autobiography, I took the idea to Larry, my publisher, and he actually said, 'Well, the first thing you're going to need to address is why so many people *hate* you.'

Can you believe that? It was his *first comment*. Not 'Oh great, I can't wait to hear you on the subject of *Blackadder*', but 'Why do so many people hate you?'. And that was from my own *publisher*, who was also a mate.

What's to address? What case am I supposed to be answering for? I pay my tax. I have campaigned all my life for a party and policies that will *raise* that tax. We sent our kids to state school. What is it that I've done that's supposed to contradict what I've said?

The funny thing was Larry thought the antagonism towards me was a relatively new phenomenon, something that had all started after I worked with Andrew Lloyd Webber. Like many people, he had this idea that I had once been respected but had frittered away my moral authority by writing a musical with a Tory.

Well, if you've got this far in the book, you know it ain't so.

Exactly the same question my publisher wanted me to address had already been asked thirty years before when I was in my sparkly suited pomp. And by no less a figure than revered and respected feature writer Lynn Barber. She did a mean and snarky profile on me for *The Observer*, in which she somewhat gracelessly conceded that, having met me, she had found me pleasant and reasonable. 'So why,' she asked her readers, 'does everyone hate him?'

I remember thinking about that. After all, my family didn't hate me. My friends didn't hate me. And of the people I didn't know not everybody could hate me because when that article came out, I had a number-one novel, my own TV show and a play opening at the Theatre Royal Haymarket.

So who did?

The answer was obvious and I wondered how Lynn Barber, such a famously astute judge of character and fearless debunker of vanity and hypocrisy, could have missed it. The people she had dinner parties with hated me. And just possibly, *she* hated me, or at least had wanted to when she met me. And why would that be? *Because* I had a number-one novel, my own TV show and a play opening at the Theatre Royal Haymarket, that's fucking why.

You would have thought she'd have spotted it.

There's this weird collective delusion in our attitude towards critics and arts media writers that they come from a place of objectivity. That's genuinely my only real problem with reviews and profiles, the fact that they present as some kind of clear and present truth as opposed to being a reflection of the opinions and personalities of the person writing the piece. That criticism, *all* criticism, is entirely and absolutely *subjective*.

Honestly, if they *just* started with 'in my opinion' before saying something's shit (or something's great for that matter) I could forgive them anything.

But they never ever do.

Is it a Jew thing?

Harry Enfield says it's a Jew thing. He's always confrontational like that; he does it for a laugh. He'll put on a hopelessly posh 'Colonel Blimp' voice and say 'We don't like uppity Jews, y'know'. I said 'Well, Stephen's as Jewish as I am and he doesn't get all that shit.' Harry's answer to this is that it's because Stephen doesn't look and act 'Jewish'. He's urbane and self-deprecating in patrician English style, whereas I'm too eager to please and too anxious to succeed. (Incidentally now that the internet has made trolling a popular sport, Stephen cops plenty without a doubt, but I'm going back decades.)

My uncle once wrote to me about the same thing. He had a lot of haters. Historians do, of course. They fight like bull ants in a jar, but he definitely seemed to provoke a particular level of ire. I went to his memorial in Cambridge and they were still slagging him off during the eulogies. It was actually funny, these crusty old gits getting their last dig in.

'Geoffrey Elton was brilliant in his way, but he was also fundamentally *WRONG!*'

Amazing. At his own memorial.

Uncle Geoff was the first historian to really look at Thomas Cromwell sympathetically, as the key player in early Tudor England, calling him the father of the English civil service. The view caught on for a while, but then went seriously out of fashion. Interestingly, it's come back now with *Wolf Hall*, but for decades, G.R. Elton copped a lot of shit in the rarefied world of academia. Anyway, he saw that I too was copping it and wrote to tell me that friends had often encouraged him to see some anti-Semitism in the criticism he got but that he absolutely refused to. I know what he meant. I've always felt the same way, believing as he did that I live in a wonderful and tolerant society, protected by an ancient democracy and the rule of law. And Britain *is* a wonderful and tolerant society. The Nazis never found fertile soil in Britain. We showed Oswald Mosley the door. Yes, we have our racists and resurgent Right and there have been many tensions as Britain transforms into a multi-cultural society, but the rivers of blood that Enoch Powell so confidently predicted have largely failed to materialize.

But one thing did give me pause for thought. I happened recently to open the Folio Society edition of Uncle Geoff's most celebrated work, *England Under the Tudors*.

Let me offer you a few quotes from the introduction. It's actually quite incredible.

He was one of a common breed: Central European intellectuals who have embraced English life . . . He adored England yet he never seemed quite at home in it . . . He showed symptoms of an inferiority complex . . . He seemed ill at ease with his appearance . . . blackly moustached, ungainly . . . with an immense bald head on which sweat seemed to suppurate . . . fidgety in encounters . . . he used language effectively but never beguilingly . . . Elton rose by merit but not by charm . . . Elton spent his life wanting to be English . . . He has seeped into the Englishness he loved.

Interesting isn't it? That's from the Folio edition introduction, which presumably is supposed to celebrate an important book and its author. And, frankly, it's fucking outrageous. Talk about a dog whistle. A *breed* of *European intellectual?* Hello? With his vast bald head *suppurating* with sweat *seeping* into English life! The writer just wants to say 'Jew. Jew! DIRTY JEW!', but of course he's *far* too English for that.

So has that been my problem? Despite having been born in Catford have I been trying to *seep into the Englishness I love*? Reading that introduction certainly made me wonder.

Look, I really don't think any of the long list of people who have found me unbearable over the last forty-five years are being anti-Semitic – some of them have been Jews themselves. I think what Harry was really talking about is snobbery. There is a prejudice against the characteristics that are sometimes *seen* as Jewish, but which are in fact merely the characteristics of any person or group trying to get from the outside in. The British establishment just doesn't like uppity people; you're supposed to be born to it, or at least make a good impression of being born to it. People who are on the outside and have no choice but to reveal their ambition and their desire to make a mark are patronized and viewed with suspicion. It's another part of the class prejudice which has robbed Britain of so much of its potential over the years.

Except for one brief shining moment in the '60s. But don't get me started on what we owe to The Beatles *again*!

The Late Teens and
Early Twenties

Saved by the Bard

And then, one day, quite unexpectedly things started to turn around. *The Wright Way* had been my nadir. There now began a period which Sophie started referring to as the Ben-aissance.

The seeds had actually been sewn in 2014 when I was surprised to be invited to dinner with Shane Allen, the new head of BBC Comedy. I say I was surprised because frankly I'd really thought TV was done with me. I had no complaints. I'd certainly had my fair share of privilege back in the day and wasn't expecting any more.

It was Bill Shakespeare who got me back in the game. The 400th anniversary of his death was to occur in 2016 and Shane wanted to talk to me about it. Shane is a total TV original, first at Channel 4 and then at the BBC. He was happy to go his own way and ruffle feathers if he wanted to. In fact, he didn't just ruffle feathers. Sometimes he throttled the whole chicken. And Shane (whom I will love for ever for this) had decided I might make a good fit for what was on his mind. He told me that BBC Drama and Arts were doing stuff around Shakespeare's death day and therefore so should BBC Comedy and would I like to think about that.

It wasn't a commission, far from it. Just a probe. But if you've got this far in this book, you know I love to grab an opportunity and throw words at it.

Shane's original thought was for a one-off comic play, but the more I read about Shakespeare himself, the more I thought the project should be a sitcom. Will Shakespeare just struck me as a classic, archetypal, old-school British sitcom hero, the endlessly put-upon, hard-working, lower-middle-class arriviste constantly aspiring to social advancement and getting roundly put down by the posh snobs of the establishment. Class is in Britain's DNA (as I know I've already mentioned) and many classic sitcom heroes have reflected its attendant conflicts, with characters deeply resenting an establishment while also wishing to be a part of it. Hancock, Sykes, Captain Mainwaring, Basil Fawlty and even Edmund Blackadder all felt aggrieved and undervalued. In fact, I took my title *Upstart Crow* from the only contemporary published review of Shakespeare and his work that survives – and it was a stinker! The reference was a vicious put-down from rival poet Robert Greene who accused Shakespeare of being an unoriginal upstart trying to clothe himself in the feathers of proper gentlemen poets. It didn't take much of a stretch for me to imagine Will's feelings on reading that!

I was excited. Really excited. To quote Churchill's comment on becoming prime minister in 1940 at the moment of Britain's greatest peril: 'I felt as if my whole life had been but a preparation for this hour.'

Maybe I didn't feel it quite *that* strongly and clearly, the stakes weren't quite as high, but I definitely felt a real kinship with the subject matter that Shane had gifted me, because leaving aside Shakespeare's cosmically greater talent, I rather empathized with Will. I couldn't help feeling that, in his day, Will would not have been considered 'cool'.

Christopher Marlowe was cool. *Beyond* cool. Apart from being a celebrated poet, Marlowe was a wild boozer, a sexual profligate, probably bisexual and a *spy* for fuck's sake. In fact, he was a double agent who got stabbed to death in a knife fight in a pub!

Now *that* is cool.

And it wasn't just Marlowe. All the other London playwrights of the Renaissance were wild boys. Every one of them was 100 per cent rock'n'roll and they all burned out quick and died young.

Will, on the other hand, was definitely not rock'n'roll. He was supremely hard working, he carefully invested his money in property, diligently supporting his wife and kids (at least financially), and even managed to retire to the country before dying in his own home with his wife and daughters around him.

And here's another thing. Without exception, all Will's contemporaries were educated at either Oxford or Cambridge. Among poets of the

English renaissance, only Shakespeare didn't get to university. He went to a municipal grammar school until getting turfed out because his dad was in court for fraud. What a character! He was just so middle-class with the requisite permanent chip on his shoulder. He even *bought* himself a coat of arms – the Elizabethan equivalent of getting a personalized number plate. He had a mother who felt she had married beneath her (and who felt her son had too; Anne Hathaway is generally thought to have been illiterate) and a dodgy dad who was endlessly on the make. Add three grumpy kids (well, all TV comedy kids are grumpy) and the Shakespeares were a perfect sitcom family. Will was even an early commuter, working in London but returning often to Stratford-upon-Avon (which the real Will must have done as he had many business interests in his home town plus a growing family). This would, of course, allow for regular commuting and travel gags ('they're filling ruts and laid on a replacement donkey service after Leamington Spa'). And, of course, the heart of it all would be the massive fun to be had with Shakespeare's plays, plots, language and reputation: the constant cross dressing; the ridiculous contrivances in which people failed to recognize each other because they were wearing a tiny mask or notice their presence because they were hiding behind a twig; the appalling sexual politics in which lovers drugged their beloveds into falling in love with donkeys or tricked them into sex by pretending to be someone else; the soliloquys during which characters eloquently expressed their innermost thoughts to empty rooms; the comedy that wasn't funny (yellow cross garters anyone?) and the tragedy that was (Hamlet is, after all, just a bored student).

Then there's the myths and presumptions that pertain to the man himself. Was he gay? Did he really write his plays? Who was the Dark Lady? Was it her 'waste of shame' that he wanted to 'expend his spirit' into or was it up the Fair Youth's?

And, on top of it all, I had Shakespeare's historical literary deification to play with: the fact that we revere him while often failing to follow a word he wrote, the common experience that every schoolkid has shared of being bored shitless by the works of someone they are assured is the greatest writer who ever lived. Also, I had at my disposal the common contemporary attitudes to the Bard with which I could lend Will a cynical hindsight, making him *aware* that the more wilfully obtuse and complex he made his language, the cleverer everybody thought he was. And, of course, there was the language he invented himself. Shakespeare famously made up many words and phrases. I would invent a few futtocking more to stick in his coddling pouch next to his cod dangle.

I felt that never before had I been working with so rich a comic canvas. And I knew *exactly* the voice I needed for Will too. I didn't know David Mitchell at the time, but it was his voice in my head from the very start.

So I suggested to Shane that what we should create was not a TV play, but a sitcom. And, God love him, he agreed. The course of my next five years was set.

We did three series, two Christmas specials and a lockdown edition. I wrote twenty-one episodes, which took an awful lot of reading and research. I certainly worked harder on the plays and poems and history of the period than I ever did at school or university. I was lucky in the support of our brilliant (and extremely well-educated) producer Gareth Edwards, who proved to be a wonderful script consultant and editor; also director Richard Boden (who directed *Blackadder Goes Forth)* and I received really diligent and focused support from Shane and other execs at the BBC.

And the cast were simply sublime, as fine an ensemble as has ever assembled before a studio audience. These included Harry Enfield, Liza Tarbuck and Paula Wilcox, all led by the incomparable Gemma Whelan and, above all, David Mitchell as Will. David became my friend, inspiration and confidant on that show, as close as a colleague can be. We were a team and working with him was an unalloyed and constant joy. I had not expected so late in life to make any really proper new close friends, but David and his equally inspiring and funny wife Victoria Coren Mitchell became just that. I call them my newest 'old' friends.

And there were plenty of old, old friends involved too. Besides Harry, Ade made a guest appearance, as did Nigel Planer, Gabby Glaister, Mina Anwar and Hannah Jane Fox. And Emma Thompson and Ken Branagh starred in separate Christmas specials. Now *those* recording nights were events in a sitcom studio.

It wasn't all plain sailing, particularly at the beginning. The days of me progressing from script to screen without pause were very long gone.

I went through the same development process that everybody else did, which meant the first thing the BBC commissioned was an afternoon table read. For which at first we didn't even have David! You'll remember that I had his voice in my mind, but Gareth and my first thought was to find a younger actor to mimic that attitude. As mentioned, I'd never met David at the time and, since my first episode featured Will at the very beginning of his career, my view was that we were looking for 'a young David Mitchell' (David was forty-two at the time). We saw a number of fine young actors but, of course, nobody who remotely had David's unique comic intelligence because, well, it's unique. Pretty quickly, we realized that the man we needed with the voice of David Mitchell was David futtocking Mitchell. Well, duh! So Gareth (who had worked with David before) sent him a script and fortunately he loved the idea. It was only then that David and I met and what a meeting of minds that was. We clicked instantly and, in my view, David's Shakespeare is as perfect an expression of my comic writing as I have ever been fortunate enough to witness. It's definitely as great as Rik's Rick or Rowan's Blackadder. The Will that David created was moving, multi-layered, conflicted, complex and hilarious. His performance truly flattered my script, doubling its value without asking to change a *single* word.

Did I mention what a lucky bastard I've been? Well, it's worth repeating.

But, as mentioned, it wasn't all plain sailing. The table read went okay-ish. But for such an expensive undertaking (a costume comedy in a live studio), Shane and the BBC needed further convincing. So they commissioned a non-broadcast pilot. This used to be a regular thing but, by 2015, it was a massive luxury (I don't imagine they happen at all now). We were to be given the chance to try the show out with a full studio production for development purposes only. This, of course, meant the BBC would have the chance at that point to cut their losses and drop it. I think the reason for their reluctance to go straight to a series was because of my stubborn reluctance to drop one idea.

Right from the start, I'd had this extra layer in mind where I wanted to *cast two principal male roles using female actors.* This was to be a sort of 'meta' joke on the Elizabethan practice of casting boys to play women. In my original script, there was no Kate the Landlady's daughter (Gemma

Whelan's role). Instead we had Will's house companion, Toby. Toby's character was that of a young male actor who played the female characters in Will's plays. My conceit was that, in a reversal of an ancient sexism, Toby would be played by a young woman. The idea wasn't that Toby was secretly a woman pretending to be a man, but that Toby was a genuine male character whom we had cast a woman to play in an act of what would shortly come to be known as gender-blind casting. A woman plays the role, but it's still a man. Get it? No. Nobody did really. Toby was played in the pilot by Beattie Edmondson and she did a really wonderful job as a dim but enthusiastic young actor (shades of Private Pike to Captain Mainwaring), but sadly everybody except me found it all too confusing – particularly since I had pushed my idea further by insisting that the character of Henry Condell, who I portrayed as a bitter old luvvie who played the female roles in Will's acting company, should also be played by a woman. Again, this would be a woman playing an actual male actor who performed woman's roles. For this role, we cast the sitcom legend Paula Wilcox (who would end up playing Will's mum).

Well, look. You know it didn't work because (I hope) you've watched *Upstart Crow*. Gareth and David *sort of* liked the idea *a bit* – or at least they understood it – which was more than can be said for our pilot audience. I was the only one who *loved* the idea. I just couldn't let go of what I thought was the delicious irony that in my version of Shakespeare, women would play men. Not women *pretending* to be men but *actual* men.

Shane hated it.

And he was right, of course. It was just too confusing a conceit and, frankly, a one-off joke that would become a burden to a whole series. After we'd made the pilot, Shane rang me.

'We *might* proceed, Ben, but there will have to be changes.'

I knew exactly what change he meant and gave up without a fight. 'All right, Shane. I'll make the Toby character an actual girl and Condell will be played by an actual man.'

And so the character of Kate (which became so utterly crucial to the show) was born and the incandescent Gemma Whelan joined our company. And this, of course, allowed me to really develop the sexism satire by having Kate be an aspiring actress always thwarted by the misogyny of the day.

> KATE: But Mr Shakespeare, surely the logical thing would be to cast a real woman to play your female roles?
> WILL: Really, Kate? And by that logic I suppose you think I should seek out real kings to play the kings and cast real fairies for the fairies.

Anyway, we got our commission and *Upstart Crow* was a hit, both in popular terms and with the critics! A rare double whammy for me.

I never expected to get such an opportunity so late in my career. A sitcom on the BBC remains for me an iconic thing and if *Upstart Crow* proves to be my last (as I imagine it will), I am beyond grateful for it.

Cancelled for a weekend

Sticking with *Crow* but jumping forward a bit to the autumn of 2019, I got heart-stoppingly, arse-clenchingly close to being cancelled. For two or three very nervous days I was staring down the barrel of professional isolation and public disgrace. And it had all started out so well. The road to hell is indeed paved with good intentions.

Phil and I had decided to present a stage play of *Upstart Crow*, which he and Lucy Ansbro would produce. This was a big challenge for me as I wasn't planning the usual type of stage TV spin-off which involves an edit of favourite episodes from the telly but a fully original new play for the stage. It seemed to me that the theatre was in some ways *Upstart Crow*'s spiritual home and I was relishing the opportunity to build on the fun I'd already been having with all the mad conventions of theatre both current and ancient. David loved the idea and so, in 2018, I sat down at my desk in Sussex and, after twisting my brain for about a fortnight, came up with a plot which centred on a comedy mash-up of *Twelfth Night*, *King Lear* and *Othello*.

It was the *Othello* bit that got me into some serious hot water.

In my play, twins Desiree and Aragon (a prince and a princess of Africa) are shipwrecked and separated off the English coast (*Twelfth Night* style) and Desiree (now disguised as a boy, of course) ends up as Will's servant in London. It transpires that Will has been thinking about casting the world premiere of his new biggie *Othello* and, thinking Desiree a man, gleefully casts her in the lead role. Will is thrilled; he has got an ethnically authentic actor for his tragic hero and so will be celebrating diversity and inclusion in theatre 400 years early. What's more, he will now avoid the nightmare performance that Richard Burbage, his usual leading man, will offer with its inevitable appalling blackfaced, offensive stereotype, racist pantomimic capering. Will reflects ruefully that he has already suffered Burbage's deeply offensive ruination of Shylock, in which the famed actor had played the Venetian Jew feasting on murdered Christian babies and wearing a false nose so huge and hooked that he had to wheel the end of it before him in a cart.

So, with Othello cast, Will must find his Desdemona, who regrettably must be played by a boy according to the custom of the time. Enter Kate, Will's housekeeper, who longs to act and so disguises herself as a boy in order to audition for Desdemona and wins the role.

Matters become complicated when Burbage turns up in blackface insisting on playing Othello. Also, Aragon, the lost African brother, arrives, now dressed as a girl.

Look, it would take too long to explain the further plot convolutions that ensued, but it ended up with a massive mix-up and Will finally presenting the first-ever *Othello* with Kate, a white woman pretending to be a man, wearing blackface in order to play Othello and Desiree, a black woman pretending to be a man pretending to be a woman, wearing whiteface and playing Desdemona.

In mixing up both gender and race, I was seeking to satirize the racist and sexist history of English theatre while exploring the themes of racism and toxic masculinity that are central to *Othello*.

To quote Will's *Upstart Crow* catchphrase, 'it's what I do'. All through my career, I've said that if you take serious and funny and put them together, you get seriously funny and that was what I wanted for my *Upstart Crow* play.

It all seemed to be going very well for a while. Everybody who read the play in its early stages of development seemed happy. Certainly nobody, including our excellent theatre director Sean Foley and the casting team, had rung any alarm bells. So they went into pre-production while I went off on tour.

Being new to the *Crow* world, the roles of Desiree and Argon would, of course, need to be cast. Scripts had gone out to agents representing various actresses and actors of colour, inviting them to read for the roles.

So it's October 2019 and I'm on my way up to Edinburgh with my tour manager to perform that night when Lucy Ansboro texted. 'Call me. Urgent.'

I soon learned that one of the actresses invited to read for Desiree had objected to the play. Well, not so much objected as condemned it utterly and very angrily. Both she and her agent had sent a very serious complaint to Lucy accusing me of having written a deeply offensive racist script. It seemed to Lucy that their intention was to take the matter further. In fact, this process had already begun. The agent concerned also represented a regular member of the *Crow* cast whom they had already alerted. Word spread fast and, over the course of the next hour, as I travelled to Edinburgh, I began to receive anguished messages from cast members explaining that they would have to resign.

I understood, absolutely. They had suddenly all found themselves in a terrible position. A young black woman was accusing an old white man of racism and doing so with great hurt and anger. There really was no way they could ignore that without incurring career-changing reputational damage themselves.

Next, David rang. He was just coming up to speed with the crisis and was totally supportive, offering to stand by me and help in any way he could. But we both knew that there wasn't much he could do beyond offering moral support. With such inflammatory accusations being levelled (and which were clearly about to go very public), we simply could not proceed with the play as matters stood.

Clearly this was my problem. I needed to fix it.

First, I asked if I could contact my accuser to try to explain, but Lucy told me that neither the actress nor her agent were prepared to speak to me. So, sitting in the back of the car hurtling north, my iPhone hotspot running red, I wrote her an email, the bulk of which I quote here.

To say that I am sorry to have caused you outrage and offence is, of course, an understatement. I have spent a lifetime in radical and progressive politics and your reaction is devastating to me.

In Upstart Crow, *I have always attempted to satirize modern sensibilities and hypocrisies through the lens of a comically imagined Elizabethan world. Of course, the original production of* Othello *would have involved an actor in blackface (as almost all Othellos were until very recently) and in this fact I saw an opportunity to create something which would speak to our modern abhorrence at such archaic practices.*

My vision of a white woman and a black woman in reverse make-up doing Othello *was intended to be confronting and empowering, to make the audience uncomfortable but also to make them think. Racism and male violence towards women are at the core of* Othello *and I had hoped to present a positive satirical vision which would turn racism and sexism on their heads. Perhaps I am naive to have thought that* any *presentation of blackface, even as a historical fact and even when placed opposite whiteface for absurdist effect, can ever work in the current age.*

I asked her to reconsider speaking to me so that I could better understand her position and adjust my play accordingly. I was at this point pretty scared, desperate to find a way to stop this situation getting onto Twitter. I knew that once that happened, I would never ever escape it no matter what I said or did.

With that appeal sent, I wrote another email to be forwarded to all the other actors who had received the script, recalling it. I explained that objections of racism had been raised and that, of course, I took this beyond seriously. The play was now off the table until such times as I could either adequately address the problems, in which case new audition scripts would be issued, or else the project would be cancelled.

By the time I got to Edinburgh, we had all the scripts back. Encouragingly, we had also had supportive messages from the other actors saying they looked forward to the new draft. A couple even went so far as to state that they personally had had no objections to the script as it stood, which I must say was a wonderful moment in an otherwise horribly bleak afternoon.

Sadly, the objecting actress and her agent let it be known they had no interest in receiving any new draft, which of course I totally respected. But with Sophie and Lucy both scanning Twitter, it seemed that they had chosen not to take their outrage further.

As mentioned, I had a gig that night (try focusing on that!), but by great good fortune, I had a day off the following day and so I got up at 5 a.m., ordered coffee on room service and sat down to rewrite my play. My ambition was to excise all the black (and white) face and to re-word all of Burbage's racist excesses, while hopefully somehow being able to hang on to the comedy and the politics of the original satirical intent.

Not fukn easy. The whole structure needed unpicking and less confronting solutions found. I worked for eleven hours without a break, by which time I had a new plot in which Burbage's blackface occurred off stage and Aragon, a black man pretending to be a woman pretending to be a man, played Othello, and Kate, a white woman pretending to be a man pretending to be a woman, played Desdemona. I was actually pretty pleased. I didn't feel that the play had lost any of its edge and nobody had to black up any more, which I understood was now simply unacceptable for actors under any circumstances. I pinged the new draft off to David, Sean and Lucy, and then, as rainy darkness gathered over Edinburgh, I went for a long, cold, lonely run up Arthur's Seat.

When I got back in sodden darkness, I found to my immense relief that they all loved the new draft and that David was happy and willing to perform it whatever the fall-out. Shortly thereafter, new audition scripts went out. The rest of the *Crow* cast all rescinded their resignations and auditions for the black roles proceeded without further upset.

Phew. With a capital PH.

Sean directed a beautiful production with a hugely happy company. The role of Desiree was played quite wonderfully by Rachel Summers and then, in the post-Covid production, by the sublime and hilarious Gloria Onitri. Aragon was thrillingly given by an endlessly inventive and compelling Jason Callender and the role of the Dancing Bear (a huge role and a massive physical challenge) was taken by Reice Weathers, who never failed to win an ovation on every exit.

The play got five-star reviews, a rare treat for me, and also an Olivier nomination for best comedy. We didn't win. Best comedy that year was won by another play featuring Shakespeare in which Shakespeare was played by a woman.

Blow winds and crack your cheeks

And my Shakespearian 'Benaissance' had a second act.

One very stormy day in 2017, Sophie and I were having a little break on the wonderful holiday island of Wadjemup (also known as Rottnest), a beautiful spot just a few miles off the coast of Perth. I say it was stormy; that's an understatement. It was closer to a cyclone. The warning had gone out the day before that the last ferries would leave that day and anyone who wasn't on one of them would be trapped for at least another three days because the seas would be far too wild for any crossings. Pretty much everybody left, but by this time, Sophie and I only had one kid left at home and he was quite capable of looking after himself, so we had the luxury of pleasing ourselves. We fancied the excitement of remaining in one of the little holiday camp-style concrete chalets, that were built in the 1950s, and riding out what promised to be a spectacular storm. And it was. The tree tops bent down to the ground in the massive wind, the rain threatened to smash the windows in and the seas simply exploded on the rocky shore. And in the middle of it all, while hunkered down with beans on toast and whisky round the little gas fire, my phone rang. The reception was pretty bad, but

I recognized Ken's voice at once and he had an exciting proposal. And one which really fitted the weather.

It was as much a challenge as a proposal. Ken wanted me to write a screenplay depicting Shakespeare in retirement, a man wrestling with the conflicts of a wife and daughters he'd long put second to his career and the still-unprocessed grief over his lost son. It would be a very different way of looking at the known facts of the great man's career than on *Upstart Crow*, which was fortunate because the biggest part of the challenge was that Ken did *not* want a comedy. He wanted a serious reflection on the subjects of ambition and grief. He also wanted me to address the creative process and what drives an artist to express themselves through their work. All without jokes. 'The humour will be there,' he said. 'You won't be able to stop yourself, but you must not at any point *try* to be funny.' I was to put aside my ruthless pursuit of the one-line gag.

I worked as hard as I knew how on that challenge, creating a plot which turned on the unresolved mystery of Hamnet Shakespeare's death, along with the lack of family closure on that tragedy and Will's emotional and physical distance from it and his wife and daughters. Also covered would be the deeply troubled lives of both daughters and sons-in-law, which involved well-documented sex scandals, and, above all, the character of Anne Shakespeare, a woman neglected by both her husband and perhaps also by history. It is fascinating to reflect that in three of Will's last great plays – *A Winter's Tale*, *The Tempest* and *King Lear* – we find a deeply conflicted old man dealing with strong and wilful daughters, but no wife and no sons.

I called my screenplay *All Is True*, which is the alternative title of Shakespeare's final play *Henry VIII*. I did this because although my plot was necessarily pure speculation, every character and every event depicted in it are matters of historical fact.

Ken loved the screenplay and resolved to make the movie. You can imagine my delight when he cast Judi Dench and Ian McKellen to play opposite him. Dame Judi I knew to be quite a fan of *Upstart Crow* and it was beyond a thrill to receive a short video from her taken on the first day of filming where she told me she had taken the role in *All Is True* because of the script.

I wish I could give you stories of hanging out with Dame Judi and Sir Ian on Sir Ken's film set, but he banned me from it. I'm making that sound a bit more dramatic than it was, but while I'm sure I could have dropped in, Ken did make it pretty clear that he didn't want me around. I understood; he had very little time to make the movie and it was a complex story. He knows me well. I think he thought were I hanging about hunched over a catering department coffee cup, I'd have the odd tuppenceworth to suggest. And, being such old friends, he would have had to expend precious seconds appearing to give some consideration to any suggestion before inevitably dismissing it. I didn't mind. In fact, I fully understood and welcomed the banishment. In my experience, unless you are in a key role, movie sets and locations are eye-wateringly boring environments. The hanging around is endless while you wait for some department or other to complete their preparations. Actors can go out of their minds. It's why they smoke and shag so much, or at least they used to. Things may have changed. Certainly regarding the smoking.

All Is True was very warmly received critically and, at one point, *The Guardian* even speculated on its Oscar chances. It never quite scaled those heights, but it was very nice to be on the right side of the critics. Although it did make me think about the old comedians' lament that if you want to be taken seriously, do something that isn't funny. Anyway, Ken made a very beautiful film and that phone call in the storm gifted me something truly special.

Failing towards America again!
Dancing all the way!

Another Ken-connected passion project from that time, but one which sadly did not arrive at quite the same lovely fruition, was an invitation to write a Bee Gees biopic, an invitation which came from Sir Barry Gibb himself, no less. Yep, the uber Bee Gee wanted me. Sadly, Hollywood didn't. But I had a lot of fun finding that out.

I think I've probably bored you enough about how I love pop music, but it doesn't come any greater than the extraordinarily eclectic and never less-than-majestic Bee Gees songbook. Barry, Robin and Maurice Gibb have never really got the credit they deserve, but their collective works represent one of the truly towering achievements of twentieth-century popular arts.

Hollywood had been trying to develop a *Bohemian Rhapsody*-style biopic for the brothers Gibb for some time. In fact, the producer was to be Graham King, who produced *Bohemian Rhapsody*. And he would be answering to no less a figure than Steven Spielberg as executive and over-all kingpin.

But they had no script. They'd commissioned several, but Barry – who, of course, had script approval – didn't like any of them. So he asked them to commission me.

That was a lovely thing. I didn't know Barry, just as I hadn't known Queen prior to *We Will Rock You.* But like Queen, Barry liked my work and thought I was the right fit. So I flew to Miami where he lives, drove over the very bridge where the rhythm created by the expansion bolts on his wheels inspired 'Jive Talking' and hung out with Sir Baz for a night. He's a truly kind, sweet and humble man and he welcomed me into the bosom of his family. Linda, his beautiful wife of more than fifty years, ordered a takeaway curry and we yarned the night away, along with various Gibb offspring and partners. Much wine and beer was drunk, although Barry stuck exclusively to his beloved saki and we all laughed uproariously.

Back in Australia, and now in the early days of lockdown, I retreated to our bush block where I just luxuriated in the Bee Gees' music, reading everything I could about the lives of three working-class boys who had overcome immense challenges and devastating personal loss. These three brothers made the world cry with their ballads and dance with their pop, and truly met triumph and disaster and treated those two imposters just the same. Barry, Maurice and Robin Gibb were all flawed humans in their own way, as all humans are, but they were also utterly magnificent and deeply admirable.

Yet again, I found in their story that same challenge I have encountered myself and which I firmly believe even Shakespeare battled – corrosive artistic snobbery and that old British canker: class. If any band should have been *cool* (again, that grim ambition), it was the Bee Gees. They weren't just working-class. They were proper *street*, three barely educated Manchester scallywags in constant trouble with the police and who only emigrated to Australia after the judge in a juvenile court suggested to Mr and Mrs Gibb that it might be the only way their eldest son Barry would avoid borstal. These accidental immigrants, barely in their teens, then sang their way around outback Australia – alongside their sister who did a snake-dancing act!

Despite scoring an Australian number one, the three boys then travelled back to London, where Robin wrote and sang the ethereal 'Massachusetts', and Barry wrote and sang 'To Love Somebody', when they were *still teenagers*. Ten years later, having fully imploded and briefly even split up before finding themselves doing cabaret on the rubber-chicken circuit, they pulled themselves together and wrote and sang a disco second coming that turned them into the biggest band on the planet.

And yet, despite all that, they never had *cred* and copped the sneers of rock's critical elite and various comics for forty years. The reasons for this were the same as they always are: their unashamed hunger for success and a good-natured desire to be liked. Those twin crimes – which the British arts establishment in particular will not lightly forgive – meant that despite having almost singlehandedly soundtracked the years of '77 and '78, their tight trousers and big hair provoked infinitely more comment than the world-moving music they produced.

So I wrote my script with love and admiration and was overjoyed when, a couple of drafts in, Ken became my script editor, having been brought in by the big studio cheeses to direct. There is nothing like working on a script with Ken Branagh. His fierce passion and forensic eye are hugely invigorating. Sadly, Barry never saw the finished result. The deal was that Graham King would only pass on to Barry scripts that Spielberg wanted to make. Barry had his veto, but so did Spielberg and he invoked it. Spielberg didn't like my script, so they paid me for it and put it on the reject pile. Overnight, me and Ken were out.

It's that brutal; many months of work ended in an instant. Then absolute silence. Just a note to your agent and you're done. Graham and I had had a great relationship, exchanging many long, detailed and very matey emails during our period of development, but after Spielberg rejected my script, I never heard from him again. I don't resent it – he's busy and that's how it's done. The American industry is brutally practical. While you're in, you're love-bombed; when you're out, you simply don't exist.

But Barry and I have stayed in touch. He doesn't email, but loves a late-night text and, once or twice a year, we exchange a couple. His last one ended 'Friendship is what matters'.

Barry Gibb has true class.

So did the Bee Gees.

Back to the future

Looking back on the year 2016, it seems almost as if I'd got into Marty McFly's time-travelling DeLorean and gone back thirty years. Suddenly, and so unexpectedly, I had a hit sitcom on the BBC, followed by a hit novel on the charts and then a sell-out stand-up tour on the road. It was the kind of slam-dunk trifecta that hadn't happened for me all at once since those first heady days back in the previous century.

Upstart Crow was first broadcast in spring 2016 and immediately found an audience. What was more, it seemed I had become so venerable that I was asked to give a lecture. That was something new. Shane Allen wanted to promote more serious discussion of the comic arts and so, as head of comedy at the BBC, he decided to stage The Ronnie Barker Memorial Lecture and asked me to deliver it. I chose to speak on the qualities and challenges of studio-based sitcoms that are recorded in front of live audiences. This is a purely television art form which has, I fear, gone almost terminally out of fashion. In fact, it is routinely derided. As if the acclaim heaped on drier, single-camera sitcoms pioneered by Ricky Gervais and Stephen Merchant's brilliant *The Office* must somehow be balanced with an equal contempt for the more heart-on-sleeve theatrical style where an audience is joining in the fun. The lecture became something of a passion project and I really worked hard on it. It was broadcast on BBC2 and it attracted two million viewers, which frankly amazed us all.

I'd also written my sixteenth novel. It was called *Identity Crisis* and my publisher was terrified because it was a satire centred in the new identity politics which, of course, included trans ideology. My publisher was having kittens. You have no idea the terror that stalks the upper echelons of the media over all things trans. You have literally only got to *say* the word and they shit themselves. And unless you're writing an achingly sincere and 100 per cent positive love letter to trans youth, then they tend to run several miles, dig a huge hole and hide in it – which seems rather strange when you reflect that we are talking about perhaps the most radical and, to many people, baffling reappraisal of what it is to be human in all our history. But I can assure you that *nobody* wants to touch it. My publisher insisted I do 'media training' before the press tour. Can you believe that? At the age of fifty-nine, and after forty years in the business, he wanted me to learn how to talk to an interviewer without getting cancelled because I'd written a novel with a trans-orientated sub plot. But I always try to be cooperative and I did talk to a very nice bloke for an hour, during which we both agreed on the bleeding obvious: it is not the *subject matter* itself which might cause offence but the treatment of it. And on that score, I was prepared to 'stand in my truth', as Gen Z would say – as I have always done.

The book was a top-five bestseller in the UK, Australia and New Zealand, and provoked none of the outrage that my publisher had feared. The book is not *remotely* 'anti' trans by the way, but nor is it slavishly supportive either. It just chronicles (among *many* other identity issues) the confusion of a well-meaning but ageing cop confronted with a male corpse which he has been instructed to treat as a female victim, along with all the attendant culture wars and political fallout that stems from that.

But the lack of offence caused by the book didn't stop the same paranoia emerging when I tried to develop *Identity Crisis* for TV. For some time, I and independent producers Michael Wrenn and Tony Ayres were in discussions for a pitch to Netflix and as part of the process the producers thought it wise for me to spend two days in a writers' room with a trans writer. Ever cooperative, I said I would be happy to, but I'd like them to find me a trans *man* writer because having done a lot of research already, I'd listened to many trans *women's* voices which were often assert-ive and loud. But the voices of trans *men* were rarer and quieter and not remotely so central to the debate. I felt that this was rather significant and that I'd appreciate the opportunity to 'unpack' it, as we now say. Well, that didn't happen. My new colleague turned out to be a trans woman as they couldn't find a trans man writer prominent in the media. Make of that what you will.

I hasten to add that my new trans colleague was absolutely lovely – talented, funny and astute. It was a fascinating two days and we both felt we learned something. We still exchange emails occasionally.

Sadly, the series never got a full commission. Donald Trump was already gearing up to run for a second term by the time we submitted the script and there was little appetite among streamers for political satire, particularly one featuring a wannabe demagogue cynically weaponizing culture wars. Fair enough, I guess. If you wanted that, you only had to turn on the news.

Back on the road again

And then I went back on the road. It was 2019 and I hadn't done stand-up since 2005. I never consciously gave up touring; I just didn't do it for close to fifteen years. I wanted to be a part of the kids growing up and being on the road for six months every year or two makes that difficult.

But with the kids all gone to uni, I was free to tour again. Sophie knew how much I'd missed the challenge and was also quite keen to see what I'd make of it after so long away, so she really encouraged me to. It was kind of nerve-wracking, I must say. Could I still cut it? Would there even be an audience still happy to come out and see me? It had, after all, been fifteen years and the world had changed beyond recognition. My shout-line for the adverts was 'The last time I toured, I was still smarter than my phone', which I thought summed it up. My previous tour had been pre-social media, pre-streaming and, above all, pre-iPhone, the device that changed the world. I felt like I was starting again, but on a different planet.

Speaking of smartphones, of course I have one and I love a bit of sat-nav but I am not, and never have been, on any social media whatsoever. This isn't some sort of grumpy old man cultural Luddism. It's just a way of safeguarding my time and my sanity. I would *love* to reap the benefits of building Instagram, Tik Tok and X (Twitter) followings. Old media is dying and it's very hard to promote stuff any more. A tour used to be sold with a few ads in local papers, a novel with an appearance on Radio 4. But those mediums now have a shadow of the outreach they once had and most artists alert their fans to any new endeavour directly. I dream of being able to tell masses of followers that I'll be appearing at this or that theatre or have a new book out. But I can't. I know I'd be on it all the time. I'd spend hours trying to think of the perfect post and then more hours agonizing over the response. And I don't need the trolling. Everybody gets trolled these days. You certainly don't need to be famous any more, but I've had a lifetime of it, avoiding the papers and radio for weeks after I've put out a book or play. It would be even harder to avoid your phone. I certainly don't want to invite hecklers directly into my fucking pocket!

Anyway, I wrote a load of new material for our brave new world and went back on the road. And, fortunately, people came and they laughed. In fact, I think I was a better comic for the long break. Just a bit calmer and less frantic.

I did have one very unpleasant experience early on on that tour. It was at a warm-up date in Grimsby. This was Autumn 2019 and Boris Johnson was gearing up for his 'Get Brexit Done' election. I was doing some material around what to my mind was the almost criminal lie that Brexit was a simple matter. I wasn't going for or against it, merely riffing on Johnson's outrageous claim that the whole thing could be easily and satisfactorily dealt with if a strong, no-nonsense bloke just cut all the legal and parliamentary crap and got on with it. One of my lines was 'This is a divorce and divorce is never simple. Blimey, Boris Johnson's left enough women. You'd have thought he'd have worked that out by now.'

I admit I was going very hard on Johnson's total lack of principle and integrity. I always draw my comedy from my personal point of view and

I despise the man, considering it to be self-evident that he is motivated exclusively by visceral self-interest, vanity and a grotesque sense of entitlement. He is a cancer on the body politic – and deeply dangerously anti-democratic in that he was prepared to trash the rule of law, parliament itself and, even more criminally, the public trust in those things for his own selfish vanity.

It all seemed to be going okay until suddenly this very big man, who had clearly been boiling with anger for some time, stood up and started hurling abuse at me. 'You are a cunt! You are a fucking disgusting cunt!' It was awful. Being a warm-up gig, the venue was pretty small (maybe 300 seats) and I could see him clearly. His blind rage was both scary and deeply sad. He was middle-aged and I guess he'd have considered himself to be working class. His strong Grimsby accent was raw with emotion as he shouted 'Yez focking cont! Yez focking basstadd!' It was a pretty stunning intervention. His wife got up at once and was trying and failing to push him towards the exit, but he just kept shouting as I tried to find a way to respond. This was real and earnest. No traditional heckler 'put downs' were appropriate. The man was in pain.

I knew what was happening. He thought I was looking down on him for wanting to believe in 'Boris'. I'd said nothing about the pros or cons of Brexit; my routine was exclusively about the idea that it was simple, but what this man heard was the voice of the 'elite' of which he'd been told so much, the latte-drinking, London-based, middle-class liberals who were *sneering* at him, who thought he was an ignorant racist thug for wanting to put his wife and family first and for fearing that the resources of his community were being stretched by a very visibly changing local population. *Nothing* I'd actually said supported this view, but his fury (which was kind of heart-breaking as well as being scary) made it clear that was what he felt. And I knew he had a lot to feel pain and anger about. I'd had a walk around earlier in the day and the derelict deprivation of the town centre was dystopian – boarded-up shops and empty, windblown precincts. Well, empty save for groups of bored youths chucking wheelies on their bikes and a few meth heads with pinned irises slumped about the place. I knew where his anger came from, but that didn't make it any less frightening or me any more responsible for it.

I felt very alone on stage. Like I say, he was a huge man in a blind fury and he was in the central aisle now. Half a dozen strides would have got him to the stage, which was easily low enough for him to step up onto and give physical vent to his resentment of me. I wanted to run but I stood my ground, trying to argue that I wasn't the problem and he was hating on the wrong guy. But he kept hurling abuse (while some of the audience started to heckle back at him) until mercifully his wife and a couple of very scared ushers slowly got him up the aisle, him walking backwards and shouting as he went.

It was fucking horrible to be the subject of such hate. And so deeply sad because it was a clear physical manifestation of what Britain's own little Trump (and his willing enablers) had unleashed with his nakedly cynical populist posturing – Johnson's gleeful weaponization of the old canard that there is a 'liberal elite' who despise 'the people'. Johnson's new normal was one in which highly educated cabinet ministers could denigrate 'experts' and serious newspapers could call High Court judges 'enemies of the people' for daring to insist that the law could not be broken just because the prime minister felt like it. And I'm talking about trying to deny the sovereign will of parliament, not fucking 'partygate' which was still in the future.

I'd never experienced anything like this incident before. The 1980s had been a deeply divided and angry decade, but in all the gigs I did back then, I never *once* encountered anything approaching the wild, inarticulate, *agonized* fury of that poor bloke on whom Johnson and his sorry crew had leached. I got through the rest of the gig okay (not an easy one to come back from), but I left the stage both scared and deeply depressed.

But that was very early on in the tour. The rest of it was really rather wonderful, not least because I still had an audience. I had honestly wondered whether, forty years into my stand-up gear, anyone would want to come out and see an old git like me. It turned out a lot of other old gits did! Unsurprisingly, my audience had largely aged with me. There were some younger punters, which was gratifying, often coming with their parents. But, on the whole, I was now an old comic with an old audience. And with the exception of the encounter in Grimsby, it all seemed much more relaxed and jollier than when I'd been thought edgy and hip. I think I was still moderately edgy, but not being the current big thing made for a much more relaxed vibe. I even picked up some rave reviews.

And the best bit of all about going back on the road was that my three children were finally able to see me do what it was that made people recognize me in the streets. They'd been pretty small when I'd last toured, but now they were adults and it was so lovely to have them there. Lottie and Fred saw me in the UK and then later Fred and Bert saw me in Melbourne. They are not uncritical of their old man when they feel that way inclined, but they loved me as a stand-up and that for me meant everything.

A proper blast from the past

That tour was supposed to finish up in New Zealand in 2020, but because of COVID, I didn't finally complete it until 2022 – and even then I wasn't quite done. In fact, I got a real echo of my '80s self when the fortieth birthday celebrations of Channel 4 led to a one-off revival of *Friday Night Live*. This hugely welcome and entirely unexpected treat came again via my latter-day champion Shane Allen. He'd left the BBC by that time and, as an independent, wanted to pitch a project for the channel's birthday. His original thought had been some sort of irreverent satire on the boorish Boris Johnson, who was the all-conquering PM at the time. My view was that Johnson was beyond satire and so I suggested instead we pitch a revival of my live '80s alternative cabaret show. Shane and Lucy Ansboro assembled a production proposal, took it to Channel 4 and we were off!

And it all worked perfectly. We had a smattering of oldies – most notably Harry reviving both Stavros and Loadsamoney for the first time in thirty-four years – plus the fantastic Jo Brand and Julian Clary. Then Lucy assembled a bunch of brilliant new young acts and also some amazing live music from Self Esteem. And, of course, there was me, in a brand-new sparkly suit, doing my old job of hosting, doing an opening topical monologue, introducing all the acts and doing a closing routine of road-tested gear. It was all *exactly* the way it had been, even down to Geoff Posner directing every bit as brilliantly as he had back in the '80s. It absolutely felt like we'd never been away and we had a truly magical night, marred only by a gaggle of Channel 4 suits (not of course that 'suits' wear suits any more) going to Harry's dressing room to tell him that they felt his Stavros tan was too dark and might be construed as 'blackface'. His makeup was actually no darker than mine (and paler than Julian Clary's), so Harry told them to fuck the fuck off and then get fucked. Except he didn't put it that politely.

Well, suits are gonna suit, I guess. And we do live in culturally paranoid times, even if much of that paranoia is self-imposed.

We knew it had gone well even in the studio, but the next morning we were actually kind of ecstatic. The 'old' media reviews were universally super-positive, with all of them calling for the return of the series proper. 'The socials' had gone wild too. I never look but Sophie often takes a sly peak at what's being said about me and it's often not pleasant. This morning was different. The show, and me in particular, were getting love-bombed. I was fully trending and in the best possible way. I admit I'd been lucky with the topicals; prime minister Liz Truss having resigned *on the afternoon of the live show*. Then again, the necessity of coming up with something original on the subject after the country had been laughing about it for seven hours had been quite a challenge. The general wisdom across the board was that a show like this was as needed now as it had ever been in the '80s. Sophie's eyes were shining as she scrolled down and down the Twitter feed. I don't get that kind of validation often and she was relishing it. We were on a train to go and see my mum, who'd just gone into a rest home, and we were the bearers of good news!

And then we only won a flipping BAFTA for it, my first since 1989. Plus a Royal Television Society Award, my first since 1991. Wow.

My name's Ben Elton. Goodnight

I think I'll leave it there. That late-life BAFTA takes me up to the spring of 2023, and it seems sensible to stop while I'm winning. Stop writing this book, that is. Not stop working. It won't surprise you to hear that I've carried on with that. In the summer of 2023, I cast myself in *We Will Rock You* for a start, and had a lovely three-month season at the London Coliseum, making what was, at sixty-three years old, my professional stage acting debut. I also wrote and directed a new musical about the life of my old friend Twiggy called *Close Up*, which did a sell-out run at London's Menier Chocolate Factory. And I wrote and embarked on a huge new stand-up tour with a show called 'Authentic Stupidity'.

I'm still on that tour as I write these words, on a train on my way to play Cheltenham Town Hall this evening. The 104th date of what will be a 105-date UK tour, my longest ever and with Australia and New Zealand still to do. I even did a couple of Euro gigs, one in Amsterdam and another in Oslo. That was new. Sophie has been with me for some of the dates as my WAG (her description, not mine) and we took a little break in Oslo. You should go – it's stunning.

And just last week I took a night off from the road for what was a very nice career moment for me. The Aardman Animation Studio run an annual comedy festival and they were giving me their Legend award. There were many lovely video tributes from many of my closest friends and colleagues, plus a couple of real surprises. Michael Palin sent one, which was pretty amazing; the Pythons are the most original, pioneering and funniest television comic artists of my lifetime, and that Michael Palin thought to pay tribute to me was a very great honour. And then came the last video. It was from Paul McCartney. To say that I was stunned is a very big understatement. I never imagined such a thing. Paul's contribution to the sum of human happiness is without equal. The whole world holds him in love and awe, and the fact that he found time in his day to congratulate me was simply mind-blowing. Sophie was in the audience and she was as thrilled and happy as I was.

And I hope I'll keep going for a bit longer too (if the currently unfolding geopolitical and environmental nightmare allows) so, who knows, perhaps in ten years I'll have had enough extra life to warrant a new extended edition of this memoir. But, for now, this is it.

I am sometimes asked in interviews if I have any remaining ambitions and I always answer that I fulfilled my ambition when I was twenty-one, the day I began to make my living as a writer. My only ambition ever since has been to keep doing it. So far, I've been ridiculously fortunate and, if it turns out that that good fortune now begins to fade, well, I've had a very good run.

Another question I am often asked is what have I written that I am most proud of. The boring truth is that I am equally proud of all my creative efforts and equally alert to their failings. I take no greater pride in *Blackadder*, which was a monster hit, than I do in *The Wright Way*, which was castigated by critics and cancelled after a single series. Everything I've ever written was a passion project at the time.

I don't really think about being proud of my projects, anyway. I just do them and move on. What I am truly proud of in my life are the friendships I have formed – and which have survived the decades – and the family that Sophie and I have made together.

And of always having done my best.

My name's Ben Elton. Goodnight!

Acknowledgements

With thanks to Richard Curtis, Amanda Ross, David Mitchell, Victoria Coren Mitchell, Jo Laurie and Adrian Edmondson.

Photo Credits

All images author's own except:

South of Watford © London Television Weekend

1984 with Madness © London Television Weekend

Alfresco © BFI Stills

The Young Ones © BBC

Happy Families © BBC

1983 Edinburgh Fringe © Mark Rusher

The Jam Tarts © Brent Sumner

Red Wedge event © Steve Rapport/Getty Images

Spice Girls © Dave Hogan

Andrew Lloyd Webber © John Stoddart/Popperfoto/Getty Images